Most Powerful Handbook for Reasoning

Shortcuts in REASONING

(Verbal, Non-Verbal & Analytical)

for Competitive Exams

- **Corporate Office :** 45, 2nd Floor, Maharishi Dayanand Marg, Corner Market, Malviya Nagar, New Delhi-110017 Tel. : 011-49842349 / 49842350

Typeset by Disha DTP Team

Printed at : Repro Knowledgecast Limited, Thane

For further information about books from DISHA,

Log on to www.dishapublication.com or email to info@dishapublication.com

Index

VERBAL REASONING

NON-VERBAL REASONING

ANALYTICAL REASONING

Analogy & Classification

ANALOGY

The meaning of analogy is 'similar properties' or similarity. If an object or word or digit or activity shows any similarity with another object or word or digit or activity in terms of properties, type, shape, size, trait etc., then the particular similarity will be called analogy. The relationship of analogy can be established in two ways :

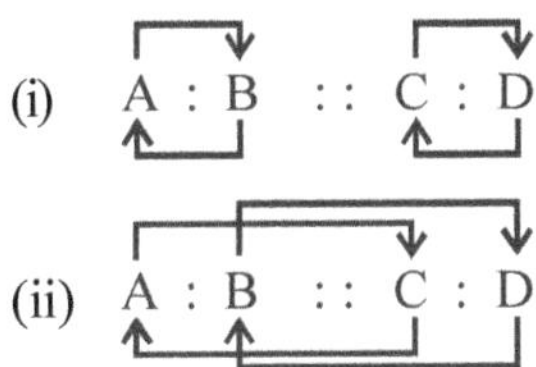

TYPES OF ANALOGY

1. **Word Analogy**
2. **Letter Analogy**
3. **Number Analogy**
4. **Mixed Analogy**

Word Analogy

In word analogy, candidates have to find the relationship between given words in a pair.

1. **TOOL & OBJECT BASED ANALOGY**

   This establishes a relationship between a tool and the object in which it works.

   EXAMPLE

   Scissors : Cloth

2. **SYNONYM BASED ANALOGY**

   In such type of analogy two words have similar meaning.

   EXAMPLE

   Huge : Gigantic

3. **WORKER & TOOL BASED ANALOGY**

   This establishes a relationship between a particular tool and the person of that particular profession who uses that tool.

   EXAMPLE

   Writer : Pen

4. **WORKER & PRODUCT BASED ANALOGY**

   This type of analogy gives a relationship between a person of particular profession and his/her creations.

   EXAMPLE

   Writer : Book

5. **CAUSES & EFFECT BASED ANALOGY**

   In such type of analogy 1st word acts and the 2nd word is the effect of that action.

   EXAMPLE

   Work : Tiredness

6. **OPPOSITE RELATIONSHIP (ANTONYM) BASED ANALOGY**

   In such type of analogy the two words of the question pair are opposite in meaning.

   EXAMPLE

   Poor : Rich

7. **GENDER BASED ANALOGY**

In such type of analogy, one word is masculine and another word is feminine of it or It is a 'male and female' or 'sex' relationship.

EXAMPLE

Man : Woman

8. **CLASSIFICATION BASED ANALOGY**

This type of analogy is based on biological, physical, chemical or any other classification. In such problems the 1st word may be classified by the 2nd word and vice-versa.

EXAMPLE

Oxygen : Gas

9. **FUNCTION BASED ANALOGY**

In such type of analogy, 2nd word describes the function of the 1st word.

EXAMPLE

Singer : Sings

10. **QUANTITY AND UNIT BASED ANALOGY**

In such type of analogy 2nd word is the unit of the first word and vice-versa.

EXAMPLE

Distance : Mile

11. **FINISHED PRODUCT & RAW MATERIAL BASED ANALOGY**

In such type of analogy the 1st word is the raw material and 2nd word is the end product of that raw material and vice-versa.

EXAMPLE

Yarn : Fabric

12. **UTILITY BASED ANALOGY**

In such type of analogy the 2nd word shows the purpose of the 1st word or vice-versa.

EXAMPLE

Pen : Writing

13. **SYMBOLIC RELATIONSHIP BASED ANALOGY**

In such type of analogy, the 1st word is the symbol of the 2nd word and vice-versa.

EXAMPLE

White : Peace

14. **ADULT & YOUNG ONE BASED ANALOGY**

In such type of analogy, the 1st word is the adult one and 2nd word is the young one of the 1st word or vice-versa.

EXAMPLE

Cow : Calf

15. **SUBJECT & SPECIALIST BASED ANALOGY**

In such type of analogy the 2nd word is the specialist of 1st word (subject) or vice-versa.

EXAMPLE

Heart : Cardiologist

16. **HABIT BASED ANALOGY**

In this type of analogy 2nd word is the habit of 1st and vice-versa.

EXAMPLE

Cat : Omnivorous

17. **INSTRUMENT AND MEASUREMENT BASED ANALOGY**

We see in this type of analogy, the 1st word is the instrument to measure the 2nd word and vice-versa:

EXAMPLE

Hygrometer : Humidity

18. **INDIVIDUAL & GROUP BASED ANALOGY**

Second word is the group of 1st word (or vice-versa) in such type of analogy.

EXAMPLE

Cow : Herd

19. STATE & CAPITAL BASED ANALOGY

1st word is the state and 2nd word is the capital of that state (1st word) (or vice-versa) in the analogy like this.

EXAMPLE

Bihar : Patna

20. ANALOGY BASED ON INDIVIDUAL & DWELLING PLACE

In such type of analogy 1st word is the individual & 2nd word is the dwelling place of that individual (1st word) and vice-versa.

EXAMPLE

Horse : Stable

21. ANALOGY BASED ON WORKER AND WORKING PLACE

In this type of analogy the 1st word represents a person of particular profession and 2nd word represents the working place of that person (1st word) and vice-versa.

EXAMPLE

Doctor : Hospital

22. ANALOGY BASED ON TOPIC STUDY

1st word is the study of the 2nd word (or vice-versa) in the analogy like this.

EXAMPLE

Birds : Ornithology

Letter Analogy

In letter analogy, candidate has to find out the relationship between given letters or group of letters.

1. FORWARD ALPHABETICAL SEQUENCE BASED ANALOGY

EXAMPLE

CD : FG : : PQ : UV

Here, CD and FG are in the natural alphabetical sequence. Similarly, PQ & UV are in the natural alphabetical sequence.

2. BACKWARD OR OPPOSITE ALPHABETICAL SEQUENCE BASED ANALOGY

EXAMPLE

DC : GF : : QP : VU

In fact this case is opposite of case I

3. VOWEL – CONSONANT RELATION BASED ANALOGY

EXAMPLE

ATL : EVX : : IPR : ORS

Here, the 1st two words start with the 1st two vowels A & E and the next two words start with the next two vowels I & O. Last two letter of every word are consonants.

4. SKIP LETTER RELATION BASED ANALOGY

EXAMPLE

ABC : FGH : : IJK : NOP

Here, between ABC & FGH two letters skip and they are D & E. Similarly, between IJK & NOP two letters skip and they are L & M.

5. JUMBLED LETTERS RELATION BASED ANALOGY

EXAMPLE

(i) LAIN : NAIL : : EVOL : LOVE

Here, the 1st term gets reveresed to produce the 2nd term and similar relation is shown in between 3rd and 4th term.

❑ *Shortcut Approach*

I: While solving the problems based on alphabet, you must have in your mind the exact positions of every letters of alphabet in forward order as well as in backward or reverse order as given below:

Letters positions in forward alphabetical order:

A	B	C	D	E	F	G	H	I	J	K	L	M	N	O	P	Q	R	S
1	2	3	4	5	6	7	8	9	10	11	12	13	14	15	16	17	18	19

S	T	U	V	W	X	Y	Z
19	20	21	22	23	24	25	26

Letters positions in backward or reverse alphabetical order:

Z	Y	X	W	V	U	T	S	R	Q	P	O	N	M	L	K	J	I
1	2	3	4	5	6	7	8	9	10	11	12	13	14	15	16	17	18

H	G	F	E	D	C	B	A
19	20	21	22	23	24	25	26

II: Just keep in mind, the following positions of the letters in the English alphabet (forward order).

(i)

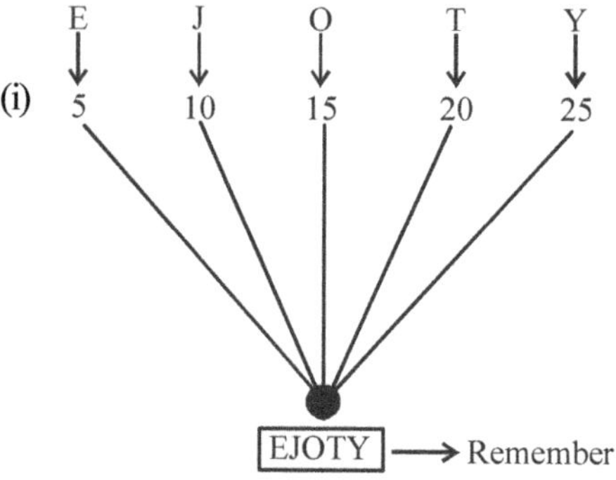

(ii)

C → 3, F → 6, I → 9, L → 12, O → 15, R → 18, U → 21, X → 24

CFILORUX ⟶ Remember

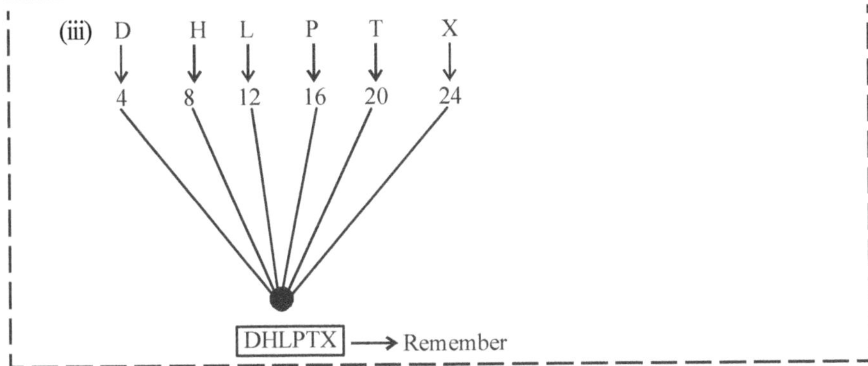

Number Analogy

In this, candidate has to find out the relationship between the numbers or group of numbers.

1. **EVEN AND ODD NUMBERS BASED ANALOGY**

   EXAMPLE 84 : 51 : : 72 : 37
   (Here, 84 & 72 are even and 51 & 37 are odd numbers respectively)

2. **ADDITION AND SUBTRACTION OF NUMBERS BASED ANALOGY**

   EXAMPLE 234 : 9 : : 136 : 10
   (Here, $2 + 3 + 4 = 9$ and $1 + 3 + 6 = 10$)

3. **MULTIPLICATION AND DIVISION OF NUMBERS BASED ANALOGY**

   EXAMPLE 3 : 21 : : 5 : 35
   (Here, $3 \times 7 = 21$ and $5 \times 7 = 35$)

4. **SQUARES & CUBES OF NUMBERS BASED ANALOGY**

   EXAMPLE 4 : 16 : : 8 : 64
   (here, $4^2 = 16$ and $8^2 = 64$)

Mixed Analogy

In this, candidate has to find out the relationship between the given group of letters and a number on one side.

EXAMPLE AB : 12 : : CD : : 34

(Here, A B ↓ ↓ 1 2 (positional value) and C D ↓ ↓ 3 4 (positional vlaue)

CLASSIFICATION

In classification we take out an element out of some given elements and the element to be taken out is different from the rest of the elements in terms of common properties, shapes, sizes, types, nature, colours, traits etc. In this way, the rest of the elements form a group and the element that has been taken out is not the member of that group as this single element does not possesses the common quality to be possessed by rest of the elements.

TYPES OF CLASSIFICATION

1. **Letter/meaningless word based classification**
2. **Meaningful word based classification**
3. **Digit based classification**
4. **General knowledge based classification**

1. LETTER/MEANINGLESS WORD BASED CLASSIFICATION

Such classifications are based on letters of English alphabet. So many groups of letters are given in the question in which one group is different from remaining groups and hence the different group will be our answer.

EXAMPLE

(a) PQT **(b) UVY**
(c) DEH **(d) IJN**
(e) FGJ

Sol. (a) Here,

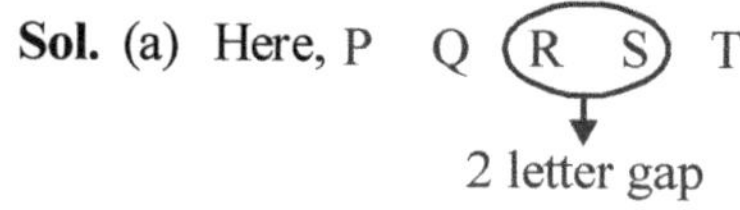

(b)

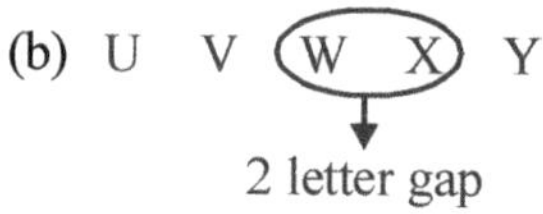

(c)

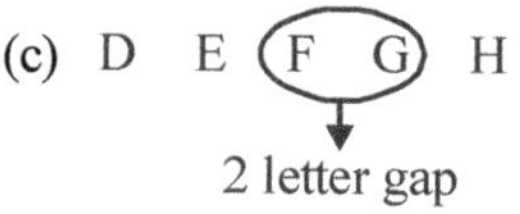

(d)

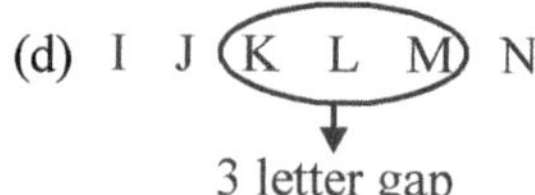

(e)

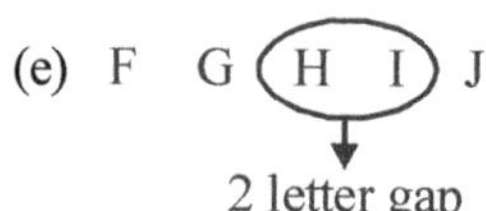

2. MEANINGFUL WORDS BASED CLASSIFICATION

In such type of classification we have to take odd word out of the given group of meaningful words.

EXAMPLE

(a) Slim **(b) Trims**
(c) Greets **(d) Grid**
(e) Fight

Sol. (a) Here, (b)

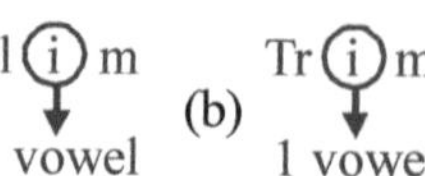

(c) Gr(ee)ts → 2 vowels (d) Gr(i)d → 1 vowel

(e) F(i)ght → 1 vowel

3. DIGIT BASED CLASSIFICATION

In such type of classifications digits or numbers are given to find out one number that is not a part of the group of remaining numbers.

EXAMPLE

(a) 122 **(b) 128**
(c) 199 **(d) 200**
(e) 388

Sol. 199 is an odd number while all the other options are even numbers.

4. GENERAL KNOWLEDGE BASED CLASSIFICATION

Such classification is done on the basis of our general knowledge. No doubts that this is a word based classification but without having general knowledge this type of questions can not be solved.

EXAMPLE

(a) Cat **(b) Dog**
(c) Tiger **(d) Octopus**
(e) Lion

Sol. Octopus is the only animal out of given options which is a water animal. Rest of the options are land animals.

❑ ***Shortcut Approach***

Step I : See all the given options with a serious eye.

Step II : Try to make relation of similarity among the given options.

Step III : Find out the one word not having the common similarity like other four options and that one word will be your answer.

PRACTICE EXERCISE

DIRECTIONS (Qs. 1-2) : *In the following six questions, select the related word/letters/number from the given alternatives.*

1. 43 : 57 : : 111 : ?
   (a) 135 (b) 133
   (c) 134 (d) 136
2. AZBY : CXDW : : EVFU : ?
   (a) GTHS (b) FUVE
   (c) ZYEU (d) BXWD

DIRECTION (Q. 3) : *In the following question, select the related word pair from the given alternatives.*

3. Power : Watt : : ? : ?
   (a) Pressure : Newton
   (b) Force : Pascal
   (c) Resistance : Mho
   (d) Work : Joule

DIRECTION (Q. 4) : *In the following question, select the related word pair from the given alternatives.*

4. 9143 : 9963 : : 6731 : ?
   (a) 1368 (b) 5666
   (c) 8964 (d) 9694

DIRECTION (Q. 5) : *In the following question, select related word pair/ number from the given alternatives.*

5. KLMN : IJKL : : TUVW : ?
   (a) RSUT (b) VWXY
   (c) STUV (d) RSTU

DIRECTIONS (Qs. 6-8) : *In the following questions, select the related word from the given alternatives.*

6. Influenza: Virus :: Ringworm: ?
   (a) Bacteria (b) Fungi
   (c) parasite (d) Protozoa
7. LMNO : NQTW :: GHIJ : ?
   (a) ILOR (b) ILRO
   (c) ILMO (d) LRMO
8. 103 : 10609 : : 106 : ?
   (a) 10606 (b) 10306
   (c) 11236 (d) 13636

DIRECTIONS (Qs. 9-12): *In the following questions, find the odd word/ letters/number pair from the given alternatives.*

9. (a) D F O U (b) N P S W
   (c) K M P T (d) D F I M
10. (a) 286 (b) 166
    (c) 495 (d) 583
11. (a) Wing Commander
    (b) Air Marshal
    (c) Captain
    (d) Group Captain
12. (a) 243 - 132 (b) 183 - 54
    (c) 108 - 97 (d) 99 - 63

DIRECTION (Q. 13) : *In the following question, select the odd word from the given alternatives.*

13. (a) Chennai (b) Daman
    (c) Raipur (d) Shimla

DIRECTIONS (Qs. 14-15): *Choose the odd word/letters number/number pair from the given alternatives.*

14. (a) Sirius
    (b) Proximacentauri
    (c) Deimos
    (d) Alpha centauri
15. (a) 2890 (b) 3375
    (c) 1728 (d) 1331

HINTS & SOLUTIONS

1. **(b)** As, $6^2 + 7 = 43$
$(7^2) + 8 = 57$
Similarly,
$(10)^2 + 11 = 111$
$(11)^2 + 12 = 133$

2. **(a)** $A \xrightarrow{+2} C$ $E \xrightarrow{+2} G$
$Z \xleftarrow{+2} X$ $V \xleftarrow{+2} T$
$B \xrightarrow{+2} D$ $F \xrightarrow{+2} H$
$Y \xleftarrow{+2} W$ $U \xleftarrow{+2} S$

3. **(d)** As, Power is measured by Watt.
Similarly, Work is measured by Joule.

4. **(c)** As,
$9143 \Rightarrow 9 + 1 + 4 + 3 = 17$
$9963 \Rightarrow 9 + 9 + 6 + 3 = 27$
Similarly,
$6731 \Rightarrow 6 + 7 + 3 + 1 = 17$
$8964 \Rightarrow 8 + 9 + 6 + 4 = 27$

5. **(d)** As,

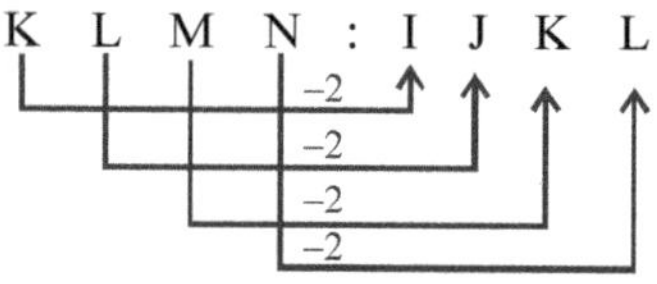

Similarly,

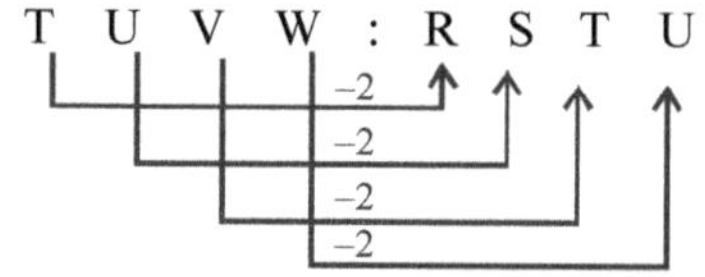

6. **(b)** As, Infuenza is caused by virus.
Similarly, Ring worm is caused by Fungi.

7. **(a)** As,

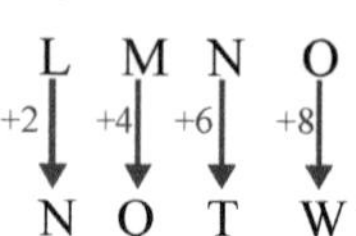

Similarly,

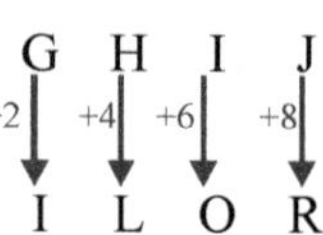

8. **(c)** As, $(103)^2 = 10609$
Similarly, $(106)^2 = 11236$

9. **(a)**
N P S W, K M P T
+2 +3 +4 +2 +3 +4

and D F I M
+2 +3 +4

But, D F O U
+2 +9 +6

10. **(b)** As, 2 ⑧ 6 = 2 + 6 = ⑧, 4 ⑨ 5 = 4 + 5 = ⑨ and 5 ⑧ 3 = 5 + 3 = ⑧
but, 1 ⑥ 6 = 1 + 6 = 7 ≠ 6

11. **(c)** Captain is odd one out.

12. **(d)** 99-63 is odd one out.

13. **(b)** Except Daman, all others are capital.

14. **(c)** Except Deimos (It is a satellite), all others are star systems.

15. **(a)** Except 2890, All are cube of a number.
$(15)^3 = 3375$, $(12)^3 = 1728$, $(11)^3 = 1331$.

Chapter 2

Series

INTRODUCTION

A series is a sequence of numbers/alphabetical letters or both which follow a particular rule. Each element of series is called 'term'. We have to analyse the pattern and find the missing term or next term to continue the pattern.

TYPES OF SERIES

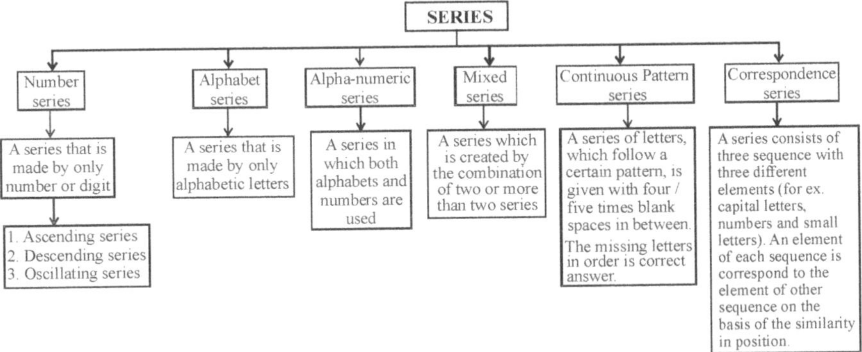

NUMBER SERIES

Number series is a form of numbers in a certain sequence, where some numbers are mistakenly put into the series of numbers and some number is missing in that series, we need to observe first and then find the accurate number to that series of numbers.

Remember

- Even and odd numbers.
- Prime and composite numbers.
- Square and square roots of a numbers.
- Cube and cube roots of a numbers.
- Arithmetic Operations
  - Addition
  - Subtraction
  - Division
  - Multiplication

Types of Number Series

1. PERFECT SQUARE SERIES

This type of series are based on square of a number which is in same order and one square number is missing in that given series.

EXAMPLE **841, ?, 2401, 3481, 4761**

Sol. $29^2, 39^2, 49^2, 59^2, 69^2$

2. PERFECT CUBE SERIES

Perfect Cube series is a arrangement of numbers in a certain order, where some number which is in same order and one cube is missing in that given series.

EXAMPLE **4096, 4913, 5832, ?, 8000**

Sol. $16^3, 17^3, 18^3, 19^3, 20^3$

3. MIXED NUMBER SERIES

Mixed number series is a arrangement of numbers in a certain order. This type of series are more than are different order which arranged in alternatively in single series or created according to any non conventional rule.

EXAMPLE **62, 64, 30, 32, 14, 16, ?**

Sol.

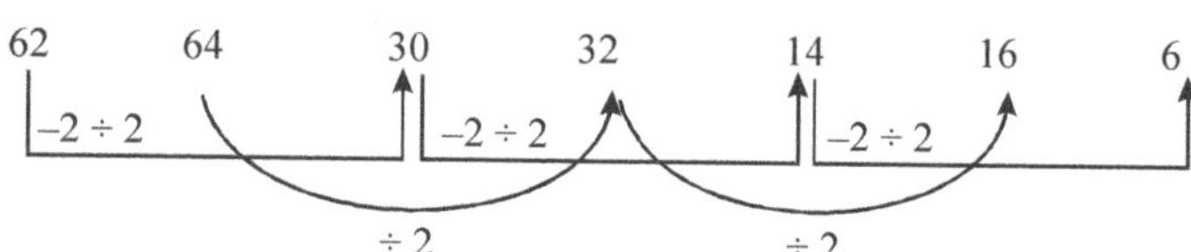

4. PRIME SERIES

When numbers are a series of prime numbers.

EXAMPLE **2, 3, 5, 7, 11, 13, __ , 19**

Sol. Here, the terms of the series are the prime numbers in order. The prime number, after 13 is 17. So, the answer to this question is 17.

5. ALTERNATE PRIMES

It can be explained by below example.

EXAMPLE **2, 11, 17, 23, __, 41**

Sol. Here, the series is framed by taking the alternative prime numbers. After 23, the prime numbers are 29 and 31. So, the answer is 31.

6. The difference of any term from its succeding term is constant (either increasing series or decreasing series):

EXAMPLE **4, 7, 10, 13, 16, 19, __, 25**

Sol. Here, the differnce of any term from its succeding term is 3.

$7 - 4 = 3$

$10 - 7 = 3$

So, the answer is $19 + 3 = 22$

7. The difference between two consecutive terms will be either increasing or decreasing by a constant number:

EXAMPLE **2, 10, 26, 50, 82, __**

Sol. Here, the difference between two consecutive terms are

$10 - 2 = 8$

$26 - 10 = 16$

$50 - 26 = 24$

$82 - 50 = 32$

Here, the difference is increased by 8 (or you can say the multiples of 8). So the next difference will be 40 (32 + 8). So, the answer is $82 + 40 = 122$

8. The difference between two numbers can be multiplied by a constant number:

EXAMPLE 15, 16, 19, 28, 55, __

Sol. Here, the differences between two numbers are
$16 - 15 = 1$
$19 - 16 = 3$
$28 - 19 = 9$
$55 - 28 = 27$
Here, the difference is multiplied by 3. So, the next difference will be 81. So, the answer is $55 + 81 = 136$

9. The difference can be multiples by number which will be increasing by a constant number:

EXAMPLE 2, 3, 5, 11, 35, __

Sol. The difference between two number are
$3 - 2 = 1$
$5 - 3 = 2$
$11 - 5 = 6$
$35 - 11 = 24$

10. Every third number can be the sum of the preceding two numbers :

EXAMPLE 3, 5, 8, 13, 21, __

Sol. Here, starting from third number
$3 + 5 = 8$
$5 + 8 = 13$
$8 + 13 = 21$
So, the answer is $13 + 21 = 34$

11. Every third number can be the product of the preceeding two numbers :

EXAMPLE 1, 2, 2, 4, 8, 32. __

Sol. Here, starting from the third number
$1 \times 2 = 2$
$2 \times 2 = 4$
$2 \times 4 = 8$
$4 \times 8 = 32$
So, the answer is $8 \times 32 = 256$

12. Every succeeding term is got by multiplying the previous term by a constant number or numbers which follow a special pattern.

EXAMPLE 5, 15, 45, 135, __

Sol. Here,
$5 \times 3 = 15$
$15 \times 3 = 45$
$45 \times 3 = 135$
So, the answer is $135 \times 3 = 405$

13. In certain series the terms are formed by various rule (miscellaneous rules). By keen observation you have to find out the rule and the appropriate answer.

EXAMPLE 4, 11, 31, 90, __

Sol. Terms are,
$4 \times 3 - 1 = 11$
$11 \times 3 - 2 = 31$
$31 \times 3 - 3 = 90$
So, the answer will be $90 \times 3 - 4 = 266$

14. TRIANGULAR PATTERN SERIES:

Sometimes the difference between consecutive terms of a series, again form a series. The differences between the consecutive terms of the new series so formed, again form a series. This pattern continues till we attain a uniform difference between the consecutive terms of the series.

EXAMPLE

2, 12, 36, 80, 150, ?

Sol. As discussed above, we may lebel the given series as I and then form series II to IV as shown, below:

Series-I: 2 12 36 80 150 ?
Series-II: 10 24 44 70 ?
Series-III: 14 20 26 ?
Series-IV: 6 6

Clearly, the pattern in series III is +6.
So, missing term in series III = 26 + 6 = 32
Missing term in series II = 70 + 32 = 102
Missing term in series I = 150 + 102 = 252
Thus the missing term = 252
(i.e. 150 + 70 + 26 + 6)

Remember

Elementry Idea of Progressions:

1. **ARITHMETIC PROGRESSION (A. P.):**
   The sequence of the form a, $a + d$, $a + 2d$, $a + 3d$, ... is known as an A.P., whose n^{th} term is $a + (n-1)d$. Here 'a' is first term and 'd' is common difference.
2. **GEOMETRIC PROGRESSION (G. P.):**
   The sequence of the form a, ar, ar^2, ar^3, ... is known a G.P., whose n^{th} term is ar^{n-1}.
3. **FIND THE WRONG NUMBER:**
   In this type of questions, a series of numbers is given which follow a certain pattern and one its term does not fit into the series. The candidate is required to identify the pattern involved in the formation of series and then find out that number which does not follow the specific pattern of the series. This particular number is the wrong term in the series.

EXAMPLE

One number is wrong in the following series. Find out this wrong number.
1, 5, 9, 15, 25, 37, 49,

Sol. The pattern is as follows

1	5	9	(15) → 17	25	37	49
↓	↓	↓	↓	↓	↓	↓
1^2	(2^2+1)	3^2	(4^2+1)	5^2	(6^2+1)	7^2

Hence number 15 is wrong and should be replaced by 17.

Shortcut Approach

(1) If numbers are in ascending order in the number series, then the numbers may be **added or multiplied** by certain numbers from the first number.

(A) 19 23 26 30 33 ?
19 23 26 30 33 37
+4 → +3 → +4 → +3 → +4 →

(B) 1 3 12 60 ?
1 3 12 60 360
×3 → ×4 → ×5 → ×6 →

(2) If numbers are in descending order in the number series, then the numbers may be **subtracted or divided** by certain numbers from the first number.

(A) 34 18 10 6 4 ?
34 18 10 6 4 3
−16 → −8 → −4 → −2 → −1 →

(B) 720 120 24 6 2 ?
720 120 24 6 2 1
/6 → /5 → /4 → /3 → /2 →

(3) If numbers are in mix order (increasing and decreasing) in the number series, then the numbers may be in **addition, subtraction, multiplication, division, square and cube** in the alternate numbers.

(A)
200 165 148 117 104 ?
200 165 148 117 104 77

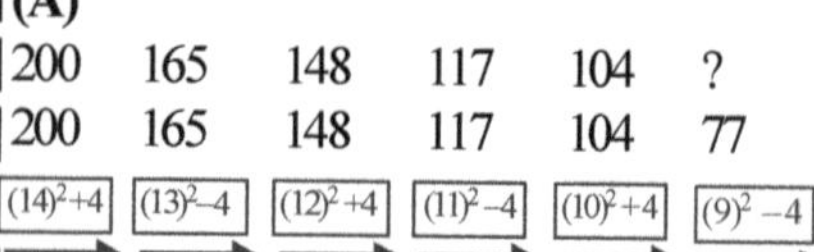
$(14)^2+4$ → $(13)^2-4$ → $(12)^2+4$ → $(11)^2-4$ → $(10)^2+4$ → $(9)^2-4$ →

(B)

14 17 31 48 ? 127

14 17 31 48 79 127

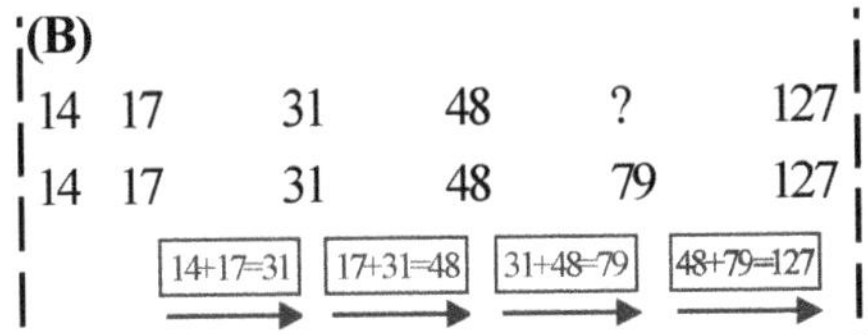

(4) Check the direct formula if any.

(5) Check whether all numbers are odd, even or prime.

(6) Check whether all the number are perfect squares or cubes.

ALPHABET SERIES

A series that is made by only alphabetic letters.

EXAMPLE **G, H, J, M, ?**

Sol.

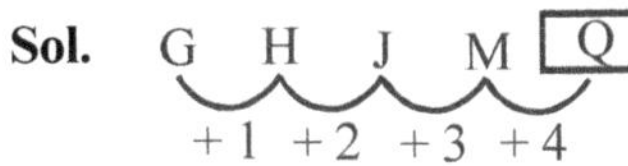

Shortcut Approach

- Remember all the alphabets and their place number.
- Intervals like :

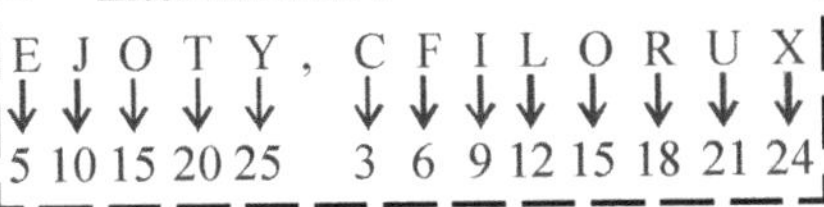

ALPHA NUMERIC SERIES

These kind of problems used both mathematical operation and position of letters in the alphabet in forward, backward order.

EXAMPLE 2 Z 5, 7 Y 7, 14 X 9, 23 W 11, 34 V 13, ?

Sol.

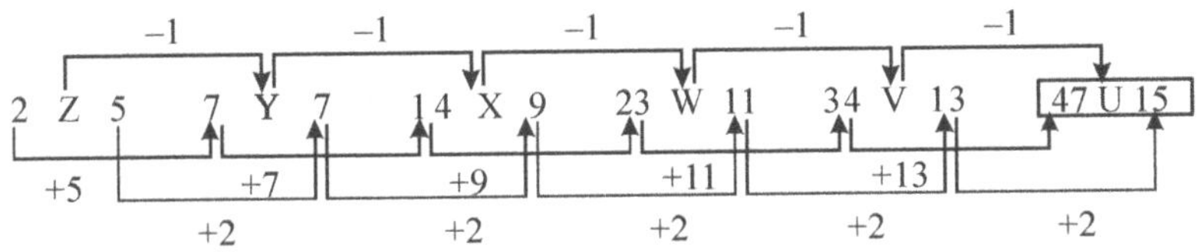

MIXED SERIES

A series formed with the combination of more than one series.

EXAMPLE A, Z, C, X, E, ?

Sol. There are two interwoven series.

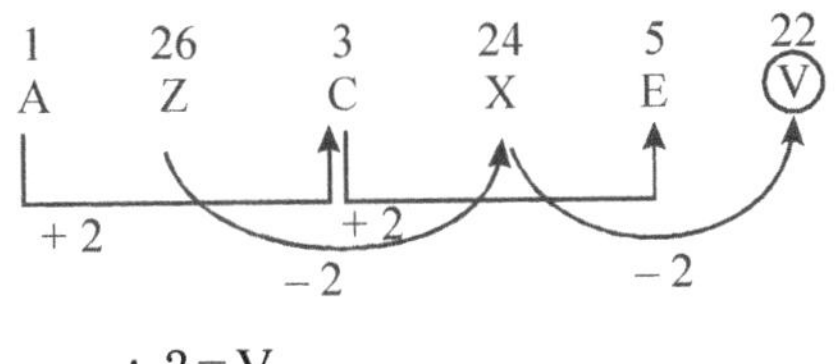

$\therefore$? = V

EXAMPLE **Z, L, X, J, V, H, T, F, __, __**

Sol. The given sequence consists of two series

(i) Z, X, V, T, __

(ii) L, J, H, F, __. Both consisting of alternate letters in the reverse order.

$\therefore$ Next term of (i) series = R, and

Next term of (ii) series = D

Reverse Order Repetition Series:

In such series, first part is written in reverse order of the second part of the series.

EXAMPLE R, A, M, S, H, H; S, E, M A, ?

Sol.

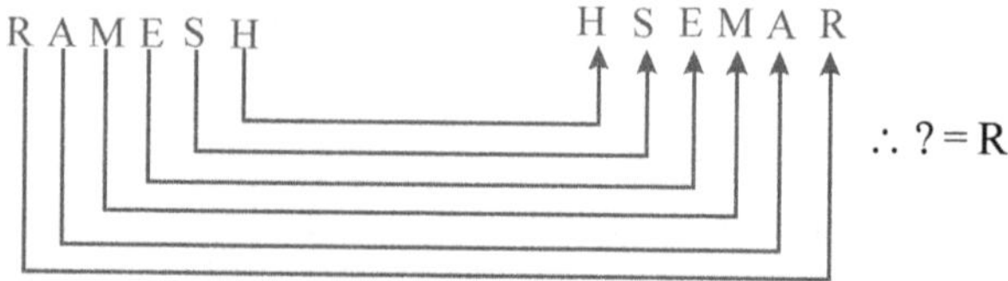

∴ ? = R

SERIES HAVING GROUP OF LETTERS AS ITS ELEMENTS:

In such series, each element consists of group of letters instead of a single letter.

EXAMPLE LDP, DPL, PLD, ?

Sol.

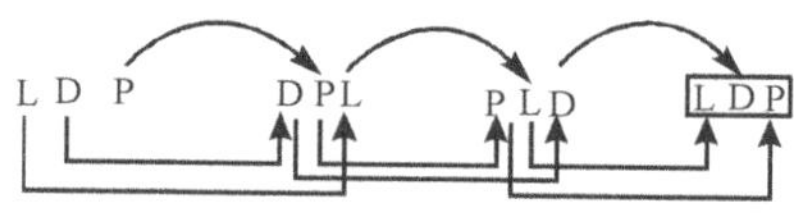

∴ ? = LDP

CONTINUOUS PATTERN SERIES

It is a series of small/capital letters that follow a certain pattern like repetition of letters.

EXAMPLE **b a a b – a b a – b b a – –**

Sol. b a a b b a / b a a b b a / b a

CORRESPONDENCE SERIES:

This type of series consists of three sequences with three different elements (usually capital letters, digits and small letters). On the basis of the similarity in position in the three sequences, a capital letter is found to correspond with a unique digit and a unique small letter, whenever it occurs. The candidate is required to trace out this correspondence and accordingly choose the elements to be filled in at the desired places.

EXAMPLE

C B – – D – B A B C C B

– – 1 2 4 3 – – ? ? ? ?

a – a b – c – b – – – –

Sol. Comparing the positions of the capital letters, numbers and small letters, we find a corresponds to c and 1 correspond to a. So, a and 1 correspond to c. b corresponds to A and 2 corresponds to b. So, b and 2 correspond to A. Also, 4 corresponds to D. Therefore, the remaining number i.e. 3 corresponds to B. Hence, BCCB corresponds to 3113.

PRACTICE EXERCISE

DIRECTIONS (Qs. 1-2): *In the following Questions, which one set of letters when sequentially placed at the gaps in the given letter series shall complete it?*

1. ccbab _ caa _ bccc _ a _
(a) babb (b) bbba
(c) baab (d) babc

2. a_ _ dba_ _bcad__ _da__ _cd
(a) bccdbcab (b) abcddcba
(c) cbcddcba (d) aabbccdd

DIRECTIONS (Qs. 3-4): *A series is given, with one term missing. Choose amongst the given responses choose the meaningful one.*

3. CUS, DVT, EWU, ____
(a) FXV (b) VXF
(c) XFV (d) XVF

4. 206, 221, 251, 296, ?, 431
(a) 326 (b) 356
(c) 311 (d) 341

5. A series is given, with one term missing. Choose the correct alternative from the given ones that will complete the series.
CAT , DBT , ECT , ?
(a) DCT (b) FDT
(c) FCT (d) FAT

DIRECTIONS (Qs. 6-10) : *What should come in place of the question mark (?) in the following number series?*

6. 2 16 112 672 3360 13440 ?
(a) 3430 (b) 3340
(c) 40320 (d) 43240
(e) None of these

7. 4 9 19 ? 79 159 319
(a) 59 (b) 39
(c) 49 (d) 29
(e) None of these

8. 4000 2000 1000 500 250 125 ?
(a) 80 (b) 65
(c) 62.5 (d) 83.5
(e) None of these

9. 588 563 540 519 ? 483 468
(a) 500 (b) 496
(c) 494 (d) 490
(e) None of these

10. 121 ? 81 64 49 36 25
(a) 92 (b) 114
(c) 98 (d) 100
(e) None of these

DIRECTIONS (Qs. 11-15) : *Each of the following number series, a wrong number is given. Find out that number.*

11. 3 5 13 43 178 891 5353
(a) 43 (b) 178
(c) 891 (d) 5353
(e) None of these

12. 80640 10080 1440 240 48 10 4
(a) 240 (b) 48
(c) 1440 (d) 10
(e) None of these

13. 3 5 10 12 17 23 24
(a) 5 (b) 17
(c) 24 (d) 23
(e) None of these

14. 1, 11, 38, 78, 175, 301
(a) 11 (b) 78
(c) 175 (d) 301
(e) None of these

15. 17, 39, 85, 179, 369, 879
(a) 369 (b) 211
(c) 179 (d) 879
(e) None of these

HINTS & SOLUTIONS

1. **(a)** c c b a/b b c a/a a b c/c c b a/b

2. **(a)** a b c d/b a c d/b c a d/b c d a/ a b c d.

3. **(a)**

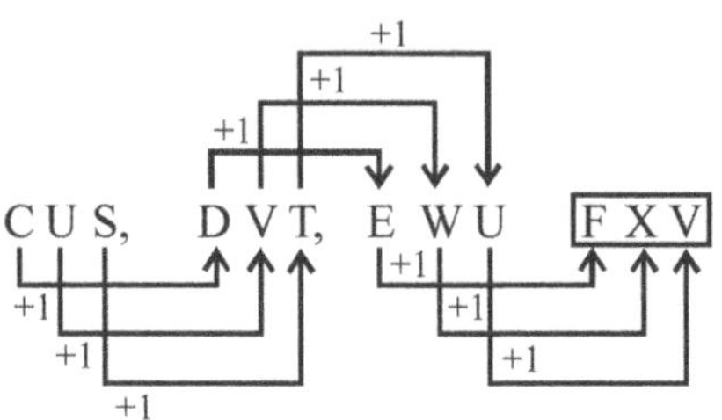

4. **(b)**

206 221 251 296 [356] 431

+15 +30 +45 +60 +75

5. **(b)**

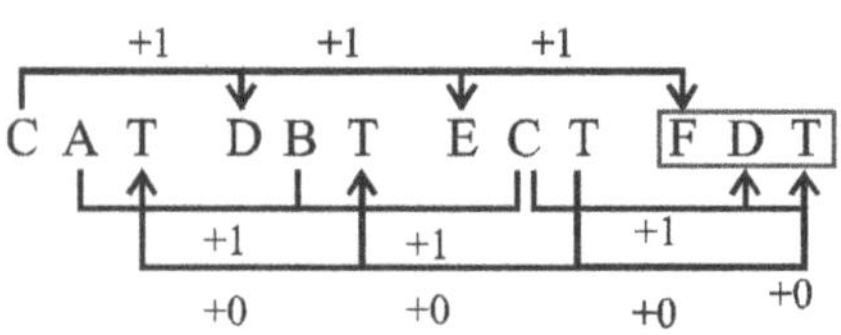

6. **(c)** Given series.

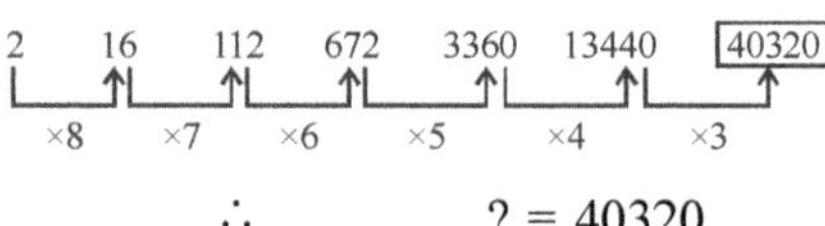

∴ ? = 40320

7. **(b)** Given series.

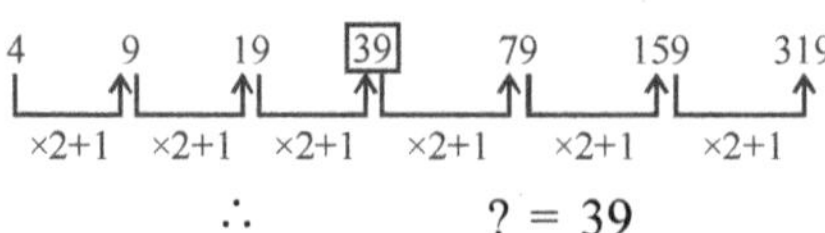

∴ ? = 39

8. **(c)** Given series

4000 2000 1000 500 250 125 [62.5]

÷ 2 ÷ 2 ÷ 2 ÷ 2 ÷ 2 ÷ 2

∴ ? = 62.5

9. **(a)** Given series.

588 563 540 519 [500] 483 468

− 25 − 23 − 21 − 19 − 17 − 15

∴ ? = 500

10. **(d)** Given series.

121	[100]	81	64	49	36	25
↑	↑	↑	↑	↑	↑	↑
$(11)^2$	$(10)^2$	$(9)^2$	$(8)^2$	$(7)^2$	$(6)^2$	$(5)^2$

∴ ? = 100

11. **(b)** $3 \times 1 + 2 = 5$
$5 \times 2 + 3 = 13$
$13 \times 3 + 4 = 43$
$43 \times 4 + 5 = 177$
Wrong No = 178
Correct Number = 177

12. **(d)** $80640 \div 8 = 10080$
$10080 \div 7 = 1440$
$1440 \div 6 = 240$
$240 \div 5 = 48$
$48 \div 4 = 12$
Wrong No = 10
Correct Number = 12

13. **(e)** First series: 3, 10, 17, 24 (increased by 7)
Second Series: 5, 14, 23 (increased by 9)
Wrong Number: 12
Correct Number: 14

14. **(b)** $1 + 3^2 + 1 = 11$
$11 + 5^2 + 2 = 38$
$38 + 7^2 + 3 = 90$
$90 + 9^2 + 4 = 175$
$175 + 11^2 + 5 = 301$
Wrong Number = 78
Correct Number = 90

15. **(d)** $7 \times 2 + 3 = 17$
$17 \times 2 + 5 = 39$
$39 \times 2 + 7 = 85$
$85 \times 2 + 9 = 179$
$179 \times 2 + 11 = 369$
$369 \times 2 + 13 = 751$
Wrong Number = 879
Correct Number = 751

Alphabet & Number Test

INTRODUCTION

As we know that English alphabet is a group of English letters, hence the problems based on alphabet are the problems based on English letters.

English Alphabet: English Alphabet has

- 26 letters
- 5 vowels (A, E, I, O, U) and 21 consonants.
- 13 letters in first half i.e. A to M
- 13 letters in second half i.e. N to Z

- **Linear arrangement of alphabets in forward order and their corresponding positions:**

A	B	C	D	E	F	G	H	I	J	K	L	M
1	2	3	4	5	6	7	8	9	10	11	12	13

N	U	P	Q	R	S	T	U	V	W	X	Y	Z
14	15	16	17	18	19	20	21	22	23	24	25	26

- **Linear arrangement of alphabets in reverse order and their corresponding positions:**

Z	Y	X	W	V	U	T	S	R	Q	P	O	N
1	2	3	4	5	6	7	8	9	10	11	12	13

M	L	K	J	I	H	G	F	E	D	C	B	A
14	15	16	17	18	19	20	21	22	23	24	25	26

- **Circular Arrangement:**

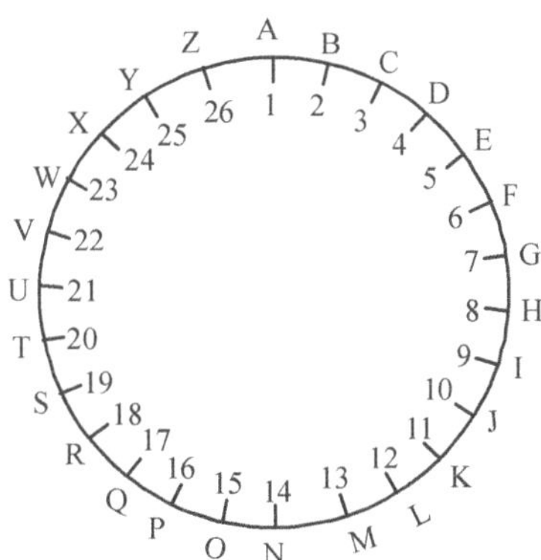

When we have to find out the letters coming before A or after Z, then linear arrangement does not work. In this case, we have to take help of circular arrangement . It is clear from circular arrangement, the letter coming just before A is Z and just after Z is A.

TYPES OF PROBLEMS

1. **General series of alphabet**
2. **Random series of alphabet**
3. **Problems of word formation**
4. **Problems of letter gap**
5. **Finding digits after rearrangement.**

General Series of Alphabet

EXAMPLE 1. Which of the following options is seventh to the right of the 13th letter from the left in a forward Alphabet series?

Sol. 1st of all we will write the forward alphabet series as given below:

A B C D E F G H I J K L M

13th letter from left

N O P Q R S T U V W X Y Z

7th letter

From the above series it is clear that M is the 13th letter from left and to the right of M (13th letter from left), T is the 7th letter.

Here, we have solved this problem with a general method. But this type of problem can also be approached through quicker method that will help you save some extra consumed time.

❑ Shortcut Approach

(a) If both the directions are same then subtraction of numbers takes place.

(b) If the directions are opposite then addition of numbers takes place.

SHORTCUT METHOD FOR ABOVE EXAMPLE:

Now, for solving the example we apply this rule. As we want to find out the 7th letter to the right of the 13th letter from the left, the directions are opposite and thus shortcut (b) will be applied here. Hence, we add $7 + 13 = 20$. Therefore, the answer will be 20th from left. Also, 20th from left less mean $26 - 20 + 1 = 7$th from right. We can easily see,

$\therefore$ 20th letter from left = T

Also 7th letter from right = T

After solving the example, you must have noticed that the above mentioned trick is to calculate the actual position of the required letter before going to search for it.

Remember

*m*th element to be counted from left to right of a series of *x* characters is equal to $(x + 1 - m)$th element to be counted from right to left of that series. This rule can be better illustrated by an example which is given below:

Let us take the forward order alphabet series,

A	B	C	D	E	F	G	H	I	J	K	L	M	N	O	P	Q	R	S	T	U	V	W	X	Y	Z
1	2	3	4	5	6	7	8	9	10	11	12	13	14	15	16	17	18	19	20	21	22	23	24	25	26

As we know that English alphabet has 26 characters, hence, we have $x = 26$.

Now suppose, we have to find out the position of K in the above given series counting from right to left.

Position of 'K' in the English alphabet from left to right is 11. Thus $m = 11$

$\therefore$ Position of K in the above given series from right to left would be $(26 + 1 - 11) = 16$

1. How to find the number of letters in the middle of two letters?

Four situations can be created under these type of problems.

1. ⟶ …?… ⟵
2. ⟶ …?… (with ⟶ above)
3. …?… ⟵ (with ⟵ above)
4. …?… ⟵ (with ⟶ above)

Let us understand through the following examples.

EXAMPLE 2. How many letters are there between 10th letter from left and 6th letter from right in the English Alphabets?

Shortcut Sol. Total number of letters in the English Alphabets = 26

10 letters
From left 10th 6th From right

Required number of letters

= 26 – (10 + 6) = 10 letters

EXAMPLE 3. How many letters are there between 18th letter from left and 7th letter from left in the English Alphabets?

Shortcut Sol. Total number of letters in the English Alphabet = 26

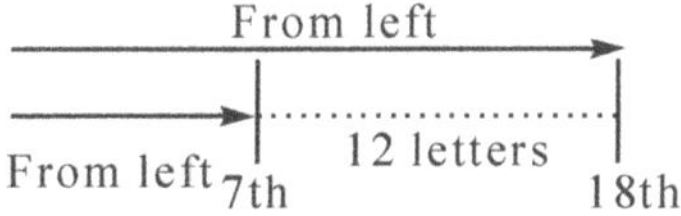

Required number of letters

= 18 – 7 – 1 = 10 letters

EXAMPLE 4. Find the number of letters between 19th letter from right and 6th letter from right in the English Alphabet.

Shortcut Sol. Number of letters in the English Alphabet = 26

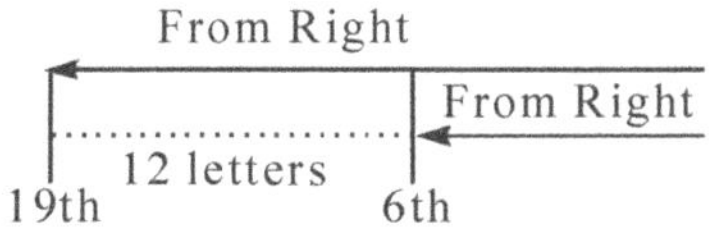

Required number of letters

= 19 – 6 – 1 = 12 letters

EXAMPLE 5. Find the number of letters between 21st letter from left and 15th letter from right in the English Alphabets.

Shortcut Sol. Number of letters in the English Alphabets = 26

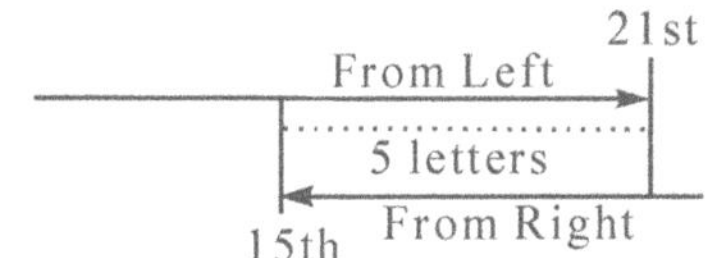

Required number of letters = 21 – 15 – 1 = 5

2. How to solve problems when letters are dropped or deleted at regular intervals?

EXAMPLE 6. If every 3rd letter from left to right of English alphabet is deleted, then what would be the 6th letter from left in the new series obtained?

Sol. General method:

A B (C) D E (F) G H (I) J K (L) M N (O) P Q (R) S T (U) V W (X) Y Z

Here, deleted letters have been encircled and we find the new series as given below:

A	B	D	E	G	H	J	K	M	N	P	Q	S	T	V	W	Y	Z
1	2	3	4	5	6	7	8	9	10	11	12	13	14	15	16	17	18

It is clear, that 6th letter from left in the new series is H.

❑ *Shortcut Approach*

No doubt, above general method gives the correct answer. But we need to save extra consumed time and this is the reason we go for a quicker approach.

As per the example, every third letter is deleted in the original series. It does mean that we are left of two letters after every deletion. Here, '2' is the key digit for us and we have to find out 6th letter from the left in the new obtained series. Therefore, we have to find a digit which is just less than 6 but divisible by 2. For this question the digit just less than 6 and divisible by 2 is 4. Now, we follow the operation given below:

6th letter from the left in the new series = $6+\frac{4}{2}$

= 8th letter from the left in the original series, which is it.

In the same manners, we can find out any letter at a particular position in the new obtained series.

∴ 16th letter from the left in the new obtained series = $16+\frac{14}{2}$

= 23rd letter from the left in the original series which is W.

18th letter from the left in the new obtained series

$= 18+\frac{16}{2}$

= 26th letter from the left in the original series which is Z.

The sample example can be asked in following way also.

"If every third letter from left to right in English alphabet is dropped (or deleted), then find out the 13th letter from right in the new obtained series".

To solve this, we find first of all the number of letters in the new obtained series.

As every third letter is dropped, hence we have

$\left(26-\frac{26}{3}\right) = 26-8 = 18$ letters in the new series.

(approximate value of $\frac{26}{3}$ is 8).

As per the example we have to find out 13th letter from right in the newly obtained series. This loss mean $(18+1-13) = 6$th letter from left which is H.

Note that : This shortcut approach can also be applied to the dropping of every 4th, 5th, 6th, 7th..... and so on letters from left to right at regular intervals.

3. How to solve problems based on the backward (reversed) alphabet series?

While solving problems based on general series of alphabet, we come across the various cases. In some cases we see that whole alphabet series is reversed but in some other cases 1st half of the series is reversed, or second half of the series is reversed or many segments of the alphabet series are reversed.

Let us take a case when a forward order alphabet series get reversed in three segments. In 1st segment 8 letters get reversed; in 2nd segment the next 8 letters get reversed and in the 3rd segment the remaining 10 letters get reversed. Just see the presentation given below:

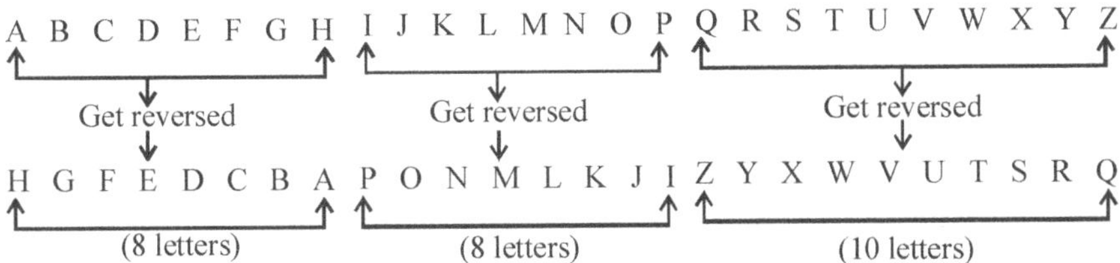

Now if you are asked to find out the 4th letter from left in the new obtained series, then through general method, we simply do counting from left in the new series and find out our required answer as 'E' because 'E' is at 4th position from left in the new obtained series. But while solving such type of problems, we have to do some time consuming formalities like (a) writing the original series (b) writing and reversing the letters of original series as per the question says and (c) counting them to get the required answer. Such time consuming processes can be avoided if we go through "**Remember**" and solve the question with shortcut approach.

❑ *Shortcut Approach*

It is clear that 4th letter from left in the new obtained series falls into first segment which has 8 letters. Hence, 4th letter in the new obtained series = $(8 + 1 - 4) = 5^{th}$ letter from the left in the original series. As we know that exact position of 5th letter from left in the original alphabet series is the position of E. Hence, E is our required answer.

If we have to find out 18th letter from left in the new obtained series, then that will be $16 + (10 + 1 - 2) = 25^{th}$ letter from left in the original alphabet series (why?) which is Y.

In fact, while finding out 18th letter, we can easily see that 18th letter is the 2nd letter of 3rd segment and hence it will be not affected by 1st two segments having 8 letters each. In other words to find out 18th letter in the new obtained series, we have to find out the 2nd letter in the 3rd segment. This is the reason we find out the 2nd letter in the 3rd segment and then add the 16 letters of 1st two segment to get the 18th letter in the new obtained series. From this, we find that 18th letter from left in the new obtained series is the 25th letter from left in the original series. As 25th letter from left in the original series is Y. So, (Y) will be our required answer.

Readers are advised to practice such type of problems as you much as possible and after a certain time will notice that you have got a skill to solve such problems in a few seconds and that too, without the use of pen and paper.

4. How to solve if positions of letters are interchanged?

There is no any rule for such type of problems. Only the hard practice can given you a skill to solve such questions in a quick time.

EXAMPLE 7. If A and C interchange their places, B and D interchange their places, F and H interchange their places and so on, then which letter will be 5th to the left of Q?

Sol. As per the question the interchanges take place as follows:

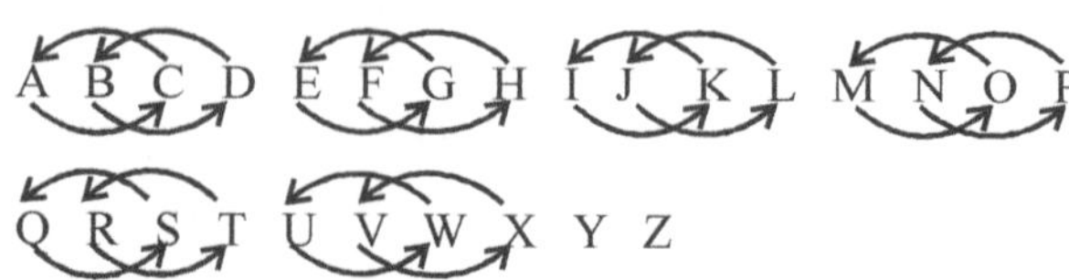

Here we can see that Q interchanges with S. Then to left of Q, the 5th letter would be P because P interchanges with N.

5. How to find the Middle Letter?

Shortcut Approach

Case I : Remember that if mth and nth letter from the left in the English alphabet are given then

Middle letter $= \left(\frac{m+n}{2}\right)$ th letter from the left.

EXAMPLE 8. Which letter will be midway between 8th letter from the left and 16th letter from the left in the English alphabet?

Sol. Here, $m = 8$ and $n = 16$

then middle letter $= \frac{8+16}{2} = \frac{24}{2}$

= 12th letter from left in the alphabet

= L

Shortcut Approach

Case II: Remember that if mth and nth letter from the right in the English alphabet are given then

Middle letter

$= \left(\frac{m+n}{2}\right)$ th letter from right

$= \left[26+1-\left(\frac{m+n}{2}\right)\right] = \left[27-\left(\frac{m+n}{2}\right)\right]$ th letter from the left in the English alphabet.

EXAMPLE 9. Which letter will be midway between 8th letter from the right and 16th letter from the right in the English alphabet.

Sol. Middle letter $= \left[27-\left(\frac{8+16}{2}\right)\right]$ th letter from left in the alphabet.

or middle letter = (27 – 12) = 15th letter from left = 0

Note : In case I and case II (m + n) must be divisible by 2.

Shortcut Approach

Case III : Remember that if the mth letter from the left and the nth letter from the right are given then middle letter

$= \left[\frac{(m-n)+27}{2}\right]$ th letter from the left in the alphabet.

EXAMPLE 10. Which letter will be midway between 8th letter from the left and 15th letter from the right?

Sol. Here, $m = 8$ and $n = 15$

Then middle letter $= \left[\frac{(8-15)+27}{2}\right]$

$= \left[\frac{20}{2}\right] = 10^{th}$

letter from left in the English alphabet = J.

Note : In case III, (m – n) + 27 must be divisible by 2.

2. Random Series of Alphabet

This series is not in the proper sequence and letters take their position in the series in jumbled manner. Further, there is also a possibility that all the 26 letters of English alphabet are not available in the series. Even same letters may be repeated in the series.

EXAMPLE 12. How many letters in the following series are immediately preceded by B but not immediately followed by D?

R S P Q B A H M A C F B A D N O P B A C D.

Sol. 

∴ Only the two times A fulfill the given condition and those A have been marked with the correct sign (✓). Those not fulfilling the condition have been marked with the cross sign (×). ∴ Required answer is 2.

3. Problems on Word Formation

In such problems, a word is given and you have to find out the number of words to be formed out of some letters drawn from that particular word.

EXAMPLE 11. How many meaningful words can be formed from the 3rd, 4th, 6th and 8th letter of the word 'CONTROVERSIAL'?

Sol.

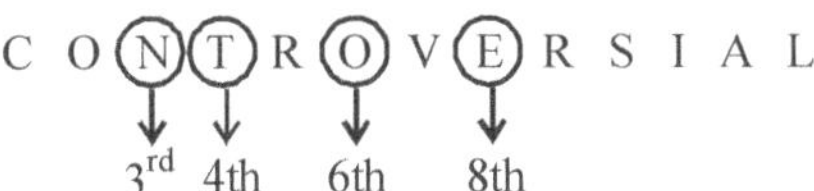

Now, from letters N, T, O and E, two words 'NOTE' and 'TONE' can be formed.

4. Problems of Letter Gap

Case I:

EXAMPLE 13. How many pairs of letters are there in the word 'DREAMLAND' which have as many letters between them as in the English alphabet?

Sol. Here, we are asked to solve problem according to English alphabet. In this case we have to count both ways. It does mean that we have to count from left to right and from right to left. Let us see the following presentation:

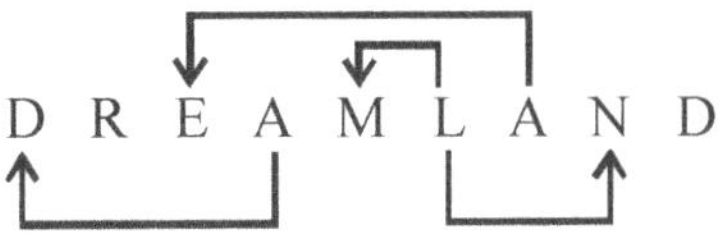

The above presentation makes it clear that the required pairs of letters are 4. (Pairs: DA, EA, ML and LN)

Case II:

EXAMPLE 14. How many pairs of letters are there in the word 'DREAMLAND' which have the same number of letters between them as in the English alphabet in the same sequence.

Sol. Here, we are asked to solve problems according to the alphabetical sequence. It does mean that we have to do counting only from left to right. Let us, see the following presentation:

D R E A M L A N D

The above presentation makes it clear that the required pair of letters is only 1 (Pair: LN)

5. Finding Digits After Rearrangement

In this type of problems, a specified order or pattern is used to rearrange the positions of digits of the number. Then, either the number of those digits is found out whose positions remain unchanged after rearrangement or the digit at particular place from left or right of the number is to be found out.

EXAMPLE : (Direction (Qs. 15-19)

Following questions are based on the five three-digit numbers given below:

713 361 458 932 724

15. If the positions of the first and the third digits are interchanged in each of these numbers, then which of these will be an even number.

Sol. According to the question,

Original Numbers : 713 361 458 932 724

New Arrangement : 317 163 854 239 427

So, here only one number is even i.e., 854.

16. What is the difference between the sum of the three digits of the highest and that of the second highest number?

Sol. Highest number = 932

Second highest number = 724

So, the required difference

$= (9+3+2)-(7+2+4)$

$= 14-13 = 1$

17. If all the three digits are arranged in ascending order (from left to right) within the number, in each of these numbers, then which of these will be second lowest ?

Sol. According to the question,

Original number : 713 361 458 932 724

New arrangement : 137 136 458 239 247

So, the second lowest number will be 137.

18. If the positions of the second and the third digits are interchanged in each of these numbers, then which of these will be exactly divisibly by 2 ?

Sol. According to the question,

Original Numbers : 713 361 458 932 724

New Arrangement : 731 316 485 923 742

So, two numbers will be exactly divisible by 2, i.e., 316 and 742.

19. If the given numbers are arranged in descending order, then what will be the square of the digits sum of the third number from the right end of the new arrangement ?

Sol. According to the question,

Original Numbers : 7 1 3 3 6 1 4 5 8 9 3 2 7 2 4

New Arrangement : 9 3 2 7 2 4 7 1 3 4 5 8 3 6 1

3rd from the right end

Now, digits sum of the 3rd number from the right

$= 7 + 1 + 3 = 11$

$\therefore$ Square of the digits sum

$= (11)^2 = 121.$

PRACTICE EXERCISE

1. If it is possible to make only one meaningful word with the first, second, fifth and sixth letters of the word PYGMALION, which of the following would be the second letter of that word from the right end? If no such word can be made, give 'X' as your answer and if more than one such word can be formed, give your answer as' Z '.
   (a) X (b) P
   (c) Y (d) A
   (e) Z
2. How many such pairs of letters are there in the word TRIBUNAL each of which has as many letters between them in the word as in the English alphabet ?
   (a) None (b) One
   (c) Two (d) Three
   (e) More than three
3. How many meaningful English words can be made with the third, fifth, seventh and ninth letters of the word DOWNGRADED, using each letter only once in each word?
   (a) None (b) One
   (c) Two (d) Three
   (e) More than three
4. Each vowel of the word BUCKSHOT is changed to the next letter in the English alphabetical order and each consonant is changed to the previous letter in the English alphabetical order. If the new alphabets thus formed are arranged in alphabetical order (from left to right). Which of the following will be fifth from the right ?
   (a) R (b) B
   (c) G (d) J
   (e) P
5. The positions of how many alphabets will remain unchanged if each of the alphabets in the word WORTHY is arranged in alphabetical order from left to right ?
   (a) None (b) One
   (c) Two (d) Three
   (e) More than three
6. Each odd digit in the number 5263187 is substituted by the next higher digit and each even digit is substituted by the previous lower digit and the digits so obtained are rearranged in ascending order, which of the following will be the third digit from the left end after the rearrangement?

(a) 2 (b) 4
(c) 5 (d) 6
(e) None of these

7. If the digits in the number 79246358 are arranged in descending order from left to right, what will be the difference between the digits which are third from the right and second from the left in the new atrangement?
(a) 1 (b) 2
(c) 3 (d) 4
(e) 5

DIRECTIONS (Qs. 8-10) : The following questions are based on five words given below:

RAT ONE BUT AND SAW

(The new words formed after performing the mentioned operations may or may not necessarily be meaningful English words.)

8. If in each of the given words, each alphabet is changed to the next letter in the English alphabetical series, in how many words thus formed have the consonants changed to vowels?
(a) One (b) Two
(c) Three (d) Four
(e) Five

9. How many such pairs of letters are there in the word highlighted in **bold,** each of which has as many letters between them in the word (in both forward and backward directions) as they have between them in the English alphabetical order?
(a) None (b) One
(c) Two (d) Three
(e) Four

10. If the first alphabet of each of the words is changed to the next alphabet in the English alphabetical series, how many meaningful English words will be formed?
(a) One (b) Two
(c) Three (d) Four
(e) Five

DIRECTIONS (Qs. 11-13) : The following questions are based on the five three digit numbers given below:

612 589 743 468 297

11. If two is added to the first digit of each of the numbers, how many numbers thus formed will be completely divisible by three?
(a) None (b) One
(c) Two (d) Three
(e) Four

12. If the position of the second and the third digits of each of the numbers are interchanged, in how many numbers thus formed will the last digit be a perfect square? ('1' is also a perfect square)
(a) One (b) Two
(c) Three (d) Four
(e) Five

13. What will be the resultant if the third digit of the second lowest number is divided by the second digit of the highest number?
(a) 4 (b) 1
(c) 6 (d) 5
(e) 2

DIRECTIONS (Qs. 14-15) : Study the following arrangement carefully and answer the questions given below.

P 7 3 G # R E $ 4 F K 1 U % W H 2 N I 5 B Q Y 6 @ H M β 8 V D

14. If all the symbols and numbers are dropped from the above arrangement, which of the following will be the fifteenth from the right end?

(a) P (b) R
(c) E (d) F
(e) None of these

15. How many such numbers are there in the above arrangement, each of which is immediately preceded by a symbol and immediately followed by a letter?

(a) None (b) One
(c) Two (d) Three
(e) More than three

HINTS & SOLUTIONS

1. (d)

Meaningful Word ⇒ PLAY

2. (e)

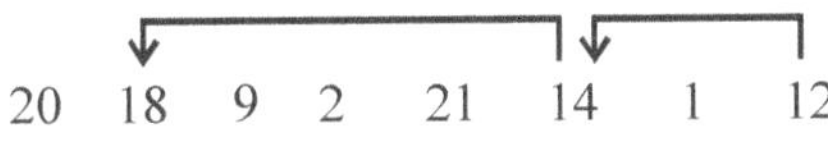

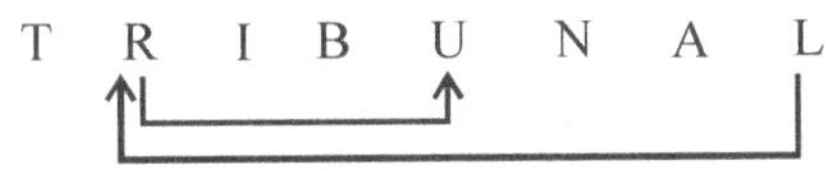

3. (b) The third, fifth, seventh and ninth letters are W, G, A, and E respectively.
Only one meaningful word can be formed using these letters which is WAGE.

4. (d) After shifting,

B U C K S H O T
↓ ↓ ↓ ↓ ↓ ↓ ↓ ↓
A V B J R G P S

After arranging in alphabet sequence.

A V B J R G P S
↓ ↓ ↓ ↓ ↓ ↓ ↓ ↓
A B G J P R S V

Hence, letter J will be fifth from the right.

5. (e) W O R T H Y
H O R T W Y

6. (b) 5 2 6 3 1 8 7
↓ ↓ ↓ ↓ ↓ ↓ ↓
6 1 5 4 2 7 8
$1<2<4<5<6<7<8$

7. (d) 7 9 2 4 6 3 5 8
9 8 7 6 5 4 3 2

Required difference = 8 – 4 = 4

Sol. (8-10) :

8. (e) RAT ⇒ SBU; ONE ⇒ POF;
BUT ⇒ CVU; AND ⇒ BOE;
SAW ⇒ TBX

9. (b) 18 1 20
R A T

10. (b) RAT ⇒ SAT; ONE ⇒ PNE;
BUT ⇒ CUT; AND ⇒ BND;
SAW ⇒ TAW
Meaningful Words
⇒ SAT, CUT

11. (b) 612 ⇒ 812; 589 ⇒ 789;
743 ⇒ 943; 468 ⇒ 668;
297 ⇒ 497

$\frac{812}{3} = 270.66; \frac{789}{3} = 263;$

$\frac{943}{3} = 314.33; \frac{668}{3} = 222.66;$

$\frac{497}{3} = 165.66$

12. (c) $612 \Rightarrow 621; 589 \Rightarrow 598;$
$743 \Rightarrow 734; 468 \Rightarrow 486;$
$297 \Rightarrow 279$

$6\,2\,\boxed{1};\ 7\,3\boxed{4}:\ 2\,7\boxed{9}$

13. (e) Second lowest number

$\Rightarrow 46\boxed{8}$

Highest number

$\Rightarrow 7\ \boxed{4}\ 3\ = \frac{8}{4} = 2$

14. (c) If all the symbols and numbers are dropped, the new arrangement is P G R E F K U W H N I B Q Y H M V D

15. (c) Only two

\$ 4 F   β 8 V

Coding-Decoding

INTRODUCTION

In this segment of commonsense reasoning, secret messages or words have to be decoded. They are coded as per a definite pattern/ rule which should be identified first. Then the same is applied to decode another coded word.

FORWARD ORDER POSITION (Left to Right)

A	B	C	D	E	F	G	H	I	J	K	L	M	N	O	P	Q	R	S	T	U	V	W	X	Y	Z
1	2	3	4	5	6	7	8	9	10	11	12	13	14	15	16	17	18	19	20	21	22	23	24	25	26

BACKWARD ORDER POSITION (Right to Left)

A	B	C	D	E	F	G	H	I	J	K	L	M	N	O	P	Q	R	S	T	U	V	W	X	Y	Z
26	25	24	23	22	21	20	19	18	17	16	15	14	13	12	11	10	9	8	7	6	5	4	3	2	1

Backward order position of any letter = 27 – Forward order position of that letter

For example,

Backward order position of C

= 27– Forward position of C

= 27 – 3 = 24

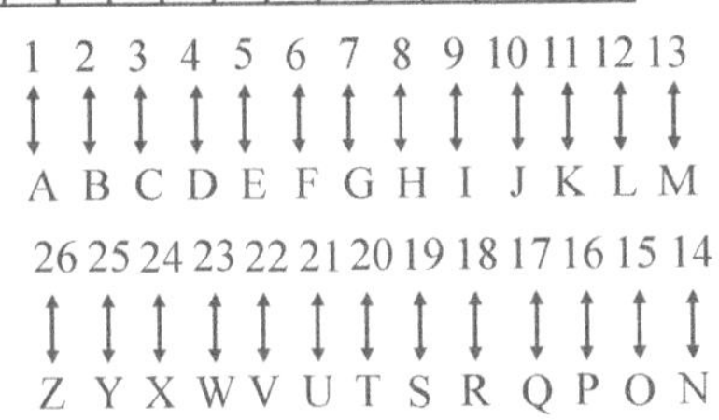

OPPOSITE LETTERS

Two letters are called opposite letters, if sum of their corresponding positions is equal to 27.

Opposite position of any letter = 27– corresponding position of that letter

For example,

Opposite position of D = 27 – Corresponding position of D = 27 – 4 = 23.

Hence D and W are opposite letters

CIRCULAR ARRANGEMENT

(i) Clockwise Arrangement

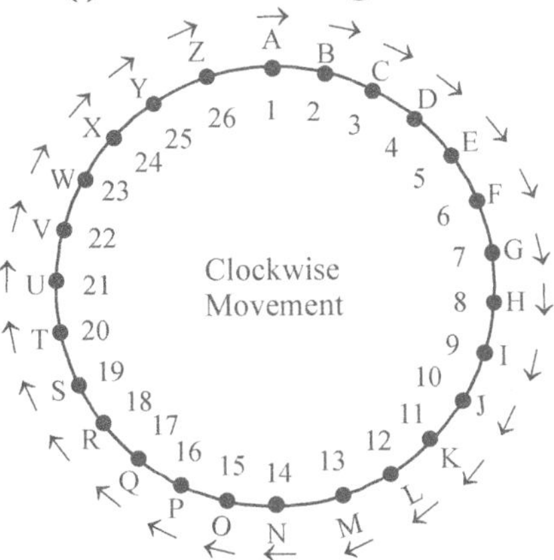

(ii) Anti-clockwise Arrangement

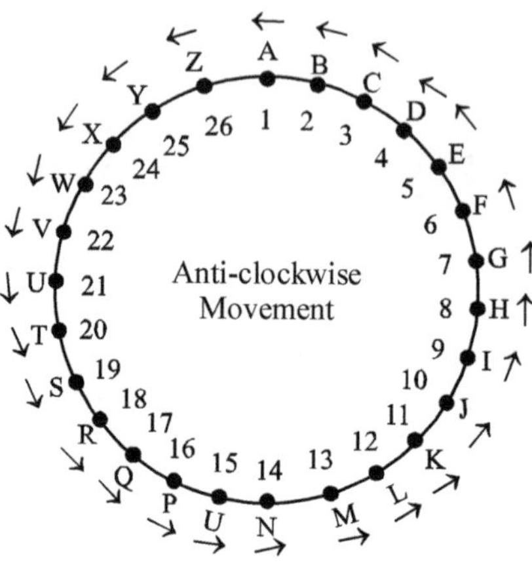

If we have to find the letter one place forward to A, then the letter will be B and this result can be found out by using either linear or circular arrangement but when one is asked to find the letter which is one letter backward of A (Z is one letter backward A) or one letter forward of Z (A is the one letter forward Z), then only circular arrangement gives such result.

TYPE-1 CODING BY LETTER SHIFTING

Pattern 1: Coding in forward sequence

EXAMPLE 1. If 'GOOD' is coded as 'HPPE', then how will you code 'BOLD'?

Sol. Here,every letter of the word 'GOOD' shifts one place in forward alphabetical sequence.

G	O	O	D
+1 ↓	+1 ↓	+1 ↓	+1 ↓
H	P	P	E

Similarly, every letter in the word 'BOLD' will move one place in forward alphabetical sequence as given below:

B	O	L	D
+1 ↓	+1 ↓	+1 ↓	+1 ↓
C	P	M	E

∴ Code for 'BOLD' will be 'CPME'.

Pattern 2: Coding in backward sequence.

EXAMPLE 2. If 'NAME' is coded as 'MZLD', then how will code 'SAME'?

Sol. Here, every letter of the word 'MZLD' moves one place in backward alphabet sequence. Let us see:

N	A	M	E
−1 ↓	−1 ↓	−1 ↓	−1 ↓
M	Z	L	D

Similarly, every letter of the word 'SAME' will move one place in backward alphabet sequence. Let us see :

S	A	M	E
−1 ↓	−1 ↓	−1 ↓	−1 ↓
R	Z	L	D

∴ Code for 'SAME' will be 'RZLD'.

Pattern 3: Coding based on skipped sequence.

EXAMPLE 3. If the word 'FACT' is coded as 'IDFW'; then how will you code 'DEEP'?

Sol. Here, every letter of the word shifts three place in forward alphabetical order.

F	A	C	T
+3 ↓	+3 ↓	+3 ↓	+3 ↓
I	D	F	W

Similarly, 'DEEP' can be coded. Let us see:

D E E P
+3↓ +3↓ +3↓ +3↓
G H H S

∴ Code for 'DEEP' will be 'GHHS'.

Pattern 4: Mixed Sequence Coding (Forward and Backword)

EXAMPLE 4. In a certain code language 'AMIT' is written as 'RAMA', then how will 'BOOT' be coded in that language ?

Sol.
A M I T
+17↓ −12↓ +4↓ −19↓
R A M A

Similarly
B O O T
+17↓ −12↓ −4↓ −19↓
S C K A

Pattern 5: Direct Letter Coding

In this type of coding, some letter group/words are assigned some codes which do not follow any rule but are direct code for a particular letter of the letter group/words. These direct codes are then used to form the codes of an another given word.

EXAMPLE 5. In a code language, 'APPLE' is written as 'PQQRS; 'RIS' is written as 'ABC' and 'MANGO' is written as 'TPXYZ'. How will 'ROSE' be written in that same code language?

Sol.

A → P	R → A	and M → T
P → Q	I → B	A → P
P → Q	S → C	N → X
L → R		G → Y
E → S		O → Z

Similarly.
R → A
O → Z
S → C
E → S

∴ ROSE ⇒ AZCS

Pattern 6: Opposite Letters Coding

In this pattern, each letter of a word is coded with its opposite letter of the alphabet.

EXAMPLE 6. If in a certain code language 'NATURAL' is coded as 'MZGFIZO' then how will 'CARE' be written in that language?

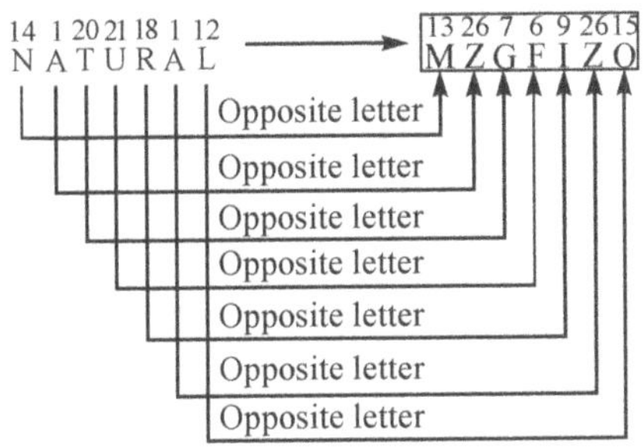

Similarly.

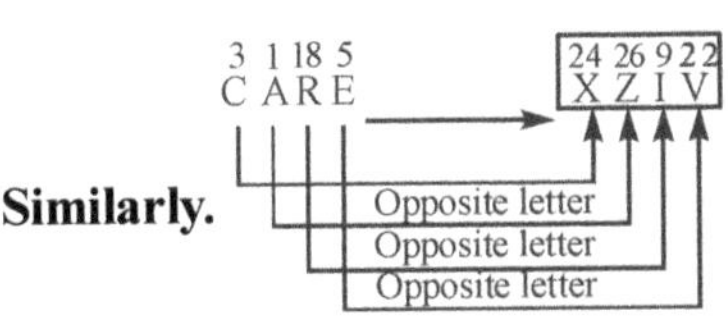

∴ CARE ⇒ XZIV

❑ Shortcut Approach

- Observe alphabets given in the code carefully.
- Find the sequence it follows whether it is ascending/descending
- Detect the rule in which the alphabets follow.
- Fill the appropriate letter in the blank given.

TYPE-2 : CODING BY SUBSTITUTION

In this coding, some words are replaced by some other words and on the basis of these new words the code is derived.

EXAMPLE 7. If 'cages' are called 'rockets', 'rockets' are called 'traps', 'traps' are called 'planets', 'planets' are called 'aeroplanes', 'aeroplanes' are called 'cycles' and cycles' are called 'cars', what is Earth

(a) Cycles (b) Rockets
(c) Planet (d) Aeroplanes
(e) Cars

Sol. Earth is a planet and here planets are called aeroplanes. So, earth will be called aeroplanes.

TYPE -3: CODING BASED ON REARRANGEMNT OF LETTERS

In this type of coding, the letter of the original word are rearranged in a particular manner to obtain the code. Such coding can be of the following types.

(a) CODING BY REVERSING LETTERS

In this coding, all letters of a word has been reversed.

EXAMPLE 8. If 'TEMPERATURE' is coded as 'ERUTAREPMET', then how will you code 'EDUCATION' following the same scheme.

Sol. Here, the word 'TEMPERATURE' has been reversed. Hence, the code for 'EDUCATION' will be 'NOITACUDE'.

(b) When letters of the word are divided into two parts and then both the parts are written in reverse order or the first part is written in reverse order at the place of second part and second part is written in reverse order at the place of first part. Following situations can arise in such cases

(i) When the number of letters of the word is even

EXAMPLE 9. In a certain code 'TEMPLE' is written as 'METELP', then how will 'ACTION' be written in that code ?

Sol. T E M P L E → M E T E L P
1 2 3 4 5 6 → 3 2 1 6 5 4

Similarly

A C T I O N → T C A N O I
1 2 3 4 5 6 → 3 2 1 6 5 4

(ii) When the number of letters of the word is odd

EXAMPLE 10. In a certain code language 'MAGICAL' is written as 'MAGILAC', then how will 'LETTERS' be written in that code?

Sol. M A G I C A L; → M A G I L A C
1 2 3 4 5 6 7 → 1 2 3 4 7 6 5

Similarly

L E T T E R S → L E T T S R E
1 2 3 4 5 6 7 → 1 2 3 4 7 6 5

(iii) When letters of the word are divided into two or more groups and then all or some particular groups are written in reverse order.

EXAMPLE 11. In a certain code language 'POSITION' is written as 'POSTIION' then how will 'LANGUAGE' be written in that code?

Sol.

P O S I T I O N → P O S T I I O N
1 2 3 4 5 6 7 8 → 1 2 3 5 4 6 7 8

Similarly

L A N G U A G E → L A N G U A G E
1 2 3 4 5 6 7 8 → 1 2 3 5 4 6 7 8

(iv) When first and last letter of the word remain at the same place but middle letters get reversed

EXAMPLE 12. In a certain code language 'RESPONSE' is written as 'RSNOPSEE' then how will DAUGHTER be written in that code?

Sol.

R E S PO N S E→R S N O P S E E
1 2 3 4 5 6 7 8 1 7 6 5 4 3 2 8

Similary

D A U G H T E R→D E T H G U A R
1 2 3 4 5 6 7 8 1 7 6 5 4 3 2 8

(v) When each letter of the word is written at a certain place

EXAMPLE 13. In certain code language 'TRANGLE' is written as 'AGTRELN', then how will 'MAGICAL', be written in that code?

Sol. T R A N GL E→ AG T R E L N
1 2 3 4 5 6 7 3 5 1 2 7 6 4

Similarly

M A G I C A L→ G C M A L A I
1 2 3 4 5 6 7 3 5 1 2 7 6 4

TYPE 4: CODING OF LETTERS BY THEIR LEFT AND RIGHT LETTERS

In this pattern, each letter of a letter group/word is coded by its left and right letters of English alphabet.

Q6. If in a certain language 'NIL' is written as 'MOHJKM' then how will 'COMB' be written in that language?

Sol.

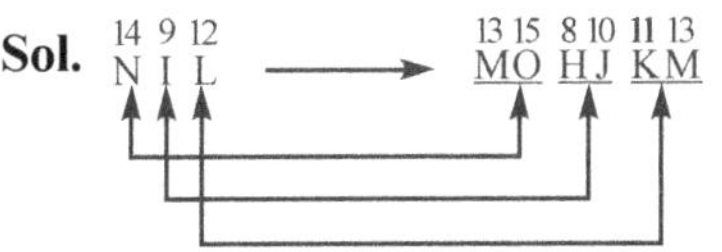

Similarly.

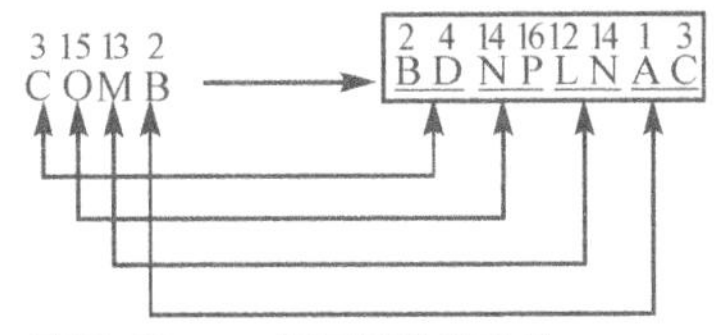

∴ COMB ⇒ BDNPLNAC

TYPE 5 : CODING IN FICTITIOUS LANGUAGE

In some cases of coding-decoding, fictions language is used to code some words. In such questions, the codes for a group of words is given. In such types of problems, codes for each word can be found by eliminating the common words.

EXAMPLE 14. In a certain code language 'over and above' is written as 'da pa ta' and 'old and beautiful' is written as 'Sa na pa'. How is 'over' written in that code language?

Sol. Over (and) above → da (Pa) ta

Old (and) beautiful → Sa na (Pa)

Clearly, 'and' is common in both and a common code is 'Pa'.

∴ Code for 'and' must be 'Pa'.

Code for 'over' = 'da' or 'ta'.

Code for above = 'da' or 'ta'.

Code for old = 'Sa' or 'na'

Code for beautiful = 'Sa' or 'na'

∴ We can't certainly say what will be exact code for 'over'. But it is sure that code for 'over' must be either 'da' or 'ta'.

Shortcut Approach

- Firstly, write the words and their codes as given in the question in straight line with an arrow in middle.

- Now, find the common words and their corresponding codes.
- Encircle each pair with the same shape.
- Finally, we have each word and its corresponding code.

TYPE-6 : CODING BASED ON NUMBERS

Pattern 1:

When numerical values are given to words.

EXAMPLE 15. If in a certain language A is coded as 1, B is coded as 2, C is coded as 3 and so on, then find the code for AEECD.

Sol. As given the letters are coded as below:

A	B	C	D	E	F	G	H	I
1	2	3	4	5	6	7	8	9

Now,

A	E	E	C	D
1	5	5	3	4

∴ Code for AEECD = 15534

Shortcut Approach

- First you have to observe the number code.
- Now, notice the position of number.
- Search the common pattern.

Pattern 2 :

When alphabetical code value are given for numbers.

EXAMPLE 16. In a certain code 3 is coded as 'R', 4 is coded as 'D', 5 is coded as 'N', 6 is coded as 'P', then find the code for '53446'.

Sol. As per the given condition

3	4	5	6
R	D	N	P

Now,

5	3	4	4	6
N	R	D	D	P

∴ Code for 53446 = NRDDP.

TYPE-7 : MATHEMATICAL OPERATIONS WITH THE POSITION NUMBERS OF LETTERS

EXAMPLE 17. In a certain code, if 'TALE' is written as 38, then how will you code 'CAME' using the same coding scheme?

Sol. Look at the numbered alphabet and write down the number corresponding to the letters of the word 'TALE'.

T A L E
20 1 12 5

The fact that the code for 'TALE' is 38, gives you a clue that the code is probably obtained by performing an arithmatical operations between the numbers related to each letter. Let us see :

$20 + 1 + 12 + 5 = 38$

Thus, the code for 'CAME' is

C A M E
$3 + 1 + 13 + 5 = 22$

∴ Code for 'CAME' = 22

EXAMPLE 18. If in a certain code language 'RAMAN' is written as '23.5', then how will 'CAPACITY' be written in that code?

Sol.

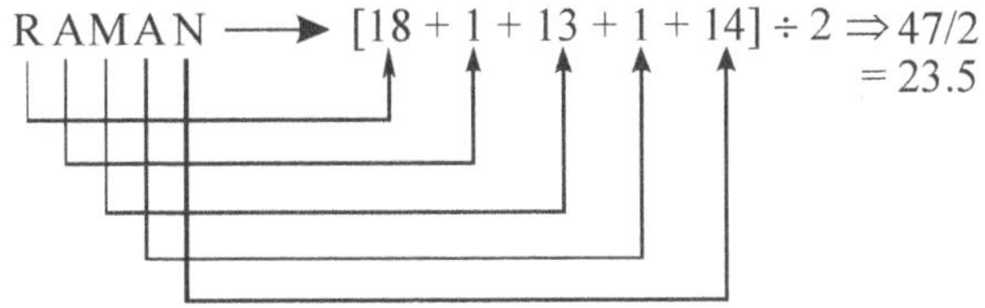

Similarly,

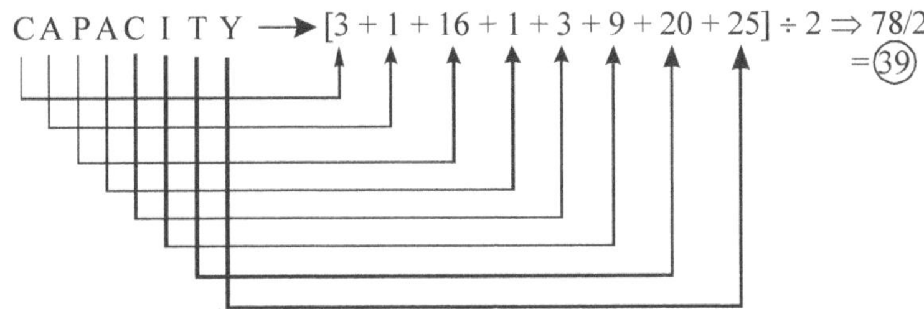

∴ CAPACITY ⇒ 39

Remember

- If more than one codes are given then likely the required code can be drived from the question itself and you will no need to solve it mathematically.
- If the code for a word is a one digit number then likely the position of the letters are added and the digits are summed up until the one digit number is arrived at.

TYPE-8 : MATRIX CODING

In this type of questions two matrices are given. In each matrix there are 25 cells and these cells contain two classes of alphabets. The columns and rows of matrix I are numbered from 0 to 4 and that of matrix II from 5 to 9. A letter from these matrices can be represented first by its row number and next by its column number. For example. 'A' Can be represented by 32 or 43.

EXAMPLE 19.

Directions: In this question find out the correct set of number pairs for the given word from the two matrices given above.

Matrix I

	0	1	2	3	4
0	I	A	U	E	O
1	E	U	O	A	I
2	O	A	I	E	U
3	E	U	A	O	I
4	E	I	O	A	U

Matrix II

	5	6	7	8	9
5	K	R	L	M	N
6	M	R	K	N	L
7	K	N	M	L	R
8	M	L	K	R	N
9	N	R	L	K	M

MONK

(a) 58, 33, 67, 98
(b) 65, 02, 59, 67
(c) 65, 04, 89, 75
(d) 65, 20, 89, 68

Sol.

A → 01, 13, 21, 32, 43
E → 03, 10, 23, 30, 40
I → 00, 14, 22, 34, 41
O → 04, 12, 20, 33, 42

U → 02, 11, 24, 31, 44
K → 55, 67, 75, 87, 98
L → 57, 69, 78, 86, 97
M → 58, 65, 77, 85, 99
N → 59, 68, 76, 89, 95
R → 56, 66, 79, 88, 96

So, 65, 04, 89, 75 is correct

TYPE 9 : SYMBOL CODING BASED ON SIMILARITY

In this coding, various symbols are assigned to the letters of a word and based upon their correlation or similarity, you have to determine the rules or pattern being followed.

EXAMPLE 20. If in a certain code language 'ROPE' is written as, '% 5 7 $', 'DOUBT' is written as '3 5 # 8 ★', and 'LIVE' is written as '@ 2 4 $', then how will 'TROUBLE' be written in that language?

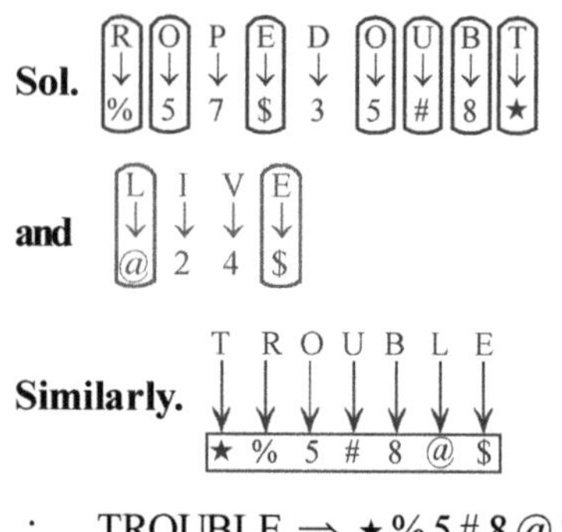

∴ TROUBLE ⇒ ★ % 5 # 8 @ $

TYPE 10 : CODING BY COMPARISON

In this coding, some words are given in one column and their codes are given in another column. But the given codes are not in the same order of words given. You have to find out the codes of words on the basis of comparison of their properties, traits, ete.

EXAMPLE

Directions (Q. Nos. 21-25) *Read the following information to answer the questions that follow. In Column I, some words are given. In Column II, their codes are given and they are arranged in the same order in which they are in Column I but the letters in the code in Column II are not in the same order in which the letters of the words are given in Column I. Study the columns and give your answer on the basis of that.*

Column I	Column II
(1) FLOUR	(A) xncap
(2) TAP	(B) ksd
(3) ROSE	(C) cmrn
(4) LOTUS	(D) smcpx
(5) SAIL	(E) kptm

21. Find the code for F.
(a) p (b) c
(c) a (d) x

22. Which letter is the code for P?
(a) k (b) s
(c) c (d) d

23. Find the code for L.
(a) n (b) c
(c) k (d) p

24. What is the code for E?
(a) c (b) m
(c) r (d) n

25. Which of the following options is the code for 0?
(a) x (b) c
(c) m (d) r

Sol.

21. (c) Clearly, the code for F is a
22. (d) Clearly, the code for P is d
23. (d) Clearly, the code for L is p
24. (c) Clearly, the code for E is r
25. (b) Clearly, the code for O is c

TYPE 11 : CONDITIONAL CODING

In this coding, letters/numbers are given and their codes are given right under them, you have to find out code for a particular letter group/number coding to the given condition.

EXAMPLE

Directions (Q. Nos. 26-27) *In each question below, is given a group of letters followed by four combinations of digits/symbols numbered (a), (b), (c) and (d). You have to find out which of the four combinations correctly represents the group of letters based on the following coding system and the conditions that follow and mark the number of that combination as your answer. If none of the combinations correctly represents the group of letters, mark (e), i.e. 'None of these'. as your answer.*

Letter	E	R	C	F	L	N	H	K	P	T	A	S	G
Code	%	3	2	5	@	7	#	6	1	8	4	%	9

(i) If the first letter is a vowel and the last letter is a consonant, both are to be coded as O.

(ii) If the first letter is a consonant and the last letter is a vowel both are to be coded as O.

(iii) If the first letter as well as the last letter are vowels, both are to be coded as the code of the last letter.

26. NFRSCA

(a) 753% 20 (b) 053%24

(c) 0232%0 (d) 053% 20

27. ARFTHE

(a) % 358#% (b) 4358#%

(c) 4358#4 (d) 96385#%

Sol.

26. (d) From Statement II.

27. (a) From Statement III.
If both the first and last letter are vowels, the both are coded as the last letter.

TYPE 12 : DECIPHERING NUMBERS AND SYMBOLS CODES FOR MESSAGES

In this type of questions, a few groups of numbers/symbols, each coding a certain message are given. Through a comparison of the given coded messages, taking two at a time, the candidate is required to find the number/symbol code for each word and then formulate the code for the given message.

EXAMPLE 28. In a certain code language. '617' means 'sweet and hot', '735' means 'coffee is sweet' and '263' means 'tea is hot'. Which of the following would mean 'coffee is hot'?

Sol. In the first and third statements, the common code digit is '6' and the common word is '*hot*', So, '6' means 'hot'

In the second and third statements, the common code digit is '3' and the common word is 'is'. So '3' means 'is'.

In the first and second statements, the common code digit is '7' and the common word is 'sweet'. So, in the second statement '5' means 'coffee'. Clearly, '536' would mean 'coffee is hot'.

PRACTICE EXERCISE

1. In a certain code language, "BAD" is written as "7" and "SAP" is written as "9". How is "BAN" written in that code language?
(a) 8 (b) 3
(c) 4 (d) 6

2. In a certain code language **"NIGHT"** is written as **"ODDGM"** and **"DARK"** is written as **"GOYC"**. How is **"GREEN"** written in that code language?
(a) IABPF (b) MCBNB
(c) OGHVL (d) FPBAI

3. A word is represented by only one set of numbers as given in any one of the alternatives. The sets of numbers given in the alternatives are represented by two classes of alphabets as shown in the given two matrices. The columns and rows of Matrix – I are numbered from 0 to 4 and that of Matrix – II are numbered from 5 to 9. A letter from these matrices can be represented first by its row and next by its column, for example, 'K' can be represented by 10, 31, etc., and 'M' can be represented by 76, 87, etc. Similarly, you have to identify the set for the word "SCAM".

Matrix – I

	0	1	2	3	4
0	S	P	K	N	C
1	K	S	C	P	N
2	P	C	N	S	K
3	N	K	S	C	P
4	C	N	P	K	S

Matrix – II

	5	6	7	8	9
5	I	R	A	J	M
6	A	J	I	M	R
7	J	M	R	A	I
8	R	A	M	I	J
9	M	I	J	R	A

(a) 00, 13, 57, 76 (b) 11, 04, 86, 59
(c) 23, 22, 99, 95 (d) 32, 40, 66, 68

4. In a certain code language **"who are you"** is written as **"432"**, **"they is you"** is written as **"485"** and **"they are dangerous"** is written as **"295"**. How is **"dangerous"** written in that code language?
(a) 2 (b) 4
(c) 5 (d) 9

5. In a certain code language, "RIVER" is written as "12351" and "RED" is written as "156". How is "DRIVER" written in that code language?
(a) 612311 (b) 612531
(c) 621351 (d) 612351

6. In a certain code language 'GUST' is coded as '@7$2' and 'SNIP' is coded as '957#' and 'GAPE' is coded as 'β$35'. How will 'SING' be coded in the same code?
(a) 9$7# (b) 59#$
(c) 9β7$ (d) 7$59
(e) $27#

7. In a certain code language, 'how can you go' is written as 'ja da ka pa,' 'can you come here' is writter as 'na ka sa ja' and 'come and go' is written

as 'ra pa sa'. How is 'here' written in that code language ?
(a) ja (b) na
(c) pa (d) Data inadequate
(e) None of these

DIRECTIONS (Qs. 8-9) : Study the following information to answer the given questions.

In a certain code, 'strong financial economy' is written as 'mo tic su', 'financial inclusion needed' is written as 'da ra su' and 'economy crisis inclusion' is written as 'ye da mo'.

8. What is the code for 'financial'?
(a) da (b) su
(c) mo (d) ra
(e) Can't be determined

9. What does 'tic' stand for?
(a) economy (b) financial
(c) strong (d) needed
(e) Either economy or strong

10. If 'yellow' means 'green', 'green' means 'white', white means 'red', 'red' means 'black', 'black' means 'blue' and 'blue' means 'violet', which of the following represents the colour of human blood ?
(a) black (b) violet
(c) red (d) blue
(e) None of these

DIRECTIONS (Qs. 11-15) : Study the information below and answer the following question:

In a certain code language,
'Thin paper neatly folded' is written as @D6, %R5, !N4, ?Y6
'Four people from USA' is written as @M4, %E6, #A3, @R4
'Urban development programme launched' is written as % E9, *T11, #N5 &D8
'Dhaya likes forties hero' is written as @S7, &S5, *A5, $O4

11. The code for the word 'People' is
(a) @M4 (b) %E6
(c) #A3 (d) @R4
(e) None of these

12. The code '*A5' denotes which of the following word ?
(a) Likes (b) Hero
(c) Forties (d) Dhaya
(e) None of these

13. The code word of 'Four' is
(a) @R4 (b) %E6
(c) @M4 (d) #A3
(e) None of these

14. '#' denotes which letter of the given words ?
(a) N (b) F
(c) L (d) D
(e) U

15. According to the given code word, what will be the code for ' Data Line reach points' ?
(a) *4A &4E @5H%6S
(b) *4A &4E !5H%6S
(c) *4A &4E #5H%6S
(d) *4A &4E $5H%6S
(e) None of these

HINTS & SOLUTIONS

1. **(a)** As,
BAD = 2 + 1 + 4 ⇒ 7
SAP = 19 + 1 + 16 = 36
⇒ 3 + 6 = 9
Similarly,
BAN = 2 + 1 + 14 = 17
⇒ 1 + 7 = 8

2. **(a)** As,

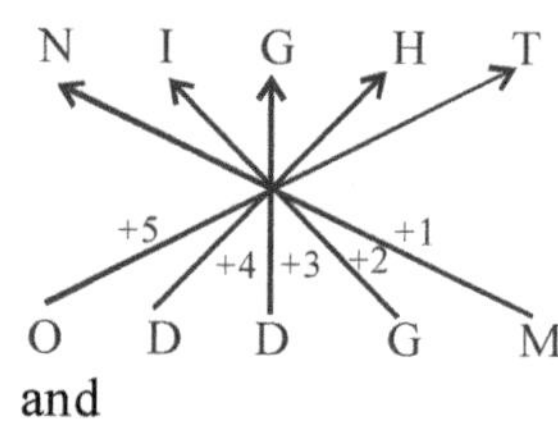

and

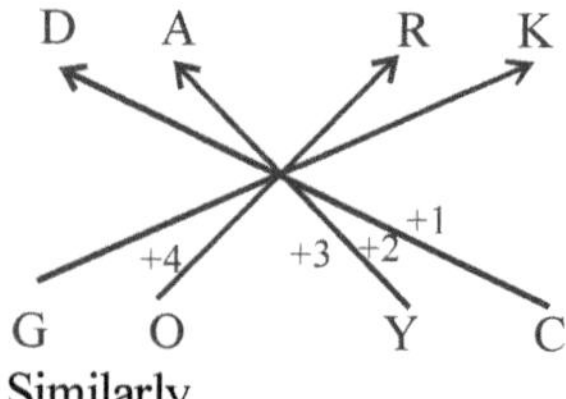

Similarly,

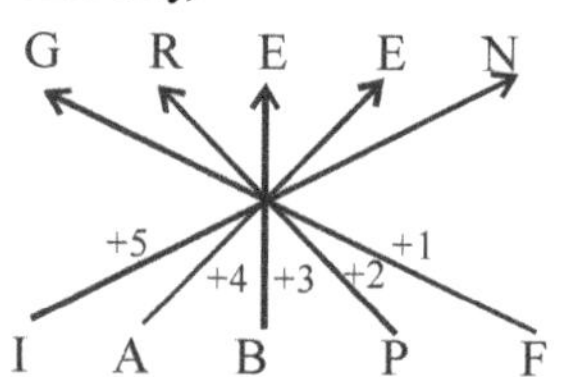

3. **(b)** Code 11, 04, 86, 59 will resemble SCAM when matched from given two matrices.

4. **(d)**

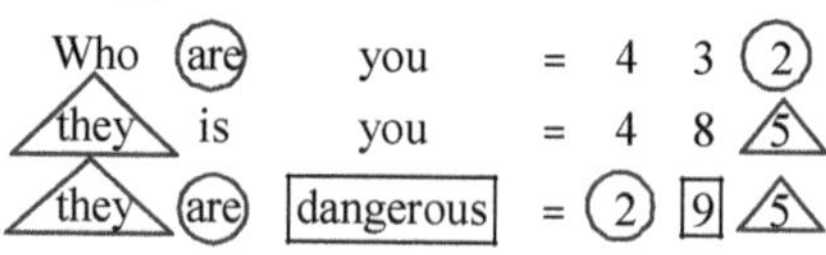

5. **(d)** As,

R I V E R → 1 2 3 5 1
R E D → 1 5 6

Similarly,

D R I V E R → 6 1 2 3 5 1

6. **(a)**

G U S T ⟶ @ 7 $ 2
S N I P ⟶ 9 5 7 #
G A P E ⟶ β $ 3 5

Therefore, S I N G ⇒ 7 9 # $

7. **(b)**

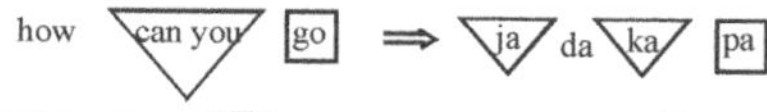

can you come here ⇒ na ka sa ja
come and go ⇒ ra pa sa

Codes are:
how ⇒ da
can ⇒ ja or ka
you ⇒ ja or ka
go ⇒ pa
come ⇒ sa
here ⇒ na
and ⇒ ra
The code for here is 'na'.

8. **(b)** 9. **(c)**

10 **(e)** The colour of human blood is red. Here *white* means *red*. Therefore *white* is our answer. Do not opt for *black* because *red* means *black* implies that black is called red.

11. **(b)** People - %E6
P - %
No of letters - 6
Last letter - E

12. **(d)** *A5 - Dhaya
D denote *
A denote Dhaya end with A 5 denote no of letter (Dhaya => 5)

13. **(a)** Four => @R4
F - @
R - last letter of the word R and Total no of letter 4

14. **(e)** T = !, P = %, N = ?, F = @, U = #, D = *, L = &, H = $

15. **(e)**

Blood Relations

INTRODUCTION

Blood relation does mean biological relation. Remember a wife and husband are met biologically related but they are biological parents of their own children. Similarly, brother, sister, paternal grandfather, paternal grandmother maternal grandfather, maternal grandmother, grandson, granddaughter, niece, cousin etc. are our blood relatives.

TYPES OF BLOOD RELATIONS

There are mainly two types of blood relatives:

(i) **Blood relation from paternal side**

(ii) **Blood relation from maternal side**

BLOOD RELATION FROM PATERNAL SIDE

This type of blood relation can be further subdivided into three types:

(a) **Past generations of father :** Great grandfather, great grandmother, grandfather, grandmother etc.

(b) **Parallel generations of father:** Uncles (Brothers of father), Aunts (sisters of father) etc.

(c) **Future generations of father:** Sons, daughters, grandsons, granddaughters etc.

BLOOD RELATION FROM MATERNAL SIDE

This type of blood relations can also be subdivided into three types:

(a) **Past generations of mother:** Maternal great grandfather, maternal great grandmother, maternal grandfather, maternal grandmother etc.

(b) **Parallel generations of mother:** Maternal uncles, maternal aunts etc.

(c) **Future generations of mother:** Sons, daughters, grandsons, granddaughters etc.

Table of Blood Relations		
1	Son of father or mother	Brother
2	Daughter of father or mother	Sister
3	Brother of father	Uncle
4	Brother of mother	Maternal uncle
5	Sister of father	Aunt
6	Sister of mother	Aunt
7	Father of father	Grandfather
8	Father of father's father	Great grand father
9	Father of grandfather	Great grandfather

10	Mother of father	Grandmother
11	Mother of father's mother	Great grandmother
12	Mother of grandmother	Great grandmother
13	Father of mother	Maternal grandfather
14	Father of mother's father	Great maternal grand father
15	Father of maternal grandfather	Great maternal grandfather
16	Mother of mother	Maternal grandmother
17	Mother of mother, mother	Great maternal grandmother
18	Mother of maternal grandmother	Great maternal grandmother
19	Wife of father	Mother
20	Husband of mother	Father
21	Wife of Grandfather	Grandmother
22	Husband of Grandmother	Grandfather
23	Wife of son	Daughter-in-law
24	Husband of daughter	Son-in-law
25	Brother of Husband	Brother-in-law
26	Brother of wife	Brother-in-law
27	Sister of Husband	Sister-in-law
28	Sister of wife	Sister-in-law
29	Son of brother	Nephew
30	Daughter of brother	Niece
31	Wife of brother	Sister-in-law
32	Husband of sister	Brother-in-law
33	Son of sister	Nephew
34	Daughter of sister	Niece
35	Wife of uncle	Aunt
36	Wife of maternal uncle	Aunt
37	Son/daughter of uncle/Aunt	Cousin
38	Son/daughter of maternal uncle/maternal aunt	Cousin
39	Son/daughter of sister of Fathar	Cousin
40	Son/daughter of sister of Mother	Cousin
41	Only son of grandfather	Father

42	Only daughter of maternal grandfather	Mother
43	Daughter of grandfather	Aunt
44	Sons of grandfather other than father	Uncle
45	Son of maternal grandfather/maternal grand mother	Maternal Uncle.
46	Only daughter in law of grandfather/ grandmother	Mother
47	Daughters in law of grandfather/ grandmother	Aunt other than mother
48	Daughters-in-law of maternal grandfather/grandmother	Aunt maternal
49	Neither brother nor sister	Self

SOME IMPORTANT INFORMATION ABOUT BLOOD RELATION

A. Without the information of gender, no relationship can be established between two people. For example, If given that R is the child of P & Q, then we can only say that P & Q are the parents of R. But we can not find out:
   (i) R is the son of P & Q or R is the daughter of P & Q.
   (ii) Who is mother of R and who is father of R.

   But if we have given that P is a male, Q is a female and R is male, then we can easily say that R is the son of P and Q. Further we can also say that P is father of R and Q is mother of R.

B. Gender can not be decided on the basis of name. For example, in Sikh community the names like Manjit, Sukhvinder etc. are the names of both male and female. Similarly, in the Hindu Community 'Suman' is the name of both male and female.

❑ ***Shortcut Approach***

- While solving blood relation based question, first of all find out that two persons between whom a relationship has to be established.
- Next, try to find out middle relation.
- Finally, find out the relationship between two persons to be identified for this purpose.

TYPES OF PROBLEMS

(1) **General Problems on Blood Relation**
(2) **Blood Relation based on Family Tree**
(3) **Coded Blood Relation**

(1) General Problem on Blood Relation

EXAMPLE 1. Pointing towards a photograph, Mr. Sharma said, "She is the only daughter of mother of my brother's sister." How is Mr. Sharma related to the lady in the photograph?

Sol. Here, we have to find relationship between Mr. Sharma & the lady in the photograph.
Mother of my brother's sister does mean my (Mr. Sharma's) mother. Only daughter of Mr. Sharma's mother does mean "sister of Mr. Sharma".

❑ ***Shortcut Approach***

Read the statement from right to left to develop the relation by using blood relation table.

(2) Blood Relation Based on Family Tree

Some symbols are used to draw family tree as below:

'↔' is used for husband & wife.
'___' is used for brother & sister
' | ' is used for parents (father or mother). Parents are put on top while children are put at the bottom.
'–' or minus sign is used for female
'+' or plus sign is used for male.

EXAMPLE 2. Q is the brother of C and C is the sister of Q. R and D are brother and sister. R is the son of A while A & C are wife and husband. How is Q related with D.

Sol. Using the symbols, we can make a family tree and solve the given problem. Let us see the family tree:

Family tree :

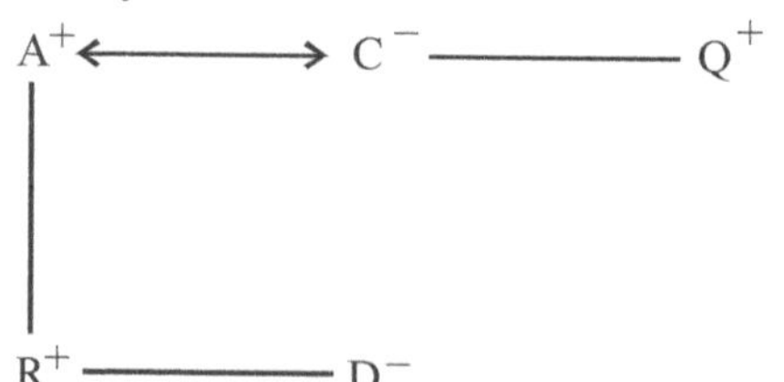

As per the question Q is the brother of C and C is the sister of Q. Hence, relation between C & Q has been presented as $\left(C^- — Q^+\right)$ where '–' sign above C makes it clear that C is a female and '+' sign above 'Q' makes it clear that Q is a male. Similarly, for R and D. The presentation $\left(\overset{+}{R} — D^-\right)$ has been made. Further according to the question, A and C are having a husband and wife relationship and hence this has been presented as $\left(\overset{+}{A} \leftrightarrow C^-\right)$. As it is already given that C is the sister of Q and A and C are wife and husband, this becomes clear that A is the male member of the family and this is the reason A has '+' as its gender sign. Lastly, the vertical line gives father and son relationship and has been presented as $\begin{pmatrix} A^+ \\ | \\ R^+ \end{pmatrix}$. Now from this family tree it becomes clear that C is the mother of R and D and as Q is the brother of C, then Q will definitely be the maternal uncle of R & D. Hence, we can say that Q is the maternal uncle of D and this is the required answer for our question.

Note : *In solving family tree based relations, make sure that your diagram is in correct representation.*

(3) Codded Blood Relations

EXAMPLE 3. If P + Q means P is husband of Q, P/Q means P is the sister of Q, P*Q means P is the son of Q. How is D related to A in D*B + C/A ?

Sol. C/A – C is sister of A.
B + C/A – B is brother-in-law of A
(Sister's husband – broter-in-law)
D*B + C/A – D is nephew of A
(Sister's husband's son means sister's son i.e., nephew)
So, D is nephew to A.

Shortcut Method :

By using symbols and generation relations :

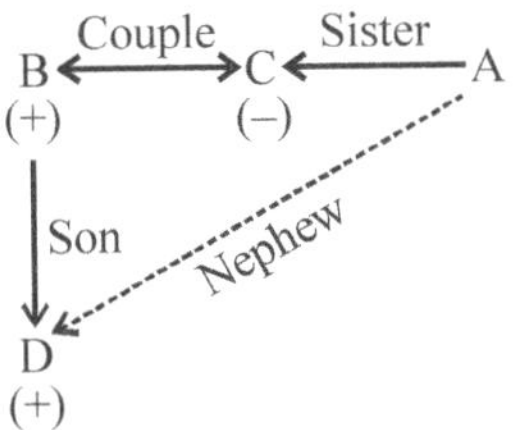

So, it is clearly shown that D is nephew to A.

❑ Shortcut Approach

- The best way to solve blood relation questions, you try and relate every statement to 'yourself'. The starting name of the statement could be assumed as your name or you.
- When the statement is very long, it can get confusing. So, break down every statement in the question into sub statements and solve the question.
- Do not assume the gender of any person in the question just based on the names given in the question.
- Draw a family tree where people of the same generation are placed at the same level and the entire diagram is in the form of a hierarchy.

Remember

- Concentrate on points which give maximum definite information.
- Read the questions carefully and try identifying the persons between whom relationship is to be established. Possibly put yourself in given character so that it becomes easy for you to understand.
- Whilst concluding the relationship between two people be careful about the gender of the person being talked about as it is possible to commit mistake by assuming the gender of the person which is not given in the data or which can't be extracted from the data/ information given.

PRACTICE EXERCISE

DIRECTIONS (Qs. 1–2): *Study the following information carefully to answer the given questions :*

'P + Q' means 'P is the sister of Q'.
'P @ Q' means 'P is the wife of Q'.
'P $ Q' means 'P is the son of Q'.
'P % Q' means 'P is the mother of Q'.

1. What is the relation between 'J and A' in the expression 'A @ F $ M % J + T' ?
(a) J is the mother-in-law of A
(b) A is the aunt of J
(c) J is the sister-in-law of A
(d) A is the husband of J
(e) None of these

2. What will come in the place of question-mark, if it is provided that 'J is the daughter-in-law of T' in the expression 'J % B ? K $ T' ?
   (a) @ (b) % (c) +
   (d) $ (e) % or +
3. 'A + B' means 'A is the son of B', 'A – B' means 'A is the wife of B'. 'A × B' means 'A is the brother of B', 'A ÷ B' means 'A is the mother of B', 'A = B' means 'A is the sister of B'. Which of the following represents P is the maternal-uncle of Q?
   (a) R × P ÷ Q (b) P × R ÷ Q
   (c) P + R ÷ Q (d) P + R × Q
   (e) None of these

DIRECTIONS (Qs. 4-5): *Study the information given below and answer the questions following it:*

Mohan is son of Arun's father's sister. Prakash is son of Reva, who is mother of Vikash and grandmother of Arun. Pranab is father of Neela and grandfather of Mohan. Reva is wife of Pranab.

4. How is Mohan related to Reva ?
   (a) Grandson
   (b) Son
   (c) Nephew
   (d) Data inadaequate
   (e) None of these
5. How is Vikash's wife related to Neela ?
   (a) Sister
   (b) Niece
   (c) Sister-in-law
   (d) Data inadaequate
   (e) None of these
6. Pointing to a photograph Shubha said, "he is the only grandson of my mother's father". How is the man in photograph related to Shuhha?
   (a) Cousin
   (b) Brother
   (c) Uncle
   (d) Cannot be determined
   (e) None of these
7. If 'A $ B' means 'A is father of B', 'A # B' means 'A is daughter of B', 'A @ B' means 'A is sister of B', then how is K related to M in H @ K $ L # M ?
   (a) Husband
   (b) Uncle
   (c) Father
   (d) Cannot be determined
   (e) None of these
8. Chanda is the wife of Bharat. Mohan is the son of Chanda. Ashish is the brother of Bharat and father of Dhruv. How is Mohan related to Dhruv?
   (a) Sister (b) Cousin
   (c) Brother (d) Mother
9. X is sister of Y. Y is brother of Z. Z is husband of P. O is father of Y. How is P related to O?
   (a) Sister
   (b) Daughter
   (c) Uncle
   (d) Daughter - in - law
10. P and Q are brothers, P is the father of S, R is the only son of Q and is married to U. How is U related to S?
    (a) Sister – in – law
    (b) Mother – in – law
    (c) Sister
    (d) Mother
11. Pointing to a lady, Rohit said "She is the sister of the daughter of my father's wife's son". How is the lady related to Rohit?
    (a) Daughter
    (b) Sister
    (c) Niece
    (d) Daughter or Niece

HINTS & SOLUTIONS

1. (c) A @ F ⇒ A is wife of F.
F $ M ⇒ F is son of M.
M % J ⇒ M is mother of J.
J + T ⇒ J is the sister of T.

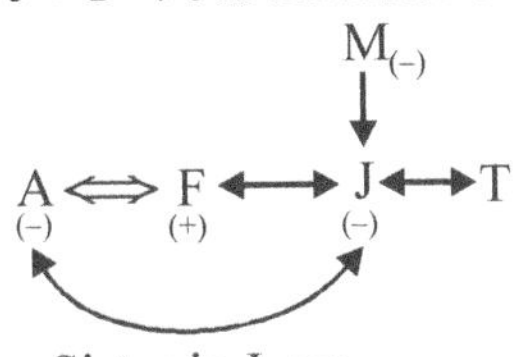

Sister-in-Law

2. (d) J % B ⇒ J is the mother of B
B $ K ⇒ B is the son of K.
K $ T ⇒ K is the son of T.
Therefore J is daughter-in-law of T.

3. (b) Consider option (b), P × R ÷ Q, it means that P is the brother of R and R is the mother of Q. So, P is the maternal uncle of Q.

Sol 4–5

Pranab (+) ⇔ Reva (–)
↓ ↓ ↓
Neela Prakash Vikash
↓
Mohan (+) Arun

4. (a) 5. (c)

6. (b)

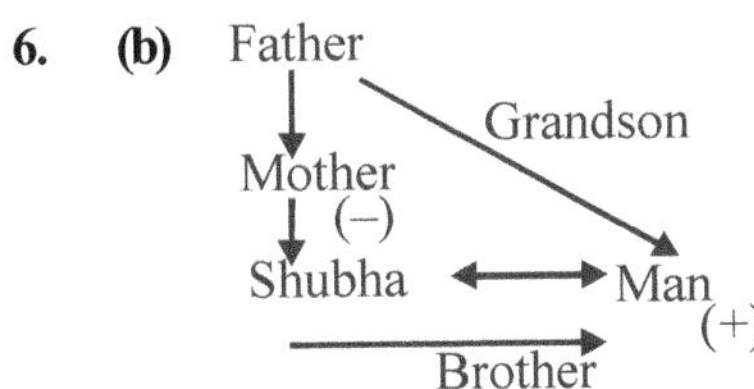

7. (a)

H (–) —— K (+) ═ M (–)
|
L (–)

So, K is husband of M

8. (b)

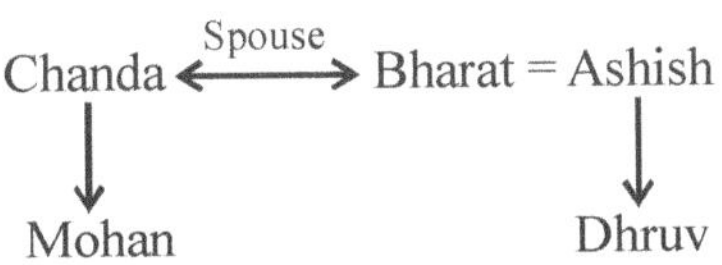

Hence, Mohan is cousin of Dhruv.

9. (d)

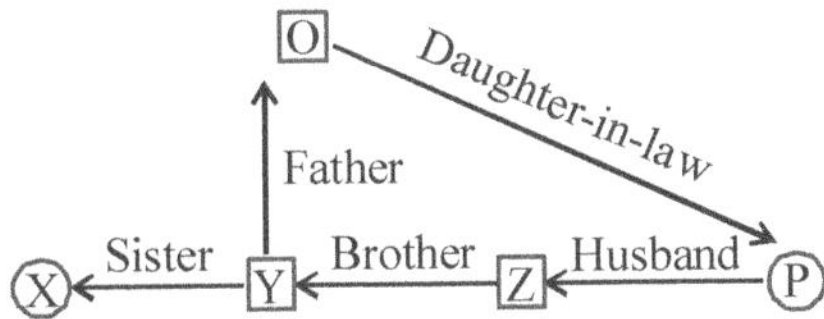

So, P is daughter -in-law of O.

10. (a)

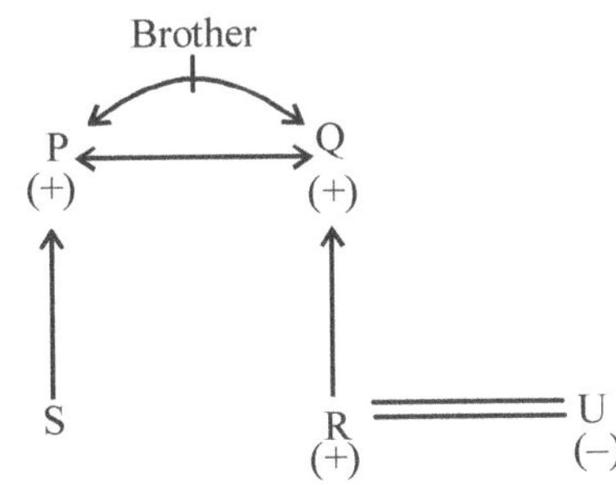

Therefore, U is sister – in – law of S.

11. (d)

Direction and Distance

INTRODUCTION

This part of reasoning comes under the category of common sense reasoning. In fact, this segment gauges the sense of direction of a candidate.

CONCEPT OF DIRECTION

In our day to day life, we make our concept of direction after seeing the position of sun. In fact, this is a truth that sun rises in the East and goes down in the West. Thus when we stand facing sunrise, then our front is called East facing while our back is called West facing. At this position our left hand is in the Northward and the right hand is in the Southward. Let us see the following direction map that will make your concept more clear.

Direction Map

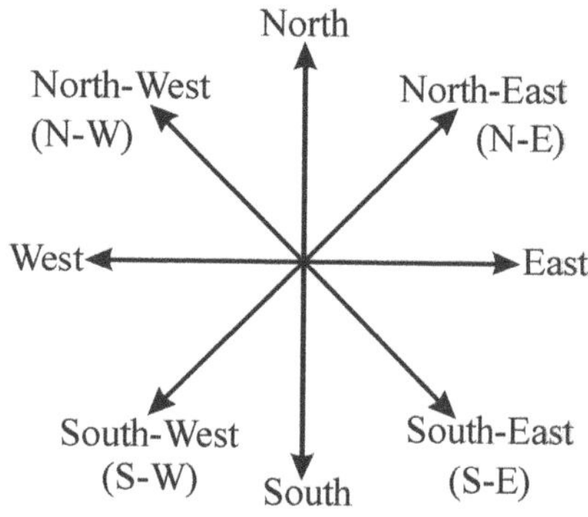

❑ Shortcut Approach

To remember four main directions, always remember the word 'NEWS.'

Note: *On paper North is always on top while South is always in bottom.*

CONCEPT OF DEGREE

Let us see the following picture:

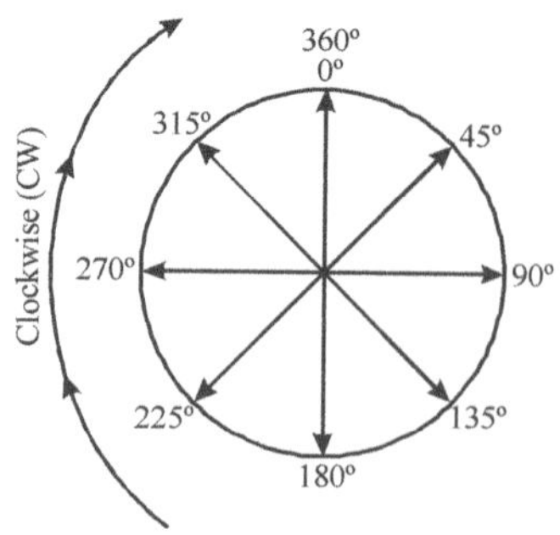

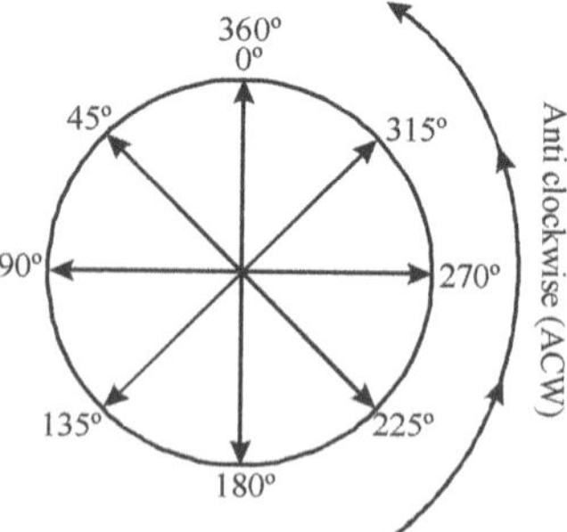

Remember

- North, East, South and West are called main directions.
- North-east, South-east, South-west and North-west are called subdirections.
- Angle between two consecutive main directions is always 90°.
- Angle between two consecutive subdirections is always 90°.
- Angle between a main direction and its adjucent subdirection is always 45°.

CONCEPT OF TURN

Right turn = Clockwise turn
Left turn = Anticlockwise turn
Let us understand it through pictorial representation:

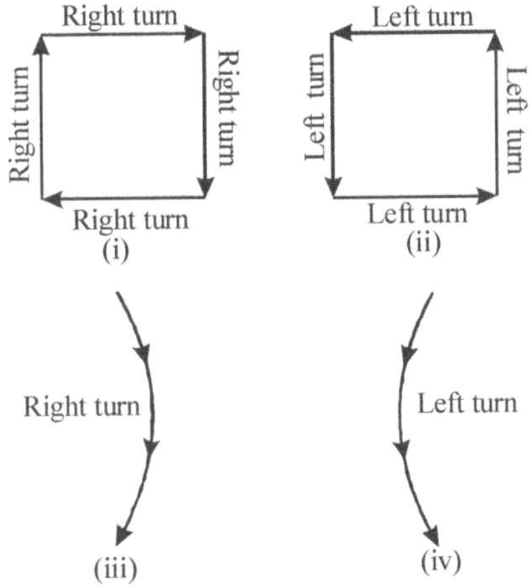

EXAMPLE 1. Raman walked 2 km West from his office and then turned South covering 4 km. Finally, he waked 3 km towards East and again move 1 km West. How far is Raman from his initial position.

Sol. Raman starts from his office A, moves 2 km West upto B, then 4 km to the South upto C, 3 km East upto D and finally 1 km West upto E, Thus his distance from the initial position AE = BC = 4 km.

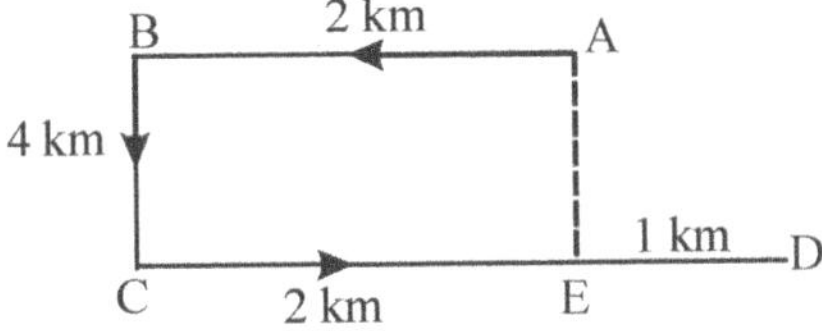

Remember

- If our face is towards North, than after left turn our face will be towards West while after right turn, it will be towards East.
- If our face is towards South, then after left turn our face will be towards East and after right turn it will be towards West.
- If our face is towards East, then after left turn our face will be forwards North and after right turn it will be towards South.
- If our face is towards West, then after left turn our face will be towards South and after right turn it will be towards North.
- If our face is towards North-West, then after left turn our face will be towards South-West and after right turn it will be towards North-East.
- If our face is towards South-West, then after left turn our face will be towards South-East and after right turn it will be towards North-West.
- If our face is towards South-East, then after left turn our face will be towards North-East and after right turn it will be towards South-West.
- If our face is towards North-East, then after left turn our face will be towards North-West and after right-turn it will be towards South-East.

Shortcut Approach

Direction before taking the turn	Direction in which the person or vehicle will be moving after taking the turn	
	Right	**Left**
(i) North	East	West
(ii) South	West	East
(iii) East	South	North
(iv) West	North	South
(v) North-West	North-East	South-West
(vi) South-West	North-West	South-East
(vii) South-East	South-West	North-East
(viii) North-East	South-East	North-West

CONCEPT OF SHORTEST/ MINIMUM DISTANCE

The shortest distance between two points may be different from the total distance covered in going from initial position to final position.

To find the minimum distance between initial and last point, many times we have to use '**Pythogoras Theorem**'.

$$h^2 = b^2 + P^2$$

where,

h = Hypotenuse

b = Base

P = Perpendicular

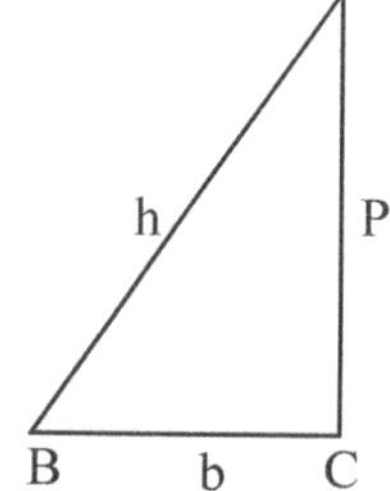

EXAMPLE 2. Rashmi walks 10 km towards North. She walks 6 km towards South then. From here she moves 3 km towards East. How far and in which direction is she with reference to her starting point?

Sol. It is clear, Rashmi moves 10 km from A towards North upto B, then moves 6 km Southwards upto C, then turns towards East and walks 3 km upto D.

Then, $AC = (AB - BC) = 10 - 6 = 4$ km

$CD = 3$km.

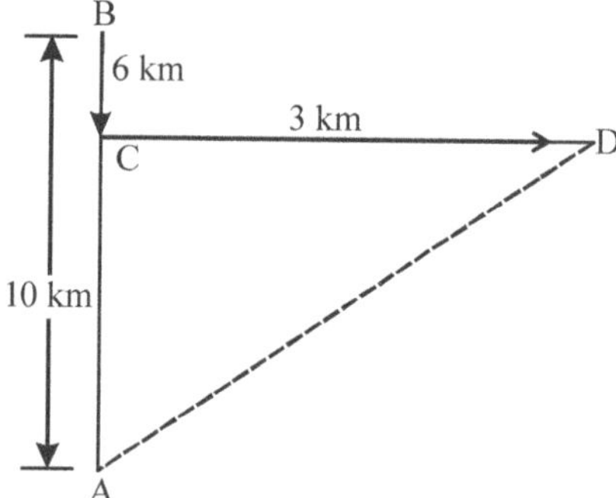

$\therefore$ Rashmi's distance from starting point A

$$= AD = \sqrt{AC^2 + CD^2} = \sqrt{4^2 + 3^2}$$

$$= \sqrt{16+9} = \sqrt{25} = 5\text{km}.$$

From figure, D is to the North-East of A.

SHADOW CASE

In Morning/Sunrise Time

(a) If a person facing towards Sun, the shadow will be towards his back or in West.

(b) If a person facing towards South, the shadow will be towards his right.

(c) If a person facing towards West, the shadow will be towards his front.

(d) If a person facing towards North, the shadow will be towards his left.

In Evening/Sunset Time

(a) If a person facing towards Sun, the shadow will be towards his back or in East.

(b) If a person facing towards North, the shadow will be towards his right.

(c) If a person facing towards East, the shadow will be towards his front.

(e) If a person facing towards South, the shadow will be towards his left.

Note : *At 12:00 noon there is no shadow because the rays of the sun are vertically downward.*

EXAMPLE 3. Early morning after sunrise, Rajesh was standing infront of his house in such a way that his shadow as falling exactly behind him. He starts walking straight and walks 5 m. He turns to his left and walks 3 m and again turning to his left walks 2m. Now in which direction is he from his starting point?

Sol. The shadow of Rajesh was falling exactly behind him. So, he was facing towards East. Diagram clearly shows that Rajesh was in North-East with reference to the starting point.

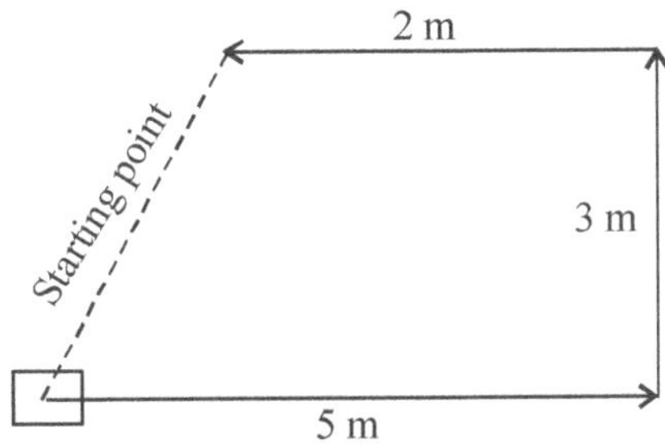

Shortcut Approach

- Draw four lines from a point (let o) repersenting four main directions.
- Think that you are the point o.
- Read the statement line by line.
- Move yourself as per statement asked and prepare a diagram as per line by line statement.
- Show, check and verify the direction and distance moved from starting point.
- Find the direction and distance of the final position.

The questions of direction and distance asked in various competitive exams are classified into the following types.

1. FINDING THE DIRECTION ONLY

(a) To determine the final direction when initial direction of movement along with various turns are given.

EXAMPLE 4. A rat runs 20' towards east and turns to right, runs 10' and turns to right, runs 9' and again turns to left, runs 5' and then to left, runs 12' and finally turns to left and runs 6'. Now, which direction is the rat facing?

(a) East (b) West
(c) North (d) South
(e) None of these

Sol. (c) The movements of rat are as shown in figure. Clearly, it is finally walking in the direction FG i.e. North.

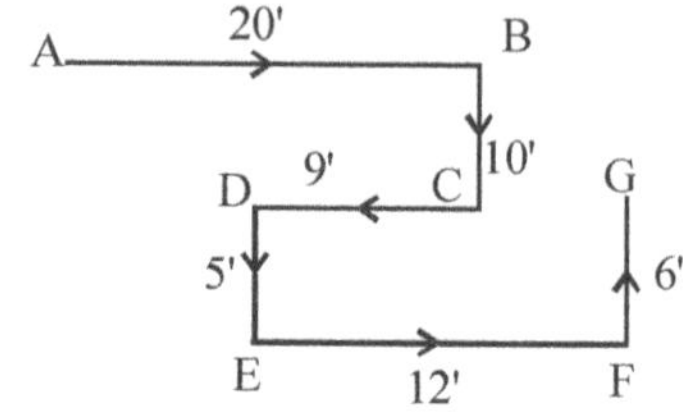

(b) To find the initial direction when various turns taken during a journey are given along with the final direction.

EXAMPLE 5. Kunal travels 10 m from his shop and turns to his left. After that he turns to right from the crossing. After moving certain yards, he turns to left and again turns to left after moving some distance. Finally, he turns to right. If at final position he is facing North direction, then which direction he was facing while coming out of his shop?

(a) South (b) West
(c) East (d) North

Sol. (c) According to the question, the direction diagram will be as follows

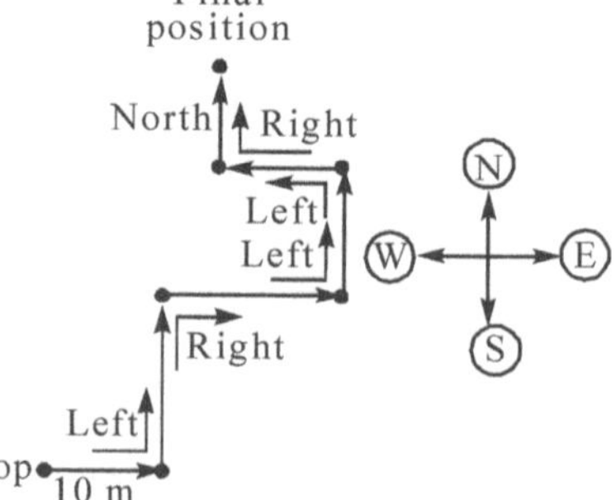

Clearly, Kunal is facing East while coming out of his shop.

(c) When one direction gets changed by some other direction, then other directions also changed accordingly. In this case we have to find the new direction of any one (or more) of the remaining directions.

EXAMPLE 6. Rohit walked 25 metres towards South. Then he turned to his left and walked 20 metres. He then turned to his left and walked 25 metres. He again turned to his right and walked 15 metres. At what distance is he from the starting point and in which direction?

(a) 35 metres East
(b) 35 metres North
(c) 40 metres East
(d) 60 metres East
(e) None of these

Sol. (a) The movements of Rohit are as shown in figure.
Rohit's distance from starting point A = AE
= (AD + DE) = (BC + DE)
= (20 + 15) m = 35 m.
Also, E is to the East of A.

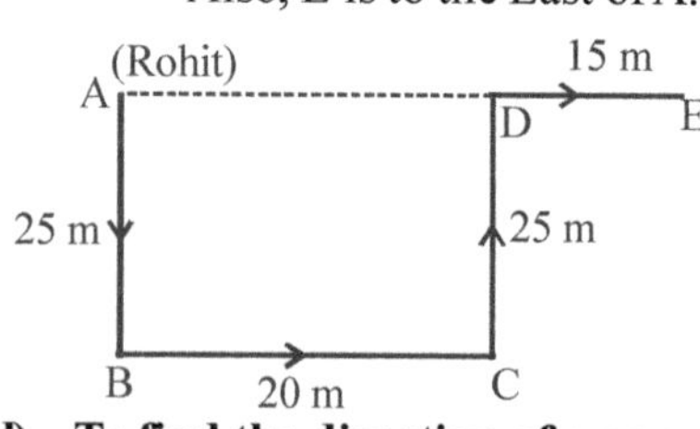

(d) To find the direction of a person when direction of a shadow form of a person in an action is given.

EXAMPLE 7. After 4 pm on a sunny day when Ramesh was returning from his school, he saw his uncle coming in the opposite direction. His uncle talked to him for some time. Ramesh saw that the shadow

of his uncle was to his right side. Which direction was his uncle facing during their talk?

(a) North
(b) South
(c) East
(d) Data inadequate
(e) None of these

Sol. (b) After 4 pm the shadow will be towards East. Now, East is to the right of Ramesh. So Ramesh faces North. And his uncle, who is opposite to him, faces South.

(e) To Find Clock Based Direction

EXAMPLE 8. If the digit 12 of a clock is pointing towards East, then in which direction will digit 9 point?

(a) South (b) West
(c) North (d) North-East

Sol. (c) According to the question, the diagrams will be as follows.

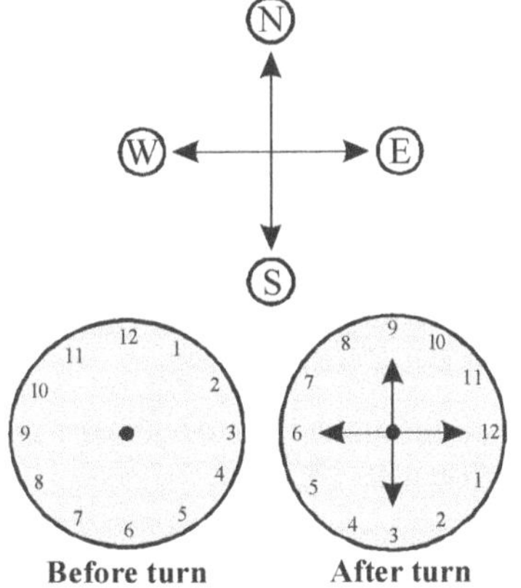

Clearly, digit 9 will point towards North.

(f) To Find Relative Direction

EXAMPLE 9. Raman starts from his house and goes towards 15 m North, then he turns his right and walks 30 m before taking right turn and moving again upto 30 m to reach a temple. In which direction is the temple with respect to Raman's house?

(a) North-West (b) South
(c) South-East (d) West

Sol. (c) According to the question, the direction diagram is as follows

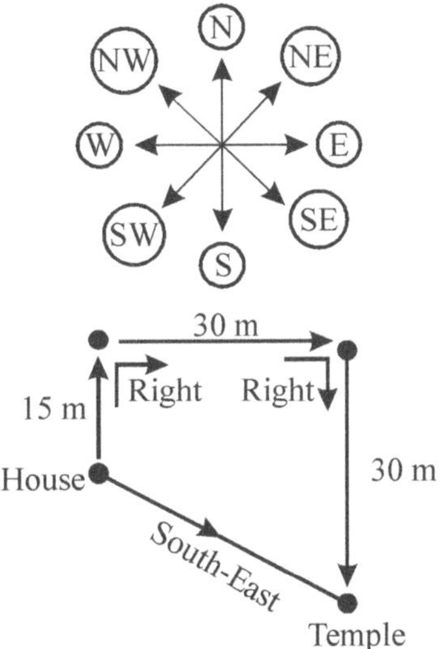

Clearly, temple is towards South-East with respect to Raman's house.

2. FINDING THE DISTANCE ONLY

EXAMPLE 10. One day, Ravi left home and cycled 10 km southwards, turned right and cycled 5 km and turned right and cycled 10 km and turned left and cycled 10 km. How many kilometres will he have to cycle to reach his home straight?

(a) 10km
(b) 15km
(c) 20km

(d) 25 km
(e) None of these

Sol. (b) Here, Ravi starts from home at A, moves 10 km southwards up to B, turns right and moves 5 km up to C, turns right again and moves 10 km upto D and finally turns left and moves 10 km up to E.

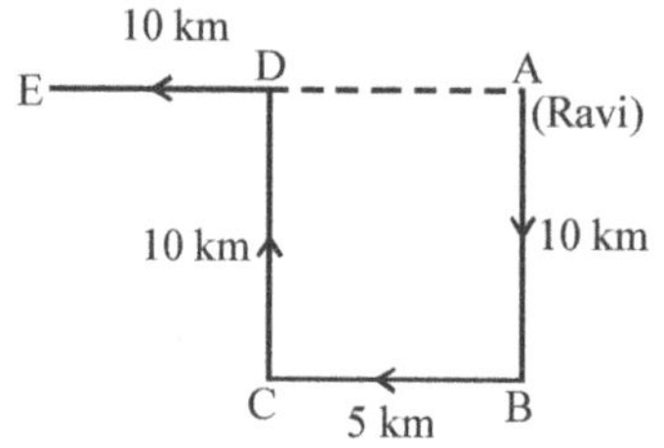

Thus, his distance from initial position A = AE
= AD + DE
= BC + DE = (5 + 10) km = 15 km.

3. FINDING BOTH THE DISTANCE AND DIRECTION

EXAMPLE 11. Sanjay's school is $10\sqrt{2}$ km in North-West direction from his house. The office of his father is 10 km in South direction from the school. The multiplex hall is 10 km towards East from the school. How far and in which direction is the multiplex hall from the office of his father?

(a) $10\sqrt{2}$ km, North-East
(b) 20 km, North-East
(c) Cannot be determined
(d) 10 km, South-East

Sol. (a) According to the question, the direction diagram will be as follows

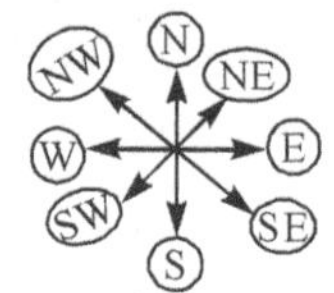

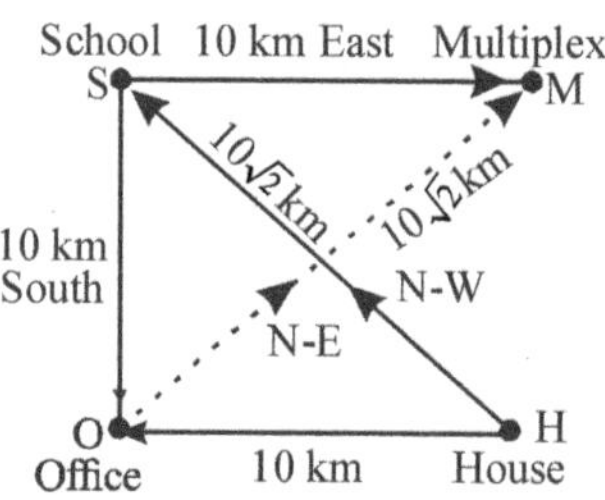

As in a square, diagonals are equal

$\therefore$ SH = OM = $10\sqrt{2}$ km

$\therefore$ Required distance, OM
= Distance between office and multiplex = $10\sqrt{2}$ km

Also, if is clear from diagram that multiplex (M) is to the North-East of O (office)

So, the multiplex is $10\sqrt{2}$ km North-East from office.

PRACTICE EXERCISE

1. Ashok started walking towards South. After walking 50 metres he took a right turn and walked 30 metres. He then took a right turn and walked 100 metres. He again took a right turn and walked 30 metres and stopped. How far and in which direction was he from the starting point?
   (a) 50 metres South
   (b) 150 metres North
   (c) 180 metres East
   (d) 50 metres North
   (e) None of these
2. Town D is towards East of town F. Town B is towards North of town D. Town H is towards South of town B. Towards which direction is town H from town F ?
   (a) East
   (b) South-East
   (c) North-East
   (d) Data inadequate
   (e) None of these
3. Mohan walked 30 metres towards South, took a left turn and walked 15 metres. He then took a right turn and walked 20 metres. He again took a right turn and walked 15 metres. How far is he from the starting point?
   (a) 95 metres
   (b) 50 metres
   (c) 70 metres
   (d) cannot be determined
   (e) None of these

DIRECTIONS (Qs. 4-5): *Study the following information to answer the given questions :*

Point P is 5 m towards the South of Point M. Point Q is 3 m towards the East of Point P. Point O is 3 m towards the East of Point M. Point N is 2 m towards the South of Point Q.

4. A person, facing North, takes a left turn from point M, walks 4m and stops. He then takes another left turn, walks 5 m and stops at point R. Which of the following points, including R, fall in a straight line?
   (a) M, O, R (b) N, R, P
   (c) R, O, Q (d) R, Q, N
   (e) Q, P, R
5. How far and towards which direction is Point O from Point N?
   (a) 5 m towards South
   (b) 7 m towards North
   (c) 8 m towards West
   (d) 7 m towards West
   (e) 5 m towards North
6. Vikas walked 10 metres towards North, took a left turn and walked 15 metres and again took a left turn and walked 10 metres and stopped walking. Towards which direction was he facing when he stopped walking?
   (a) South
   (b) South-West
   (c) South-East
   (d) Cannot be determined
   (e) None of these

7. While facing East, I turn to my left and walk 10 m, then turn to my left and walk 10 m. Now, I turn 45 degrees towards my right in North-West direction and cover 25 m. At this point, in which direction am I from my starting point?
   (a) South-East (b) South-West
   (c) North-East (d) North-West
   (e) None of these
8. Vijay started walking towards South. After walking 15m, he turned to the left and walked 15 m. He again turned to his left and walked 15 m. How far is he from his original position and in which direction?
   (a) 15 m, North (b) 15 m, South
   (c) 30 m, East (d) 15 m, West
   (e) None of these
9. Two Person P and Q are separated by a distance of 20 meter in west-east direction respectively. Now P and Q start walking in north and south direction respectively and walked for 5 meter. Now P and Q took a right turn and walked 10m each. Now P and Q took left turn and after walking 5 meter both of them stopped. Find the distance between them
   (a) 15 (b) 25
   (c) 30 (d) 35
   (e) None of these
10. Mohan walked 30 metres towards South, took a left turn and walked 15 metres. He then took a right turn and walked 20 metres. He again took a right turn and walked 15 metres. How far is he from the starting point?
   (a) 95 metres
   (b) 50 metres
   (c) 70 metres
   (d) Cannot be determined
   (e) None of these

HINTS & SOLUTIONS

1. **(d)**

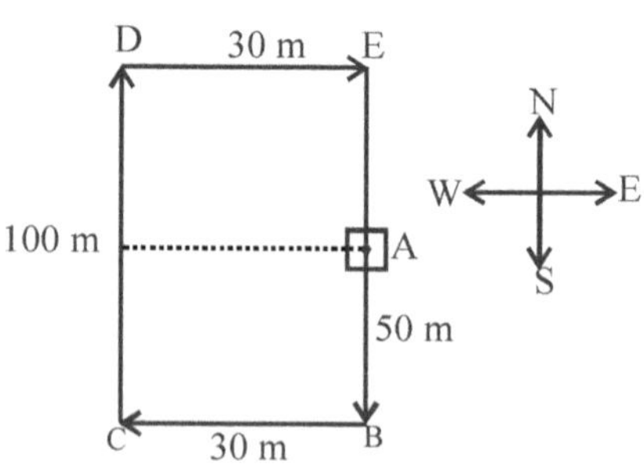

Required distance = (BE – AB) = (100 – 50) m = 50 m

Direction ⇒ North

2. **(d)**

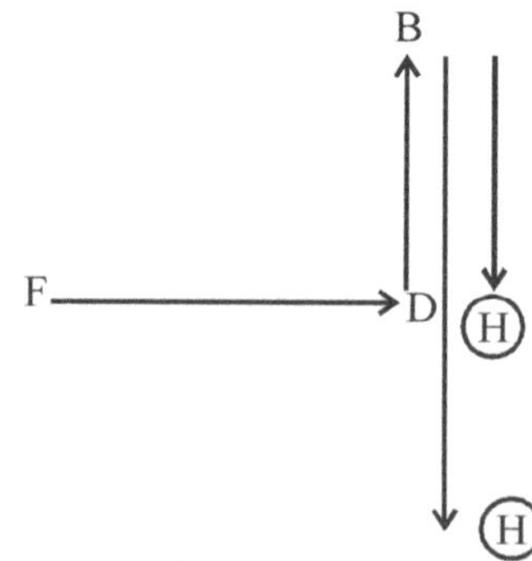

So there is no sufficient data to determine the direction of Town H.

3. **(b)** As per conditions given

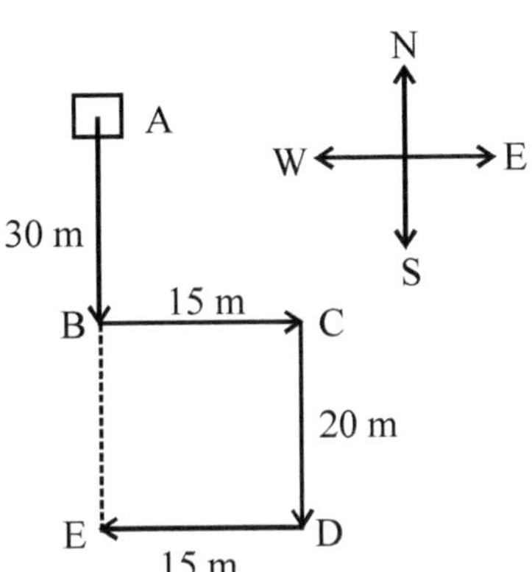

Required distance = AE = AB + BE = (30 + 20) m = 50 m

4. **(e)**

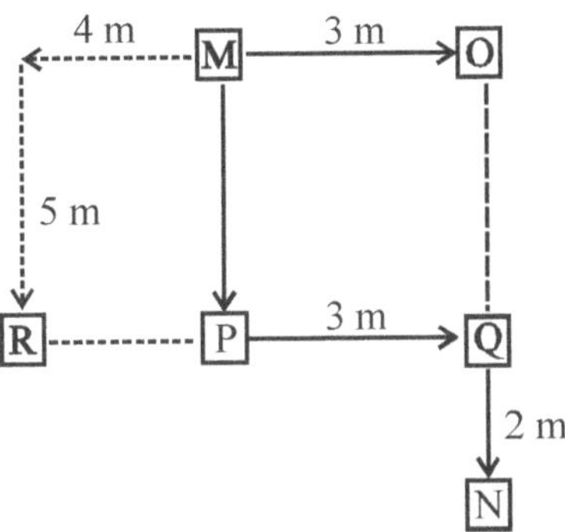

Points R, P and Q are in a straight line.

5. **(b)** Points O is 7 metres towards North of Point N.

6. **(a)**

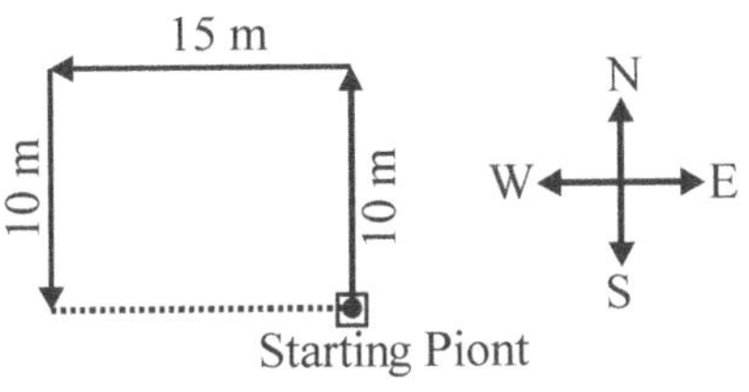

7. **(d)**

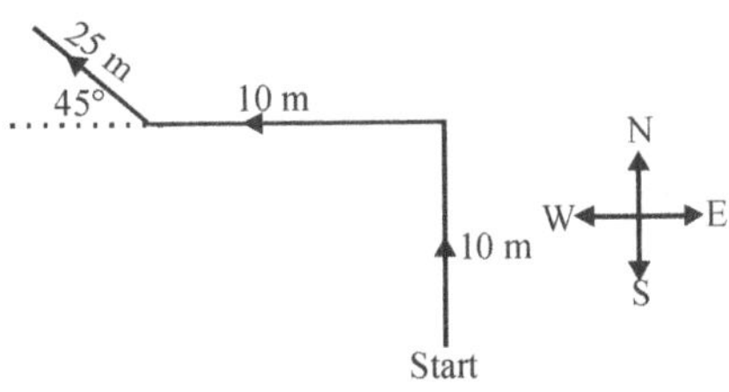

So, the person is in North-West direction from starting point

8. **(e)** Follow the given movements,

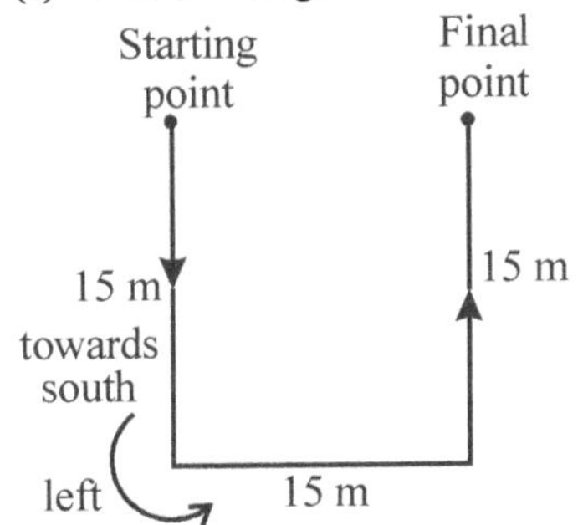

Hence, he is 15 m to the East from the starting point.

9. **(e)**

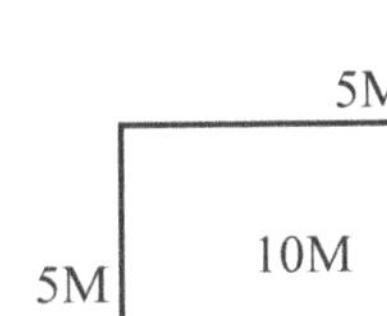

∴ Required distance = 20 meter.

10. **(b)**

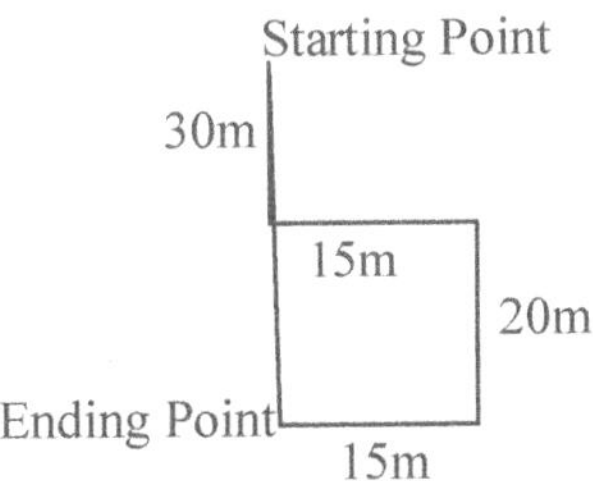

Time Sequence, Number, Ranking Test & Position Test

TIME SEQUENCE

In time sequence, we have to detect exact time/a particular day/a particular day on the basis of several statements provided in the question.

To solve problems related to time sequence, let us gather first the following informations :

1 Minute = 60 seconds
1 Hour = 60 minutes
1 Day = 24 hours
1 Week = 7 days
1 Month = 4 weeks
1 Year = 12 months
1 Ordinary year = 365 days
1 Leap year =366 days
1 Century = 100 years

Remember

- A day is the period of the earth's revolution on its axis.
- A 'Solar year' is the time taken the earth to travel round the sun. It is equal to 365 days, 5 hours, 48 minutes and $47\frac{1}{2}$ seconds nearly.
- A 'Lunar month' is the time taken by the moon to travel round the earth. It is equal to nearly 28 days.

Leap Year

- If the number of a given year is divisible by 4, it is a leap year. Hence, the years like 1996, 2008, 2012 are leap years. But years like 1997, 1991, 2005, 2007 are not divisible by 4 and therefore, such years are not leap years.
- In a leap year, February has 29 days.
- A leap year has 52 weeks and 2 days. Therefore, a leap year has 2 odd days.

Ordinary year

- An ordinary year has 12 months.
- An ordinary year has 365 days.
- An ordinary year has 52 weeks and 1 day. Therefore, an ordinary year has 1 odd day.

Century (100 years)

- A century has 76 ordinary years and 24 leap years.
- A century has 5 odd days.

Odd days

Odd days in an ordinary year = 1
Odd days in a leap year = 2
Odd days in 100 years = 5
Odd days in 200 years = (5×2)
= 1 week + 3 days = 3
Odd days in 300 years = (5×3)
= 2 weeks + 1 day = 1
Odd days in 400 years = $(5 \times 4 + 1)$
= 21 days
= 3 weeks + 0 day = 0

Similarly, each 800, 1600, 2000, 2004, etc. has 0 odd days.

EXAMPLE 1. Neena returned home after 3 days earlier than the time she had told her mother. Neena's sister Veena reached five days later than the day Neena was supposed to return. If Neena returned on Thursday, on what day did Veena return ?

Sol. Neena returned home on Thursday. Neena was supposed to return 3 days later, i.e., on Sunday. Veena returned five days later from Sunday. i.e., on Friday.

NUMBER TEST

In such test, generally you are given a long series of numbers. The candidate is required to find out how many times a number satifying the conditions specified in the question occurs.

EXAMPLE 2. How many 8s are there in the following number sequence which are immediately preceded by 5 but not immediately followed by 3?

3 8 5 8 4 5 8 3 9 8 8 5 8 8 8 9 3

Sol. Let use see the following :

3 8 5 8 4 5 **8** 3 9 8 8 5 **8** 8 8 93

Clearly, two such 8s are there.

Remember

There is no rule as how to attempt these questions but we can practice these questions :

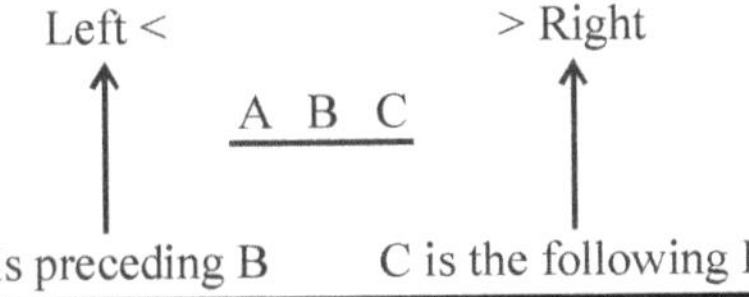

RANKING TEST

Ranking involves determining the sequencial order of one or more persons/objects based on comparison of parameters such as height, weight, age, length, position, merits etc.

For comparison, generally following symbols are used:

(i) A > B (means A is greater/heavier / taller / higher /more than B)

(ii) A < B (means A is smaller / lighter / shorter / lower / less than B)

Questions based on ranking are generally given with a set of information in jumbled form based on which the candidates are required to systematically arrange the given information and determine the sequencial order of arrangement of the various persons/objects.

EXAMPLE 3. N is more intelligent than M. M is not as intelligent as Y. X is more intelligent than Y but not as good as N. Who is the most intelligent of all?

(a) N (b) M
(c) X (d) Y

Sol. (a) According to the question,

N > M
Y > M
N > X > Y

On arranging the above data, we get

∵ Ⓝ > X > Y > M

So, N is the most intelligent among them.

EXAMPLE 4. Shailendra is shorter than Keshav but taller than Rakesh, Madhav is the tallest. Aashish is a little shorter than Keshav and little taller than Shailendra. If they stand in the order of increasing heights, who will be the second?

(a) Aashish (b) Shailendra
(c) Rakesh (d) Madhav

Sol. (b) According to the question,

K > S > R

[K = Keshav
S = Shailendra
R = Rakesh
M = Madhav
A = Aashish]

Madhav is the tallest.

K > A > S

On arranging the above data, we get

∴ M > K > A > S > R

or

R < Ⓢ < A < K < M
↓ ↓ ↓ ↓ ↓
1 2 3 4 5

Hence, Shailendra will be the second.

POSITION TEST

In this type of problems, the position of a person from either of the two ends of a row (or column) is given and it is asked to determine number of persons to the left / right (or above / below) of a partienlas person or total number of persons in the group etc. Sometimes, such questions are given in the form of a puzzle involving interchanging of seats by two or more persons.

Position of a Person from Left/ Right/Top/Bottom

❑ Shortcut Approach

Formulas to determine the position of a person in a horizontal row

(1) Left + Right = Total + 1
(2) Left = Total + 1 – Right
(3) Right = Total + 1 – left
(4) Total = left + Right – 1

EXAMPLE 5.

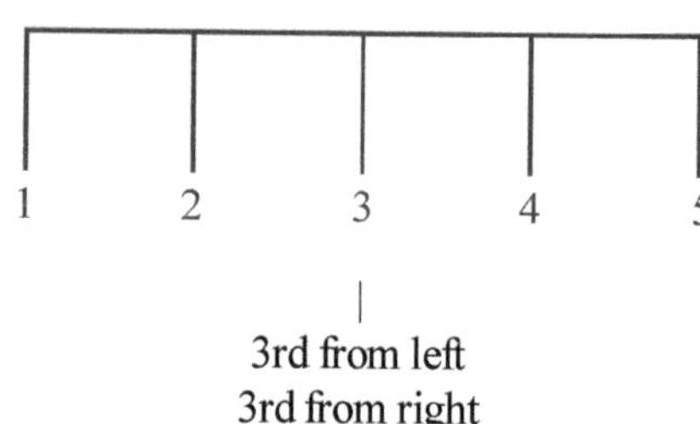

3rd from left
3rd from right
Total = 3 + 3 – 1

❑ Shortcut Approach

Formula to determine the position of a person in a vertical column

(1) Total + 1 = Top + Bottom
(2) Top = Total + 1 – Bottom
(3) Botom = Total + 1 – Top
(4) Total = Top + Bottom – 1

Note : *The above formulas are only for a single person's position*

EXAMPLE 6. In a vertical column of 40 students, A is 13th from the top end, find the rank from bottom end.

Sol. Total = 40

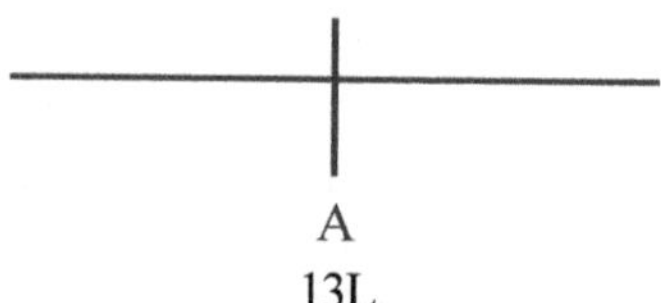

A
13L

A's rank from bottom
= Total + 1 – top
= 40 – 13 + 1
= 27 + 1
= 28

New Position of a Person(s) after Interchanging of Positions between Two Persons

In this type of questions, the positions of two persons are interchanged and it is asked to determine their new positions (from left or right)

Shortcut Approach

(i) New position of the first person from left after the interchanged

= [Difference of two position of second person from right] + [Initial position of first person from left]

(ii) New position of the second person from right after the interchanged

= [Difference of two positions of first person from left] + [Initial position of second person from right]

EXAMPLE 7. In a row of girls Ankita is sixth from the left and Rashami is nineth from the right. When they exchange their positions, then Ankita

becomes eighteenth from left. What will be Rashami new position from the right?

Shortcut Sol.

Rashami new position from the right
$= (18 - 6) + 9$
$= 21 = 21\text{st}$ position

Number of Persons between the Original and New Position of a Person

Shortcut Approach:

Total number of persons between two positions = (New position) – (original position) – 1.

EXAMPLE 8. In a row of boys, Kartik is 5th from left and Ganesh is 15th from right. If the position of Kartik and Ganesh are interchanged then new position of Kartik 20th from left. Find the number of boys between Kartik and Ganesh.

Shortcut Sol.

Total number of boys between two position of Kartik
$= 20 - 5 - 1 = 14$

Maximum and Minimum Number of Persons in a Row

Shortcut Approach:

If position of two persons from the two opposite ends and the total number of places between these two positions is given, then

(i) Maximum number of persons in the row =

$$\begin{bmatrix}\text{Sum of position} \\ \text{of both persons}\end{bmatrix} + \begin{bmatrix}\text{Number of places} \\ \text{in the middle}\end{bmatrix}$$

(ii) Minimum number of persons in the row

$$= \begin{bmatrix}\text{Sum of positions} \\ \text{of both persons}\end{bmatrix} - \begin{bmatrix}\text{Number of places} \\ \text{in the middle}\end{bmatrix} - 2$$

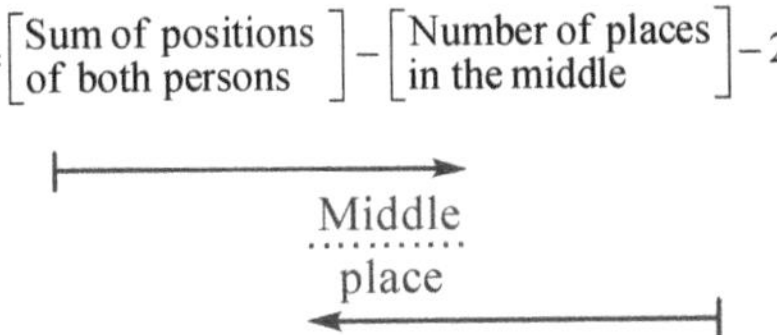

EXAMPLE 9. In a row, Sakashi is 10th from left and Sonia is 15th from right and there are 4 girls between Sakashi and Sonia, then find the maximum and minimum number of girls in the row.

Shortcut Sol.

Maximum number of girls $= (10 + 15) + 4 = 29$

Minimum number of girls
$= (10 + 15) - 4 - 2 = 19.$

PRACTICE EXERCISE

1. Pratap correctly remembers that his mother's birthday is before twenty third April but after nine teenth April, whereas his sister correctly remembers that their mother's birthday is not on or after twenty second April. On which day in April is definitely their mother's birthday?
   (a) Twentieth
   (b) Twenty-first
   (c) Twentieth or twenty-first
   (d) Cannot be determined
   (e) None of these

2. Among five friends, P, Q, R, S and T, each scored different marks in the examination. P scored more than Q but less than R. S scored more than' only T. Who amongst the following scored the second highest marks?
(a) P (b) Q
(c) R (d) S
(e) T

3. In a class of 25 students. Lata's rank is 13th from the top and Parul's rank is 19th from the bottom. If Vishal's rank is exactly between Lata's and Parul's rank what is Vishal's rank from the top ?
(a) 10th (b) 8th
(c) 9th (d) 7th
(e) Cannot be determined

4. Among P, Q, R, S, T and U. R is taller than only P and U. S is shorter than only T and Q. If each of them has a different height, who among them will be the third from top when they are arranged in descending order of their height ?
(a) R (b) P
(c) S (d) Q
(e) None of these

5. Anish's mother remember that her wedding day after 10th February 2010,but before 20th February 2010.According to her brother after 13th February 2010 but before 17th February 2010. Anish wedding day on which date? (Note: DATE Should be odd number)
(a) February 12 (b) February 13
(c) February 14 (d) February 15
(e) February 16

6. In a row of boys, Srinath is 7th from the left and Venkat is 12th from the right. If they interchange their positions, Srinath becomes 22nd from the left. How many boys are there in the row ?
(a) 19 (b) 31
(c) 33 (d) 34

7. After 9'O clock at what time between 9 p.m. and 10 p.m. will the hour and minute hands, of a clock point in opposite direction?
(a) 15 min. past 9
(b) 16 min. past 9
(c) $16\frac{4}{11}$ min. past 9
(d) $17\frac{1}{11}$ min. past 9

8. If John celebrated his victory day on Tuesday, 5th January 1965, when will he celebrate his next victory day on the same day?
(a) 5th January 1970
(b) 5th January 1971
(c) 5th January 1973
(d) 5th January 1974

9. If the 5th date of a month is Tuesday, what date will be 3 days after the 3rd Friday in the month?
(a) 17 (b) 22
(c) 19 (d) 18

10. In a row of students, if John , who is 16th from the left, and Johnson, who is 8th from the right, interchange their positions, John becomes 33rd from left. How many students are there in a row?
(a) 38 (b) 39
(c) 40 (d) 41

HINTS & SOLUTIONS

1. (c) According to Pratap his mother's birthday may be on 20th, 21st or 22nd April. According to Pratap's sister their mother's birthday may be from 1st April to 21st April. Common Dates ⇒ 20th and 21st

2. (a) R > P > Q > S > T
P scored the second highest marks.

3. (a) $\xrightarrow{6}$ [P] ‖ [V] ‖ [L] $\xleftarrow{12}$
Vishal's rank from the top is 10th.

4. (c) R > P, U
T, Q > S
T, Q > S > R > P, U

5. (d) Mother: 11 12 13 14 15 16 17 18 19
Brother: 14 15 16
15 is coming in common and also a odd number.Hence Anish's wedding day is on February 15.

6. (c)

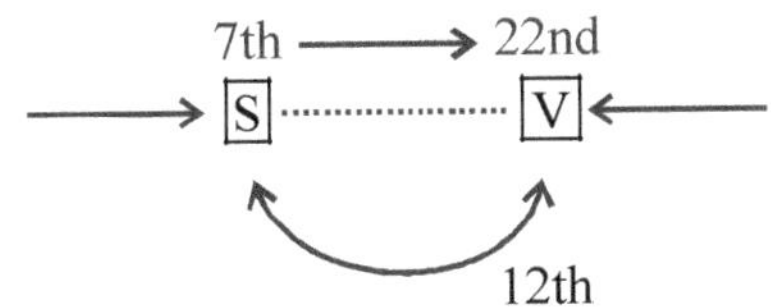

Total number of boys in the row

= 22 + 12 – 1 = [33]

7. (c) At 9 O'clock, the minute hand is 9 × 5 = 45 minute – spaces behind the hour hand. Therefore, the minute hand will have to gain 45 – 30 = 15 minute space over the hour hand.
∵ Gain of 55 minute spaces equal 60 minutes.
∴ Gain of 15 minute spaces equals

$$= \frac{60}{55} \times 15 = \frac{180}{11} = 16\frac{4}{11}$$

Therefore, hour and minute hands of a clock point in opposite direction after 9 O'clock at $16\frac{4}{11}$ minutes past 9.

8. (b) 5 January 1965 ⇒ Tuesday
5 January 1966 ⇒ Wednesday
5 January 1967 ⇒ Thursday
5 January 1968 ⇒ Friday
5 January 1969 ⇒ Sunday
Since, 1968 is a leap year.
5 January 1970 ⇒ Monday
5 January 1971 ⇒ Tuesday

9. (d) 5th date of a month is Tuesday.
Friday will be on = 5 + 3
= 8th of a month
1st Friday is on 1st of a month
2nd Friday is on 8th of a month
3rd Friday will be on 15th of a month
3 days after 15th = 15 + 3 = 18

10. (c) When John interchange his position, new

Position will be 33 from left and 8 from Right
Total = 33 + 8 – 1 = 40

Logical Sequence of Words

INTRODUCTION

In this particular type of problems, certain inter-related words are given and numbered, followed by various sequences of the numbers denoting them, as alternatives.

TYPES OF SEQUENCE

(i) Sequence of occurence of events or various stages in a process.

EXAMPLE
1. Consultation
2. Illness
3. Doctor
4. Treatment
5. Recovery

Sol. Clearly illness occurs first. One then goes to a doctor and after consultation with him, undergoes treatment to finally attain recovery.

(ii) Sequence of objects in a class or group

EXAMPLE
1. Member
2. Country
3. Community
4. Family
5. Locality

Sol. Member $\rightarrow$ Family $\rightarrow$ Community $\rightarrow$ Locality $\rightarrow$ Country

(iii) Sequence in Ascending or Descending order

EXAMPLE
1. Furniture
2. Forest
3. Wood
4. Country
5. Trees

Sol. Country $\rightarrow$ Forest $\rightarrow$ Trees $\rightarrow$ Wood $\rightarrow$ Furniture.

(iv) Sequential order of words According to Dictionary

EXAMPLE
1. Direct
2. Divide
3. Divest
4. Devine
5. Divisons

Sol. Devine $\rightarrow$ Direct $\rightarrow$ Divest $\rightarrow$ Divide $\rightarrow$ Divisons.

❑ Shortcut Approach

- Remember all English alphabets in forward and reverse order
- Knowledge of our nature or surroundings

PRACTICE EXERCISE

1. Arrange the following words according to the dictionary ?
1. Inventory 2. Involuntary
3. Invisible 4. Invariable
5. Investigate
(a) 4, 2, 5, 3, 1 (b) 4, 5, 1, 3, 2
(c) 2, 5, 4, 1, 3 (d) 4, 1, 5, 3, 2

2. Which one of the given responses would be a meaningful order of the following words ?
A. Family B. Community
C. Member D. Locality
E. Country
(a) C, A, D, B, E (b) C, A, B, D, E
(c) C, A, B, E, D (d) C, A, D, E, B

3. Which one of the given responses would be a meaningful order of the following?
1. Sentence 2. Word
3. Chapter 4. Phrase
5. Paragraph
(a) 4, 3, 1, 2, 5 (b) 2, 3, 5, 4, 1
(c) 3, 5, 1, 4, 2 (d) 1, 3, 2, 4, 5

4. Arrange the following words according to dictionary order:
1. Banquet 2. Bangle
3. Bandage 4. Bantam
5. Bank
(a) 3, 2, 4, 5, 1 (b) 3, 5, 2, 1, 4
(c) 3, 2, 1, 5, 4 (d) 3, 2, 5, 1, 4

5. Arrange the given words in a meaningful order:
1. INFANT
2. ADOLESCENT
3. CHILD
4. OLD
5. ADULT
(a) 3, 1, 2, 4, 5 (b) 1, 3, 2, 5, 4
(c) 3, 2, 4, 5, 1 (d) 5, 4, 3, 2, 1

6. Arrange the following words in their ascending order:
1. Millenium
2. Diamond Jubilee
3. Silver Jubilee
4. Centenary
5. Golden Jubilee
(a) 2, 3, 5, 4, 1 (b) 2, 5, 3, 1, 4
(c) 3, 5, 2, 4, 1 (d) 2, 3, 5, 1, 4

7. Arrange the following words as per order in the dictionary.
(i) Forge (ii) Forget
(iii) Forgo (iv) Forgive
(v) Format
(a) (v), (ii), (iv), (iii), (i)
(b) (i), (iv), (iii), (ii), (v)
(c) (iii), (iv), (v), (ii), (i)
(d) (i), (ii), (iv), (iii), (v)

8. Arrange the following words as per order in the dictionary.
1. Obscure 2. Objective
3. Objection 4. Obligation
5. Oblivion
(a) 3, 2, 4, 5, 1 (b) 3, 2, 5, 4, 1
(c) 3, 2, 5, 1, 4 (d) 5, 2, 1, 3, 4

9. Arrange the following words as per order in the dictionary :
1. Command 2. Commit
3. Connect 4. Conceive
5. Conduct 6. Commerce
(a) 6 2 1 5 4 3 (b) 6 1 2 4 5 3
(c) 1 6 2 4 5 3 (d) 1 2 6 5 3 4

10. Which one of the given responses would be meaningful order of the following in ascending order?
1. Phrase 2. Alphabet
3. Sentence 4. Word
(a) 2, 1, 4, 3 (b) 1, 2, 3, 4
(c) 2, 4, 1, 3 (d) 2, 4, 3, 1

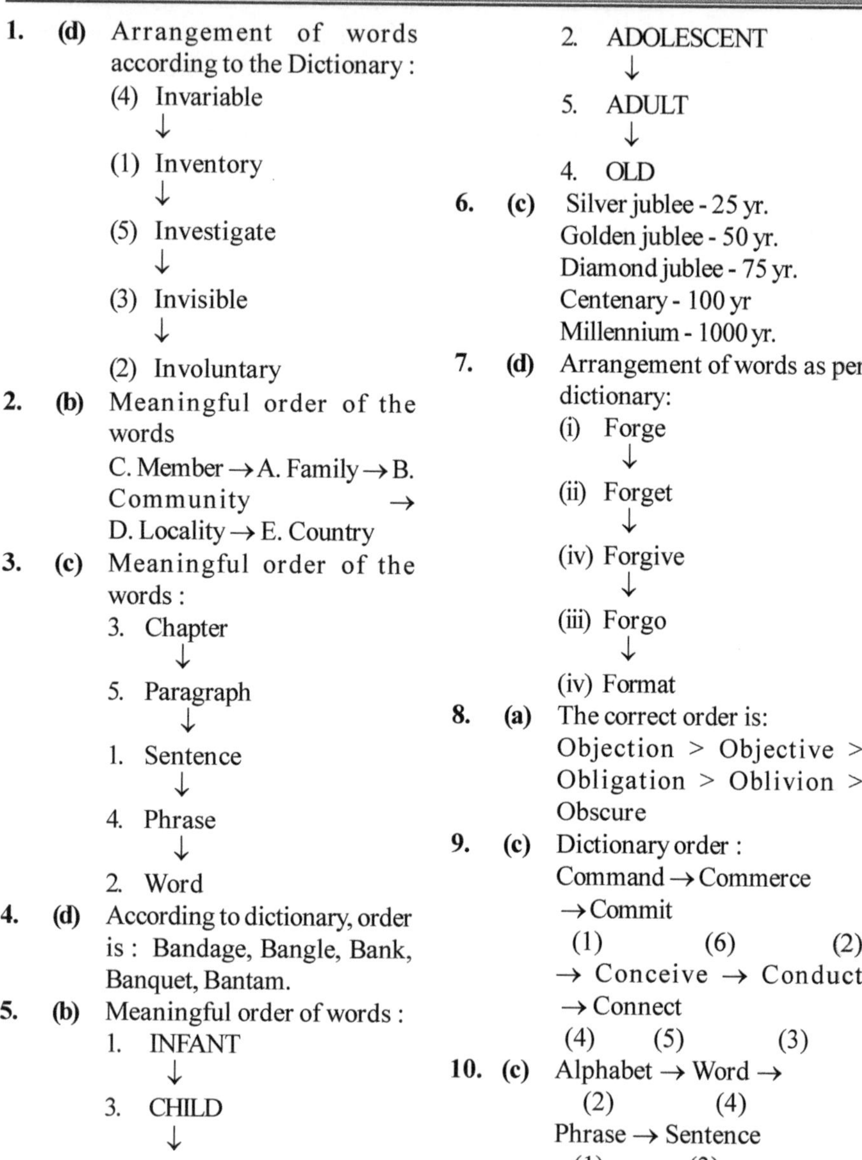

HINTS & SOLUTIONS

1. **(d)** Arrangement of words according to the Dictionary :
   (4) Invariable
   ↓
   (1) Inventory
   ↓
   (5) Investigate
   ↓
   (3) Invisible
   ↓
   (2) Involuntary

2. **(b)** Meaningful order of the words
   C. Member → A. Family → B. Community → D. Locality → E. Country

3. **(c)** Meaningful order of the words :
   3. Chapter
   ↓
   5. Paragraph
   ↓
   1. Sentence
   ↓
   4. Phrase
   ↓
   2. Word

4. **(d)** According to dictionary, order is : Bandage, Bangle, Bank, Banquet, Bantam.

5. **(b)** Meaningful order of words :
   1. INFANT
   ↓
   3. CHILD
   ↓
   2. ADOLESCENT
   ↓
   5. ADULT
   ↓
   4. OLD

6. **(c)** Silver jublee - 25 yr.
   Golden jublee - 50 yr.
   Diamond jublee - 75 yr.
   Centenary - 100 yr
   Millennium - 1000 yr.

7. **(d)** Arrangement of words as per dictionary:
   (i) Forge
   ↓
   (ii) Forget
   ↓
   (iv) Forgive
   ↓
   (iii) Forgo
   ↓
   (iv) Format

8. **(a)** The correct order is:
   Objection > Objective > Obligation > Oblivion > Obscure

9. **(c)** Dictionary order :
   Command → Commerce → Commit → Conceive → Conduct → Connect
   (1) (6) (2) (4) (5) (3)

10. **(c)** Alphabet → Word → Phrase → Sentence
    (2) (4) (1) (3)

Number Puzzles

INTRODUCTION

In this particular type of problems, questions are based on different number. This type of problem having figure which follows a particular rule for their different number. We have then asked to find a missing number by using same rule.

TYPES OF NUMBER PUZZLE

PATTERN 1 : SINGLE FIGURE PATTERN

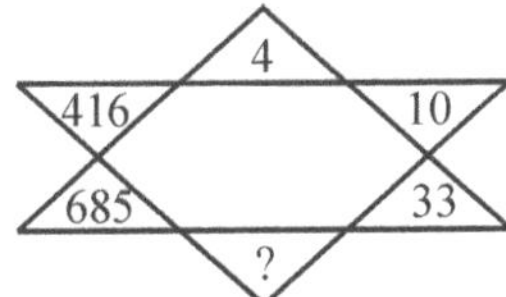

Here, a clockwise pattern is being followed. If we move clockwise we can see that numbers are increasing. If we observe it more closely, we can crack the pattern which is

As, $4 \times 2 + 2 = 10$, $10 \times 3 + 3 = 33$

So, $33 \times 4 + 4 = 136$

PATTERN 2 : MULTIPLE FIGURE PATTERN

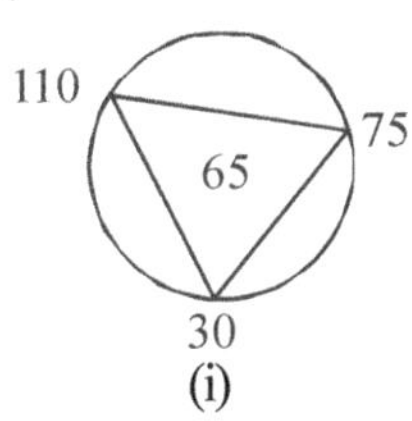

(i)

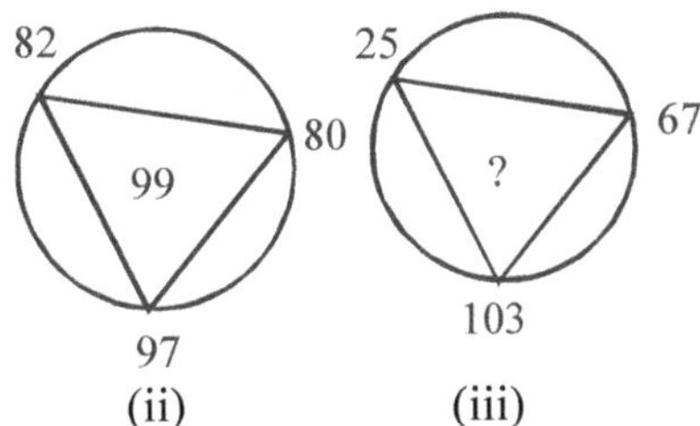

(ii) (iii)

Here, a series of figure is given. Checking the pattern in the first two figures, we have to find missing number in the third. If we observe the first two figure properly, we get an idea of the pattern.

As, $110 + 30 - 75 = 65$, $97 + 82 - 80 = 99$

So, $103 + 25 - 67 = 61$.

❑ Shortcut Approach

- The first step is to observe the figure and check if there is any familiar pattern in the given question.
- The second step is finding out the pattern.
- There is no need to memorize any pattern.
- You need to understand the concept and decode the pattern.

PRACTICE EXERCISE

1. Find the missing number from the given responses:

5	6	12
4	3	4
2	3	?
18	27	96

(a) 4 (b) 5
(c) 3 (d) 6

2. Find the missing number from the given response:

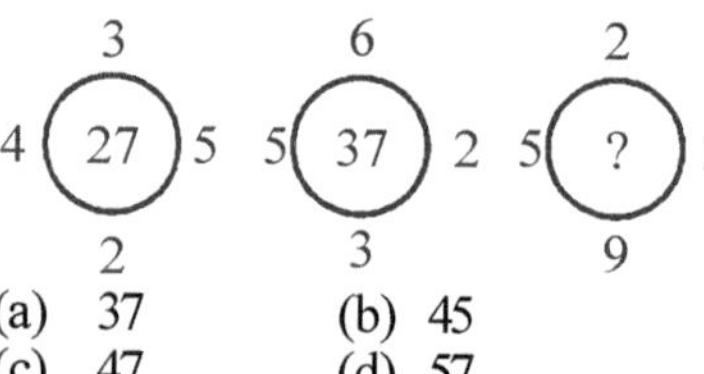

(a) 37 (b) 45
(c) 47 (d) 57

3. Select the missing number from the given responses:

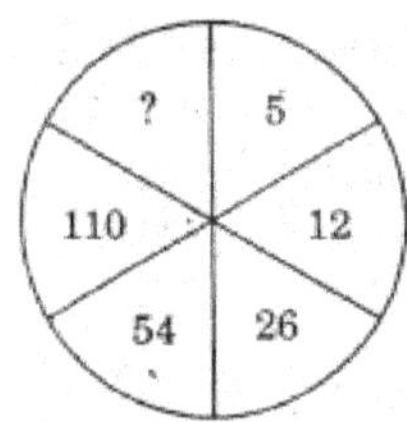

(a) 132 (b) 122
(c) 222 (d) 212

DIRECTIONS (Qs. 4 - 5) : *In questions below, select the missing number from the given responses*

4.

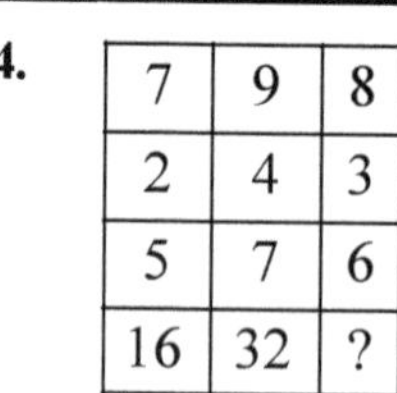

7	9	8
2	4	3
5	7	6
16	32	?

(a) 17 (b) 23
(c) 47 (d) 73

5.

3 9 7 81 5 | 2 8 4 64 6 | 4 7 ? 49 5

(a) 1 (b) 8
(c) 6 (d) 16

6. Select the missing number from the given responses.

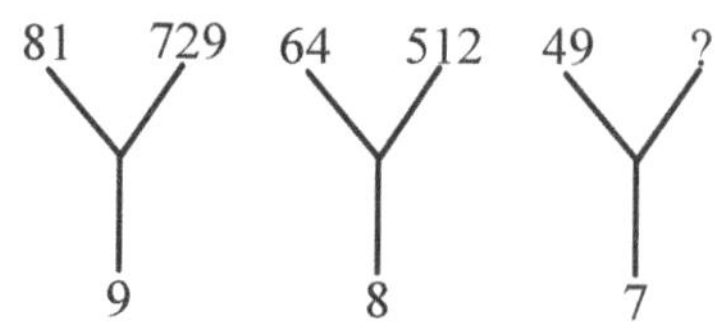

(a) 444 (b) 515
(c) 343 (d) 373

DIRECTIONS (Qs. 7 - 8) : *Select the missing number from the given responses.*

7.

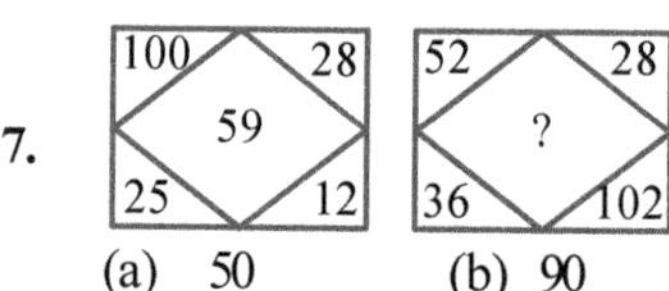

(a) 50 (b) 90
(c) 218 (d) 64

8.

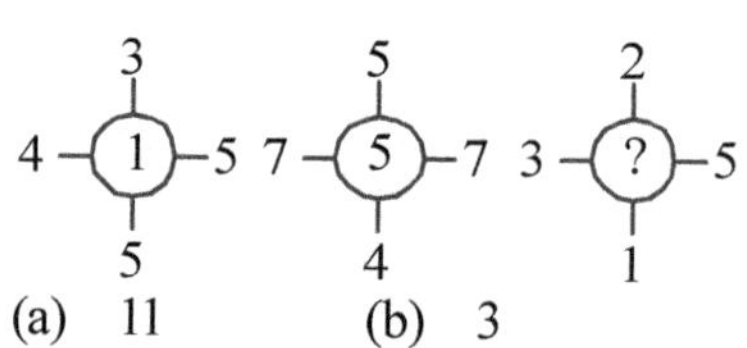

(a) 11 (b) 3
(c) 1 (d) 5

9. In the following questions, select the missing number from the given responses.

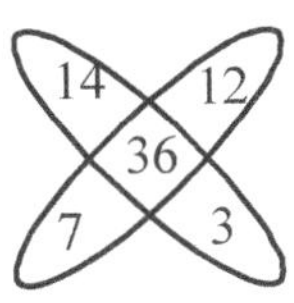

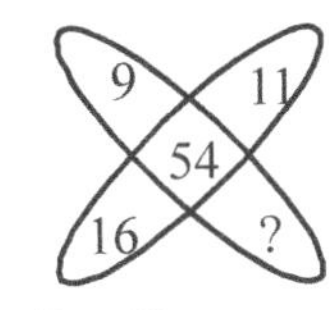

(a) 12 (b) 17
(c) 18 (d) 16

10. In the following question, select the number which can be placed at the sign of question mark (?) from the given alternatives.

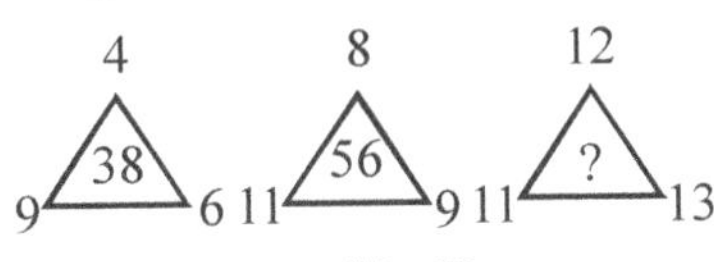

(a) 72 (b) 78
(c) 108 (d) 90

HINTS & SOLUTIONS

1. **(d)** $5+4=9$ and $9\times 2=18$
$6+3=9$ and $9\times 3=27$
$12+4=16$ and ?
$=\dfrac{96}{16}=\boxed{6}$

2. **(c)** First Figure
$3+5+2+4=14$
$\Rightarrow 14+13=27$
Second Figure
$6+2+3+5=16$
$\Rightarrow 16+21=37$
Third Figure
$2+2+9+5=18$
$\Rightarrow 18+29=\boxed{47}$

3. **(c)** Moving clockwise, the terms are :
$5\times 2+2=12$
$12\times 2+2=26$
$26\times 2+2=54$
$54\times 2+2=110$
So, missing number $=110\times 2+2$
$=\boxed{222}$

4. **(b)** $7+2^2+5=16$
$9+4^2+7=32$
$8+3^2+6=(23)$

5. **(c)** $3+9-5=7, 2+8-6=4$
$4+7-5=(6)$

6. **(c)** $81\times 9=729,\ 64\times 8=512$
$49\times 7=\boxed{343}$

7. **(b)** $(100+12)-(28+25)=59$
Similarly,
$(102+52)-(36+28)=90$

8. **(d)** $(4+5)-(3+5)=1$
$(7+7)-(5+4)=5$
$(3+5)-(2+1)=\boxed{5}$

9. **(c)** $(36)-(14+12+7)=3$
$(54)-(9+11+16)=\boxed{18}$

10. **(a)** As, $(4+6+9)\times 2=38$
$(8+9+11)\times 2=56$
Similarly,
$(12+13+11)\times 2=72$

Chapter 10

Venn Diagram

INTRODUCTION

Venn diagrams are pictorial way of represent the set of article. There are different regions which needs proper understanding for solving problems based on given Venn diagrams.

TYPES OF VENN DIAGRAM

(i) Analysis Based Venn Diagram-

In this type, generally a venn diagram comprising of different geometrical figures is given. Each geometrical figure in the diagram represents a certain class.

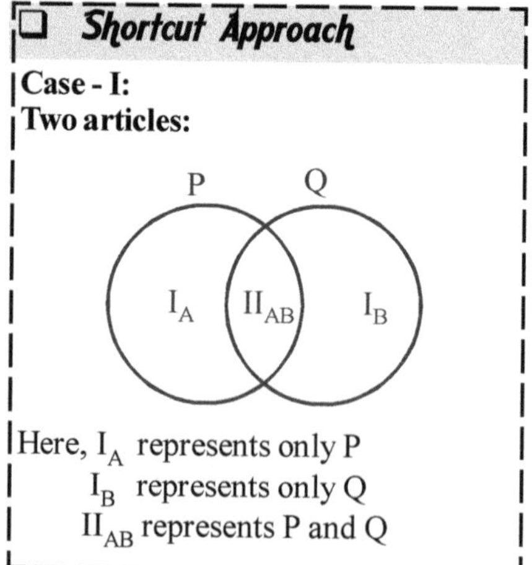

Shortcut Approach

Case - I:
Two articles:

Here, I_A represents only P
I_B represents only Q
II_{AB} represents P and Q

EXAMPLE

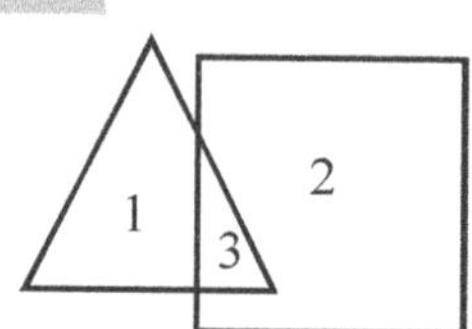

△ – represents student passed in English

□ – represents student passed in Reasoning.

1 – represents student passed in English only

2 – represents student passed in Reasoning only

3 – represents student passed in both English Reasoning both.

EXAMPLE 1.

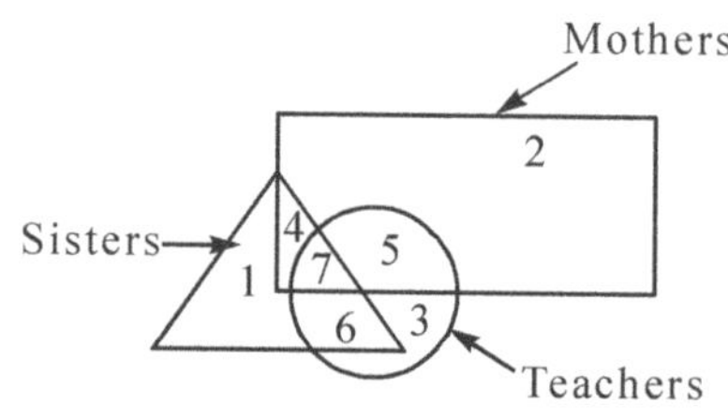

The diagram consists of three groups sisters, mothers and teachers, represented by a triangle, a rectangle and a circle respectively. There are seven regions represented by numbers from 1 to 7.

Region-1: represents only sisters

Region-2: represents only mothers

Region-3: represents only teachers

Region-4: represents those sisters who are mothers also but not teacher
Region-5: represents those mothers who are teachers also but not sister.
Region-6: represents those teachers who are sisters also but not mothers
Region-7: represents those teachers who are sisters as well as mothers.

❑ **Shortcut Approach**

Case: - II Three articles

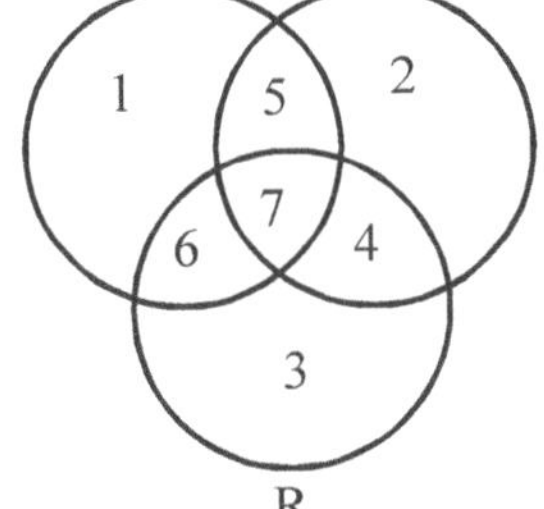

1 – represents P only
2 – represents Q only
3 – represents R only
4 – represents Q and R (not P)
5 – represents P and Q (not R)
6 – represents P and R (not Q)
7 – represents P, Q and R

EXAMPLE 2.

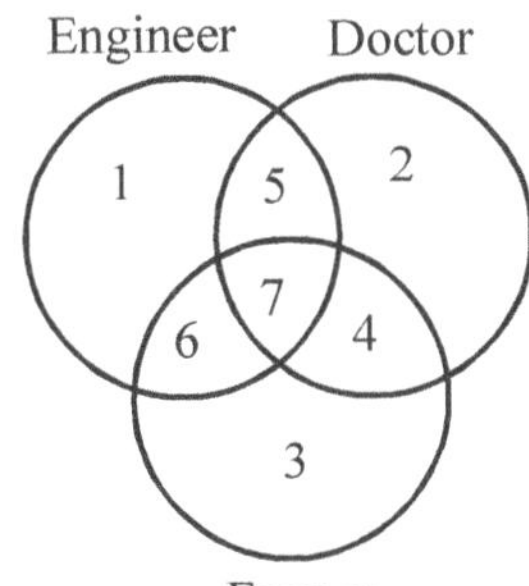

1 → Engineer

2 → Doctor

3 → Farmer

4 → Doctor who is farmer also

5 → Engineer who is doctor also

6 → Engineer who is farmer also

7 → Person who is Engineer, doctor and farmer.

(ii) Identification of Relation Based Venn Diagram -

In this type, some standard representations for groups of three items with different cases of venn diagrams are given.

❑ **Shortcut Approach**

When one class of items is completely included in the another class of item then it is represented by the given diagram

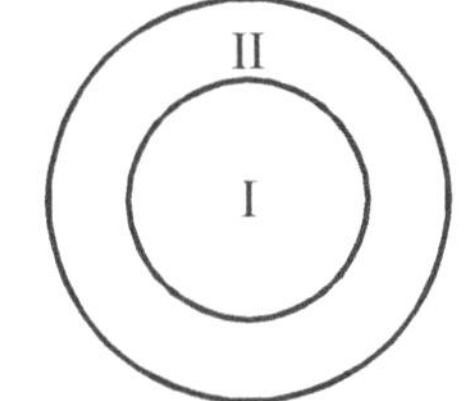

EXAMPLE 3.

I – Mango
II – Fruit
Here, all mango are fruit.

❑ **Shortcut Approach**

If two classes of item are completely different from each other but they all are completely included in third class then the relationship is represent of the diagram.

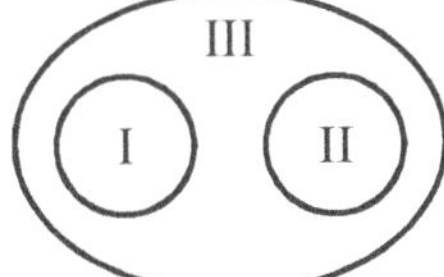

EXAMPLE 4.

I – represent potato

II – represent onion

III – represent vegetable

Shortcut Approach

- **If two group of items having some common relationship and both of them are all included in third class then the relationship is represented by the diagram.**

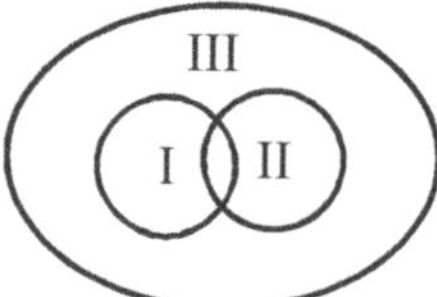

EXAMPLE 5. Brother, Father, Male.

I → Brother

II → Father

III → Male

Some Brother may be Father and all are male.

Shortcut Approach

When one class of item is completely included in another group while third is not related to both of them then such condition are diagrammatically represented by

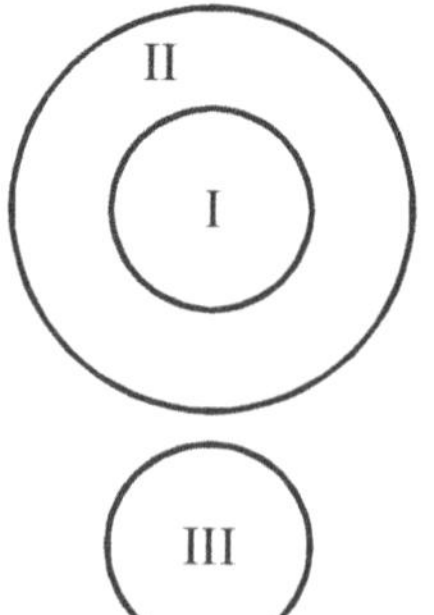

EXAMPLE 6.

Cricketer, player and farmer

I – Cricketer

II – Player

III – Farmer

All cricketers are players but farmers not.

Shortcut Approach

If three group of things are related to each other

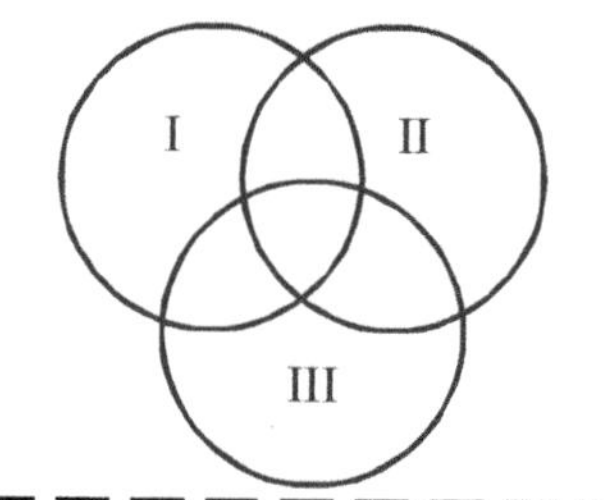

EXAMPLE 7.

Graduate, Engineer and Doctor

Graduate may be Engineer and Doctor.

Shortcut Approach

When two group of items are completely unrelated to each other while they are partly related with third group of item

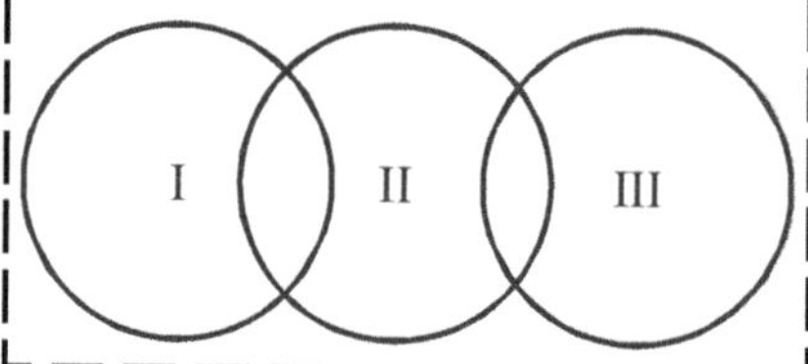

EXAMPLE 8. Cloth, Red, Flowers.

Some cloth are Red and also some Flowers are red.

❑ Shortcut Approach

When group of items are completely different from each other

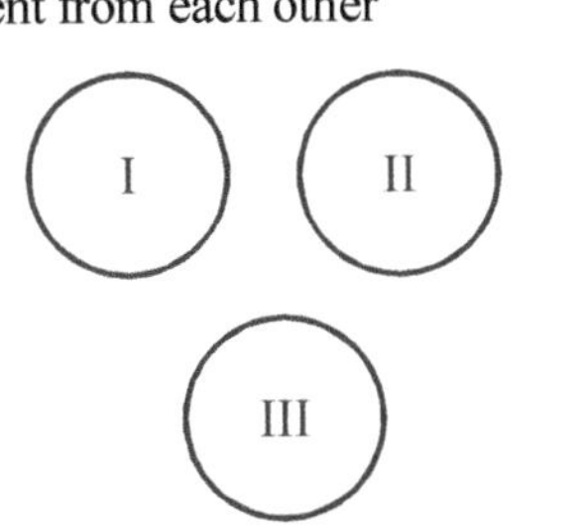

EXAMPLE 9.

Red, Yellow, Black

These are all different colour.

PRACTICE EXERCISE

1. Find out which of the diagrams given in the alternatives correctly represents the relationship stated in the question. Sharks, Whales, Turtles

(a) 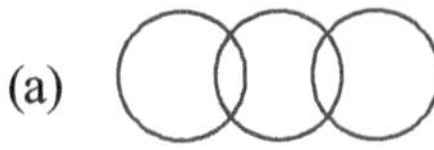

(b) 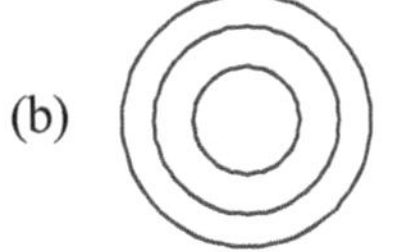

(c) 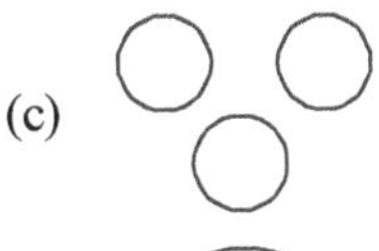

(d) 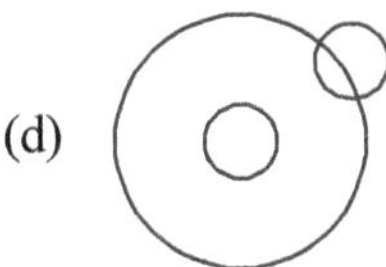

2. Which one of the following diagrams represents the correct relationship among 'Judge', 'Thief' and 'Criminal'?

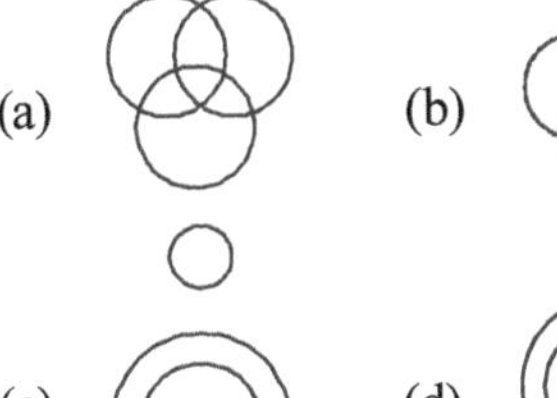

3. Which number space indicated Indian teachers who are also advocates?

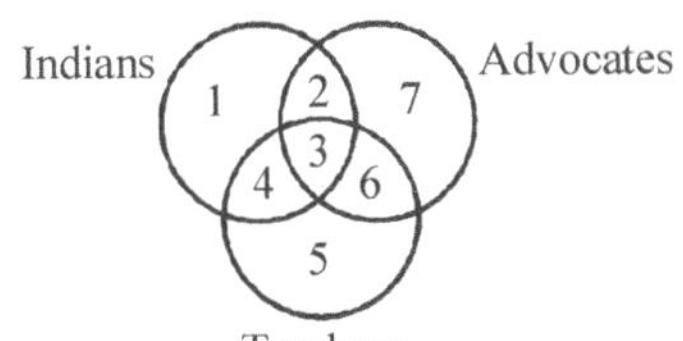

(a) 2 (b) 3
(c) 4 (d) 6

4. In the following figure, how many educated people are employed ?

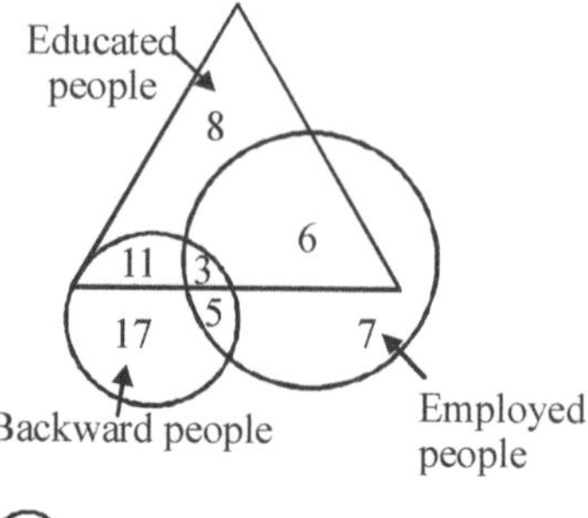

(a) 18 (b) 20
(c) 15 (d) 9

5. In the given diagram, Circle represents strong men, Square represents short men and Triangle represents military officers. Which region represents military officers who are short but not strong?

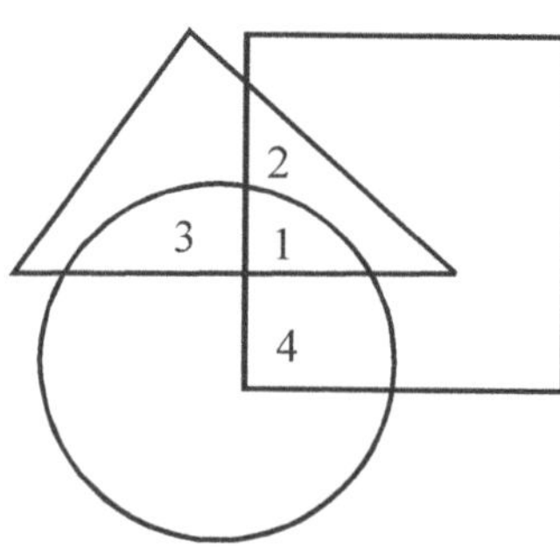

(a) 2 (b) 3
(c) 4 (d) 1

6. In the given figure, circles represent students studying three different subjects. How many students study all the three subjects?

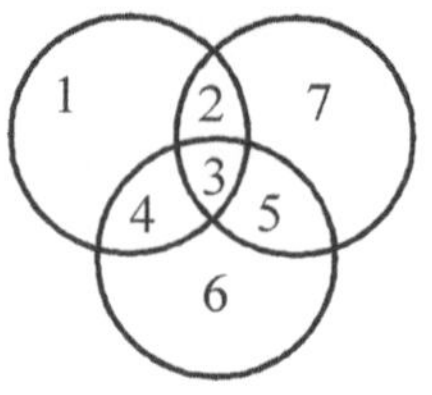

(a) 2 (b) 3
(c) 4 (d) 1

7. The diagram represents Teachers, Singers and Players. Study the diagram and find out how many teachers are also singers.

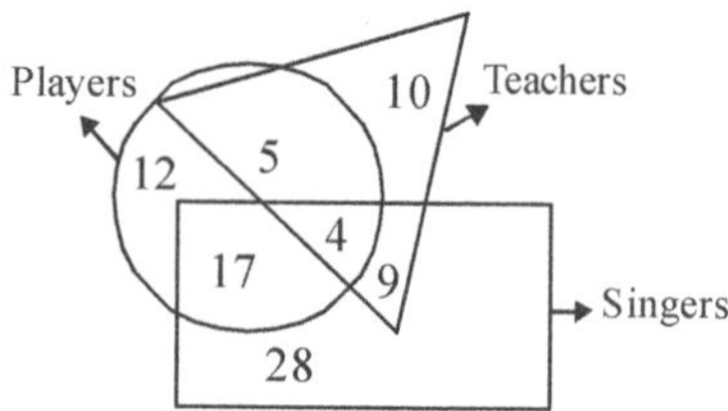

(a) 4 (b) 5
(c) 9 (d) 13

8. Identify the diagram that best represents the relationship among classes given below :
Food, Curd, Spoons

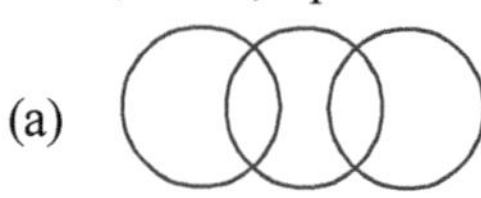

9. In the given figure, which letter represents carnivorous plants which are not green?

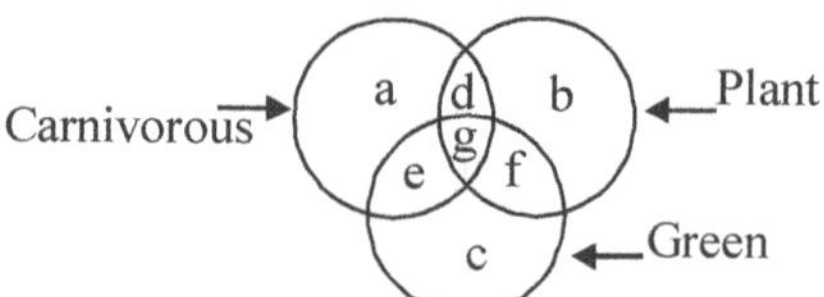

(a) d (b) g
(c) e (d) f

10. In the given figure, How many water are either tap or shower?

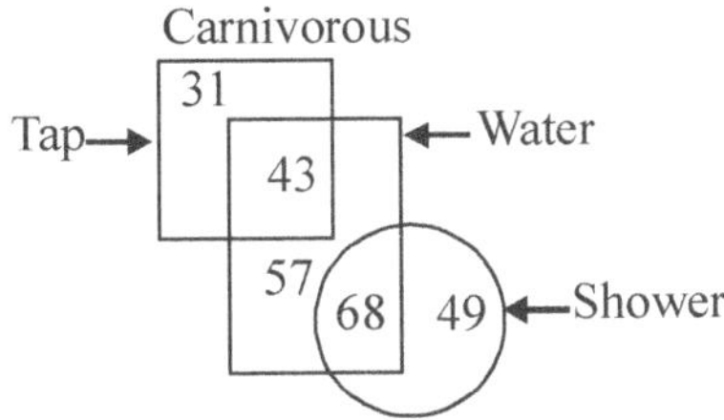

(a) 168 (b) 111
(c) 125 (d) 108

HINTS & SOLUTIONS

1. **(c)** Sharks belong to class pisces. Whale is a mammal and Turtle belongs to class reptiles.

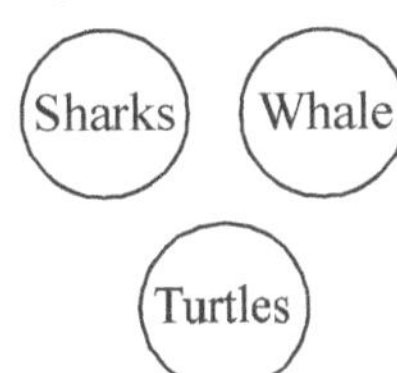

2. **(c)** Judge is different from both the thief and criminal.

The thief comes under the class criminal.

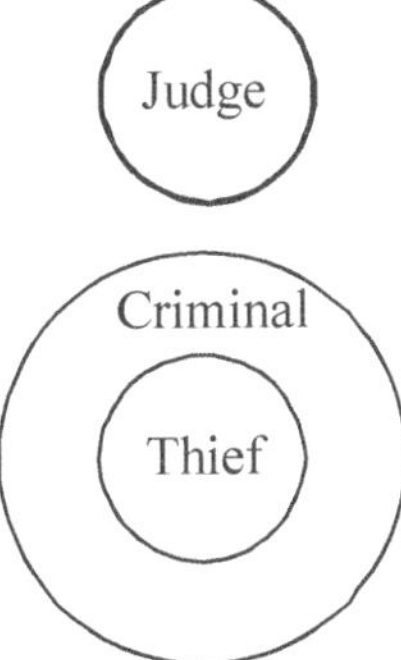

3. **(b)** The number '3' space represents Indian teachers who are also advocates as this number is common to given condition.

4. **(d)** $3+6=9$

5. **(a)**

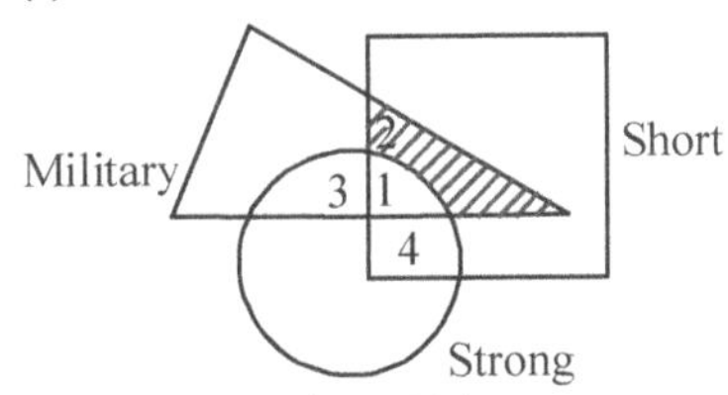

6. **(b)** The number '3' is common to all the three circles.

7. **(c)**

Persons	Numbers						
	4	5	9	10	12	17	28
○ Players	✓	✓	×	×	✓	✓	×
△ Teachers	✓	✓	✓	✓	×	×	×
□ Singers	✓		✓	×	×	✓	✓

Number of teachers who are also singers = 9

8. (d) 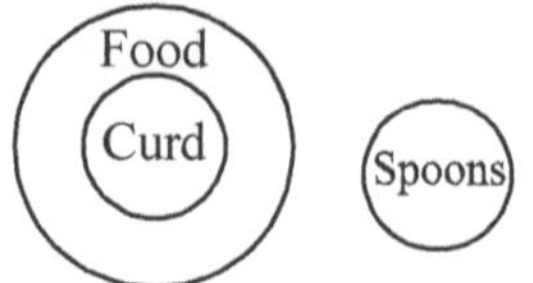

9. (a) According to figure,
'd' letter represents carnivorous plants which are not green.

10. (b) According to figure,
Total number of water are either tap or shower = (43 + 68) = 111.

Mathematical Operation Arithmetical Reasoning

INTRODUCTION

In this type of problem, usually mathematical symbol are converted into another form by either interchanging the symbol or using different symbol in place of usual symbol and then calculate the equation according to the given condition.

Remember

While simplifying a mathematical problem follow 'VBODMAS' rule

V - Viniculum bracket

B - Bracket

O - Of

D - Division

M - Multiplication

A - Addition

S - Subtraction

TYPES OF MATHEMATICAL OPERATION

(i) Symbol Substitution

In this, various mathematical symbols, followed by a question involving calculation of an expression. It is required to put the real signs in the given equation and then solve the question.

EXAMPLE 1. If '+' stands for division, '×' stands for addition, '–' stands for multiplication, and '÷' stands for subtraction, then which of the following equation is correct?

(a) $36 \times 6 + 7 \div 2 - 6 = 20$

(b) $36 + 6 - 3 \times 5 \div 3 = 24$

(c) $36 \div 6 + 3 \times 5 - 3 = 45$

(d) $36 - 6 + 3 \times 5 \div 3 = 74$

Sol. (d) $36 \times 6 \div 3 + 5 - 3$

$\Rightarrow$ $36 \times 2 + 5 - 3 = 74$

(ii) Interchange of Signs & Numbers

In this, the given equation becomes correct and fully balanced when either two signs of the equation or both the numbers and the signs of the equations are interchanged.

EXAMPLE 2. Given interchange : sign '+' and '–' and numbers 5 and 8. Which of the following is correct?

(a) $82 - 35 + 55 = 2$

(b) $82 - 35 + 55 = 102$

(c) $85 - 38 + 85 = 132$

(d) $52 - 35 + 55 = 72$

Sol. (a) $52 + 38 - 88 = 2$

(iii) Balancing the Equation

In this, the signs given in one of the alternatives are required to fill up the blank spaces for the signs in order to balance the given equation.

EXAMPLE 3. Select correct combination of mathematical sign to replace '*' sign to balance the equation.

9 * 4 * 22 * 14

(a) × = –

(b) × – =

(c) = – ×

(d) – × =

Sol. (b) 9 * 4 * 22 * 14

$9 \times 4 - 22 = 14$

Shortcut Approach

- Begin with replacing coded operators with their meanings. Write the entire expressions with correct operators and operand.
- When sowing always remember VBODMAS.
- If any interchnages are suggested, apply then before you start soling.

ARITHMETICAL REASONING

Arithmetical Reasoning tests the ability to solve basic arithmetic problems encountered in everyday life. These problems require basic mathematical skills like addition, subtraction, multiplication, division etc. The tests include operations with whole numbers, rational numbers, average, ratio and proportion, interest, percentage, and measurement. Arithmetical reasoning is one factor that helps characterize mathematics comprehension, and it also assesses logical thinking.

EXAMPLE 4 : The total of the ages of Amar, Akbar and Anthony is 80 years. What was the total of their ages three years ago?

Sol. Here, required sum = (80 – 3 x 3) years = (80 – 9) years

= 71 years.

Shortcut Approach

- If ages of n persons in a group are $x_1, x_2, x_3, \ldots, x_n$ yrs, then total of their ages befor t years

  $= x_1 + x_2 + x_3 + \ldots + x_n - nt$
- If ages of n persons in a group are $x_1, x_2, \ldots, x_n$ yrs; then total of their ages after t years

  $= x_1 + x_2 + .. + x_n + nt$

To Find the Resultant Number in a Row

In this type of questions, two rows of numbers are given along with certain rules. On the basis of these rules, you have to find out resultant number in each row separately and question below the row is to be answered.

Directions (Q. Nos. 5-9) *In each of the following questions two rows of numbers are given. The resultant number in each row is to be worked out separately based on the following rules and the questions below the rows of numbers are to be answered. The operations of numbers progress from left to right.*

Rules

(i) If an odd number is followed by another composite odd number, they are to be multiplied.

(ii) If an even number is followed by an odd number, they are to be added.

(iii) If an even number is followed by a number which is a perfect square, the even number is to be subtracted from the perfect square.

(iv) If an odd number is followed by a prime odd number, the first number is to be divided by the second number.

(v) If an odd number is followed by an even number, the second one is to be subtracted from the first one.

5. 58 17 5
85 5 n
If 'n' is the resultant of the first row, what is the resultant of the second row?
(a) 255 (b) 32
(c) 49 (d) 34
(e) None of these

6. 24 64 15
m 11 15
If 'm' is the resultant of the first row, what is the resultant of the second row?
(a) 165 (b) 75
(c) 20 (d) 3
(e) None of these

7. 7 21 3
d 7 33
If 'd' is the resultant of the first row, what will be the resultant of the second row?
(a) 40 (b) 138
(c) 231 (d) 80
(e) None of the above

8. 73 34 13
32 p 15
If 'p' is the resultant of the first row, what is the resultant of the second row?
(a) 713 (b) 50
(c) 20 (d) 525
(e) None of these

9. 14 5 19
24 w 88
If 'w' is the resultant of the first row, what is the resultant of the second row?
(a) 171 (b) 283
(c) 195 (d) 107
(e) None of these

Sol. (5 to 9)

Rules

(i) (Odd number) × (Composite odd number)

(ii) (Even number) + (Odd number)

(iii) (Even number) → (Perfect square number), then (Perfect square number) – (Even number)

(iv) (Odd number) ÷ (Prime odd number)

(v) (Odd number) – (Even number)

5. (a) **1st Row** 58 17 5 $\Rightarrow 58 + 17 = 75$ [rule (ii)]
$75 \div 5 = 15 = n$ [rule (iv)]
2nd Row 85 5 n $\Rightarrow$ 85 5 15
$\Rightarrow 85 \div 5 = 17$ [rule (iv)]
$\Rightarrow 17 \times 15 = 255$ [rule (i)]
$\therefore$ Resultant of second row = 255

6. (b) **1st Row** 24 64 15
$\Rightarrow 64 - 24 = 40$ [rule (iii)]
$\Rightarrow 40 + 15 = 55 = m$ [rule (ii)]
2nd Row m 11 15 $\Rightarrow$ 55 11 15
$55 \div 11 = 5$ [rule (iv)]
$\Rightarrow 5 \times 15 = 75$ [rule (i)]
$\therefore$ Resultant of second row = 75

7. (c) **1st Row** 7 21 3 $\Rightarrow 7 \times 21 = 147$ [rule (i)]
$\Rightarrow 147 \div 3 = 49 = d$ [rule (iv)]

2nd Row d 7 33 $\Rightarrow$ 49 7 33

$\Rightarrow$ $49 \div 7 = 7$ [rule (iv)]

$\Rightarrow$ $7 \times 33 = 231$ [rule (i)]

$\therefore$ Resultant of second row = 231

8. (d) **1st Row** 73 34 13 $\Rightarrow$ 73–34 = 39 [rule (v)]

$\Rightarrow$ $39 \div 13 = 3 = p$ [rule (iv)]

2nd Row 32 p 15 $\Rightarrow$ 32 3 15

$\Rightarrow$ $32 + 3 = 35$ [rule (ii)]

$\Rightarrow$ $35 \times 15 = 525$ [rule (i)]

$\therefore$ Resultant of second row = 525

9. (d) **1st Row** 14 5 9 $\Rightarrow$ $14 + 5 = 19$ [rule (ii)]

$19 \times 9 = 171 = w$ [rule (i)]

2nd Row 24 w 88 $\Rightarrow$ 24 171 88

$\Rightarrow$ $24 + 171 = 195$ [rule (ii)]

$\Rightarrow$ $195 - 88 = 107$ [rule (v)]

$\therefore$ Resultant of Second row = 107

Trick Based Mathematical Operations

The questions are based on simple mathematical operations that do not come under any of the above given types covered. These questions can be based on several different patterns.

EXAMPLE 10. If $2 + 6 + 9 = 926$, $1 + 8 + 2 = 218$, then 4+3+1 =?

Sol.

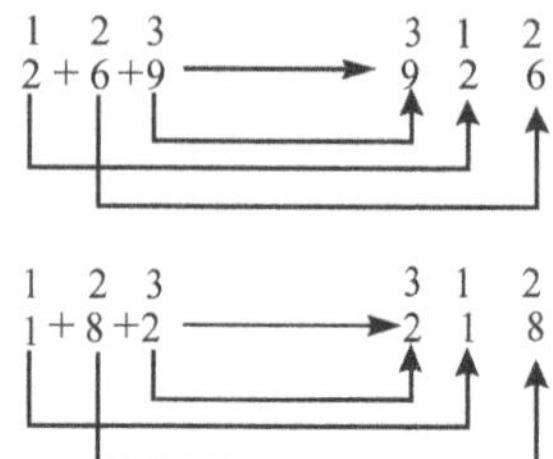

Similarly,

1 2 3 → 3 1 2

4 + 3 + 1 → 1 4 3

$\therefore$? = 143

EXAMPLE 11. If $73 + 82 = 14$, $19 + 21 = 11$, then $86 + 24 = ?$

Sol. $73 + 82 = 14$

$\Rightarrow (7 - 3) + (8 + 2) = 14$

$\Rightarrow 14 = 14$

And $91 + 21 = 11$

$\Rightarrow (9 - 1) + (2 + 1) = 11$

$\Rightarrow 11 = 11$

Similarly, $86 + 24 = (8 - 6) + (2 + 4)$

$= 2 + 6 = 8$

PRACTICE EXERCISE

1. After interchanging $\div$ and +, 12 and 18, which one of the following equations becomes correct?
   (a) $(90 \times 18) + 18 = 60$
   (b) $(18 + 6) \div 12 = 2$
   (c) $(72 \div 18) \times 18 = 72$
   (d) $(12 + 6) \times 18 = 36$

2. If '–' stands for '÷' '+' stands for '×', '÷' for '–' and '×' for '+', which one of the following equations in correct?
   (a) $30 - 6 + 5 \times 4 \div 2 = 27$
   (b) $30 + 6 - 5 \div 4 \times 2 = 30$
   (c) $30 \times 6 \div 5 - 4 + 2 = 32$
   (d) $30 \div 6 \times 5 + 4 - 2 = 40$

3. Some equations have been solved on the basis of a certain system. Find the correct answer for the unsolved equation on that basis. If $9 * 7 = 32, 13 * 7 = 120, 17 * 9 = 208$, then $19 * 11 = ?$
(a) 150 (b) 180
(c) 210 (d) 240

4. If L denotes × M denotes ÷ ; P denotes + ; Q denotes – then 16 P 24 M 8 Q 6 M 2 L 3 = ?
(a) 10 (b) 9
(c) 12 (d) 11

5. Class A has students twice that of class B. After adding 20 students to class A and 30 students to class B, the total number of students in both the classes is 140. What is the number of students in class A in the beginning?
(a) 30 (b) 60
(c) 80 (d) 140

6. At present, the ratio between the ages of Arun and Deepak is 4 : 3. After 6 years, Arun's age will be 26 years. What is the age of Deepak at present?
(a) 15 years
(b) 19 years
(c) 24 years
(d) 12 years

7. If '+' means '÷', '×' means '+', '–' means '×' and '÷' means '–', then which of the following equations is correct?
(a) $36 + 6 - 3 \times 2 = 20$
(b) $36 \times 6 + 3 - 2 < 20$
(c) $36 \times 6 + 3 \times 2 > 20$
(d) $36 + 6 \times 3 + 2 = 20$

8. If × stands for addition, < for subtraction, + stands for division, > stands for multiplication, – stands for equal, ÷ stands for greater than, and = stands for less than, state which of the following is true?
(a) $3 \times 2 < 4 \div 16 > 2 + 4$
(b) $5 > 8 + 4 = 10 < 4 \times 8$
(c) $3 \times 4 > 2 - 9 + 3 < 3$
(d) $5 \times 3 < 3 \div 8 + 4 \times 1$

9. Select the correct combination of mathematical signs to replace * signs and to balance the given equation.
$15 * 24 * 3 * 6 * 17$
(a) $+ \times = \div$
(b) $- \times = +$
(c) $- \div + =$
(d) $+ \div - =$

10. If + = ×, – = ÷, × = +, ÷ = –, then which is the correct equation out of the following?
(a) $18 \div 6 + 4 - 2 \div 3 = 22$
(b) $18 + 6 - 4 \times 2 \div 3 = 26$
(c) $18 \times 6 - 4 + 7 \times 8 = 47$
(d) $18 - 6 \times 7 \div 2 + 8 = 63$

HINTS & SOLUTIONS

1. **(d)** $(12 + 6) \times 18 = 36$
$\Rightarrow (18 \div 6) \times 12 = 36$
$\Rightarrow 3 \times 12 = \boxed{36}$

2. **(a)** $30 - 6 + 5 \times 4 \div 2 = 27$
$\Rightarrow 30 \div 6 \times 5 + 4 - 2 = 27$
$\Rightarrow 25 + 4 - 2 \Rightarrow 27 = 27$, option (a) is correct
$30 + 6 - 5 \div 4 \times 2 = 30$
$\Rightarrow 30 \times 6 \div 5 - 4 + 2 = 30$
$\Rightarrow 36 - 4 + 2 \neq 30$, option (b) is wrong

$30 \times 6 \div 5 - 4 + 2 = 32$

$\Rightarrow 30 + 6 - 5 \div 4 \times 2 \neq 32$, option (c) is wrong

$\Rightarrow 30 \div 6 \times 5 + 4 - 2 = 40$

$\Rightarrow 30 - 6 + 5 \times 4 \div 2 \neq 40$

option (d) is wrong.

3. (d) $9 + 7 = 16; \quad 9 - 7 = 2$

$16 \times 2 = 32$

$13 + 7 = 20; \quad 13 - 7 = 6$

$20 \times 6 = 120$

$17 + 9 = 26; \quad 17 - 9 = 8$

$26 \times 8 = 208$

$19 + 11 = 30; \quad 19 - 11 = 8$

$30 \times 8 = \boxed{240}$

4. (a)

L ⇒ ×	M ⇒ ÷
P ⇒ +	Q ⇒ −

16 P 24 M 8 Q 6 M 2 L 3 = ?

$\Rightarrow ? = 16 + 24 \div 8 - 6 \div 2 \times 3$

$\Rightarrow ? = 16 + 3 - 3 \times 3$

$\Rightarrow ? = 16 + 3 - 9 = \boxed{10}$

5. (b) Suppose, in the beginning the number of students in Class B = x

Therefore, the number of Students in Class A = 2x

Now,

$2x + 20 + x + 30 = 140$

$\Rightarrow 3x = 140 - 50$

$\therefore x = \frac{90}{3} = 30$

Number of Students in Class A $= 2x = 2 \times 30 = 60$

6. (a) Suppose the present age of Arun is $4x$ years and that of Deepak is $3x$ years.

6 years hence,

Arun's age $= 4x + 6 = 26$

$\Rightarrow 4x = 26 - 6$

$x = \frac{20}{4} = 5$

$\therefore$ Present age of Deepak $= 3x =$ 15 years

7. (a) By checking options

$36 \div 6 \times 3 + 2 = 6 \times 3 + 2 \Rightarrow 20 = 20$

8. (*)

× ⇒ +	< ⇒ −	+ ⇒ ÷	> ⇒ ×
− ⇒ =	÷ ⇒ >	= ⇒ <	

Option (a)

$3 \times 2 < 4 \div 16 > 2 + 4$

$\Rightarrow 3 + 2 - 4 > 16 \times 2 \div 4$

$\Rightarrow 5 - 4 > \frac{16 \times 2}{4} \Rightarrow 1 > 8$

(not possible)

Option (b)

$5 > 8 + 4 = 10 < 4 \times 8$

$\Rightarrow 5 \times 8 \div 4 < 10 - 4 + 8$

$\Rightarrow 5 \times 2 < 18 - 4 \Rightarrow 10 < 14$

Option (c)

$3 \times 4 > 2 - 9 + 3 < 3$

$\Rightarrow 3 + 4 \times 2 = 9 \div 3 - 3$

$\Rightarrow 3 + 8 \neq 3 - 3$

Option (d)

$5 \times 3 < 3 \div 8 + 4 \times 1$

$\Rightarrow 5 + 3 - 3 > 8 \div 4 + 1$

$\Rightarrow 8 - 3 > 2 + 1$

$\Rightarrow 5 > 3$

Both options (b) and (d) are correct.

9. (d) 15 * 24 * 3 * 6 * 17

$\Rightarrow 15 + 24 \div 3 - 6 = 17$

$\Rightarrow 15 + 8 - 6 = 17$

10. (b) $18 \times 6 \div 4 + 2 - 3 = 18 \times 1.5 + 2 - 3 = 27 + 2 - 3 = 26$

Inequalities

INEQUALITIES

As we know,

$$3 \times 3 = 9$$

Now, we can say that the result of multiplication between 3 and 3 is equal to 9. Therefore, $3 \times 3 = 9$ is a case of equality. But when we multiply 3×4, we get 12 as a result of this multiplication. It does mean that

$$3 \times 4 \neq 9$$

As 3×4, is not equal to 9, it is a case of inequality.

When, we come to know that one thing is not equal to another; there can be only two possibilities:-

(i) One thing is greater than another thing.

or

(ii) One thing is less than the another thing.

When, we denote (i) and (ii) mathematically, then we will write.

(i) One thing > another thing.

or

(ii) One thing < another thing.

where '>' denotes 'greater than'.

and '<' denotes 'less than'

Hence, you can write,

$$3 \times 4 > 9$$

$$4 \times 1 < 9$$

$(3 \times 4 > 9)$ means 'Product of 3 and 4 is greater than 9'.

$(4 \times 1 < 9)$ means 'Product of 4 and 1 is less than 9'.

Sometimes we come across two numbers where, we do not know the exact state of inequality between them.

Let us see :

$m \geq n$ means m is either greater than or equal to n.

$m \leq n$ means n is either less or equal to m.

Hence, we can summarise the signs to be used in inequalities as below:

Important Signs			
Signs	**Meaning**	**Example**	**Explanation**
=	Equal to	A = B	A is equal to B.
>	Greater than	A > B	A is greater than B.
<	Less than	A < B	A is less than B.
≥	Greater than or equal to	A ≥ B	A is greater than or equal to B.
≤	less than or equal to	A ≤ B	A is less than or equal to B.

In inequalities different sets of elements are given using the inequalities symbols. The candidate is required to analyse the given statements and then decide which of the relations given an alternatives follows from those given in the statements. But before solving the problems of inequalities, first you have to learn more about the inequalities

CHAIN OF INEQUALITIES

Sometimes two or more inequalities are combined together to create a single inequality having three or more terms. Such combination is called chain of inequalities.

Conditions for Combining Two Inequalities

Condition I: Two inequalities will be combined if and only if they have a common term.

Condition II: Two inequalities will be combined if and only if the common term is greater than (or 'greater' than or equal to') one and less than (or 'less than or equal to') the other.

EXAMPLE 1: $14 > 13$, $13 > 12$ can be easily combined as '$14 > 13 > 12$'.

Here,

$$14 > \textcircled{13} > 12$$

↓
Common term

Clearly, $14 > 13$ and $13 > 12$ have common term 13 and this common term is greater than 12 and less than 14. Hence, $14 > 13$ and $13 > 12$ have been combined into $14 > 13 > 12$ as per the conditions I and II.

EXAMPLE 2. $17 < 19$, and $19 < 20$ can be easily combined as $17 < 19 < 20$.

Here,

$$17 < \textcircled{19} < 20$$

↓
Common term

Clearly, $17 < 19$ and $19 < 20$ have common term 19 and this common term is greater than 17 and less than 20. Hence, $17 < 19$ and $19 < 20$ have been combined into $17 < 19 < 20$ as per the conditions I and II.

Now, let us see some examples of inequalities which can not be combined. Some such examples are given below:

i. $14 > 12, 19 > 18$
ii. $18 < 20, 22 < 25$
iii. $100 > 99, 80 > 77$
iv. $100 < 115, 118 < 119$

Clearly, (i), (ii), (iii) and (iv) can not be combined as they do not have any common term and therefore, they do not follow condition I and condition II.

How to Derive Conclusions from a Combined Inequalities?

To derive conclusion from a combined inequality, you have to eliminate the common term.

For example,

(a) If we have

$m > \ell > n$

then, our conclusion is

$$\boxed{m > n}$$

(b) When, we have

$m < \ell < n$

then, our conclusion is

$m < n$

(c) When, we have '≥' signs in the combined inequalities then you have to think a little bit more. Let us consider the combined inequality given below:

$m \geq \ell > n$

Here, m is either greater than ℓ or equal to ℓ.

Hence, the minimum value for m is equal to ℓ. But ℓ is always greater than n. Therefore, m is always greater than n.

∴ Our conclusion is $m > n$

(d) When, we have the following inequalities:-

$m > \ell \geq n$

In this case, m is always greater than ℓ and ℓ is either greater than n or equal to it. When ℓ is greater than n; m will obviously be greater than n. Even when ℓ is equal to n; m will be greater than n as m is always greater than ℓ.

∴ Our conclusion is $m > n$

(e) When, we have combine inequality

$m \geq \ell \geq n$

Here, m is either greater than ℓ or equal to ℓ.

When m is greater than ℓ; we have $m > \ell \geq n$, which gives the conclusion.

$m > n$ — (A)

When m is equal to ℓ; we have $m = \ell \geq n$, which gives the conclusion

$m \geq n$ — (B)

Combining (A) and (B), we have the final conclusion as

$m \geq n$

From (a), (b), (c), (d) and (e), we get a rule for deriving conclusions from a combined inequality, we may say it 'Golden Rule'.

GOLDEN RULE

> The conclusion inequality will have an '≥' sign or a '≤' sign if and only if both the signs in the combined inequality are '≥' or '≤' sign respectively
> In all other cases, there will be a '>' or a '<' sign in the conclusion.

Clearly, in (a), (b), (c) and (d) only one inequality and (e) ($m \geq l \geq n$) has '≥' as its both the sign.

Remember

- If $m > n$, then $n < m$ must be true.
- If $m < n$, then $n > m$ must be true.
- If $m \geq n$, then $n \leq m$ must be true.
- If $m \leq n$, then $n \geq m$ must be true.

EITHER CHOICE RULES

When your derived conclusion is of the type $m \geq n$ (or $m \leq n$) then check both the conclusions

$m > n$ and $m = n$ (or, $m < n$ and $m = n$).

I. If both the conclusions are true, then choice "either follows" is true.

II. If none of the conclusions seems correct. Then check wheather the conclusions form a complementary pair. The conclusions form a complementary pair in the 4 cases given below:

(i) $m \geq n$ and $m < n$
(ii) $m > n$ and $m \leq n$
(iii) $m \leq n$ and $m > n$
(iv) $m < n$ and $m \geq n$

If the conclusions form a complementry pair then the choice "either follows" is correct.

DIRECT INEQUALITY

In this type of questions, direct relation between two or more than two elements are given in a meaningful inequality. Candidates are required to establish the relation between elements with the help of used signs between the elements.

Shortcut Approach:

DEFINITE CONCLUSION

(i) A > B = C ⇒ a > B
(ii) A ≥ B = C ⇒ A ≥ C
(iii) A ≥ B > C ⇒ A > C
(iv) A < B > C ⇒ A < C
(v) A ≤ B = C ⇒ A ≤ C
(vi) A ≤ B < C ⇒ A < C
(vii) A < B = C ≤ D ⇒ A < D
(viii) A > B = C ≥ D ⇒ A > D

INDEFINITE CONCLUSION

(i) a > b < c ⇒ No conclusion
(ii) a > b ≤ c ⇒ No conclusion
(iii) a ≥ b ≤ c ⇒ No conclusion
(iv) a ≥ b < c ⇒ No conclusion

EXAMPLE 3 : Which of the following symbols should replace the question mark in the given expression in order to make the expressions. 'I > L' as well as 'M ≥ K' definitely true?

I > J ≥ K ? L ≤ N = M

(a) > (b) <
(c) ≤ (d) =
(e) Either < or ≤

Sol. (d) On putting sign (=) in place of question mark (?)

I > J ≥ K = L ≤ N = M

⇒ means I > L and M ≥ K

EXAMPLE 4 :

Statement : H = W ≤ R > F
Conclusion : I. R = H, II. R > H — Either Or

Statement : H > L = E < T
Conclusion : I. H ≤ T, II. H > T — Either Or

Statement : S < T ≥ R ≥ M
Conclusion : I. M < T, II. M = T — Either Or

Statement : I ≥ H = T > S ≤ R
Conclusion: I. I > T, II. I = T — Either Or

(B) NEITHER NOR :
If 2 conclusions are wrong and variables in the two conclusions are different then write it as 'Neither Nor'

EXAMPLE 5 :

Statement : P > Q ≥ S = R
Conclusion : I. P ≥ R, II. R > Q — Neither nor

Statement : L = T ≤ J ≥ K
Conclusion : I. L > K, II. T ≤ K — Neither nor

Statement : V < L ≥ J ≤ T
Conclusion : I. V < J, II. L = T — Neither nor

Statement : G ≤ K ≤ F < M
Conclusion: I. G > F, II. K ≤ M — Neither nor

CODED INEQUALITY

In the coded inequalities, all the signs of inequalities (>, <, =, ≥, ≤) are in coded form i.e. substituted symbols are used in place of real symbols. The candidates are required to replace the codes (like @ / © / * / $ / # etc.) with real signs and then solve the questions in the same way as the questions of inequalities are solved.

❑ Shortcut Approach

Steps for Solving Problems

Step I: Decode the given symbols like @, $, δ, #, *, etc.

Step II: Take one conclusion at a time and make an idea that which statements are relevant for evaluating it.

Step III: Use conditions I and II and the 'Golden Rule' to combine the relevant statements and derive a conclusion from it.

After performing the above mentioned three steps, if a conclusion is established and verified, it is well and good. But if does not happen so, then you have to perform 4 more new steps given below:

New Step I: Check if the given conclusion directly follows from anyone single statement.

New Step II: Check if the conclusion – inequality you get is essentially as same as the given conclusion but written differently.

New Step III: Check if the derived conclusion follows 'Either choice Rule I'.

New Step IV: If neither of the conclusions has been proved correct till now, then check 'Either choice Rule II'.

EXAMPLE 6: In the following question, the symbols ©, @, =,* and $ are used with the following meanings :
P © Q means 'P is greater than Q';
P @ Q means 'P is greater than or equal to Q';
P = Q means 'P is equal to Q';
P * Q means 'P is smaller than Q';
P $ Q means 'P is either smaller than or equal to Q '.

Now in the following question, assuming that the given statements are true. Find which of the two conclusions I and II given below them is/are definitely true. Give answer :

(a) if only conclusion I is true;
(b) if only conclusion II is true;
(c) if either I or II is true;
(d) if neither I nor II is true.
(e) if both I and II are true.

Statements : P © T, M $ K, T = K

Conclusions : I. T © M
II. T = M

Sol. (c) Given statements :
$P > T, M \le K, T = K.$
$T = K, K \ge M \Rightarrow T \ge M$
$\Rightarrow T > M$ or $T = M$
$\Rightarrow$ T © M or T = M
So, either I or II is true.

PRACTICE EXERCISE

DIRECTIONS (Qs. 1-4): *In the following questions, the symbols @, $, ★, # and δ are used with the following meaning as illustrated below:*

'P $ Q' means 'P is not smaller than Q'.
'P @ Q' means 'P is neither smaller than nor equal to Q'.
'P # Q' means 'P is neither greater than nor equal to Q'.
'P δ Q' means P is neither greater than nor smaller than Q'.
'P ★ Q' means 'P is not greater than Q'.
Now in each of the following questions assuming the given statements to be true, find which of the four conclusions I, II, Ill and IV given below them is/are **definitely true** and give your answer accordingly.

1. **Statements:**
   H @ T, T # F, F δ E, E ★ v
   Conclusions: I. V $ F
   II. E @ T
   III. H @ V
   IV. T # V
   (a) Only I, II and III are true
   (b) Only I, II and IV are true
   (c) Only II, III and IV are true
   (d) Only I, III and IV are true
   (e) All I, II, III and IV are true
2. **Statements:**
   D # R, R★ K, K @ F, F $ J
   Conclusions: I. J # R
   II. J # K
   III. R # F
   IV. K @ D
   (a) Only I, II and III are true
   (b) Only II, III and IV are true
   (c) Only I, III and IV are true
   (d) All I, II, III and IV are true
   (e) None of these
3. **Statements:**
   N δ B, B $ W, W # H, H ★ M
   Conclusions: I. M @ W
   II. H @ N
   III. W δ N
   IV. W # N
   (a) Only I is true
   (b) Only III is true
   (c) Only IV is true
   (d) Only either III or IV is true
   (e) Only either III or IV and I are true
4. **Statements:**
   R ★ D, D $ J, J # M, M @ K
   Conclusions:
   I. K # J
   II. D @ M
   III. R # M
   IV. D @ K
   (a) None is true
   (b) Only I is true
   (c) Only II is true
   (d) Only III is true
   (e) Only IV is true
5. Which one of the following symbols should be placed in the blank spaces(from left to right) in order to complete the given expression in such a manner that both N > L and G ≥ K definitely true?
   N_G_P_L_K
   (a) ≤, =, >, < (b) ≥, ≤, =, <
   (c) >, =, ≥, ≥ (d) <, =, ≤, ≥
   (e) None of these
6. Which one of the following will be definitely true if the expression 'Q < S > V = W ≥ O ≥ R' is definitely true?
   (a) S ≥ O (b) O ≥ Q
   (c) W < Q (d) R ≤ V
   (e) None of these
7. In Which of the following expressions does the expression 'L < T' to definitely hold true?
   (a) K > L > R = P < S ≤ T
   (b) U ≥ T ≥ M = F ≤ A ≥ L
   (c) L ≥ C > Q ≥ B = N ≤ T
   (d) G ≥ L = A < B ≤ S ≤ T
   (e) T ≥ E = G ≥ W = Y ≥ L

DIRECTIONS (Qs. 8-10): *In the given questions, assuming the given statements to be true. Find which of the given two conclusions numbered I, II is/are definitely true and give your answer accordingly.*

8. **Statement:** $M > U > L \le N; L \ge Y > A$
   Conclusions:
   I. $Y < N$
   II. $Y = N$
   (a) Both I and II are true
   (b) Only II
   (c) Only I is true
   (d) Either I or II is true.
   (e) None is true.

9. **Statement:** $J \ge A > D = E; L < A < M$
   Conclusions:
   I. $M < J$
   II. $J > L$
   (a) Only II is true.
   (b) Either I or II are true.
   (c) Both I and II are true
   (d) Only I is true.
   (e) None is true.

10. **Statement:** $M \le K > L = Y; P \le T > M$
   Conclusions:
   I. $P > Y$
   II. $T < L$
   (a) Only II is true
   (b) Only I
   (c) Either I or II are true
   (d) Both I and II are true
   (e) None is true

HINTS & SOLUTIONS

1. **(b)** $H @ T \Rightarrow H > T$
   $T \# F \Rightarrow T < F$
   $F \delta E \Rightarrow F = E$
   $E ★ V \Rightarrow E \le V$
   Therefore, $H > T < F = E \le V$
   Conclusions
   I. $V \$ F \Rightarrow V \ge F$: True
   II. $E @ T \Rightarrow E > T$: True
   III. $H @ V \Rightarrow H > V$: Not True
   IV. $T \# V \Rightarrow T < V$: True
   So conclusion I, II & IV follow

2. **(e)** $D \# R \Rightarrow D < R$
   $R ★ K \Rightarrow R \le K$
   $K @ F \Rightarrow K > F$
   $F \$ J \Rightarrow F \ge J$
   Therefore, $D < R \le K > F \ge J$
   Conclusions
   I. $J \# R \Rightarrow J < R$: Not True
   II. $J \# K \Rightarrow J < K$: True
   III. $R \# F \Rightarrow R < F$: Not True
   IV. $K @ D \Rightarrow K > D$: True
   So only conclusion II & IV follow

3. **(e)** $N \delta B \Rightarrow N = B$
   $B \$ W \Rightarrow B \ge W$
   $W \# H \Rightarrow W < H$
   $H ★ M \Rightarrow H \le M$
   Therefore, $N = B \ge W < H \le M$
   Conclusions
   I. $M @ W \Rightarrow M > W$: True
   II. $H @ N \Rightarrow H > N$: Not True
   III. $W \delta N \Rightarrow W = N$: Not True
   IV. $W \# N \Rightarrow W < N$: Not True
   W is either smaller than or equal to N. Therefore either III or IV and I are true.

4. **(a)** $R ★ D \Rightarrow R \le D, D \$ J \Rightarrow D \ge J$
   $J \# M \Rightarrow J < M, M @ K \Rightarrow M > K$
   Therefore, $R \le D \ge J < M > K$
   Conclusions
   I. $K \# J \Rightarrow K < J$: Not True
   II. $D @ M \Rightarrow D > M$: Not True
   III. $R \# M \Rightarrow R < M$: Not True
   IV. $D @ K \Rightarrow D > K$: Not True
   So none of the conclusion follows

5. **(c)** 6. **(d)** 7. **(d)**

Sol. (8-10) :

8. **(d)** Either I. $Y < N$ or II. $Y = N$
9. **(a)** $J > L$ is true.
10. **(e)** None is true.

Problem Solving (PUZZLES)

INTRODUCTION

In this chapter you will see some typical problems in which you would be given a series of interlinked information and on the basis of those informations you would be expected to reach certain conclusions.

TYPES OF INFORMATIONS IN A GIVEN PROBLEM

1. **Basic Informations**

   (Useful secondary informations): It is given in first couple of sentences of given data which are such that they give you some basic information that is essential to give you general idea of the situation.

2. **Actual Informations**

   Whatever remains after the basic informations are known as actual information.

   While trying to solve a problem one should begin with actual information keeping useful secondary information in mind.

3. **Negative Informations**

   Actual informations having negative sentences are called negative information. A negative information does not inform us anything exactly but it gives a chance to eliminate a possibility.

TYPES OF PROBLEMS

1. Simple problems (based on categorisation)
2. Problems based on arrangement (Linear, circular, rectangular/ square)
3. Problems based on comparison
4. Problems based on blood relations
5. Blood relations and profession based problems
6. Problems based on conditional selection

1. Simple Problems Based on Categorisation

Tips to Solve Problems

These type of problems can easily be solved by constructing a table.

EXAMPLE 1. Directions : Read the following information carefully and answer the question that follows:

1. There are six cities L, M, N, O, P and Q.
2. L is not a hill station.
3. M and P are not historical places.
4. O is not an industrial city.
5. L and O are not historical cities.
6. L and M are not alike.

Q. Which two cities are historical places ?

Sol. It can be solved by preparing a table in the manner given below:

	L	M	N	O	P	Q
Historical place						
Industrial city						
Hill station						

(2), (3), (4), (5) are negative informations. Therefore as per such informations. We put 'x' (not) mark wherever applicable. As a result the table looks like the one below.

	L	M	N	O	P	Q
Historical place	×	×		×	×	
Industrial city				×		
Hill station	×					

As above table gives definite informations about L and O. L is neither a historical place nor a hill station. So, it must be an industrial city. In the same manner O is neither a historical nor an industrial city. So, O must be a hill station. Hence, we put '✓' mark at the appropriate place which give the table following look:-

	L	M	N	O	P	Q
Historical place	×	×		×	×	
Industrial city	✓			×		
Hill station	×			✓		

Now, as per the condition (6), L and M are not alike, hence M can not be an Industrial city. Also M is not a historical place. Therefore, it is very obvious that M is a hill station.

Again, in the given problem there is no negative information about N. Hence, we can assume that N is a hill station as well as a historical place and an industrial city. In the same way, we find the conclusion about other cities. N, P and Q. Finally we find the following table.

	L	M	N	O	P	Q
Historical place	×	×	✓	×	×	✓
Industrial city	✓	×	✓	×	✓	✓
Hill station	×	✓	✓	✓	✓	✓

Now, after analysing the given question we get the answer 'N and Q are two historical places.'

2. Problems Based On Arrangement

In such problems a group of people, objects, etc, may have to be arranged in a row, or in a circle or any other way.

LINEAR ARRANGEMENT

One Row Sequence

(A) When direction of face is not clear, then we take ourself as base and then the diagram will be as follows

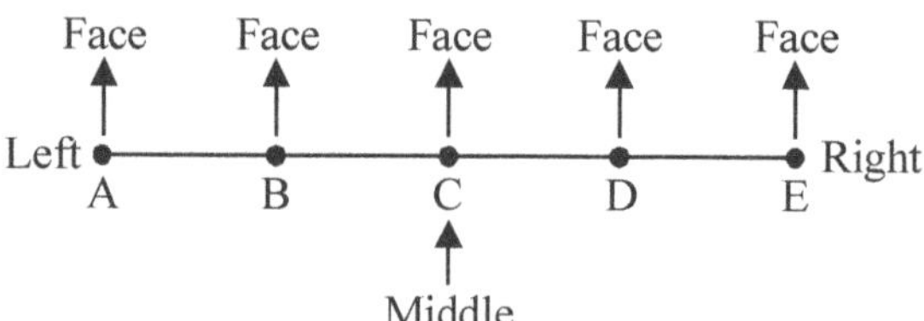

From the above diagram, it is clear that

(i) B, C, D, E are **right** of A but **only** B is the **immediate right** of A.

(ii) D, C, B, A are **left** of E but **only** D is the **immediate left** of E.

(B) When direction of face is towards you, then the diagram will be as follows

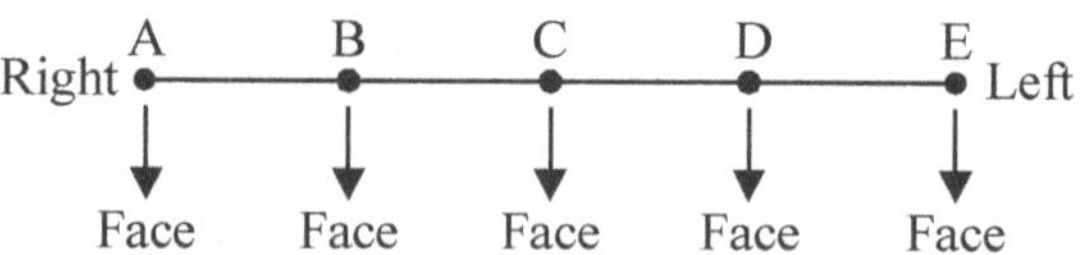

From the above diagram, it is clear that

(i) B is **immediate left** of A, C is **immediate left** of B; D is **immediate left** of C and E is **immediate left** of D.

(ii) D is **immediate right** of E; C is **immediate right** of D; B is **immediate right** of C; and A is **immediate right** of B.

TWO ROWS SEQUENCE

Let us see 6 persons seating in two rows

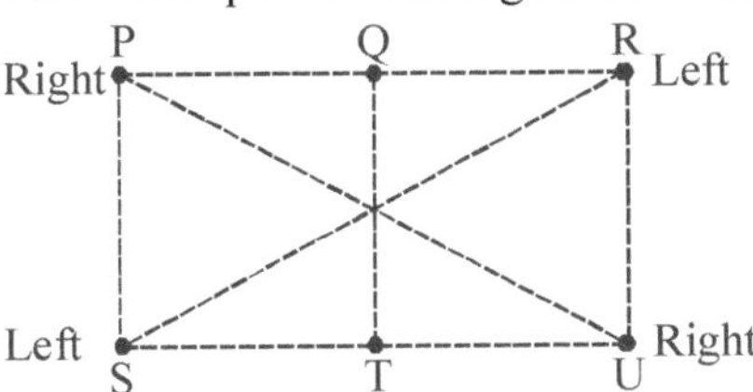

From the above diagram, it is clear that

(i) P is sitting **opposite** S.

(ii) Q is sitting **opposite** T.

(iii) R is sitting **opposite** U.

(iv) P and U are sitting at **diagonally opposite** positions.

(v) S and R are sitting **diagonally opposite** positions.

In arrangement problems, the actual information can be classified into 2 categories:-

(a) Definite information

A definite information is one when the place of object/man is definitely mentioned.

(b) Comparative information

In such information the place of object/man is not mentioned definitely but only a comparative position is given. In other words the positions of objects/men are given in comparision to another objects/men.

❑ Shortcut Approach

Step I. Sketch a diagram of empty places

Step II. Fill up as many empty places as possible using all the definite informations.

Step III. With the help of comparative information consider all possibilities and select the possibilities which does not violate any condition.

EXAMPLE 2. Directions : Just read the following information carefully to answer the questions given below it:

Five friends P, Q, R, S and T are sitting on a bench.

(1) P is sitting next to Q.

(2) R is sitting next to S.

(3) S is not sitting with T.

(4) T is on the last end of the bench.

(5) R is on the 2nd position from the right.

(6) P is on the right of Q and T.

(7) P and R are sitting together.

Q. At what position is P sitting?

Sol.

Here, 4th and 5th sentences constitute definite information: Comparative informations are: 1st, 2nd, 6th and 7th sentences while 3rd is a negative information.

Now, start with definite information, sketch the following arrangement:-

T __ __ R __

Now, this is the time to look for the comparative informations that tell about T and R. Such informations are 2nd, 6th and 7th sentences. Take the 7th and the 1st sentence. If P and R are together and also Q and P are together, then P must be between Q and R. Now the arrangement take the form as:-

T Q P R ____

By the virtue of the 2nd sentence:

T Q P R S

So, P is sitting at the middle position.

Directions (Qs. 3-5) : *The following questions consist of two words having a certain relationship to each other. Select the alternative whose words are having the same relationship amongst them.*

Q. 3 Stare: Glance

(a) Gulp: Sip (b) Confide: Tell
(c) Hunt: Stalk (d) Step: Walk

Sol. (a) Both are synonyms of each other.

Q. 4. Cloth: Texture

(a) Body: Weight (b) Silk: Cloth
(c) Wood: Grains (d) Ornaments: Gold

Sol. (a) As 'Cloth' has 'Texture' in the same way 'Body' has 'Weight'.

Q. 5. Nuts: Bolts

(a) Nitty: Gritty (b) Bare: Feet
(c) Naked: Clothes (d) Hard: Soft

Sol. (c) As 'Nuts' are covered with 'bolts', in the same way a 'Naked' is covered with 'Clothes'.

CIRCULAR ARRANGEMENT

Circle is the most important case from the exam point of view. Most of the times Circle kind of statements are there in exams.

From the exam point of view, in most cases they give 8 persons sitting in the circle. But before solving the important thing is their ' Sitting Position '.

Step 1. Knowing NEWS! N= North , E= East , W=West , S= South

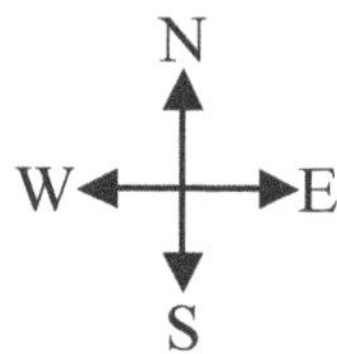

Step 2 : Picking Left & Right :

Facing Center

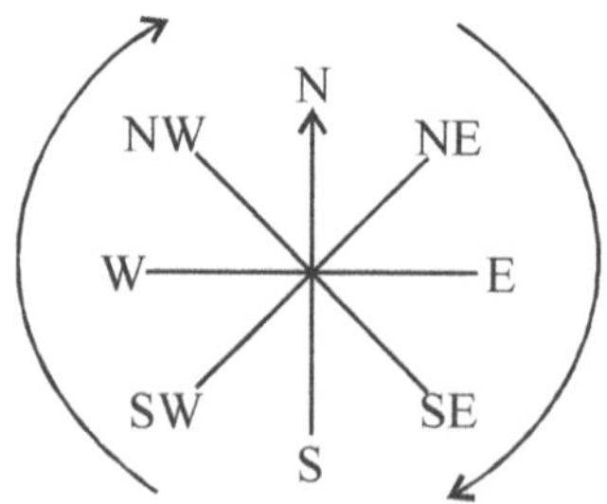

Facing Outside

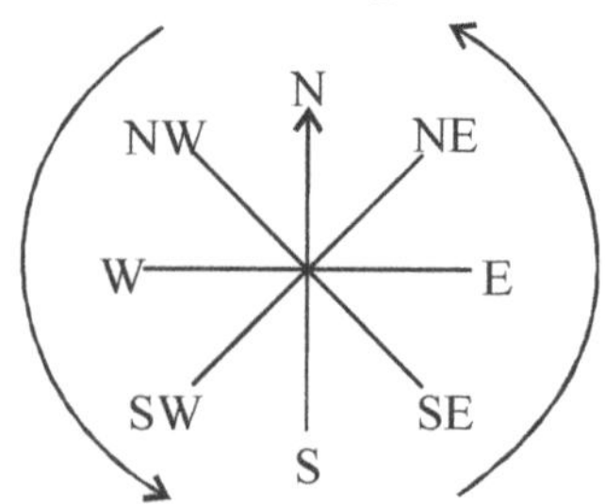

If it is mention in the statement that all is facing outside then just do opposite of above like this:

Clock wise = Right

Step 3 : Solving step wise the statement or Following the statement.

❑ *Shortcut Approach*

- Imagine yourself as one of the persons given in the question.
- Count how many people are mentioned in the question. Then draw a circle with those many people.

- Imagine yourself at the position shown by the box.
- Now your left hand is the left side and right hand is the right side.
- Now, if in question it is given, P is second to the right of Q, approach as follows.

  → Imagine yourself as Q.

→ Now, P is second to right of Q. The right of Q is your right side. So, place P is second place from Q towards its right.

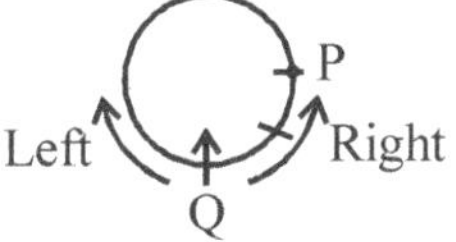

EXAMPLE 6. Directions : Study the following information carefully and answer the question given below.

Bunty, Dev, Manav, Kavya, Payal, Qasturba, Wasir and Himmat are sitting around a circle facing at the centre. Manav is to the immediate right of Bunty who is 4th to the right of Kavya. Payal is 2nd to the left of Bunty and is 4th to the right of Wasir. Qasturba is 2nd to the right of Dev who is 2nd to the right of Himmat.

Q. Who is 3rd to the right of Bunty?

Sol.

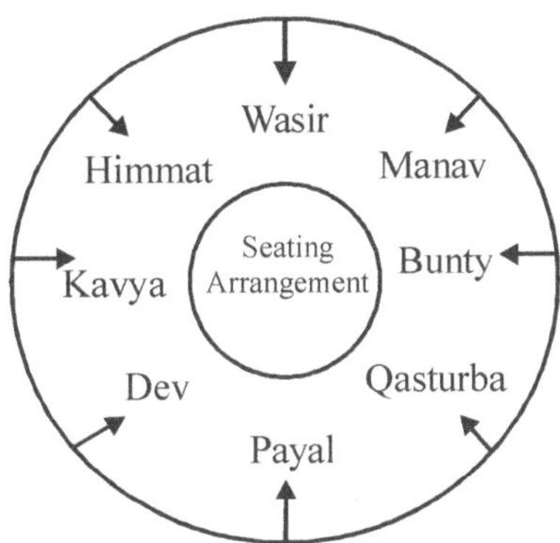

To give the answer, see the setting position. You can easily found the Himmat is 3rd to the right of Bunty.

3. Problems Based On Comparison

In such problems comparison of different objects or persons has to be made. Such comparisions are done on the basis of marks, ages heights, etc.

Method to Solve

If you give a serious look to the problem you will find that such problems are as same as the arrangement problems. Therefore, we have to go like arrangement problem while solving problems based on comparison.

EXAMPLE 7. Directions : Read the informations given below to answer the given question:

(1) 7 students A, B, C, D, E, F and G take a series of tests.

(2) No two students obtain the same marks.

(3) G always scores more than A.

(4) A always scores more than B.

(5) Each time either C scores the highest and E gets the least, or alternatively D scores the highest and F or B scores the least.

Q. If D is ranked 6th and B is ranked 5th, then what will be the rank of F?

Sol.

In this case, we see there is no definite information. Sentence 5 gives a definite information but it is conditional. Still, we draw all the possibilities based on sentence 5.

(1) C _ _ _ _ _ _ _ _ _ E

or, (2) D _ _ _ _ _ _ _ _ _ F

or, (3) D _ _ _ _ _ _ _ _ _ B

We see that the two additional informations (3) and (4) are inadequate to reach a definite conclusion. Hence, keeping these in mind. We move on to the given questions.

D is ranked 6th and B is 5th. This does mean that possibilities (2) and (3) are violated. Hence, possibility (1) must be true. Thus, we have:

C ______ B D E

Also by virtue of (3) and (4) we can have only one arrangement for G, A and B which is GAB. Accordingly, there are three possibilities:

C F G A B D E

C G F A B D E

and C G A F B D E

So, if D is ranked 6th and B is ranked 5th, then F is ranked 2nd, 3rd or 4th.

4. Problems Based On Blood Relation

Such problems involves analysis of certain blood relations.

Shortcut Approach

(i) Vertical/diagonal lines to represent parent-child relationships.

(ii) Single/double horizontal line like ($\leftrightarrow / \Leftrightarrow$) to represent marriages.

(iii) A dashed line (—) for brother and sister relationship.

(iv) '+' sign for male and '–' sign for female

For example.

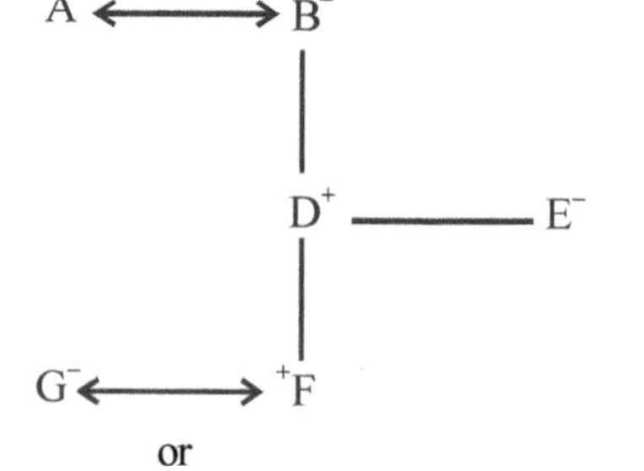

or

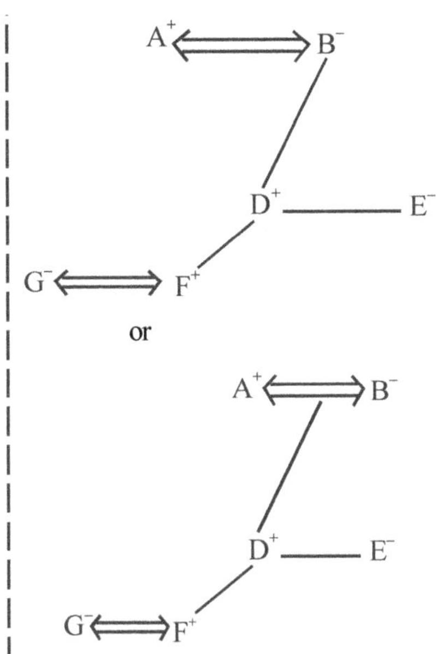

The above diagrams tells us:-

(a) A and B are couple; A is the husband while B is the wife.

(b) D is son of A and B while E is daughter of A and B.

(c) D is the brother of E and E is the sister of D.

(d) D has a son F

(e) F and G are couple; F is the husband and G is the wife.

(f) F is the grandson of A and B.

(g) G is the daughter in law of D.

(h) E is the aunt (Bua) of F

(i) There are 3 males (A, D and F) and 3 females (B, E, G)

EXAMPLE 8. Directions : Read the following information carefully and answer the question given below:

All 6 members M, N, O, P, Q, R of a family are travelling together. N is the son of O but O is not the mother of N. M and O are a married couple. Q is the brother O. P is the daughter of M. R is the brother of N.

Q. How many male members are there in the family?

Sol. Here, all the sentences are actual information except the first. Out of these statements, the 2nd and the fifth sentences give information on parent child relationship. We can begin with either of the two. Let us begin with the 6th sentence. Our diagram will be as

As, we do not want to make many diagrams, we would prefer to only add to the existing diagsams. Therefore, we should look for sentences that talk of M or P. The 3rd sentence talks about M. Hence, we add this information, that M and O are married couple in our diagram.

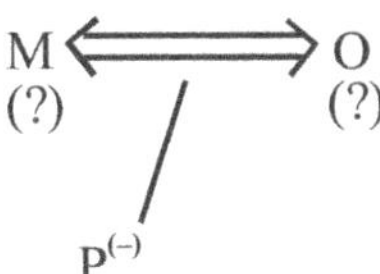

Now, the 2nd sentence talks about O. It says that N is the son of O but O is not the mother of N. Obviously, O must be the father of N. This means O is a male and hence M must be a female. Now our diagram takes the form as following:-

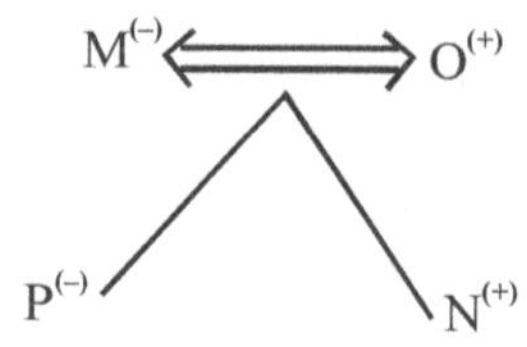

Now, we add the two sentences 'Q is the brother of O' and 'R is the brother of N' and we get the final diagram as below:-

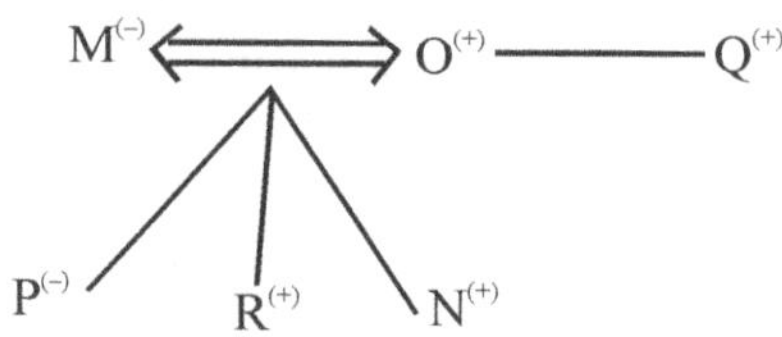

Number of '+' sign is four.. therefore, there are 4 male members in the family.

5. Problems Based On Blood Relations and Profession

Such problems are very much similar to the problems related to blood relation. What makes it different is the addition of new data:- the professions of family members. You will get the more clear idea about this type of problem.

EXAMPLE 9. Directions : Read the following information carefully and answer the question given below it:

(1) A, B, C, D, E and P are members of a family.

(2) There are two married couples.

(3) B is an engineer and the father of E

(4) P is the grandfather of C and is a lawyer.

(5) D is the grandmother of E and is a housewife.

(6) There is one engineer, one lawyer, one teacher, one housewife and two students in the family.

Q. Who is the husband of A?

Sol. Here, (1), (2), and (6) are useful secondary informations. While (3), (4) and (5) are the actual informations. We start with the 3rd sentence because it mentions a parent child relationship. Its diagram can be made as the following:-

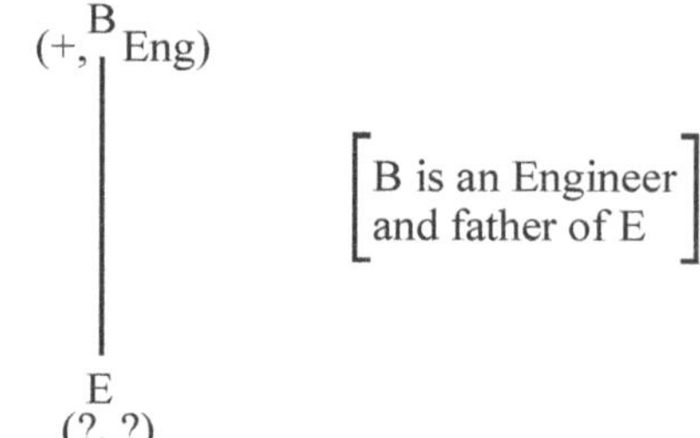

Now, we move on to another sentence that involves either B or E. You see that the 5th sentence gives some information about E. It says that D is the grandmother E. Point to be noted that if D is the grandmother of E, then the son of D must be father of E and hence B is the son of D. Now, the diagram takes the following form.

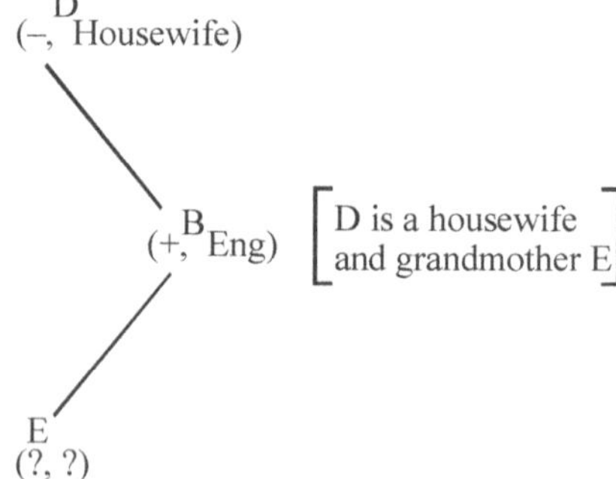

Now, the 4th sentence has the remaining information and diagram for it is given below:-

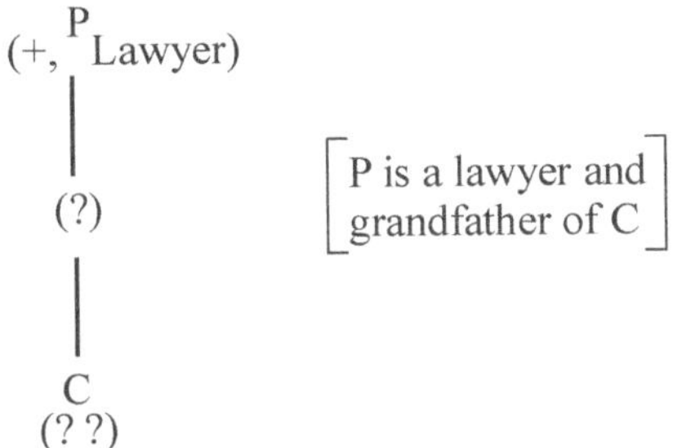

Now, we see that we have ended up with two different component. Then how to resolve this deadlock? The answer is simple: - to resolve it, we make use of the given useful secondary information (USI).

"There are two married couple in the family." Clearly, the two possible pairs are of grandfather, grandmother and father, mother. Therefore, we combine the two diagrams into the following way.

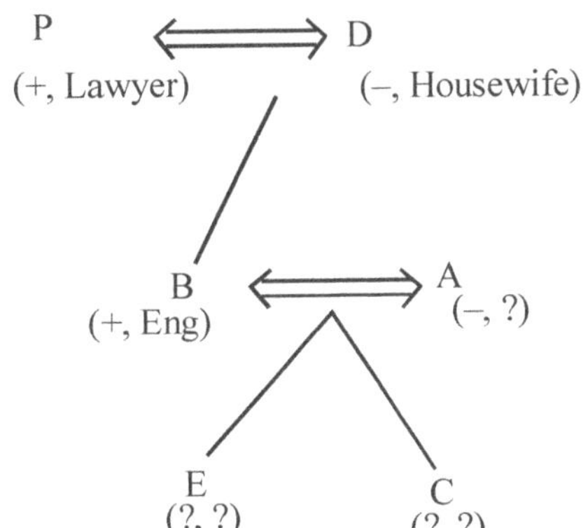

Point to be noted that the professions of A, E and C are yet unknown. However, using the 6th sentence with reasonable justification, we may assume that the mother (A) should be the teacher and the two children E and C should be students. But this conclusion can be challenged and has no reason at all.

Apart from that the sexes of E and C can not be determined.

From the above diagram, it is clear that B is husband of A.

6. Problems Based On Conditional Selection

In this type of problems, a group of objects/persons has to be selected from a given larger group, as per the given restrictions. You will get the better idea of such type of problems from the problem given below:-

EXAMPLE 10. Directions : Study the following information carefully and answer the question given below it:

From, amongst 6 boys J, K, L, M, N & O and 5 girls P, Q, R, S and T, a team of 6 is to be selected under the following conditions:

(i) J and M have to be together.

(ii) L can not go with S.

(iii) S and T have to be together.

(iv) K can not be teamed with N.

(v) M cannot go with P.

(vi) K and R have to be together.

(vii) L and Q have to be together.

Q. If there be 5 boys in the team, then the lone girl member is ------

Sol. Make the group of all the pairs that have to be together on one side and the pairs that must not be together on the other side. Next, read each of the questions and treat that as an additional information. Finally, analyse the possibilities and choose the possibilities that satisfies all the conditions. Let us see the process below.

Firstly, we can summarise the conditions in the following way.

J, M	S, T
(+)(+)	(–)(–)
K, R	L, Q
(+)(–)	(+)(–)

→ Group 'must be together'

L, S,	K, N,	M, P
(+)(–)	(+)(+)	(+)(–1)

→ Group 'never be together'

Here, number of boys are 5. We see than K and N can never be together. Therefore, there are only two ways of selecting 5 boys – JKLMO and JNLMO. But if K would select then R should also select, and if L goes than Q should also go. Hence, JNLMO is the only possibility in which L's friend Q would be the lone girl member.

PRACTICE EXERCISE

DIRECTIONS (Qs. 1-5): *Study the following information carefully to answer the given questions.*

Eight persons - J, K, L, M, N, O, P, Q are sitting around a circular table facing the centre with equal distances between each other (but not necessarily in the same order). Each of them is also related to N in some way or the other.

K sits third to the left of N. Only one person sits between N and Q. N's sister sits to the immediate right of Q. Only two people sit between N's sister and N's mother. J sits to the immediate right of N's mother. P sits to the immediate right of M. N's brother sits third to the right of P. N's wife sits second to the left of N's brother. Only three people sit between N's wife and L. N's son sits second to the right of N's father. Only two people sit between N's father and N's daughter.

1. Who amongst the following is the son of N?
   (a) Q (b) P
   (c) K (d) J
   (e) M
2. How many people sit between N and K, when counted from the right of K?
   (a) Five (b) Two
   (c) Four (d) Three
   (e) None
3. Who sits to the immediate right of Q?
   (a) J (b) N's sister
   (c) N (d) N's Wife
   (e) K
4. Which of the following statements is true with respect to the given information?
   (a) All the given options are true
   (b) P sits to the immediate left of J

(c) N's mother sits to the immediate left of N
(d) M is the mother-in-law of Q
(e) N is an immediate neighbour of his father.

5. How is J related to L?
(a) Sister (b) Uncle
(c) Sister-in-law (d) Father
(e) Daughter

DIRECTIONS (Qs. 6-10): *Study the following information Carefully to answer the given questions*

P, Q, R, S, T, U, V, W and X are sitting in a straight line, facing North. Three of them are not males. Two females sit adjacent to each other. Q is fourth to the left of V, who is second to the right of R, who is not the immediate neighbour of P.

- U is fourth to the right of R and is second to the left of X. S is not an immediate neighbour of either X or Q.
- S is not male. One of the persons sitting on the extreme ends is a female. T is not an immediate neighbour of either V or U.
- No female is an immediate neighbour of U. W does not sit second to the left of P. The immediate neighbour of S are male

6. Which of the following is a group of females ?
(a) QTS (b) TXP
(c) SVR (d) UWX
(e) None of these

7. Who is sitting to the immediate left of S ?
(a) V (b) Q
(c) W (d) R
(e) None of these

8. In which of the following combinations is the third person sitting between the first and the second person ?
(a) PWU (b) QTR
(c) RST (d) WUP
(e) None of these

9. If Q and R, V and U interchange their position then how many persons are sitting between R and V?
(a) Four (b) Five
(c) Six (d) Two
(e) None of these

10. Who among the following sits third to the left of P ?
(a) W (b) V
(c) R (d) X
(e) None of these

DIRECTIONS (Qs. 11-15): *Study the information given below and answer the question based on it.*

Seven persons P, Q, R, S, T, U and V watched movies on different days starting from Monday to Sunday. They watch i.e. Logan, Avatar, Inception, Superman, Thor, Avengers and Batman, but not necessarily in the same order. 3 persons watched movie between U and the one who watched Avengers and U watched movie before the one who watched Avengers but not on Monday. P watched Inception with a gap of a day, before the one who watched Avengers. One person watched movie between P and the one who watched Logan. Q watched Avatar just before U. One person watched movie between Q and T. T didn't watch movie on Thursday. S watched Batman before R who watched Thor.

11. Who among the following watched on Monday?

(a) P (b) Q
(c) T (d) U
(e) V

12. T watched which of the following movie?
(a) Superman
(b) Avengers
(c) Logan
(d) Batman
(e) None of these

13. How many persons watched movie between P and R?
(a) None (b) 1
(c) 2 (d) 3
(e) 4

14. 'Superman' is related to Monday in the same way as 'Avengers' is related to Thursday. Likewise, 'Thor' would be related to?
(a) Friday
(b) Saturday
(c) Sunday
(d) Tuesday
(e) Wednesday

15. Which of the following is true regarding 'V'?
(a) 'V' watches 'Inception'
(b) 'V' does not watch the movie on 'Saturday'.
(c) 'V' watches the movie on Thursday
(d) Both 'A' & 'B'
(e) None of these

DIRECTIONS (Qs. 16-20): *Study the following information carefully and answer the questions given below:*

P, Q, R, S, T, U, V and W are eight friends who live in an eight-storey building. The ground floor is numbered one and the topmost floor is numbered eight. Each of them belong to different cities, Jaipur, Kolkata, Delhi, Mumbai, Pune, Raipur, Ranchi and Patna but not necessarily in the same order. There is only one floor between P and the one who belongs to Patna lives. The person who belongs to Patna does not live on floor numbered 1. S lives just below Q. The one who belongs to Jaipur lives an even numbered floor and just above the floor on which the one who belongs to Pune lives. The person who belongs to Raipur lives on an even numbered floor but not on the 8th floor. Neither S nor W lives on the 1st floor. Only one person lives between the one who belongs to Ranchi and S. P lives on an odd-numbered floor and T lives just above P. Q lives on the fourth floor. Only two persons live between the person who belongs to Raipur and P. U lives just below the one who belongs to Pune. S belongs to neither Pune nor Patna. The one who belongs to Delhi does not live on an odd-numbered floor. V does not belong to Kolkata. There are two floors between the floor on which W lives and the floor on which T lives. Only two persons live between the one who belongs Mumbai and the one who belongs to Delhi.

16. Who among the following belongs to Kolkata?
(a) S (b) R
(c) P (d) V
(e) None of these

17. How many persons are there between T and Q?
(a) One (b) Two
(c) Three (d) Four
(e) None of these

18. Who among the following lives on the topmost floor?
(a) The one who belongs to Jaipur

(b) The one who belongs to Pune
(c) The one who belongs to Delhi
(d) The one who belongs to Mumbai
(e) None of these

19. Which of the following combinations is/are true?
(a) Floor no. 2- S- Mumbai
(b) Floor no. 5- U- Patna
(c) Floor no. 1- R-Kolkata
(d) Floor no. 8- T- Jaipur
(e) None of these

20. P belongs to which of the following city?
(a) Delhi (b) Mumbai
(c) Jaipur (d) Pune
(e) None of these

HINTS & SOLUTIONS

Sol. (1-5):

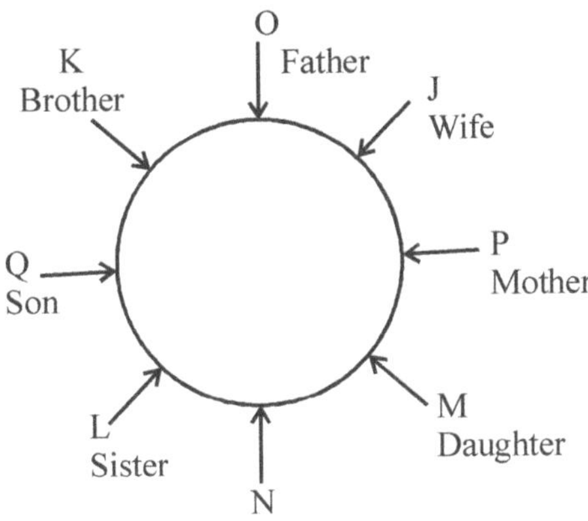

1. **(a)** **2.** **(b)** **3.** **(b)** **4.** **(b)** **5.** **(c)**

Sol. (6-10) :

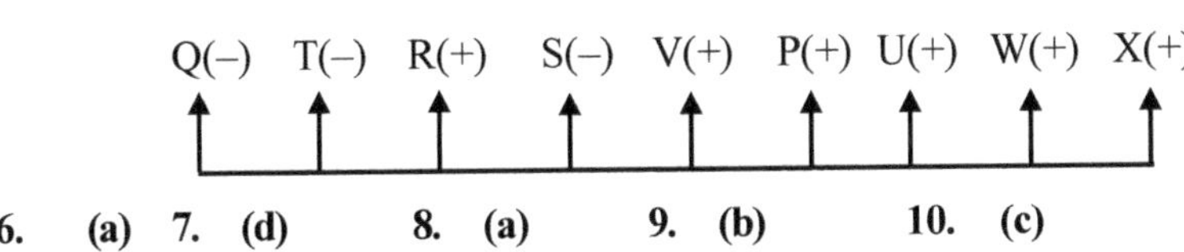

6. **(a)** **7.** **(d)** **8.** **(a)** **9.** **(b)** **10.** **(c)**

Sol. (11-15) :

Day	Person	Movie
Monday	Q	Avatar
Tuesday	U	Logan
Wednesday	T	Superman
Thursday	P	Inception
Friday	S	Batman
Saturday	V	Avengers
Sunday	R	Thor

11. (b) 12. (b) 13. (c) 14. (a) 15. (e)

Sol. (16-20) :

Floor	Person	City
8	T	Jaipur
7	P	Pune
6	U	Delhi
5	W	Patna
4	Q	Raipur
3	S	Mumbai
2	R	Kolkata
1	V	Ranchi

16. (b) 17. (c) 18. (a) 19. (d) 20. (d)

Input and Output

INTRODUCTION

Problems related to input-output are frequently asked questions in various graduate level competitive examinations. They are not very tough stuff but take a good deal of time to be solved or sometimes students do not attempt to solve them because of time consuming impression of such type of questions. But proper understanding of the subject makes you believe that such problems are not as tough and time consuming as they seem.

CONCEPT OF INPUT-OUTPUT PROBLEMS

In such problems:

(a) It is imagined that there is some kind of computer/word processing machine.

(b) An input is given to the computer/word processing machine

(c) The computer/word processing machine performs repeated operations as per a certain pattern to give different output in different steps.

TYPES OF PROBLEMS

(i) Problems of shifting

(ii) Problems of arrangement

(iii) Problems of mathematical operation

(iv) Miscellaneous.

Problem of Shifting

We know that in such type of problems, a word/number processing machine generate output through shifting. Shifting does mean an operation in which words or numbers of a given input give outputs in different steps through shifting their place to different place as per a fixed pattern.

> ***Note :*** In shifting problems, the previous step of any step can possibly be determined, so we can move in backward or reverse order which is not possible in some of the other type of problems.

Methods to Solve

Lets take an example

Input : Blue Cat Good Other Have Cake
Step 1 : Blue Other Good Cat Have Cake
Step 2 : Blue Other Have Cat Good Cake
Step 3 : Cake Other Have Cat Good Blue
Step 4 : Cake Cat Have Other Good Blue
Step 5 : Cake Cat Good Other Have Blue
Step 6 : Blue Cat Good Other Have Cake

Shifting of element can easily be understood by making them equivalent to number like

Blue = 1, Cat = 2, Good = 3, Other = 4, Have = 5, Cake = 6

Input can be written as

1	2	3	4	5	6
Blue	Cat	Good	Other	Have	Cake

Step-1 : 2 and 4 interchanged
Step-2 : 3 and 5 interchanged
Step-3 : 1 and 6 interchanged
Step-4 : 1, 2 and 3 are repeated again.

Input :	1	2	3	4	5	6	Step-3 :	6	4	5	2	3	1
Step-1 :	1	4	3	2	5	6	Step-4 :	6	2	5	4	3	1
Step-2 :	1	4	5	2	3	6	Step-5 :	6	2	3	4	5	1
							Step-6 :	1	2	3	4	5	6

Problems on Arrangements

1. Word Arrangement from Left Side:

EXAMPLE :

Input:	mango	tango	orange	banana	pear
Step I:	banana	mango	tango	orange	pear
Step II:	banana	mango	orange	tango	pear
Step III:	banana	mango	orange	pear	tango

Here, we start arrangement from the word that comes 1st in the dictionary; then comes the word coming 2nd in the dictionary, then comes the word coming 3rd in the dictionary and so on. In this case, the arrangement start from left side. This is the reason in step I banana comes 1st as it comes 1st in the dictionary. In the 2nd step, orange comes at 3rd place because after the arrangement of step I the next word coming in the dictionary is mango but it get arranged automatically and hence there is no need to arrange it in step II. This is the reason after arranging banana in step I, we directly come to the word orange (coming 3rd in the dictionary) in step II. In the 3rd step, we arrange the word 'pear' (coming 4th in the dictionary) and the word tango get arranged automatically.

2. Word Arrangement from Right:

EXAMPLE :

Input:	Name	Fame	Game	Shame	Jam
Step I:	Name	Game	Shame	Jam	Fame
Step II:	Name	Shame	Jame	Game	Fame
Step III:	Shame	Name	Jam	Game	Fame

In this case, the arrangement starts from right side. The word coming 1st in the dictionary comes at the 1st position from right. At the 2nd position from right comes the word coming 2nd in the dictionary and the process goes on till the arrangement gets completed. In the above given example, 'Fame' is the 1st word coming in the dictionary and hence it comes at the 1st position from right in the step I. In the step II, the 2nd word coming in the dictionary (Game) comes at the 2nd position from right. Point to be noted that the word coming third in the dictionary will come at the 3rd position from right and this word is 'Jam'. But 'Jam' automatically get arranged as per the given pattern when we arrange the word 'Game' in II step. This is the reason why we don't arrange 'Jam' in the third step and jump directly to arrange the word. 'Name' that comes 4th in the dictionary. 'Name' occupies 4th position from right and the word 'Shame' automatically get arranged in the 5th step. Hence, the word 'Shame' does not need to get arranged.

3. Word Arrangement from the Left-Right Alternate:

EXAMPLE :

Input:	Sachin	is	a	great	cricket	player
Step I:	a	Sachin	is	great	cricket	player
Step II:	a	is	great	cricket	player	Sachin
Step III:	a	cricket	is	great	player	Sachin
Step IV:	a	cricket	great	is	player	Sachin

Here, the arrangement is made by putting the alphabetically first word at 1st place, then alphabetically last word at last place, then alphabetically second word at second place from left and the further arrangements goes on in the same manner. In the other words, words are positioned from the left and from the right alternately. In the step I the word coming 1st in the dictionary is 'a' and it takes 1st position from left. In the step II, the last word coming alphabetically is Sachin and it takes last position (1st from right). In step III, the word coming 2nd in dictionary is 'cricket' that comes at 2nd position from left. In step IV, the word coming 3rd last in the dictionary takes the 3rd position from right. After the step IV, all the words get arranged in alphabetical order. Point to be noted that after step IV, there is no need to arrange the word 'great' as it get arranged automatically is step IV.

4. Arrangement in Increasing or Decreasing Order:

EXAMPLE :

Input:	25	17	18	58	100	35
Step I:	17	25	18	58	100	35
Step II:	17	18	25	58	100	35
Step III:	17	18	25	35	58	100

This arrangement gives a clear idea of arrangement of numbers in increasing order. In step I, the smallest number (17) comes at the 1st position from left pushing the remaining to the right. In step II, the 2nd smallest number (18) comes at 2nd position from left pushing the remaining number to the right. In step III, the 4th smallest number (35) takes 4th position from left and the other two numbers 58 and 100 get arranged automatically.

Now, let us see decreasing order arrangement:

Input:	25	17	18	58	100	35
Step I:	100	25	17	18	58	35
Step II:	100	58	25	17	18	35
Step III:	100	58	35	25	17	18
Step IV:	100	58	35	25	18	17

The same arrangement can take place from right side (or in the reverse order) as follow:

Input:	25	17	18	58	100	35
Step I:	25	18	58	100	35	17
Step II:	25	58	100	35	18	17
Step III:	58	100	35	25	18	17
Step IV:	100	58	35	25	18	17

5. Number Arrangment from Left-Right Alternate:

Like words left-right alternate arrangement, number arrangement also takes place. The process of this arrangement is exactly the same as the arrangement takes place in case of words. Just see the following cases:

Case I :

Input:	100	125	26	10	15	35
Step I:	10	100	125	26	15	35
Step II:	10	100	26	15	35	125
Step III:	10	15	100	26	35	125
Step IV:	10	15	26	35	100	125

Here, the smallest number (10) takes 1st position from left in step I. In step II the largest number takes the last (1st from right) position. Again in step III the 2nd smallest number (15) comes at the 2nd position from left. In the step IV, the 2nd largest number (100) comes at the 2nd position from right and the remaining number (26 and 35) get arranged automatically.

Case II :

Input:	100	125	26	10	15	35
Step I:	100	26	10	15	35	125
Step II:	10	100	26	15	35	125
Step III:	10	26	15	35	100	125
Step IV:	10	15	26	35	100	125

In case II, the arrangements take place in the same way as the arrangements take place in case I. But the difference here is that case I is a left-right arrangement and case II is the right-left arrangement. In case II, the arrangement starts with the largest number (125) coming at the 1st position from right and this is step I. In step II, the smallest number (10) comes at the 1st position from left. In step III the 2nd largest number (100) comes at the 2nd position from right. In step III, the third largest number (35) automatically comes at the 3rd position from right. In 4th step, the 2nd smallest number (15) comes at the 2nd position from left and 26 get arranged automatically coming at 3rd position from left.

> ***Note***: Left-right (or right-left) arrangement of numbers also take place in the same manner when numbers are arranged in decreasing order.

6. Arrangement of Words and Numbers Simultaneously:

Just see the following outputs produced by a word and number machine.

Case I

Input:	50	32	Vandana	Prerna	Aradhna	100
Step I:	32	50	Vandana	Prerna	Aradhna	100
Step II:	32	Aradhna	50	Vandana	Prerna	100
Step III:	32	Aradhna	50	Prerna	Vandana	100
Step IV:	32	Aradhna	50	Prerna	100	Vandana

In such case, numbers and words get arranged alternately. In step I, the smallest number (32) comes at the 1st position from left pushing the remaining members of input towards right. In the step II, the word coming 1st alphabetically (that is the word 'Aradhna') takes the 2nd position from left pushing the remaining member rightward. Point to be noted that the 2nd smallest number automatically comes at the third position from left while arranging the word 'Aradhna' and hence, there is no need to arrange the 2nd smallest number '50'. In step III, the word (Prerna) coming 2nd alphabetically comes at the 4th position from left pushing the other members to the right. In step IV, the largest number (100) occupies the 5th position from left and the word (Vandana) coming last alphabetically comes at last position automatically finishing the complete arrangement.

Let us see some other cases of this type:

Case II:

Input:	50	32	Vandana	Prerna	Aradhna	100
Step I:	100	50	32	Vandana	Prerna	Aradhna
Step II:	100	Vandana	50	32	Prerna	Aradhna
Step III:	100	Vandana	50	Prerna	32	Aradhan

In this case, largest number and the word coming last alphabetically get arranged alternately. Then the 2nd longest number and the word coming 2nd last alphabetically get arranged alternately and the process goes on till the arrangements of all the numbers and words get completed. In this case, arrangement completes in step III.

Case III:

Input:	50	32	Vandana	Prerna	Aradhna	100
Step I:	Aradhna	50	32	Vandana	Prerna	100
Step II:	Aradhna	32	50	Vandana	Prerna	100
Step III:	Aradhna	32	Prerna	50	Vandana	100

In this case, arrangement starts with the word coming 1st alphabetically and such word is 'Aradhna' that comes at the 1st position from left is step I. In step II, the smallest number (32) comes at the 2nd position from left. Then, in step III, the word Prerna coming 2nd alphabetically comes at the 3rd position from left and all the other members get arranged automatically.

Case IV:

Input:	50	32	Vandana	Prerna	Aradhna	100
Step I:	Vandana	50	32	Prerna	Aradhna	100
Step II:	Vandana	100	50	32	Prerna	Aradhna
Step III:	Vandana	100	Prerna	50	32	Aradhna
Step IV:	Vandana	100	Prerna	50	Aradhna	32

In this case, word coming last alphabetically comes 1st from left in step I and such word is 'Vandana'. In step II, the largest number (100) comes at the 2nd position from left. In step III, the word coming 2nd last alphabetically occupies the 3rd position from left, and such word is 'Prerna'. As the 2nd largest number (50) automatically get arranged as per the pattern going on and hence this is not needed to arranged in step IV. In step VI, the word coming Ist alphabetically comes at the 5th position from left and such word is 'Aradhna'. The smallest number (32) get arranged automatically coming at the last position from left in step IV. Thus, it is clear that in this case the word coming lst alphabetically and the greatest number get arranged alternately in 1st two steps; then 2nd last word alphabetically and 2nd largest number get arranged alternately finishing the whole arrangement in step IV.

Case V:

Input:	50	32	Vandana	Prerna	Aradhna	100
Step I:	32	50	Vandana	Prerna	Aradhna	100
Step II:	32	Vandana	50	Prerna	Aradhna	100
Step III:	32	Vandana	50	Prerna	100	Aradhna

In this case, the smallest number comes at the 1st position from left in step I and such number is 32. In step II, the word (Vandana) coming last alphabetically occupies the 2nd place from left. In the 2nd step, the 2nd smallest number (50) takes the 3rd position from left automatically and also the word coming 2nd last alphabatically takes the 4th position from left automatically. Hence, there is no need to arrange '50' and 'Prerna'. In the III step, the largest number (100) occupies the 5th position from left completing the whole arrangement.

Case VI:

Input:	50	32	Vandana	Prerna	Aradhna	100
Step I:	100	50	32	Vandana	Prerna	Aradhna
Step II:	100	Aradhna	50	32	Vandana	Prerna
Step III:	100	Aradhna	50	Prerna	32	Vandana

In this case, the logic is that the greatest number (100) comes at the 1st position from left in step I. In step II the word coming 1st alphabetically takes the 2nd position from left and the 2nd largest number (50) gets arranged automatically. Hence, in step III, we direct arrange the word coming 2nd last alphabetically (that word is 'Prerna') occupies the 4th position from left and the other two members (32 and 'Vandana') get arranged automatically finishing the whole arrangement.

7. Arrangement Based on the Number of Letters in Words:

Just have a look at the following patterns:

Case I :

Input:	let	pattern	love	fried	be	mature
Step I:	be	let	pattern	love	fried	mature
Step II:	be	let	love	pattern	fried	mature
Step III:	be	let	love	fried	pattern	mature
Step IV:	be	let	love	fried	mature	pattern

Here, the words get arranged as per increasing number of letters. In other words, the word having least number of letters comes 1st from left in step I and such word is 'be'. The word 'let' is bigger than 'be' and smaller than other words letterwise and hence, it takes 2nd position from left but it gets arranged automatically when the word 'be' is arranged in step I. In 2nd step, the word 'love' comes at the 3rd position from left as it is bigger than word 'let' letterwise. In step III, the letterwise bigger word (fried) than love comes at the fourth position from left. Similarly, mature comes at the 5th position from left and pattern comes at the last position automatically while arranging the word 'mature'.

Case II :

Input:	let	pattern	love	fried	be	mature
Step I:	pattern	let	love	fried	be	mature
Step II:	pattern	mature	let	love	fried	be
Step III:	pattern	mature	fried	let	love	be
Step IV:	pattern	mature	fried	love	let	be

In this case, the words get arranged in decreasing order in terms of letters. In other words, the word having the largest number of letters comes 1st from left, then comes the word having 2nd largest number of letters, then comes the word having 3rd largest number of letters and the process goes on till the word having the least number of letters occupies the last position from left.

Case III:

Input:	let	pattern	gate	a	set	be	hope
Step I:	a	let	pattern	gate	set	be	hope
Step II:	a	be	let	pattern	gate	set	hope
Step III:	a	be	let	set	pattern	gate	hope
Step IV:	a	be	let	set	gate	pattern	hope
Step V:	a	be	let	set	gate	hope	pattern

Have you noticed something here? Here, the words get arranged in increasing number of letters. But when it comes to the case of two or more words having equal number of letters the priority is given alphabetically. It does mean that the word coming 1st as per the alphabet will be put before the word coming 2nd. Similarly, the word coming 2nd alphabetically will be put before the word coming third. This is the reason why 'let' has been put before 'set' and 'gate' has been put before 'hope'.

Case IV:

Input:	let	pattern	gate	a	set	be	hope
Step I:	pattern	let	gate	a	set	be	hope
Step II:	pattern	hope	let	gate	a	set	be
Step III:	pattern	hope	gate	let	a	set	be
Step IV:	pattern	hope	gate	set	let	a	be
Step V:	pattern	hope	gate	set	let	be	a

In this case, the words get arranged in decreasing number of letters. But when it comes to the case of two or more words having equal number of letters the priority is given to the word that comes later alphabetically. It does mean that the word coming 1st alphabetically will be put after the word coming 2nd and the word coming 2nd will be put after the word coming 3rd. This is the reason why 'hope' has been put before 'gate' and 'set' has been put before 'let'.

Important Note: *The case of arrangement discussed so far are the cases of push. In all the cases a new word jumps from its place in every step, occupies its new and due place and gives the remaining words a push either towards left or right as per the requirement of the pattern. But in some cases of arrangement interchange does take place and that format is given below:*

8. Arrangement with Interchange:

EXAMPLE

Input:	the	most	beautiful	girl	is	Vandana
Step I:	beautiful	most	the	girl	is	Vandana
Step II:	beautiful	girl	the	most	is	Vandana
Step III:	beautiful	girl	is	most	the	Vandana

In this case, the word (beautiful) coming 1st in alphabetical order comes at the 1st position from left interchanging its place with the word 'the' and this is step I. In step II, the word (girl) coming 2nd in alphabetical order occupies the 2nd position from left interchanging with the word 'most'. In step III, the word coming 3rd (is) comes at the third position from left interchanging with the word 'the' and finishing the complete arrangement in alphabetical order.

This type of cases can also be seen in number arrangements and in the arrangements of numbers and words simultaneously. The examples of these type of arrangements are given below:

EXAMPLE (Increasing order number arrangement)

Input:	25	11	50	20	35
Step I:	11	25	50	20	35
Step II:	11	20	50	25	35
Step III:	11	20	25	50	35
Step IV:	11	20	25	35	50

Presentation :

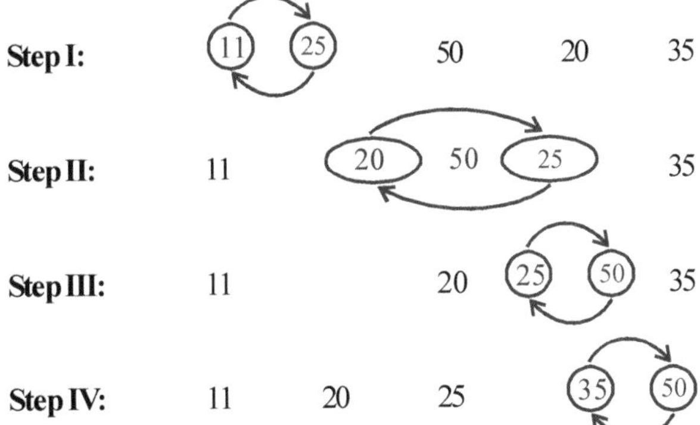

The presentation gives you the clear idea of how interchange takes place in every step.

EXAMPLE (Decreasing order number arrangement)

Input:	25	11	50	20	35
Step I:	50	11	25	20	35
Step II:	50	35	25	20	11

Presentation:

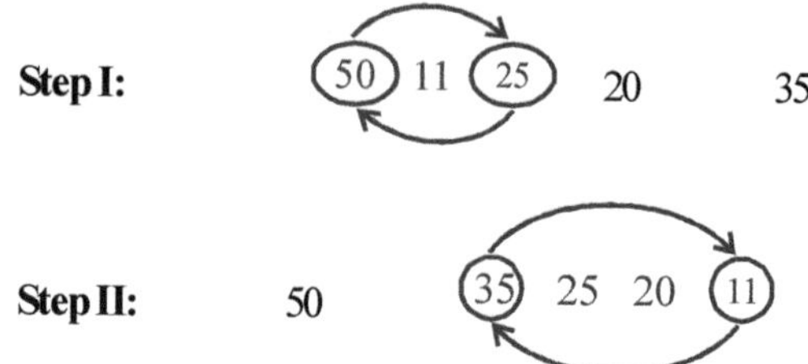

Problems of Mathematical Operation

In this type of problems, the input has some numbers. Different steps are obtained by taking the numbers of the input and different arithmetic operations are performed after that.

EXAMPLE

Input :	44	35	18	67	22	28	36
Step I :	36	27	10	59	14	20	28
Step II :	16	15	8	42	4	16	18
Step III :	132	105	54	201	66	84	108
Step IV :	50	41	24	73	28	34	42
Step V :	8	8	9	4	4	1	9
Step VI :	64	64	81	169	16	100	81
Step VII :	20	19	12	46	8	20	22

In this case, in step I (each number of the input – 8). In step II, product of the digits of each number of the input. In step III, each number of the input is multiplied by 3. In step IV, each number of the input is added by 6. In step V, keep adding the digits of each number of the input till they are converted into single digit. In step VI, (digit sum of each number of input)^2. In step VII, each number of step II is added by 4.

Miscellaneous Problems

In this type of problems, there is no fixed pattern of questions coming under this category. Infact, questions under this category comes before you as a real surprise.

EXAMPLE

Input:	every	now	and	then	same
Step I:	very	ow	nd	hen	ame
Step II:	ever	no	an	the	sam
Step III:	vry	nw	nd	thn	sm
Step IV:	ee	o	a	e	ae
Step V:	ery	w	d	en	me

In this case, in step I, first letter disappear. In step II, last letter disappear. In step III, vowels disappear. In step IV, consonants disappear. In step V, first two letters disappear.

Shortcut Approach

1. First of all, observe the given input line of words or numbers and the last step of rearrangement, so that candidate may get an idea about the changes effected in various steps of rearrangement.
2. In order to know what changes have been made in each step, observe two consecutive steps carefully.
3. Now, correlate the input, the last step and anyone of the middle steps. This will enable you to identify the rule of arrangement.
4. In shifting problems, it is possible to determine the previous/earlier steps including input. We can proceed/move backward or in reverse direction in shifting problems.
5. In shifting problems for convenience, we assign numeric value to given words.

PRACTICE EXERCISE

DIRECTIONS (Qs. 1-5) : Study the following information and answer the given questions. A word arrangement machine, when given an input line of words, rearrange them following a particular rule in each step. The following is an illustration of input and the steps of rearrangement.

Input Go for to though by easy To Access at

Step I Access go for to though by easy To at

Step II Access at go for to though by easy To

Step III Access at by go for to though easy To

Step IV Access at by easy go for to though To

Step V Access at by easy for go to though To

Step VI Access at by easy for go though to To

Step VII Access at by easy for go though To to (and step VII is the last step for this input). As per the rules followed in the above steps, find out in the following questions the appropriate step for the given output.

1. **Input** Together over series on feast the so which of the following steps will be the last but one?
   (a) II (b) III
   (c) IV (d) V
   (e) None of these
2. **Input** Every and peer to an for which of the following steps would be 'an and every for peer to?
   (a) II (b) IV
   (c) V (d) III
   (e) None of these
3. The step II of an input is an follows: 'and Do pet to an that'. Which of the following would definitely be the input?
   (a) Do and pet to an that
   (b) Do pet to and that on
   (c) Do on pet to and that
   (d) Cannot be determined
   (e) None of these
4. **Input** 'Over Go for through at are'. Which steps will be the last step of the above input?
   (a) II (b) VI
   (c) IV (d) VII
   (e) III
5. **Input** 'Story for around on was He at'.
   Which of the following will be step IV for the given input?
   (a) around at He for story on was
   (b) around at for He story on was
   (c) around at for He on story was
   (d) around at for He on was story
   (e) None of these

DIRECTIONS (Qs. 6-10): Study the following information carefully and answer the given question:

A word and number arrangement machine when given an input line of words and numbers rearrange them following a particular rule in each step. The following is an illustration of input and rearrangement. (All the numbers are two-digit numbers).

Input : gate 20 86 just not 71 for 67 38 bake sun 55

Step I: bake gate 20 just not 71 for 67 38 sun 55 86

Step II: for bake gate 20 just not 67 38 sun 55 86 71

Step III: gate for bake 20 just not 38 sun 55 86 71 67

Step IV: just gate for bake 20 not 38 sun 55 86 71 67

Step V: not just gate for bake 20 sun 86 71 67 55 38

Step VI: sun not just gate for bake 86 71 67 55 38 20

Steps VI: is the last step of the arrangement the above input.

As per the rule followed in the above steps, find out in each of the following questions the appropriate step for the given input.

Input: 31 rise gem 15 92 47 aim big 25 does 56 not 85 63 with moon

6. How many steps will be required to complete the rearrangement?

(a) Eight (b) Six
(c) Seven (d) Five
(e) None of these

7. Which words numbers would be at 7th position from the left in step IV?

(a) rise (b) aim
(c) big (d) 15
(e) 47

8. Which step number is the following output?

rise not moon gem does big aim 15 with 92 85 63 56 47 31 25

(a) Step V (b) Step VII
(c) Step IV (d) Step VIII
(e) There is no such step

9. Which of the following represents the position of '92' in step VI ?

(a) Ninth from the left
(b) Fifth from the right
(c) Sixth from the right
(d) Ninth from the right
(e) Seventh from the left

10. Which words numbers would be at 5th position from the right in the last step?

(a) gem (b) 63
(c) 56 (d) 85
(e) does

DIRECTIONS (Qs. 11-15): Study the following information carefully and answer the given questions.

When a word and number arrangement machine is given an input line of words and numbers, it arranges them following a particular rule. The following is an illustration of Input and rearrangement. (All the numbers are two digit numbers).

Input : Daily 79 do diverse 57 14 dear 86 63 domain 42 dog

Step I: diverse daily 79 do 57 dear 86 63 domain 42 dog 41

Step II: domain diverse daily 79 do 57 dear 86 63 dog 41 24 75

Step III: daily domain diverse 79 do dear 86 63 dog 41 24 75

Step IV: dear daily domain diverse 79 do 86 dog 41 do 75 36

Step V: dog dear daily domain diverse do 86 41 24 75 36 97

Step VI: do dog dear daily domain diverse 41 24 75 36 97 68

Step VI: is the largest step of above arrangement as the indended arrangement as the intended arrangement is obtained

As per the rules followed in the given steps, find out the appropriate steps for the Input.

Input : table 63 tour 19 typhoon 72 25 to tea 48 tablet 56

11. Which elelment comes exactly between 'typhoon' and ' tour' in step III of the given input?

(a) 63 (b) to
(c) 91 (d) table
(e) 56

12. Which of the following combinations represent the sixth and eight element in Step II of the given input from left end?
(a) 63 and tablet
(b) tea and 63
(c) 72 and tablet
(d) 72 and tea
(e) 48 and table

13. If in the last step '2' is added to each of the odd numbers and '1' is subtracted from each of the even numbers, then how many numbers multiple of '3' will be formed?
(a) Two (b) One
(c) None (d) Three
(e) More than three

14. Which element is fourth to the left of one which is ninth from the left end in second last step?
(a) Table (b) 72
(c) typhoon (d) 91
(e) tablet

15. If the step IV, '72' interchange its position with 'table' and 'typhoon' also interchanges its position with '91' then which element will be to the immediate right of '91'?
(a) 63 (b) to
(c) 52 (d) typhoon
(e) 72

DIRECTIONS (Qs. 16-20): Study the given information carefully and answer the given questions.

An input-output is given in different steps. Some mathematical operations are done in each step. No mathematical operation is repeated in next step but it can be repeated with some other mathematical operation (as multiplication can be used with subtraction in step 1 and same can be used with addition in step 2)

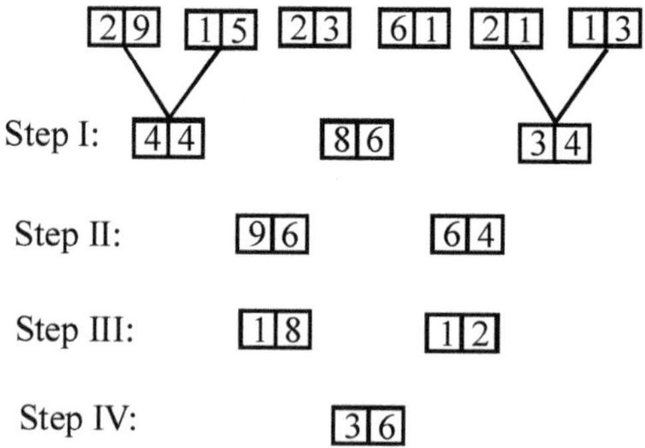

As per the rules followed in the steps given above, find out in each of the following questions the appropriate step for the given input.

12 41 17 19 23 11

16. Find the addition of the three numbers obtained in step I?
(a) 123 (b) 124
(c) 125 (d) 126
(e) None of these

17. Find the multiplication of two numbers obtained in Step III?
(a) 600 (b) 500
(c) 550 (d) 575
(e) None of these

18. Find the difference between the two numbers obtained in Step II?
(a) 28 (b) 17
(c) 37 (d) 27
(e) None of these

19. Find the square of number which is obtained in Step IV?
(a) 729 (b) 676
(c) 525 (d) 625
(e) 1000

20. If digit is exchanged within the each block then find the multiplication of two new numbers obtained in step II?
(a) 1525 (b) 1456
(c) 1460 (d) 1458
(e) None of these

HINTS & SOLUTIONS

1. **(d)** **Step I** feast Together over series on the so
Step II feast on Together over series the so
Step III feast on over Together series the so
Step IV feast on over series Together the so
Step V feast on over series so Together the
Step VI feast on over series so the Together

2. **(d)** Using the above rule, we observe that 'are and every for peer to' will be the III and last step for the given input.

3. **(d)** For the given step we cannot definitely find out the input because the position of the words in input cannot be determined.

4. **(c)** **Step I** are over Go for through at
Step II are at over Go for through
Step III are at for over Go through
Step IV are at for Go over through

5. **(b)** The step IV for the given input will be 'around at for He story on was'.

Sol. (6-10) : After careful analysis of the given input and various steps of re-arrangement it is evident that in each step one word and one number are rearranged.
The word are rearranged from left in alphabetical order and the numbers are rearranged from the right in descending order but in the final step the word get rearranged in alphabetical order in reserves manner and number appear in descending order.

Input : 31 rise gem 15 92 47 aim big 25 does 56 not 85 63 with moon
Step I: aim 31 rise gem 15 47 big 25 does 56 not 85 63 with moon 92

Step II: big aim 31 rise gem 15 47 25 does 56 not 63 with moon 92 85

Step III: does big aim 31 rise gem 15 47 25 56 not with moon 92 85 63

Step IV: gem does big aim 31 rise 15 47 25 not with moon 92 85 63 56

Step V: moon gem does big aim 31 rise 15 25 not with 92 85 63 56 47

Step VI: not moon gem does big aim rise 15 25 with 92 85 63 56 47 31

Step VII: rise not moon gem does big aim 15 with 92 85 63 56 47 31 25

Step VIII: with rise not moon gem does big aim 92 85 63 56 47 31 25 15

6. **(a)** **7.** **(d)** **8.** **(b)**
9. **(c)** **10.** **(c)**

Sol. (11-15):

Input: table 63 tour 19 typhoon 72 25 to tea 48 tablet 56

Step I: typhoon table 63 tour 72 25 to tea 48 tablet 56 91

Step II: tablet typhoon tablet 63 tour 72 to tea 48 56 91 52

Step III: table tablet typhoon 63 tour 72 to tea 56 91 52 84

Step IV: tour table tablet typhoon 63 72 to tea 91 52 84 65

Step V: tea tour table tablet typhoon 72 to 91 52 84 65 36

Step VI: to tea tour table tablet typhoon 91 52 84 65 36 27

11. **(a)** **12.** **(d)** **13.** **(a)**
14. **(c)** **15.** **(a)**

Sol: (16-20):

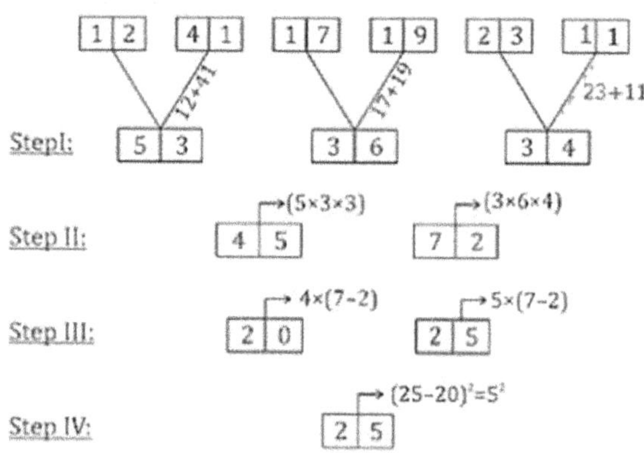

16. **(a)** Addition of number in Step I is = 34 + 36 + 53 = 123

17. **(b)** Multiplication of number in Step III- 25×20 = 500

18. **(d)** Difference between the number obtained in Step II- 72 – 45 = 27

19. **(d)** Number obtained in Step IV is 25
Square of 25 is 625

20. **(d)** Numbers obtained in Step II – 45, 72
If digits are exchanged then new numbers are 54, 27
Multiplication of new number = 54 × 27 = 1458

Syllogism

INTRODUCTION

Syllogism is a Greek word that does mean 'inference' or 'deduction'. The problems of syllogism are based on two parts :

1. Proposition / Propositions
2. Conclusion / Conclusions drawn from given proposition/ propositions

PROPOSITION

Just consider the sentences given below:

(i) 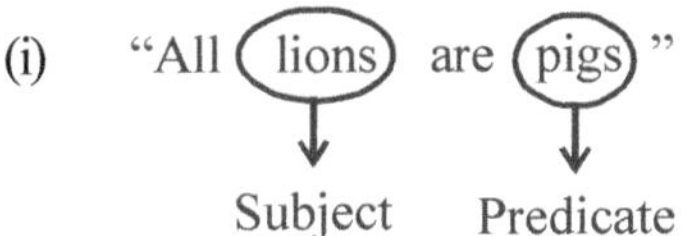

(ii) 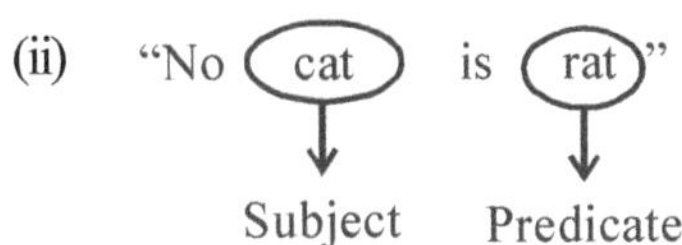

(iii) 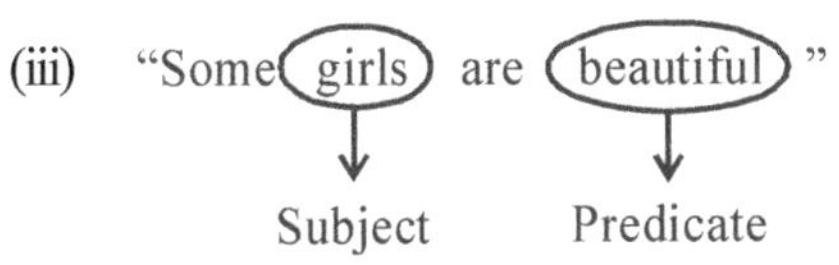

(iv) 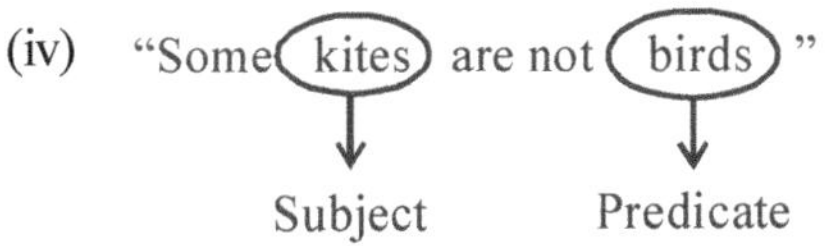

All the sentences mentioned above are proposition which give a relation between subject and predicate. Here, it is clear from the sentences that a subject is the part of a sentence something is said about, while a predicate is the term in a sentence which is related to the subject.

Now, let us define the proposition :

A proposition is a sentence that makes a statement giving a relation between two terms. It has three parts :

(a) The subject
(b) The predicate
(c) The relation between subject and predicate

CATEGORICAL PROPOSITION

Let us see the sentences given below :

"All M are P"
"No M are P"
"Some M are P"
"Some M are not P"

What we notice in all above-mentioned sentences that they are **condition free**. These type of sentences are called **Categorical Propositions**. In other words a categorical proposition has no condition attached with it and it makes direct assertion. It is different from non-categorical proposition which is in the format

"If M then P"

TYPES OF CATEGORICAL PROPOSITION:

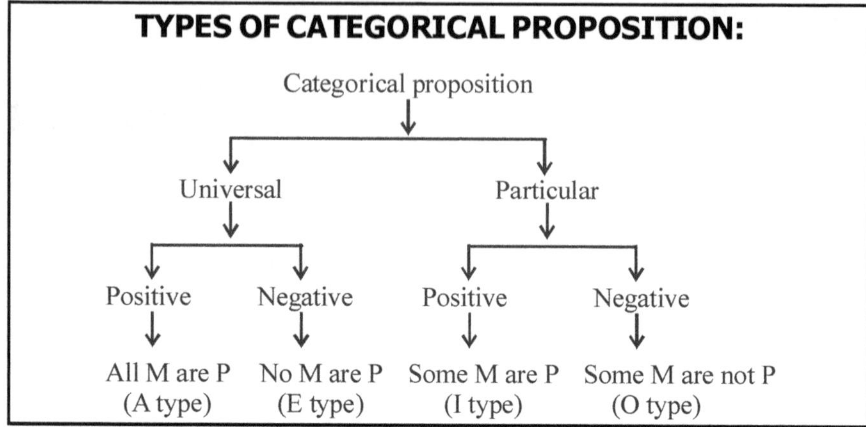

Therefore, it is clear, that universal propositions either completely include the subject (A type) or completely exclude it (E type). On the other hand, particular propositions either only partly include the subject (I type) or only partly exclude the subject (O type).

Now, we can summarise the four types of propositions to be used while solving the problems of syllogism :

Format	Type
All M are P	A
No M are P	E
Some M are P	I
Some M are not P	O

❑ *Shortcut Approach*

All M are P (A type):

No M are P (E type):

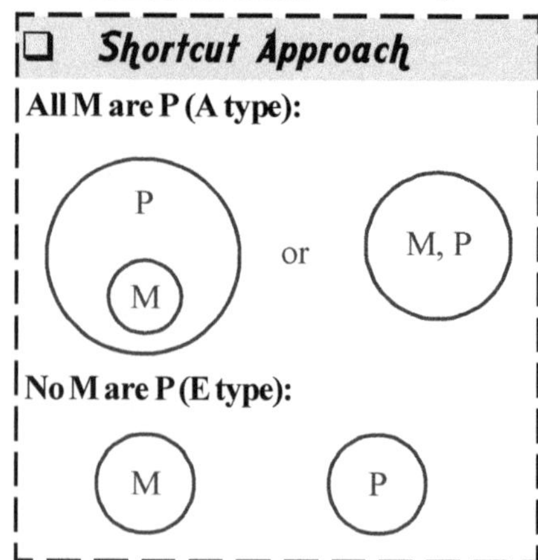

Some M are P (I type):

Some M are not P (O type):

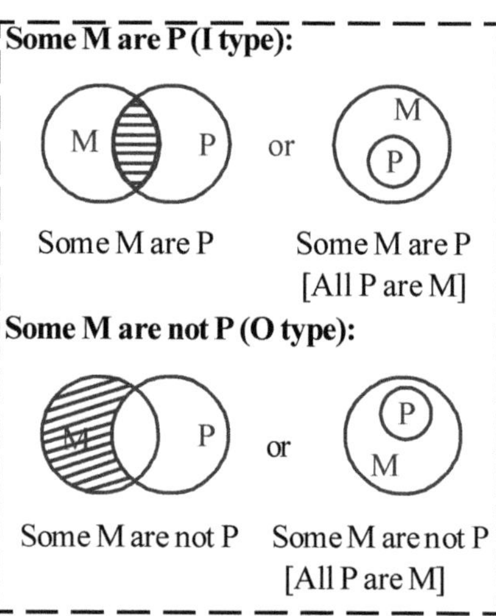

HIDDEN PROPOSITIONS

(A) A type:

Apart from 'all' it starts with every, each and any.

EXAMPLE

Every girl is beautiful.
[All girls are beautiful.]

(i) A positive sentence with a particular person as its subject is A type.

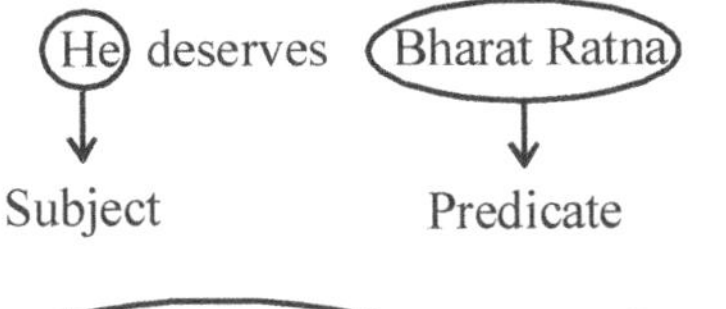

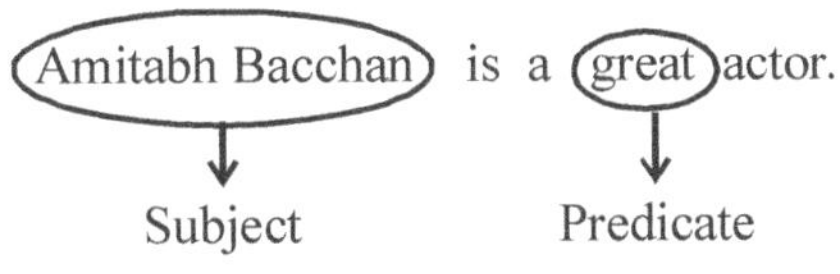

(ii) A sentence in with a definite exception is A type :

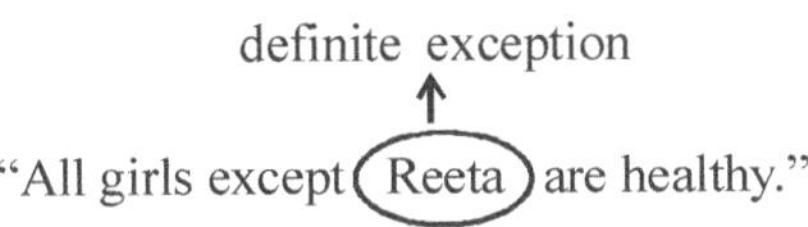

(B) E type:

Apart from 'no' this type of propositions starts from 'no one', 'none', 'not a single' etc.

EXAMPLE

No one (student) is studious.
[No student is studious]

(i) A negative sentence with a particular person as its subject is E type propoistion.

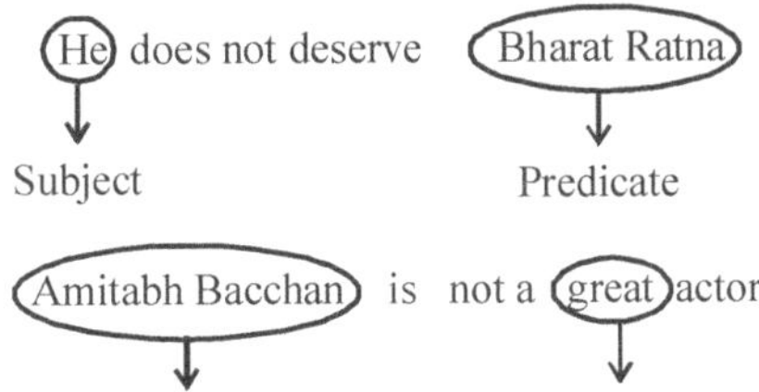

(ii) Sentences in following formats are E type :

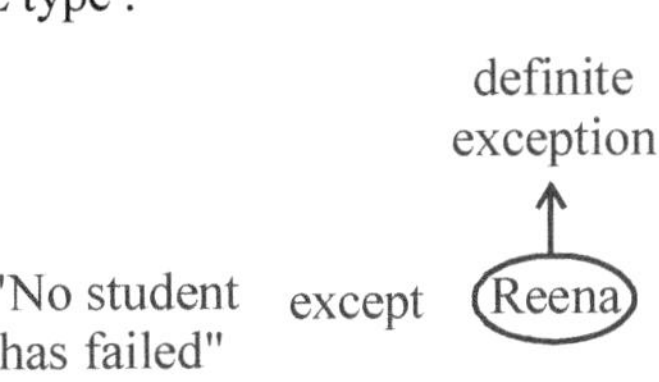

"Is there any truth left in the world"
[No truth is left in the world.]

(C) I type:

Apart from some it also starts with words such as often, frequently, almost, generally, mostly, a few, most etc.

EXAMPLE

(i) Almost all the girls are beautiful.
[Some girls are beautiful].

(ii) Most of the garments are handmade.
[Some of the garments are handmade].

It is clear from the above examples that negative sentences begining with words like 'few', 'rarely', 'seldom', etc. (Also 'hardly', 'scarcely', 'little' etc.) are to be reduced to I type.

Just see the other formates given below

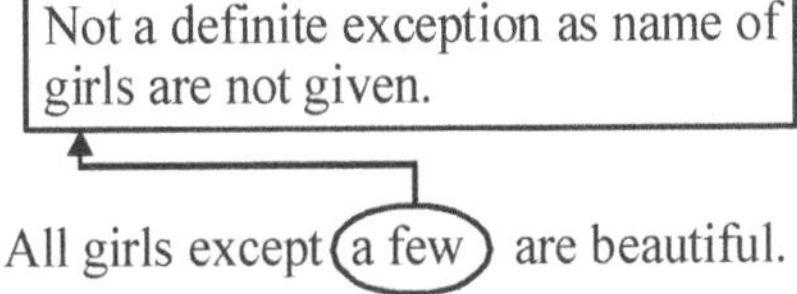

[Some girls are beautiful]

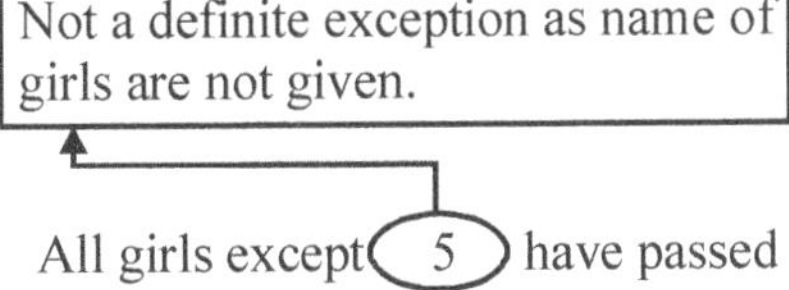

[Some girls have passed]

Therefore, a positive proposition with an indefinite exception is reduced to I type.

(D) O type :

Apart from "Some .... not' this type of statements start with words like 'all', 'every', 'any', 'each', etc.

EXAMPLE

(i) All girls are not beautiful.
[Some girls are not beautiful]

(ii) Poor are usually not healthy.
[Some poor are not healthy]

Now, it is clear from the above mentioned examples that negative propositions with words such as 'almost', 'frequently', 'most', 'mostly', 'a few', generally, etc. are to be reduced to the O–type propositions.

Again, positive propositions starting with words like 'few', 'scarcely', 'rarely', 'little', 'seldom' etc. are said to be O–type.

EXAMPLE

Seldom are women jealous.
[Some women are not jealous]

Also, see the following formates :

No definite exception as name of girls are not given.

No girls except (three) are beautiful.

[Some girls are not beautiful.]

No definite exception as name of women are not given.

No women except (a few) are housewife.

Therefore, a negative proposition with an indefinite exception, is reduced to O type.

EXCLUSIVE PROPOSITIONS

Such propositions start with 'only', 'alone', 'none else but', 'none but' etc. and they can be reduced to either A or E or I format.

EXAMPLE

Only graduates are Probationary Officers.

⇒ No graduate is Probationary Officer (E type)

⇒ All Probationary Officers are graduates. (A type)

⇒ Some graduates are Probationary Officers (I type)

General format of sentences given in the examinations :

All M are P	(A type)
No M are P	(E type)
Some M are P	(I type)
Some M are not P	(O type)

Note : General format given above are frequently asked formats in the examinations. But students must be ready for other hidden formates of A, E, I and O types of propositions as problems in hidden formates can also be given in question papers.

CONVERSION OF PROPOSITIONS

Before solving the problems of syllogism it is must to know the conversion rules of all A, E, O, and I types of propositions :

(i) Conversion of A type:

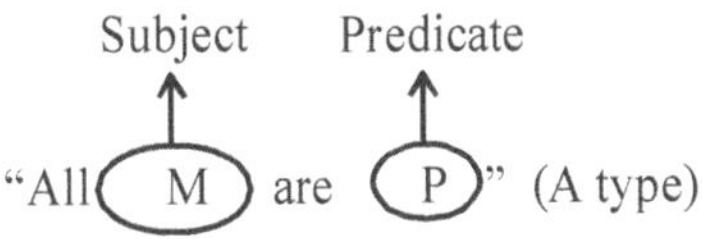

After conversion it becomes.

Subject Predicate

"Some P are M" (I type)

Therefore, it is clear that A type of propositions get converted into I type.

(ii) Conversion of E type :

Subject Predicate

"No M are P "(E type)

After conversion it becomes

Subject Predicate

"No P are M" (E type)

Therefore, E gets converted into E.

(iii) Conversion of I type :

Subject Predicate

"Some M are P " (I type)

After conversion it becomes

Subject Predicate

"Some P are M " (I type)

Therefore, I gets converted into I.

(iv) Conversion of O type:

O type of proposition can't be converted.

Note : In each conversion, subject becomes predicate and predicate becomes subject.
In fact, conversion is an immediate inference that is drawn from a single proposition while inference drawn from two propositions are called mediate inference.

❑ *Shortcut Approach*

Table of conversion :

Type of proposition	Get converted into
A	I
E	E
I	I
O	Never get converted

Rule to draw conclusion :

After knowing conversion of propositions, we must learn the rules to draw conclusions. In problems of syllogism, conclusions are drawn either from single propositions or from two proposition or from both. But a conclusion from single proposition is just a conversion of that proposition while to get conclusion from two propositions a certain table is used that tells us what type of conclusion (in form of proposition) we get out of two propositions. To understand it, let us see the following conclusion table :

Conclusion Table		
I - Proposition	**II - Proposition**	**Conclusion**
A	A	A
A	E	E
E	A	$(O)^R$
E	I	$(O)^R$
I	A	I
I	E	O

Note :

(a) Apart from above 6 pairs of propositions, no other pair will give any conclusion.

(b) The conclusion drawn out of two propositions is itself a proposition and its subject is the subject of the Ist statement while its predicate is the predicate of the 2nd statement. The common term get disappeared.

(c) $(O)^R$ does mean that the conclusion is O type but is in reverse order. In this case, the subject of the inference or conclusion is the predicate of the 2nd proposition and the predicate of the conclusion is the subject of the Ist sentence or statement.

(d) The conclusion table gives correct conclusions or inference if and only if the two propositions are aligned properly.

WHAT IS ALIGNING ?

Let us see the following examples :

EXAMPLE

Statements :

I. All (girls) are beautiful.

II. Some (girls) are Indian.

EXAMPLE

Statements :

I. No (pen) is chair.

II. Some tables are (pen).

EXAMPLE

Statements :

I. Some women are (men).

II. No (men) is chair.

In all the above mentioned example, we notice that in two statements of every example, there is a common term. In example 1 the word 'girl' is common; in example 2 the word 'pen' is common while in example 3 the word 'men' is common.

Now, the aligning of the two statements (propositions) does mean that the pair of statements must be written in such a way that the common term is the predicate of the 1st sentence and the subject of the 2nd.

Just think over the following examples :

Statements :

I. Some girls are (cute).

II. All (cute) are tall.

Here, the common term cute is the predicate of the I statement and subject of the 2nd statement. Therefore, the two statements (I & II) are properly aligned. But see another example.

Statements :

I. Some (bats) are chairs.

II. Some cats are (bats).

Here, the sentences are not aligned as the predicate of the 1st statement is not the subject of the 2nd.

Then how to align it ? In such type of cases we change the order of sentences. In another words we put I sentence in place of II and II in place of I :

II. Some cats are (bats).

I. Some (bats) are chairs.

Therefore, as per the requirement and nature of the sentence the alignment is done.

(i) only by changing the order of sentences.

or

(ii) only by converting the sentences.

or

(iii) By changing the order of the statements and then converting one of the sentences.

IEA Rule

Alignment must be done in IEA order. It does mean that if the two statements are I & E then the conversion must be done for I and for E & I it will be done for E.

After discussing all the minute things about this chapter, now we have come at the position of solving the problems of syllogism.

METHODS:
(1) By Analytical Method
(2) By Venn Diagram

(1) **Analytical method :**

This method has two main steps:

(a) Aligning the pair of sentences.

(b) Using conclusion table to draw conclusion.

EXAMPLE **Statements :**

I. All rats are cats.

II. All rats are men.

When aligned it takes the form as

I. Some cats are (rats) [I type]

II. All (rats) are men [A type]

Now we use the conclusion table given in this chapter that says

I + A = I type of conclusion.

Therefore, the drawn conclusion must be

"Some cats are men"

It is clear that the conclusion drawn "Some cats are men" is a mediate inference as it is the result of two propositions. But in actual problem immediate inferences are also given in conclusion part and that format is given below :

EXAMPLE **: Statements:**

I. All rats are cats.

II. All rats are men.

Conclusion:

(i) Some cats are men.

(ii) Some men are cats.

(iii) Some rats are cats.

(iv) Some cats are rats.

(v) Some rats are men.

(vi) Some men are rats.

Here, all the options are correct. **conclusion** (i) follows because it is the mediate inference of statements I & II.

Conclusion (ii) is the conversion of conclusion (i), conclusion (iii) is the immediate inference (conversion) of statement I while conclusion (iv) is the conversion of conclusion (iii).

Conclusion (v) is the immediate inference (conversion) of statement II while conclusion (vi) is the conversion of conclusion (v).

Further, in some problems complementary pairs are also seen in the conclusion part in the forms of sentence given below:

(a) (i) Some cats are rats.
(ii) Some cats are not rats] I-O pair

(b) (i) All cats are rats.
(ii) Some cats are not rats.] A-O pair

(c) (i) Some cats are rats.
(ii) No cats are rats.] I-E pair

Apart from I - O, A - O and I - E pair, the two sentences must have some subject and predicates as are the above mentioned pairs. For these pairs we write the form 'Either (i) or (ii) follows.

METHOD TO SOLVE

(a) First step is aligning the sentences.
(b) Second step is using conclusion table.
(c) Third step is checking immediate inferences.
(d) Fourth step is checking through the conversion of immediate inferences & mediate inferences.
(e) First step is checking the complementary pairs.

(2) **Venn diagram method for solving problems :**

Students will have to adopt three steps to solve the syllogism problems through Venn diagram method :

METHOD TO SOLVE

(a) 1st step is sketching all possible pictorial representation for the statements separately.
(b) 2nd step is combining possible pairs of these representations of all the statements into one.
(c) 3rd and final step is making interpretation of this combined figure.
Conclusions are true if they are supported by all the combined figures in 2nd step.

EXAMPLE

Statements :

A. All chairs are books.
B. All books are ties.

Conclusions :

I. Some ties are books.
II. Some ties are chairs.

1st Step :

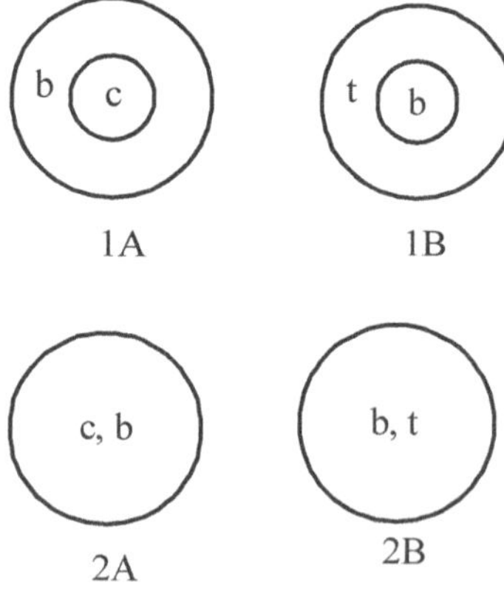

Here, 1A and 2A are representations for statement A while 1B and 2B are representations for statement B. In these representations

b = books
c = chairs
t = ties

2nd step :

Let us combine all the possible pairs of this pictorial representations :

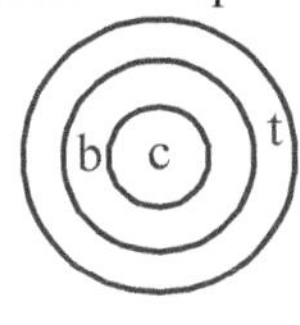

(1A + 1B)

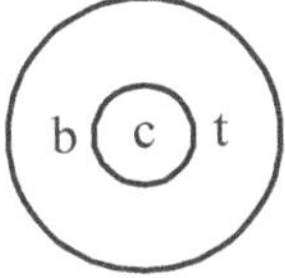

(1A + 2B)

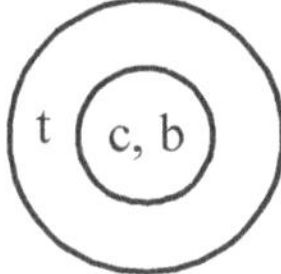

(2A + 1B)

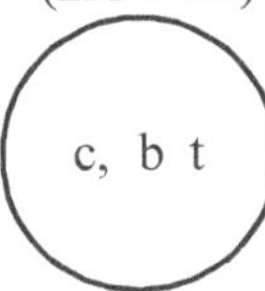

(2A + 2B)

3rd step :

When we interpret the pictures in step II, we find that all the pictures support both the conclusions. Therefore, conclusion I :
"Some ties are books" and
conclusion II.
"Some ties are chairs"
both are true.

> ***Note :*** *In the Venn diagram method, any conclusion given with any problem will be true if and only if it is supported by all the combined pictorial representations through 2nd step. If any pictorial representation contradicts the given conclusion, it will be put in the category of incorrect or wrong conclusion.*

POSSIBILITY

Generally, the meaning of possibility is probability, *viz*. possibility exists where nothing is certain between the objects. Let's understand below table in which possibility exists where no definite relation occurs between the objects and definite or proper relation between the objects eliminate existance of any possibility. In simple way given condition eliminates the possibility and improper condition favours the possibility. Here, we can go through with an example which will also clear the term possibility.

Condition	Possibility
Given facts	cannot be determined
Imaginary facts	can be determined

EXAMPLE

Statements Some boxes are trees
Some trees are hens.

Conclusions

I. Some boxes being hens is a possibility

II. All trees being hens is a possibility

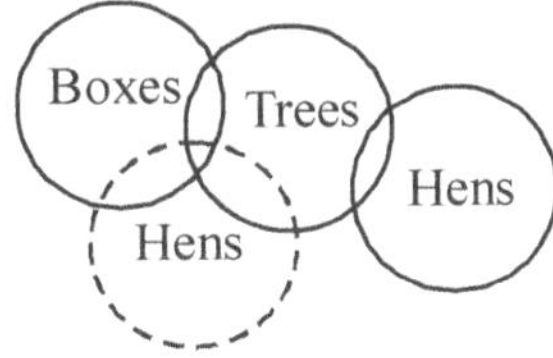

In Conclusion I, before deciding the possibility between boxes and hens, we must notice the relation between both, we find that there is no relation between boxes and hens, so possibility exists and the conclusion I is true for possibility. Now in conclusion II we must notice the relation between trees and hens. We find that both have some type of relation between them so the possibility of 'All between trees and hens is true. Hence, both the Conclusions I and II follow.

❑ Shortcut Approach

Given Exclusive Proposition	Desired Proposition	Possibility
All	All	×
Some	Some	×
No	No	×
No	Some not	×
Some	All	✓
No proper relation	Some / All	✓

SPECIAL CASES OF EXCLUSIVE PROPOSITION

If the statement is of	Conversion	Illustration	Meaningful Conversion
Much, more, many, very, a few, most, almost	Some	Most A are B. A few X are Y.	Some A and B. Some X or Y.
Atleast	Some	Atleast some A are B.	Some A and B.
Definitely	No use	Some A are definitely B. Some X are definitely not Y.	Some A are B. Some X are not Y.
Only		Only A are B.	All B are A.
1% to 99%	Some	38% A are B. 98% X are Y.	Some A are B. Some X are Y.

PRACTICE EXERCISE

DIRECTIONS (Qs. 1-3): *In each of the following questions two/three statements are given and these statements are followed by two/three/four conclusions. You have to take the given statements to be true even if they seem to be at variance from commonly known facts. Read the conclusions and then decide which of the given conclusion logically follows from the two given statements, disregarding commonly known facts.*

1. Statements :

All petals are flowers.
Some flowers are buds.
Some buds are leaves.
All leaves are plants.

Conclusions:

I. Some petals are not buds.
II. Some flowers are plants.
III. No flower is plant.

(a) Only I follows
(b) Either II or III follows
(c) I and II follow
(d) Only III follows
(e) None of the above

2. Statements:

Some apartments are flats.
Some flats are buildings.
All buildings are bungalows.
All bungalows are gardens.

Conclusions:

I. All apartments being building is a possibility.
II. All bungalows are not buildings
III. No flat is garden.

(a) None follows
(b) Only I follows
(c) Either I or III follows
(d) II and III follow
(e) Only II follows

3. Statements:

All chairs are tables.
All tables are bottles.
Some bottles are jars.
No jar is bucket.

Conclusions :

I. Some tables being jar is a possibility.
II. Some bottles are chairs.
III. Some bottles are not bucket.

(a) Only I follows
(b) I and II follow
(c) All follow
(d) Only II follows
(e) None of these

DIRECTIONS (Qs. 4-5) : *In each questions below are given three statements followed by three Conclusions I, II and III. You have to take the given statements to be true even if they seem to be at variance from commonly known facts. Read all the conclusions and then decide which of the given conclusion logically follows from the given statements disregarding commonly known facts.*

4. Statements:

Some nurses are doctors.
All doctors are medicines.
Some medicines tablets.

Conclusions:

I. Atleast some tablets are doctors.
II. Some medicine being doctors is a possibility.
III. Some medicine are definitely nurses.

(a) All follow
(b) II and III follow
(c) Only II follow
(d) Either III or Iv follows
(e) None of these

5. **Statements:**
All files are folders.
All folders are boxes.
All boxes are drawers.
Conclusions:
I. All folders being drawers is a possibility.
II. All boxes are files.
III. All files are definitely drawers.
IV. Atleast some drawers are folders.
(a) I and II follow
(b) III and IV follow
(c) II and III follow
(d) All follows
(e) None of these

DIRECTIONS (Qs. 6-7): *In each of the questions below are the two conclusions followed by four statements numbered a, b, c & d , you have to take the given statements to be true even if they seem to be at variance from commonly known facts. Read the answers and then decide which of the given statements definitely follows from the given conclusions*

6. **Conclusion:** Some boy is good. Some good is milk.
Statements:
(a) Some boy is book. All book is good. Some good is text. Some text is milk.
(b) All boy is good. Some good is text. All text is book. Some book is milk.
(c) All boy is text. All text is good. Some good is book. All book is milk.
(d) All book is boy. Some boy is text. Some text is good. All good is milk.
(e) None of these

7. **Conclusion:** No play is field. Some field is green.
Statements:
(a) Some play is green. Some green is field. All field is blue. Some blue is virus.
(b) Some play is green. No green is field. Some field is blue. All blue is virus.
(c) None of these
(d) All play is virus. No virus is field. Some field is blue. All blue is green.
(e) All play is green. No green is field. Some field is virus. All virus is blue.

DIRECTIONS (Qs. 8-9): *Question consists of five statements followed by five conclusions. Consider the given statements to be true even if they seem to be at variance with commonly known facts. Read all the conclusions and then decide which of the given conclusions does not logically follow from the given statements using all statements together.*

8. **Statements:** All violet is orange. Some orange is time. Some time is women. No women are boy. Some boy is apple.
Conclusions:
(a) All violet being women is a possibility.
(b) Some time is not boy.
(c) Some violet is women.
(d) All women being orange is a possibility.
(e) All time being violet is a possibility.

9. **Statements:** All wild are the animal. Some animal is the forest. No forest is fire. Some fire is end. No end is a life.

Conclusions:

(a) All animal being life is a possibility.

(b) All wild being the forest is a possibility.

(c) All forest being life is a possibility.

(d) All end being forest is a possibility.

(e) All forest being end is a possibility.

DIRECTION (Q. 10): *Each of the following question consists of six statements followed by options consisting of three statements put together in a specific order. Choose the options that indicates a combination where the third statement can be logically deduced from the first two statements and that option will be your answer.*

---

10. i. Some X is Y.

ii. All Y is Z.

iii. No Z is W

iv. Some W are Y

v. All Y are T.

vi. Some T are X.

(a) [ii, iii, iv]

(b) [vi, i, v]

(c) [iv, ii, iii]

(d) [iv, iii, ii]

(e) None is correct

HINTS & SOLUTIONS

1. **(b)** According to question,

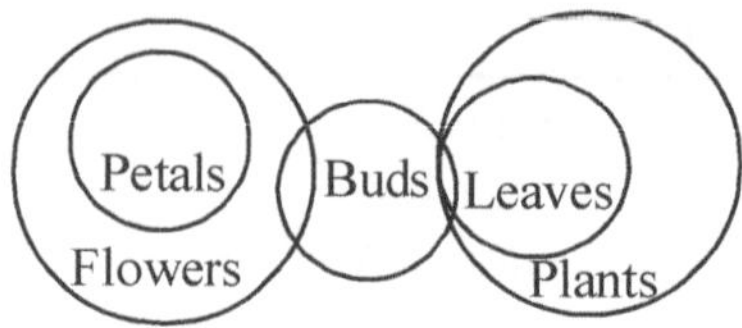

or

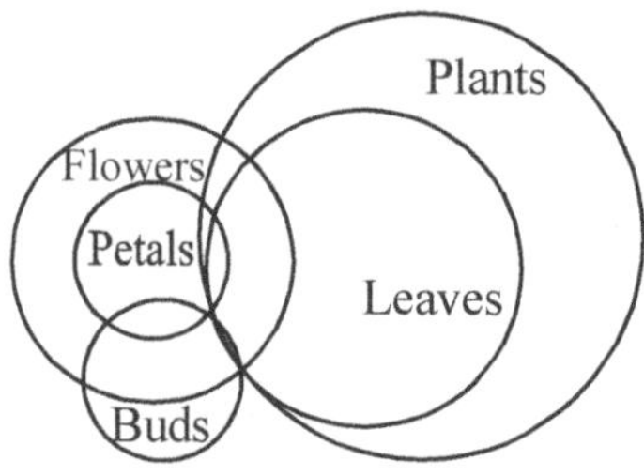

Conclusions:I. False
Conclusions:II.False ⌉ or
Conclusions:III.False ⌋
Hence, only either II or III follows.

2. **(b)** According to question,

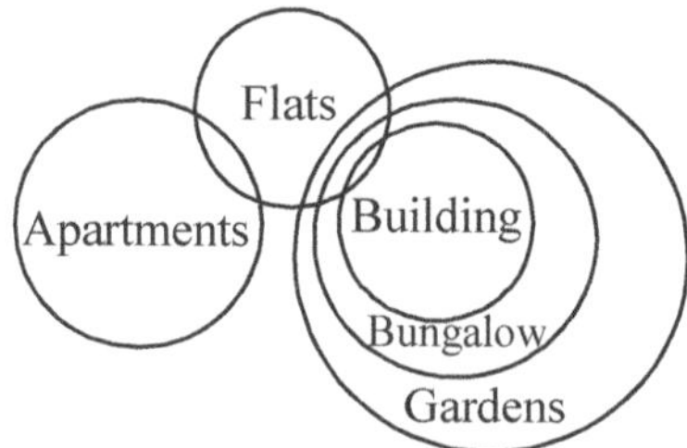

Or

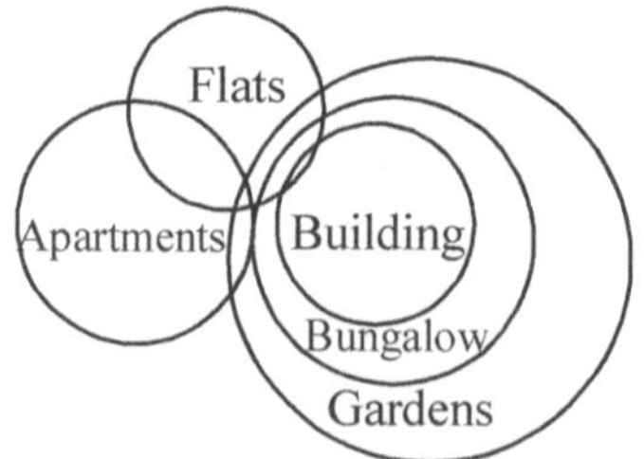

Conclusions:I. True
Conclusions:II.False
Conclusions:III.False
Hence, only conclusion I follows.

3. **(c)** According to question,

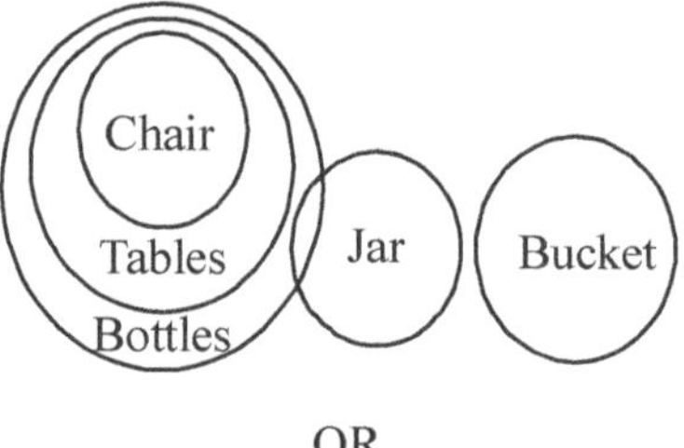

OR

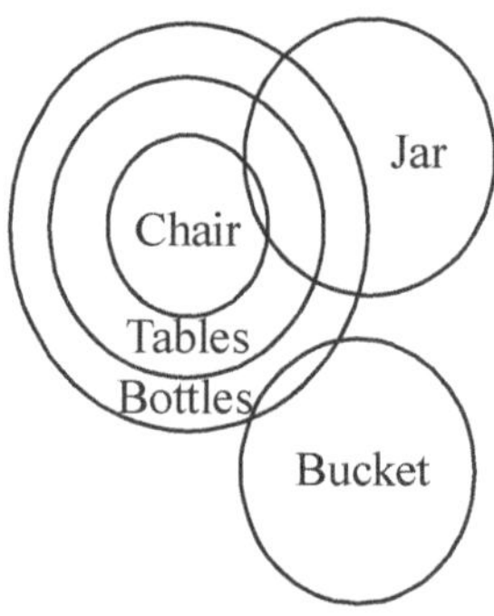

Conclusions:I.True
Conclusions:II.True
Conclusions:III.True
Hence, All I, II and III follow.

4. **(e)** According to given information

Hence, only Conclusions III follows.

5. **(b)** According to given information,

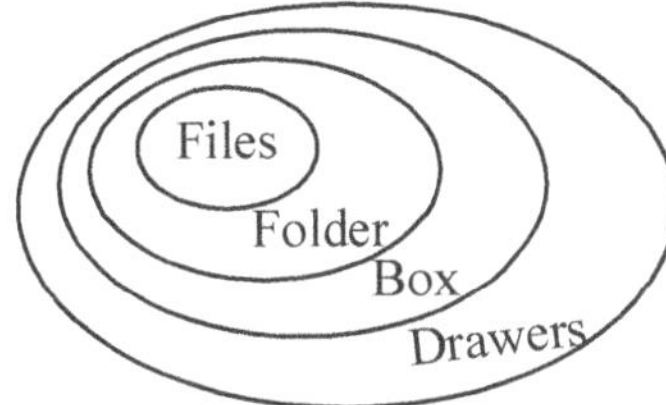

Hence, Conclusions III and IV follow.

6. **(c)**

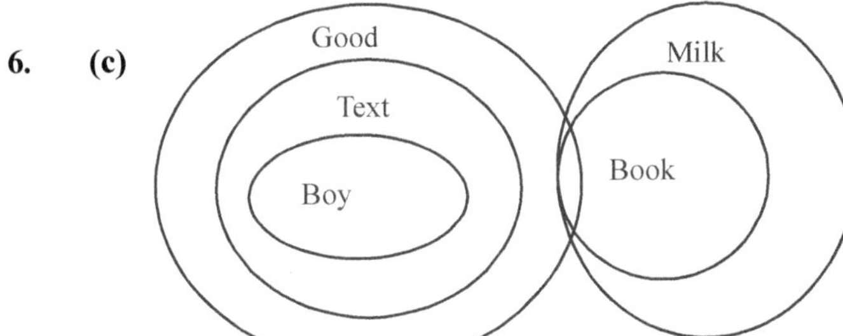

7. **(d)**

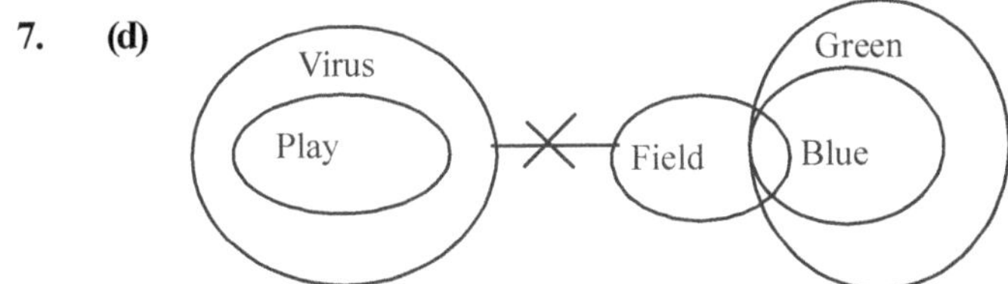

8. **(c)**

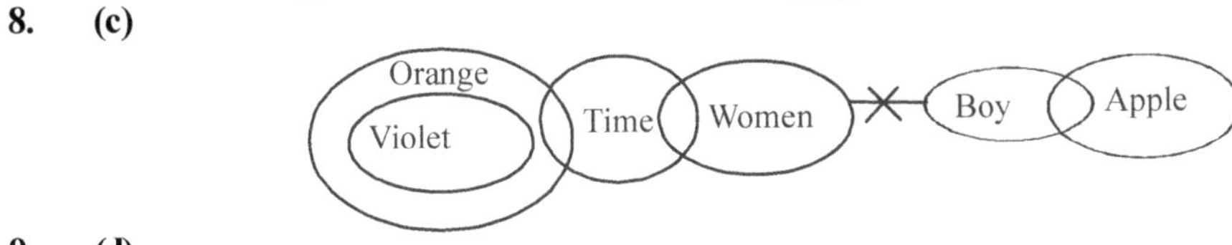

9. **(d)**

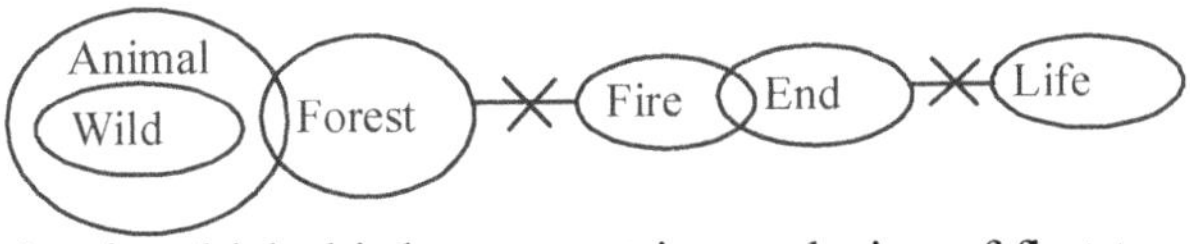

10. **(e)** There is no option in which third statement is conclusion of first two statements.

Chapter 16

Cube & Dice

CUBE

Introduction

A cube is three dimensional object whose length, breadth and height are equal and any two adjacent faces are inclined to each other at 90°. It has 6 faces, 8 corners and 12 edges.

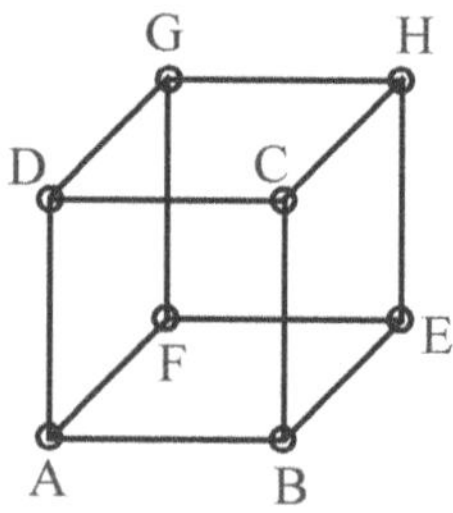

- Corners of the cube are A, B, C, D, E, F, G and H.
- Edges of the cube are AB, BE, EF, AF, AD, CD, BC, EH, CH, GH, DG and FG.

Faces of the cube are ABCD, EFGH, CDGH, BCHE, ABEF and ADFG.

When a cube is painted on all of its faces with any colour and further divided into various smaller cubes of equal size, we get following results :

(i) Smaller cubes with no face painted will present inside faces of the undivided cube.

(ii) Smaller cubes with one face painted will present on the faces (except edges) of the undivided cube.

(iii) Smaller cubes with two faces painted will present on the edges (except corner) of undivided cube.

(iv) Smaller cubes with three faces painted will present on the corners of the undivided cube.

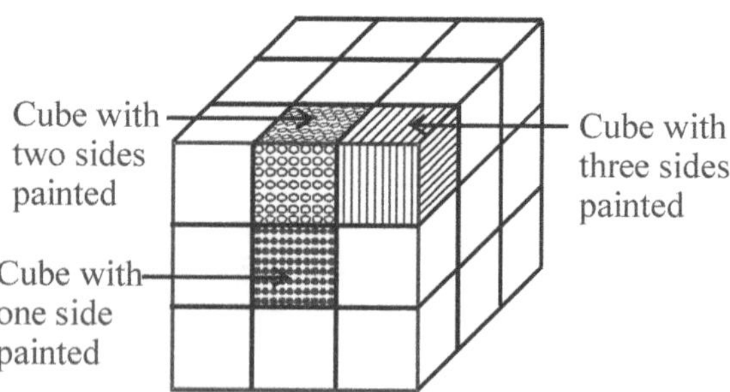

The above figure may be analysed by dividing it into three horizontal layers :

Layer I or top layer :

The central cube has only one face coloured, four cubes at the corner have three faces coloured and the remaining 4 cubes have two faces coloured.

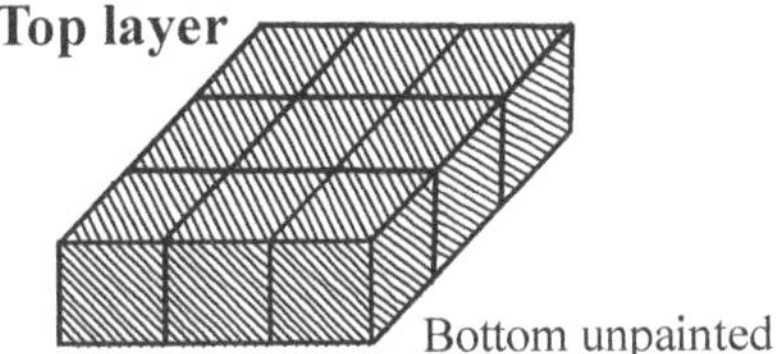

Layer II or middle layer :

The central cube has no face coloured, the four cubes at the corner have two faces coloured and the remaining 4 cubes have only one face coloured.

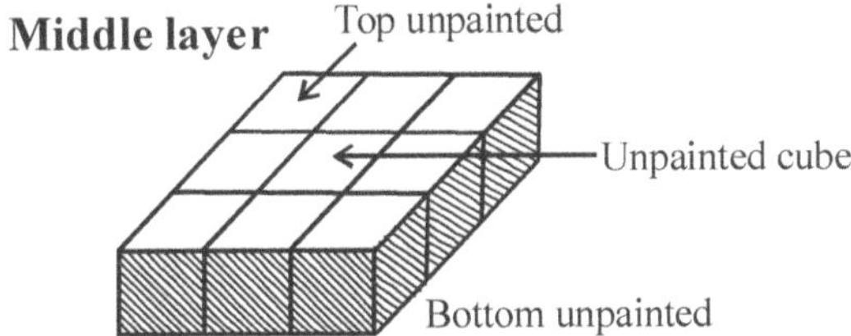

Layer III or bottom layer :

The central cube has only one face coloured, four cubes at the corner have three faces coloured and the remaining 4 cubes have two faces coloured.

Bottom layer

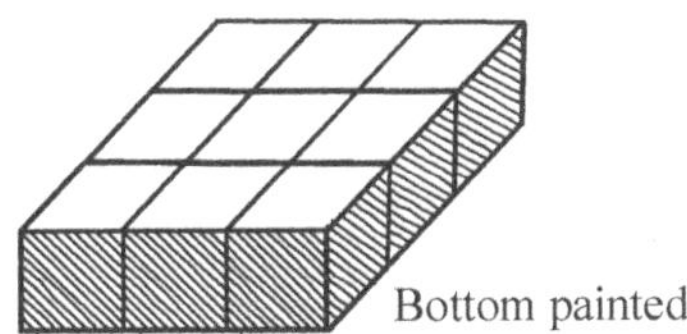

Also, number of divisions on the faces of cube,

$$n = \frac{\text{Length of the edge of undivided cube}}{\text{Length of the edge of one smaller cube}}.$$

❑ Shortcut Approach

- Total number of smaller cubes = $(n)^3$
- Number of smaller cubes with no face painted = $(n-2)^3$
- Number of smaller cubes with one face painted = $(n-2)^3 \times 6$
- Number of smaller cubes with two faces painted = $(n-2) \times 12$
- Number of smaller cubes with three faces painted = 8

EXAMPLE 1. A cube is painted blue on all faces is cut into 125 cubes of equal size. Now, answer the following question :

How many cubes are not painted on any face?

Sol. Since, there are 125 smaller cubes of equal size, therefore,
n = number of divisions on the face of undivided cube = 5.
Number of cubes with no face painted = $(n-2)^3$
$= (5-2)^3 = 27$

DICE

Introduction

A dice is three-dimensional object with 6 surfaces. It may be in the form of a cube or a cuboid.

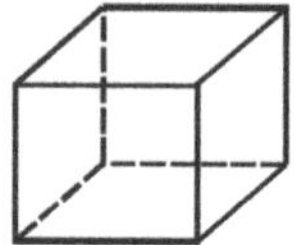

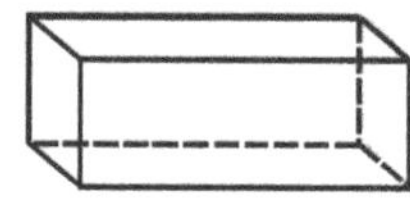

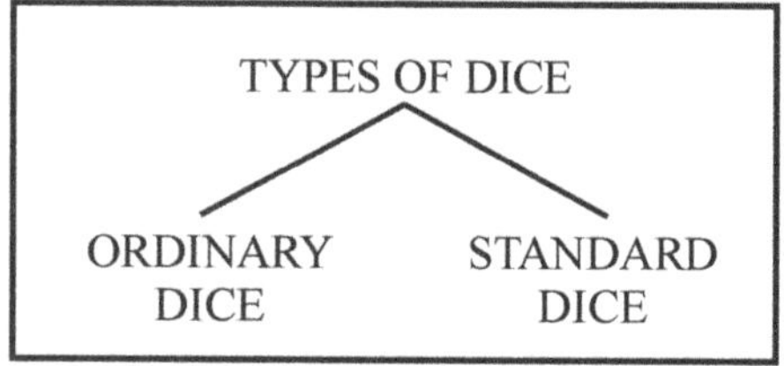

1. Ordinary Dice:

In this type of dice, the sum of numbers on opposite faces is not 7 but the sum of numbers on two adjacent sides are seven.

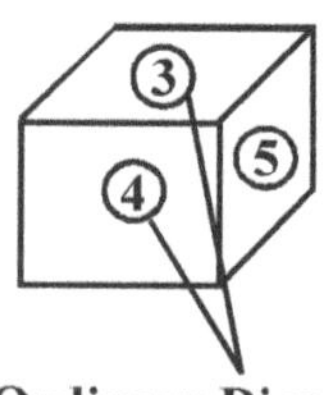

Ordinary Dice

4+3 = 7

2. Standard Dice:

In such type of dice, the sum of numbers on opposite faces is 7 or sum of numbers on adjacent faces is not 7.

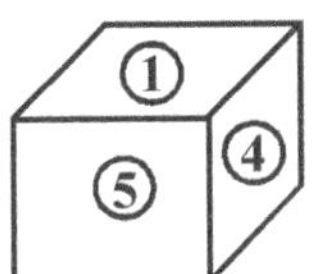

Here,
1+4 =5
4+5=9
1+5=6

Standard Dice

Opposite of 1 ....6 (since 1+6 =7)
Opposite of 5 ....2 (since 5+2 =7)
Opposite of 3 ....4 (since 3+4 =7)

IMPORTANT RULES

When Two Positions of a Single Dice are Given

Case-I: Digits are different in both position as follow.

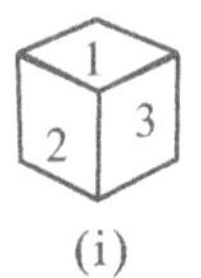

(i) (ii)

In such case any digit in position (i) can be opposite to any of the three digits in position (ii) and vice-versa as given below:

1 Can be opposite to 4, 5 or 6
2 Can be opposite to 4, 5 or 6
3 Can be opposite to 4, 5 or 6
4 Can be opposite to 1, 2 or 3
5 Can be opposite to 1, 2 or 3
6 Can be opposite to 1, 2 or 3

Case II: When one digit is common in both position and at the same face as follows.

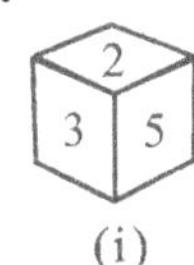

(i) (ii)

In this case, except the common digit, the digits on the other faces are opposite to each other and the face opposite to the common digit will have that digit which is invisible.

Hence,
2 and 1 are opposite
3 and 4 are opposite
5 and 6 are opposite

Case III: When one digit is common in both positions but not at same face as follows

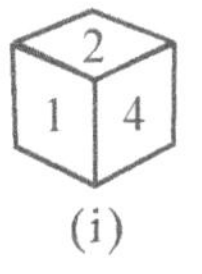

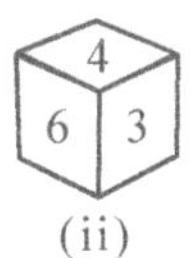

(i) (ii)

In this case list the numbers on both the dices in either clockwise or anti-clockwise starting from common digit, on comparing the numbers obtained from both dices will give you the digit on opposite faces on two position.

In the above figures, number 4 is common in both positions, Now writting the digits in both position in clock-wise starting from 4, we get

4 1 2 [Position (i)]
4 3 6 [Position (ii)]

Thus 1 is opposite to 3
2 is opposite to 6
and 4 is opposite to 5

Note that in this case digit opposite to common digit is the digit which are not seen (invisible) in the two positions.

Case IV: When two digits are common in both the positions as follows.

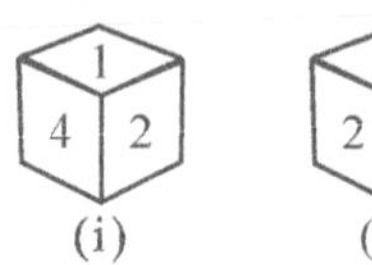

(i) (ii)

In this case,

(i) There is a probability of coming digits on the faces opposite to the faces having common digits are invisible.

(ii) Uncommon digits in each dice are opposite to each other. Hence
3 is opposite to 2 or 4
5 is opposite to 2 or 4
2 is opposite to 3 or 5
4 is opposite to 3 or 5
1 is opposite to 6

UNFOLDED DICE

When a dice is unfolded, then the following four presentation of the unfolded dice can be possible.

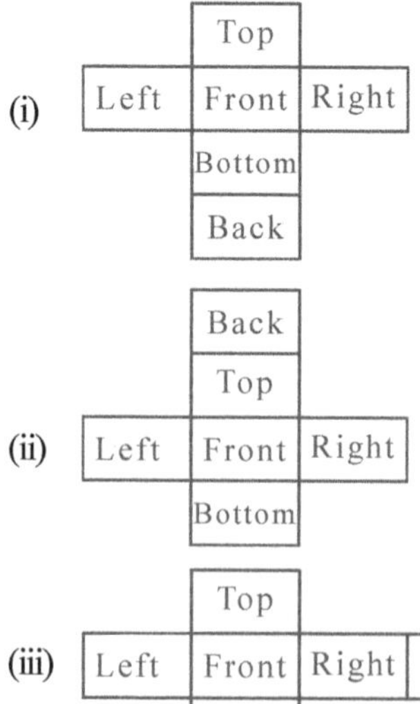

			Top	
(iv)	Back	Left	Front	Right
			Bottom	

Opposite Faces of Unfolded Dice

- Top face and Bottom face are opposite faces
- Left face and Right face are opposite faces
- Front face and Back face are opposite faces

How to Fill Unfolded Faces with Digits ?

When the unfolded faces of any dice is filled up with digit, then any question based on dice can be solved very easily. Two positions of a dice are given below and by the help of these dice, the unfolded faces have been filled up by the digits.

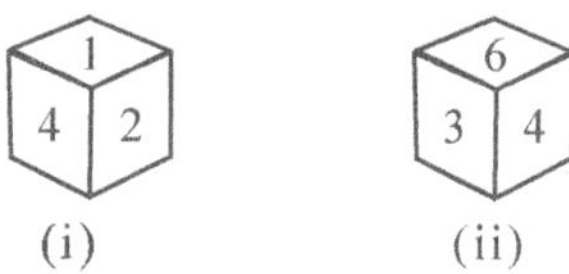

(i) (ii)

Now we will fill faces of the following unfolded dice with digits with the help of the two positions of a dice shown below

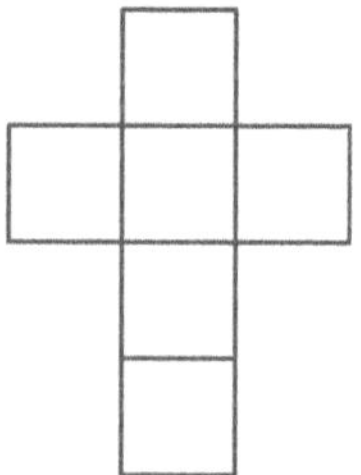

(i) Now, write the common digit (4) at the front face.

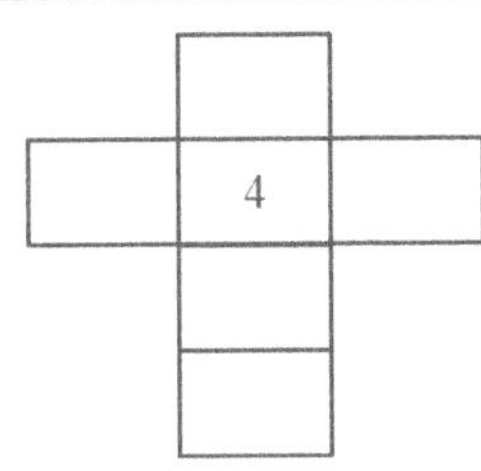

(ii) Now going anti-clockwise direction through the digits from the common digit 4 in position (i). We get 4, 2 and 1 in order. Write 2 and 1 in unfolded dice in anti-clockwise direction as shown in the figure.

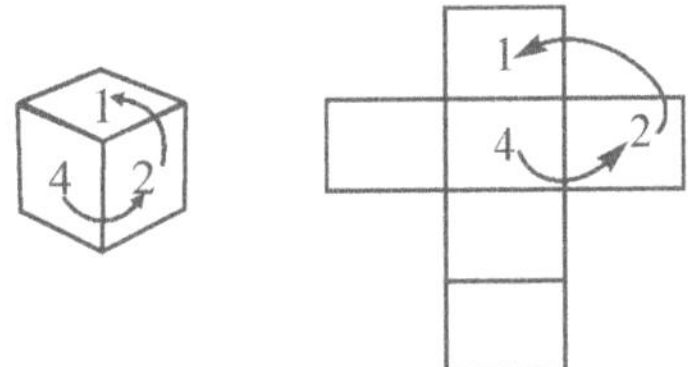

(iii) Now going anti-clockwise direction through the digits from the common digits 4 in position (ii). We get 4, 6 and 3 inorder. Write 6 and 3 in unfolded in anti-clockwise direction as shown in the figure.

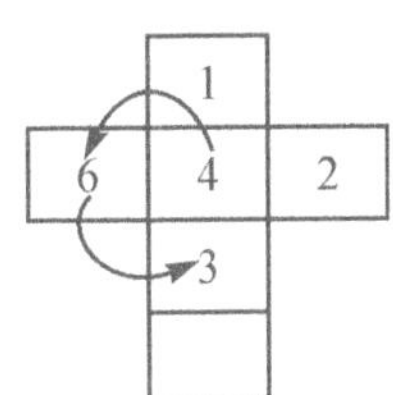

(iv) Fill the remaining blank face with the hidden digit 5

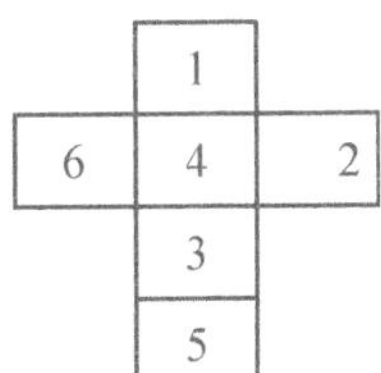

Dice Formation

A Dice is formed by folding a sheet of paper. These forms may be in the following form.

Form 1:

	1	
2	3	4
	5	
	6	

Number 1 is opposite to 5.
Number 2 is opposite to 4.
Number 3 is opposite to 6.

Form 2:

1	2	
	3	
	4	
	5	6

Number 1 is opposite to 6.
Number 2 is opposite to 4.
Number 3 is opposite to 5.

Form 3:

1	
2	
3	4
	5
	6

Number 1 is opposite to 3.
Number 2 is opposite to 5.
Number 4 is opposite to 6.

Form 4:

Number 1 is opposite to 4.
Number 2 is opposite to 6.
Number 3 is opposite to 5.

Form 5:

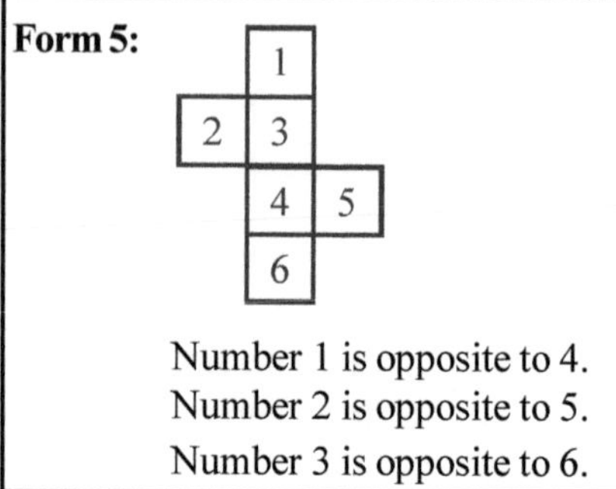

Number 1 is opposite to 4.
Number 2 is opposite to 5.
Number 3 is opposite to 6.

PRACTICE EXERCISE

1. A dice is thrown four times and its four different positions are given below. Find the number on the face opposite the face showing 2.

(a) 4 (b) 5
(c) 6 (d) 3

2. Four different positions of dice are as shown below. What number is opposite to face 3?

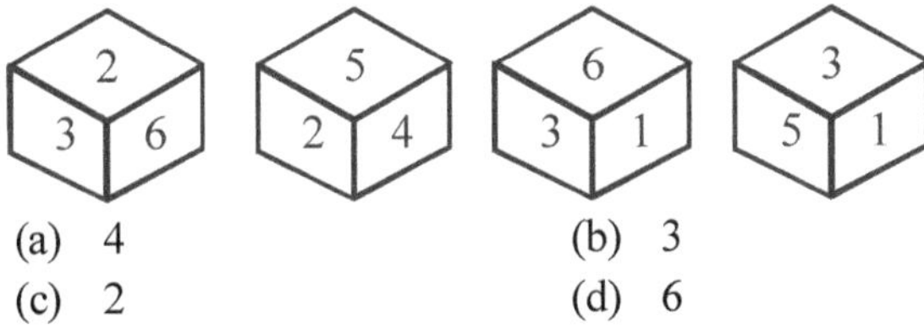

(a) 4 (b) 3
(c) 2 (d) 6

3. Which one of the following box can be created by folding the given key design?

Question Figure :

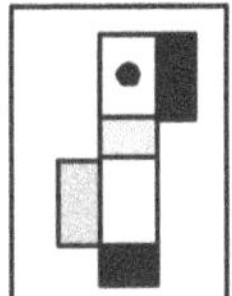

Answer Figures :

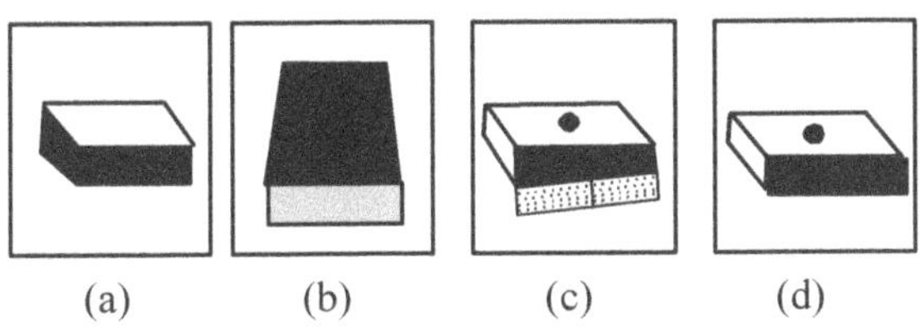

4. Which of the following cubes can be created by folding the given figure?

Question Figure.

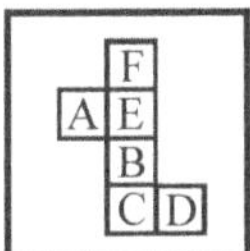

Answer Figures.

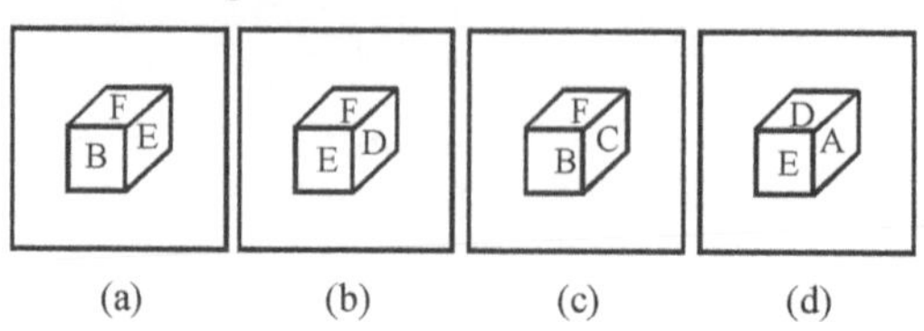

(a) (b) (c) (d)

5. Two positions of a dice are given. Which number would be at the top when bottom is 2?

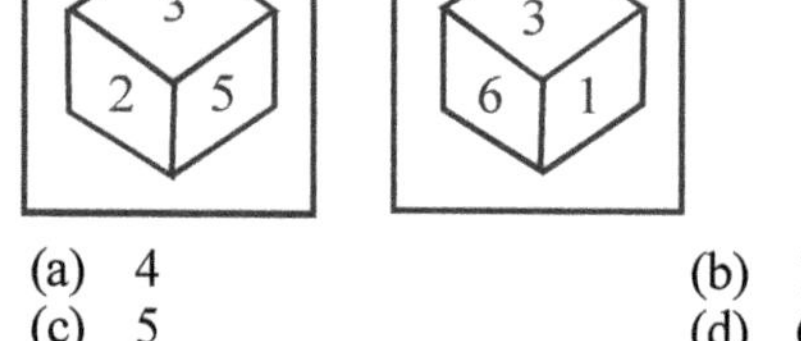

(a) 4 (b) 1
(c) 5 (d) 6

6. Which one of the four boxes given below is created by folding the given key design in the question figure?

Question figures:

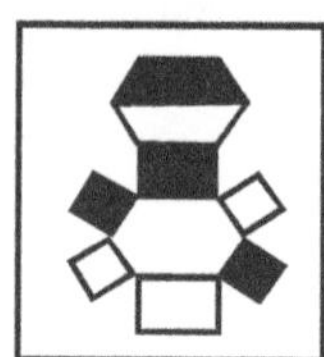

Answer figures:

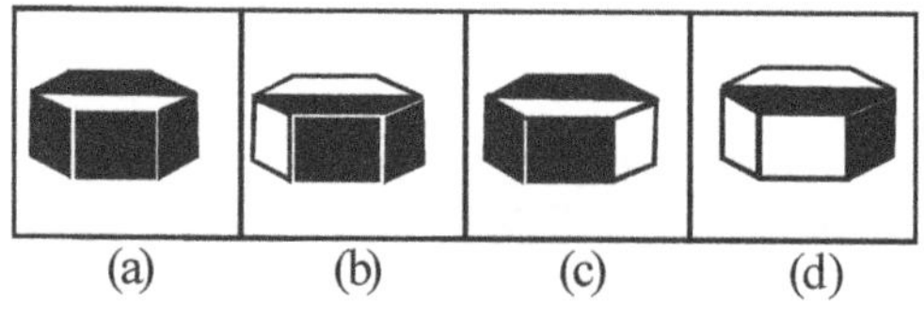

(a) (b) (c) (d)

7. Two positions of a dice are shown below. If 1 is at the bottom, which number will be on top?

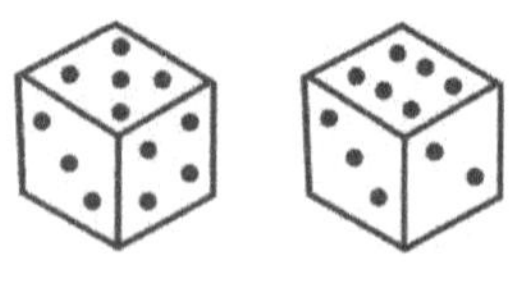

(a) 4 (b) 3 (c) 8 (d) 5

8. 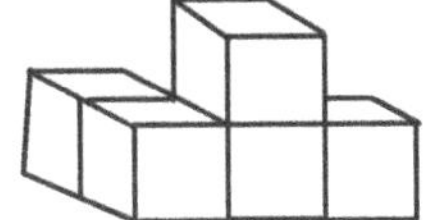

The solid so formed by joining unit cubes is rotated to obtain different positions, which of these cannot be the shape after it has turned?

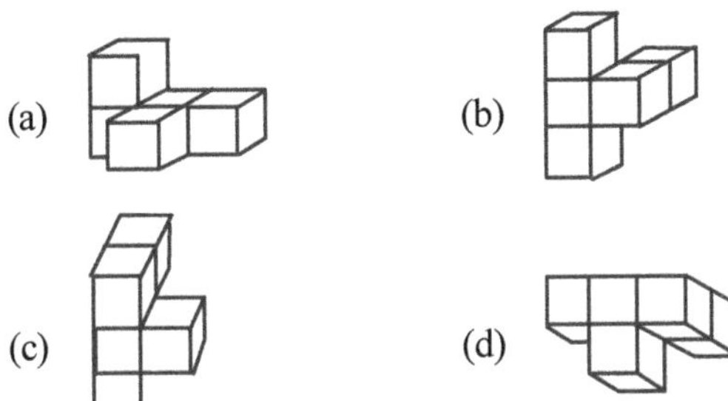

9. The figure given on the left hand side is folded to form a box. Choose from the alternatives (1), (2), (3) and (4) the boxes that is similar to the box formed.

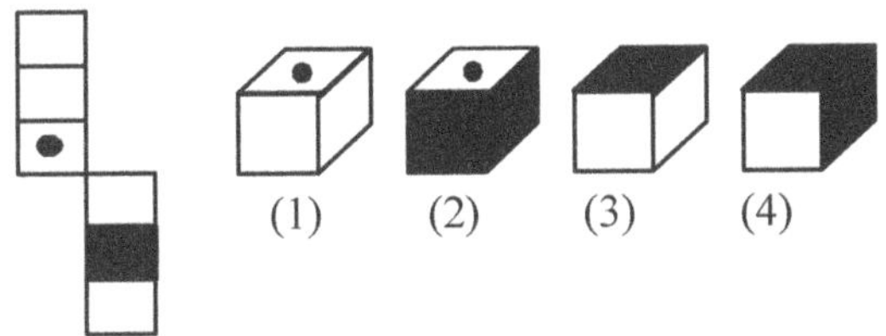

(a) (2) and (3) only (b) (1), (3) and (4) only
(c) (2) and (4) only (d) (1) and (4) only

10. In the given cubes, which colour is opposite to purple?

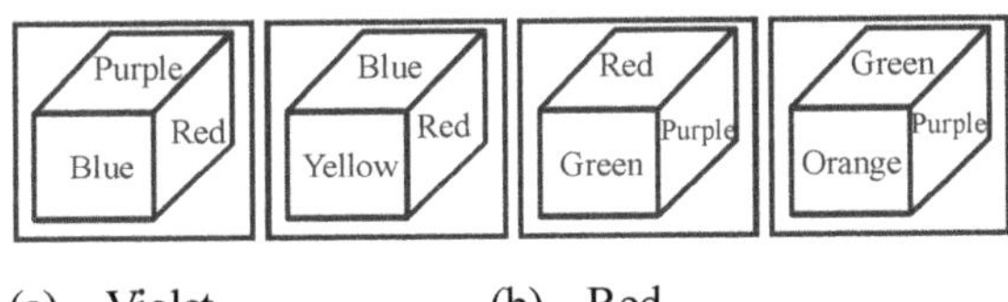

(a) Violet (b) Red
(c) Yellow (d) Blue

HINTS & SOLUTIONS

1. (b) 1, 3, 4 and 6 are adjacent 2. Therefore number 5 on the face opposite to 2.

2. (a) The numbers 1, 2, 5 and 6 are on the adjacent faces of the number 3. So, the number 4 lies opposite 3.

3. (d) The shaded parts are narow. So, answer figure (b) is invalid.

   The white part is larger. So, answer figure (c) is invalid.

   If dot is on the top surface, then the visible surface can not be white. So, answer figure (a) is invalid.

4. (b) When folded in the form of a cube, then 'F' appears opposite 'B', 'E' appears opposite 'C' and 'A' appears opposite 'D'.
   In option (a) 'F' is adjacent to 'B'
   In option (c) 'E' is adjacent to 'C'.
   In option (d) 'E' is adjacent to 'A'.

5. (d) The numbers 1, 2, 5 and 6 are on the adjacent faces of number 3. Therefore. the number 4 lies opposite 3.
   The numbers 3, 4 and 6 can not be on the faces opposite to 1. Therefore, 5 lies opposite 1.
   Now, 2 lies opposite 6.

6. (c)

7. (b) By looking, the dice position, we can say that 2, 4, 5 and 6 are adjacent faces of 3. therefore, if 1 number is at the bottom then 3 will be on the top.

8. (a) Option (a) is correct.

9. (b) The given figure can be numbered like this:

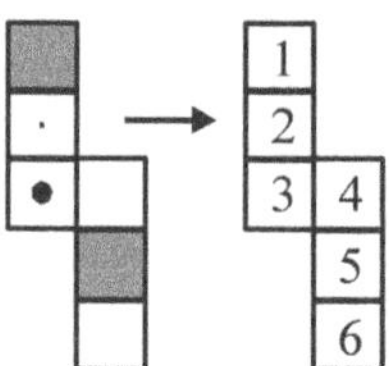

   In this figure:
   1 lies opposite 3; 2 lies opposite 5;
   4 lies opposite 6.
   When the sheet of question figure is folded to form a cube, then the face bearing a dot lies opposite to one of the shaded faces.
   Therefore, figure (2) which has both the shaded faces adjacent to the face bearing the dot, cannot be formed.
   Hence, the cubes shown in figures (1), (3) and (4) can be formed.

10. (c) Purple → Red, Blue, Yellow, Green, Orange
   Green, Orange, Red, Blue are adjacent to purple

Analytical Decision Making

INTRODUCTION

Analytical decision making is a process in which a final outcome is derived by evaluating and analysing the given information. In this chapter mainly two types of questions are covered.

(i) Eligibility Test and (ii) Passage based decision making.

These questions are designed to judge the decision making capability of the condidates.

In first type of questions, condition regarding the selection or non-selection of a candidate along with the biodata are given based on which his eligibility has to be decided. In second type of questions, a paragraph of informations is given based on which the question are to be answered.

FORMAT OF THE QUESTION OF ELIGIBILITY TEST

Example (Directions): Read carefuly the informations given below and answer the questions based on it:

The following are the given conditions for the recruitment of a candidate as a family member in a computer institute:

(i) The candidate must be in the age range of 23 years to 28 years as on 1st November, 2013.

(ii) The candidate must have work experience as a teacher or programming experience of at least 2 years.

(iii) The candidate must have a PG degree in computer application, [MCA, M.Tech. or M.Sc. (computer science)] with not less than 60% marks.

(iv) Out of total 50 marks in the interview, the candidate must obtain 50%.

(v) In the case when a candidate fulfils the above conditions, he/she shall be appointed as senior teacher.

(vi) Has less than 60% but more than 50% marks in his/her PG degree in computer application, he/she will be appointed as junior teacher.

(vii) If the age is more than 28 years but less than 32 years as on 1st November, 2013, the case may be reffered to the GM of the institute.

On the basis of the above mentioned conditions and information about each of the candidates in the question below, you have to decide which of the following courses of action should be taken against each candidate. Point to be noted that nothing extra will be assumed except the given information. The decision must be based only on the data provided.

Mark your answer:

(a) If the candidate is to be selected as a Junior teacher

(b) If the candidate is to be selected as a Senior teacher
(c) If the case will be reffered to the GM of the institute.
(d) If the data are inadequate
(e) If the candidate is not to be selected.

QUESTIONS

1. **Mukesh Verma** was born on 31st July, 1985. He is an M.Tech. in computer engineering with 70% marks. He has been working in an institution as a programmer for the last 7 years.

2. **Karishma Tiwari** is MCA with 72% marks. Her date of birth is 14th August, 1990. She has worked as a computer teacher for 4 years. She has got 35 marks in interview.

What You See in the given Question Format?

In the given format you can see the following things:

(1) Informations about some candidates have been provided.
(2) Some conditions have been given for candidates to fulfil in order to get selected for a particular job/ post. In case of the given format, four conditions have been given.
(3) When a candidate fulfils all the criteria except some, then different course of action has to be taken for him.

Some more things to understand

Basic conditions: In the given question format, there are four basic conditions (i), (ii), (iii) and (iv). They are called basic conditions because they are the original conditions.

Additional conditions: In the given question format, there are two more conditions apart from the basic conditions and they are (vi) and (vii). point to be noted that (v) will not be on additional condition as it does not talk of exceptions. In fact (v) is only a totality of the four basic or original conditions given in the question format.

What is data inadequacy?

As one of the answer is given as 'data inadequate' we must be clear about what exactly does data inadequacy mean? When details given about any candidate provide no information as required by the basic conditions/additional conditions then this would be the case of data inadequacy, For example, let us see the first question given in the format. No information is given about what marks have been obtained by Mukesh Verma in the interview. Hence, the data is inadequate here.

How to solve a given problem?

Let us consider the questions given in the format and start one stepwise process.

STEP I

Write the name of the candidates in the left side and then write the symbols (i, ii, iii, iv) of the basic conditions to the top right. Now, put the symbols of the additional conditions (vi and vii) below the symbols of that basic condition with which these might be related. For example, (vi) is a condition about educational qualification and so, it is an exception of (iii). Hence (vi) should be written below (iii). Similarly, (vii) should be written below (i). Now, after the completion of step I, the following format will be prepared:

		i (vii)	ii	iii (vi)	iv
1	Mukesh Verma				
2	Karishma Tiwari				
3	Brijesh Shankar				
4	Mansi Ranjan				
5	Subodh Saxena				

Note that three more names are added in the table only for better understanding.

NOTE : *To differentiate between basic conditions and additional conditions. The additional conditions have been encircled.*

STEP II

At the 2nd step just see the given answer choices carefully and decide which combination of the conditions leads to which conclusion. If we see the given question format with serious eye, we find that the following combination can be formed.

i + ii + iii + iv → b [Senior teacher]

vii + ii + iii + iv → c [Case will be reffered to GM]

i + ii + vi + iv → a [Junior teacher]

When we have decided the above three combination giving answer choices (a), (b) and (c), two answer choices remains and they are answer choice (d) and answer choice (e). The answer choice (e), which says that the candidate is not to be selected, should be chosen when any one or more of the given conditions (a), (b), (c) is violated. The answer choice (d), which tells that the data are inadequate, should be chosen when no information is given about any one or more conditions (a), (b), (c).

How to examine data?

After step II, you are required to read all the statements carefully. Just take each question one by one and compare then with the given conditions. Examinees are suggested to use following symbols while doing this comparision:

I If a basic condition is fulfilled mark '✓' sign below it.

II If a basic condition is violated and it is not attached with an additional condition then mark 'x' sign below it.

III If a basic condition is violated but it is attached with an additional condition, then

(A) Mark a '(×)' sign below it if additional condition is also violated.

(B) Mark a '(✓)' sign below it if additional condition is fulfilled.

IV In case of unavailability of any information about any condition, a mark '?' will be put below that condition.

After comparison, you can easily examine the data.

STEP III

(i) One by one, read the questions very carefully and compare the facts given with the various condition.

(ii) Mark the appropriate sign or '✓', '×' ,(✓), (×) or ? as required

(iii) When a '×' or a (×) sign is obtained, then stop examining further and without any hesitation select the answer choice "not to be selected" for that particular question. It so happens because, if a condition as well as its additional condition is violated, it does mean that one necessary requirement is not being fulfilled. Hence, we reach at a conclusion that the selection is not possible even if other conditions are fulfilled.

STEP IV

Now, this is the time to select your answer choices on the pattern given below:

(i) If find a '×' or (×) below any condition, go for the answer choice "not to be selected"

(ii) If you find no cross mark but there is a question mark below any condition, your answer choice would be "data are inadequate".

(iii) If you find neither any cross mark nor any question mark, than compare the combination with the three answer combinations obtained in step II and select the answer choice accordingly.

After understanding the above steps, now we are at a position of solving the question given in the question format. Let us see the solution:

Solution:

Question No.		(i) / (vii)	(ii)	(iii)/ (vi)	(iv)
1	Mukesh Verma	(✓)	✓	✓	?
2	Karishma Tiwari	✓	✓	✓	✓
3	Brijesh Shankar	(×)	✓	(✓)	✓
4	Mansi Ranjan	✓	✓	(✓)	×
5	Subodh Saxena	✓	✓	(✓)	✓

Condition (vii) is attached to (ii) while the additional condition is (vi) attached with the basic condition (iii).

STEP WISE EXPLANATION OF ABOVE TABLE

Step I

At the step I level, we read the question carefully and find out that there are four, basic conditions (i), (ii), (iii) and (iv) and two additional conditions (vii) and (vi). Further, it is clear that (vii) is attached to (i) and (vi) is attached to (iii). Now we write the name of the candidates in extreme left and then put the basic conditions (i), (ii), (iii) and (iv) at the top-right of the candidate. Next, we write additional condition (vii) below (i) and additional condition (vi) below (iii).

Step II

At the step II level, we look at the answer choices and prepare answer combinations accordingly. This will be:

i + ii + iii + iv ⇒ b

vii + ii + iii + iv ⇒ c

i + ii + vi + iv ⇒ a

Step III

At the step III level, we read every question carefully and compare the facts given in it with the various conditions.

Let us see the detailed analysis of every candidate question wise.

Mukesh Verma

He is an M.Tech in computer engineering with 70% marks. This fulfills condition (iii). Hence we write '✓' mark below (iii). Next, his date of birth is 31st July, 1985. Here, we do a mental calculation that on 31st July, 2013 he turned 28th. This is the reason that on 1st November 2013, he is more than 28 years. Therefore, (i) is violated, but the additional condition of (i) is (vii) which is fulfilled and we write (✓) mark here. Further, Mukesh Verma is having a programming experience of 7 years (more than 2 years). So we mark '✓' below (ii). Lastly, there is no information about marks of Mukesh in the interview. Thus the sign of question mark '?' is put below (iv).

Karishma Tiwari

Karishma is an MCA with 72% marks. This fulfills (iii), so we put the mark '✓' below (iii). Her date of birth is 14th August, 1990, So on 1st November, 2013, she is more than 23 years but less than 28 years. This fulfills (i) and hence we put a '✓' mark below (i). She is a computer teacher from last 4 years. This fulfils (ii) and hence we put '✓' mark below (ii). Lastly, she has obtained 35 marks in the interview. This marks is more than the required 50% (25 marks out of 50 marks), therefore (iv) is also fulfilled and we put '✓'mark below (iv).

NOTE: *Mark '✓', '×', '(✓)', and '(×)' against the three additional persons are just assumed for better understanding.*

Step IV

At the step IV level we select the answer choices.

Sol. 1. No cross mark ⇒ d But a question mark is available. Hence, data is inadequate.

Sol. 2. i + ii + iii + iv ⇒ b [step II]
So, the candidate is to be selected as a senior teacher.

❑ Shortcut Approach

- For selection all basic conditions must be fulfilled.
- For rejection atleast one independent basic condition must be violated/basic and additional condition must be violated.
- If a basic condition is violated but an additional condition attached with it is fulfilled and all other remaining basic conditions are fulfilled, then the case will be referred to the person given in the questions.
- Once the symbol ×/(×) is put in the table, there is no need to check further conditions as person is declared rejected at this stage only.
- If for one basic condition, the data is not given while all other basic conditions are fulfilled, it means data is inadequate.
- If any information is not given and answer choices don't have data inadequate option, then condition related to that particular information is supposed to be violated.

PASSAGE BASED DECISION MAKING QUESTION

DIRECTIONS (Qs. 1-3): *Read the following caselet carefully and answer the questions that follow.*

Marathe is a Vice-President in a construction equipment company in the city of Mumbai. One day, his subordinate Bhonsle requested that Kale, a project manager, be transferred to the Chennai office from the Mumbai office. In Chennai, Kale would work alone as a researcher. Bhonsle gave the following reasons for his request" Kale is known to frequently fight with his colleagues. 'Kale is conscientious and dedicated only when working alone. He is friendly with seniors but refuses to work with colleagues, in a team. He cannot accept criticism and feels hostile and rejected. He is over bearing and is generally a bad influence on the team.'

Marathe called upon Gore, another project manager and sought further information on Kale. Gore recalled that a former colleague, Lakhote (who was also Kale's former boss) had made a few remarks on his appraisal report about Kale. In his opinion, Kale was not fit for further promotion as he was emotionally unstable to work in groups though he had seven years of work experience. Lakhote had described Kale as too authoritative to work under anyone. Lakhote had further told Gore that Kale had an ailing wife and an old mother, who does not want to stay with his wife.

1. Consider the following solutions to the problem mentioned above

I. Marathe should transfer Kale to Chennai office.

II. Marathe should try and verify the facts from other sources as well.

III. Kale should be sacked.

IV. Kale should be demoted.

V. Marathe should suggest Kale to visit a family counselor.

Which of the following would be the most appropriate sequence of decisions in terms of immediacy starting from immediate to a longer term solution?

(a) II, I and V
(b) I, IV and II
(c) II, III and IV
(d) II, V and I
(e) II, V and IV

2. Marathe sought an appointment with Lakhote to find out ways to help Kale. Lakhote is of the opinion that the company's responsibility is restricted to the workplace and it should not try to address the personal problems of employees. If Marathe has to agree to Lakhote's opinion, which of the solutions presented in the previous question would be weakened?

(a) Only I (b) Only II
(c) Only III (d) Only IV
(e) Only V

3. Which of the following statements, if true would weaken the decision to sack Kale the most?

(a) A Government of India study established that employees with 5-10 year of work experience tend to have conflicting responsibilities at home and office. However, these conflicts wither away after 10 year of experience

(b) Another article published in the magazine, Xaviers Quarterly, highlighted that employees' problems at home affect their performance at work

(c) In the latest issue of a reputed journal, Xaviers Business Review, it was published that most top managers, find it difficult to work in a group

(d) It was published in Xaviers Management Review (another reputed journal) that individuals who cannot work in terms find it difficult to adjust to a new location

(e) Bhonsle was of the opinion that emtionally unstable persons, find it difficult to get back to normal working life

Sol. 1. Marathe should try to verify the facts from other sources as well becasuse there might be some jealousy feeling between Kale and his colleague due to which he is having such bad raputation in his office. Marathe should not easily believe on Gore, he should verify it from other sources.

After collecting the infromation about Kale, he should be suggested to visit the family counselor which might help him in improving his personality. If still, he is not been able to adjust with his colleagues he should take transfer to the Chennai office.

2. Concerning it as a personal problem of employees, Marathe left no right to interfere it.

3. Bhosle was of the opinion that emotionally unstable persons find it difficult to get back to normal working life.

PRACTICE EXERCISE

DIRECTIONS (Qs. 1-5): *Study the following information carefully and answer the questions given below:*

An organization wants to recruit system analysts. The following conditions apply.

The candidate must

(i) be an engineering graduate in computer/IT with at least 60% marks.

(ii) have working experience in the field of computer at least for 2 yr after acquiring the requisite qualification.

(iii) have completed minimum 25 yr and maximum 30 yr of age as on 1.12.2013.

(iv) be willing to sign a bond for ₹50000.

(v) have secured minimum 55% marks in selection test. However, if a candidate fulfils all other conditions

Except

A. at (i) above, but is an Electronics Engineer with 65% or more marks the case is to be referred to the General Manager (GM)-IT.

B. at (iv) above, but has an experience of atleast 5 yr as a Software Manager, the case is to be referred to the VP.

In each question below, detailed information of candidate is given. You have to carefully study the information provided in each case and take one of the following courses of actions based on the information and the conditions given above. You are not to assume anything other than the information provided in each question. All these cases are given to you as on 01.12.2013.

You have to indicate your decision by marking answers to each question as follows:

Give Answer:

(a) If the case is to be referred to VP

(b) If the case is to be referred to GM

(c) If the data provided is not sufficient to take a decision

(d) If the candidate is to be selected

(e) If the candidate is not to be selected

1. Ms. Suneeta is an IT Engineer with 60% marks at graduation as well as in selection test. She is working as a Software Engineer for last 3 yr after completing engineering degree and has completed 27 yr of age. She is willing to sign the bond of II ₹50000.

2. Rakesh Rao is a Computer Engineer Graduate and thereafter is working as a Software Manager for last 6 yr. He has secured 72% marks at graduation and 67% marks in selection test. His date of birth is 5th December, 1984. He is not willing to sign the bond for ₹50000.

3. Ramkumar is an Engineering graduate in computers with 78% marks passed out in 2007 at the age of 23 yr. Since, then he is working as a Software Manager in an engineering firm. He doesn't want to sign the bond for ₹50000. He has cleared the selection test with 72% marks.

4. Nishant is an Electronics Engineer passed out in June, 2010 at the age of 22 yr. Since, then he is working as a Programmer in a software company. He has passed the selection test with 66% marks and is willing to sign the bond.

5. Kalyani is an Engineer with 72% marks in Telecommunication. She has just completed 27 yr of age. She has cleared the selection test with 59% marks. She is willing to sign the bond.

DIRECTIONS (Qs. 6-10): *Study the following information carefully and answer the questions given below :*

Following are the conditions for selecting Marketing Manager in an organisation :

The candidate must :

(i) be at least 30 years old as on 01.03.2013

(ii) have secured at least 55 per cent marks in graduation

(iii) have secured at least 60 per cent marks in Post graduate Degree/ Diploma in Marketing.

(iv) have post qualification work experience of at least five years in the Marketing Division of an organisation.

(v) have secured at least 45 per cent marks in the selection process.

In the case of a candidate who satisfies all other conditions **except -**

(A) at (iv) above, but has post qualification work experience of at least two years as Deputy Marketing Manager, the case is to be referred to GM-Marketing.

(B) at (ii) above, but has secured at least 65 per cent marks in Post graduate Degree/Diploma in Marketing Management, the case is to be referred to Vice President-Marketing.

In each question below is given details of one candidate. You have to take one of the following courses of actions based on the information provided and the conditions and subconditions given above and mark your answer accordingly. You are not to assume anything other than the information provided in each question. All these cases are given to you as on 01.03.2013.

Mark answer (a) if the candidate is not to be selected.

Mark answer (b) if the candidate is to be selected.

Mark answer (c) if the data are inadequate to take a decision.

Mark answer (d) if the case is to be referred to Vice President -Marketing.

Mark answer (e) if the case is to be referred to GM-Marketing.

6. Suresh Mehta has secured 58 per cent marks in graduation. He was born on 19th May 1979. He has secured 50 per cent marks in the selection process. He has been working for the past seven years in the Marketing division of an organ-isation after completing his Post Graduation with 62 per cent marks.

7. Sudha Gopalan has secured 50 per cent marks in both selec-tion process and graduation. She has been working for the past six years in the Marketing division of an organisation after completing her Post Graduate Diploma in Marketing with 70 per cent marks. She was born on 14th October. 1982.

8. Divya Kohli has been working for the past five years in Marketing division of an organisation after completing her Post Graduate Diploma in Marketing with 65 per cent marks. She has secured 55 per cent marks in graduation and 50 per cent marks in the selection process. She was born on 2nd April 1979.

9. Navin Marathe was born on 8th April 1979. He has secured 60 per cent marks in both graduation and Post-Graduate Degree in Marketing. He has been working for the past six years in the Marketing division of an organisation after com-pleting his PG Degree in Marketing. He has secured 50 per cent marks in the selection process.

10. Varun Malhotra was born on 3rd July 1980. He has been working as Deputy Marketing Manager in an organisation for the past three years after completing his Post Graduate Degree in Marketing with 65 per cent marks. He secured 55 per cent marks in both graduation and selection process.

HINTS & SOLUTIONS

Sol. (1-5):

Candidate	i	ii	iii	iv	v	(A)	(B)
Suneeta	✓	✓	✓	✓	✓		
Rakesh	✓	✓	✓	–	✓		✓
Ram Kumar	✓	✓	✓	–	✓		✓
Nishant	–	✓	✓	✓	✓		
Kalyani	×	✓	✓	✓	✓		

1. **(d)** Suneeta fulfils all conditions so, she is to be selected.
2. **(a)** Rakesh Rao fulfils condition (B) instead of (IV) so, his case is to be referred to VP.
3. **(a)** Ramkumar fulfils condition (B) instead of (IV) so, his case is to be referred to VP.
4. **(c)** Percentage marks of Nishant in graduation is not given so, data is insufficient.
5. **(e)** Kalyani is telecommunication engineer so, she is not to be selected.

Sol. (6-10) :

CANDIDATE	CRITERIA							
	(i)	(ii) or B		(iii)	(iv) or A		(v)	Ans
Suresh	✓	✓	–	✓	✓	–	✓	b
Sudha	✓	–	✓	✓	✓	–	✓	d
Divya	×	✓	–	✓	✓	–	✓	a
Navin	✓	✓	–	✓	✓	–	✓	b
Varun	✓	✓	–	✓	–	✓	✓	e

6. **(b)** Suresh Mehta satisfies all the conditions (i), (ii), (iii), (iv) and (v). Therefore, he can be selected.
7. **(d)** Sudha Gopalan satisfies the conditions (i), (B), (iii), (iv) and (v). Therefore, her case would be referred to Vice-president -Marketing.
8. **(a)** Divya Kohli does not satisfy condition (i). Therefore, she cannot be selected.
9. **(b)** Navin Marathe satisfies all the conditions (i), (ii), (iii), (iv) and (v). Therefore, he can be selected.
10. **(e)** Varun Malhotra satisfies the conditions (i), (ii), (iii), (A) and (v). Therefore, his case should be referred to GM-Marketing.

Series

INTRODUCTION

The word **"series"** is defined as anything that follows or forms a specific pattern or is in continuation of a given pattern or sequence.

In this type of non-verbal test, two sets of figures pose the problem. The sets are called Problem Figures and Answer Figures. Each problem figure changes in design from the preceding one.

❑ *Shortcut Approach*

- **Directions** – There are eight directions as follows :

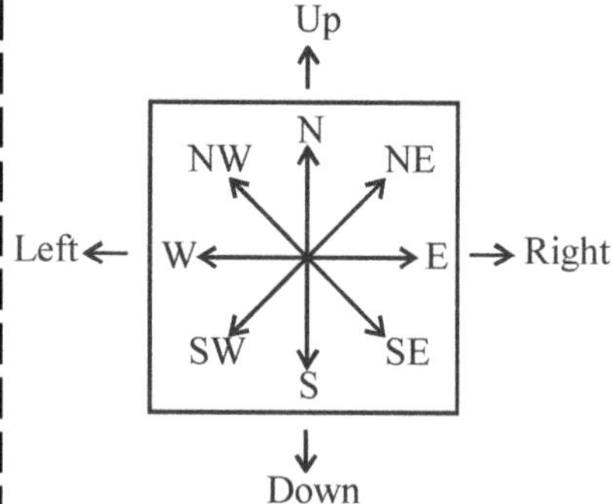

- **Rotational Directions** –
There are two rotational directions as follows :

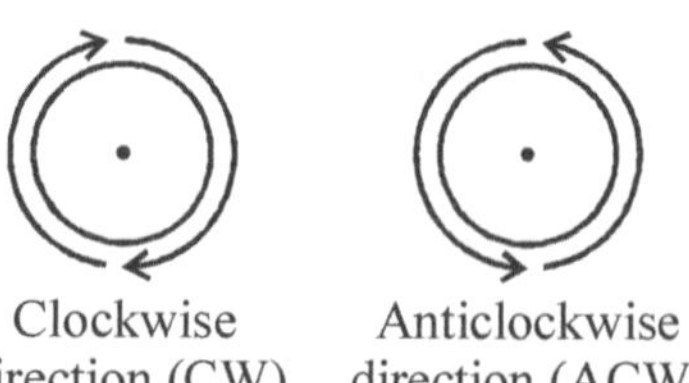

Clockwise direction (CW) Anticlockwise direction (ACW)

- **Positions of Elements** –

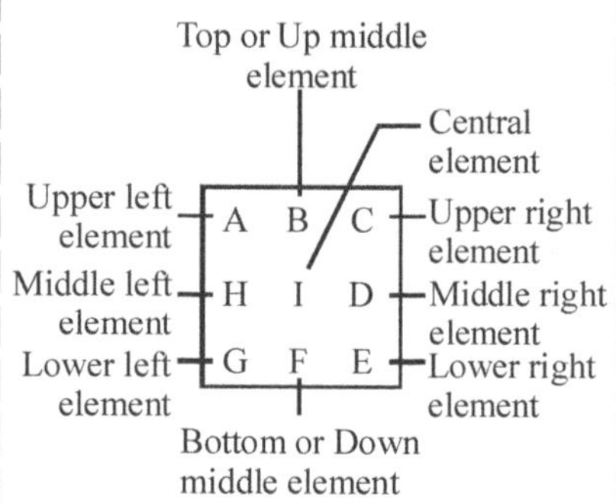

- **Movement of Elements Through Distance** –

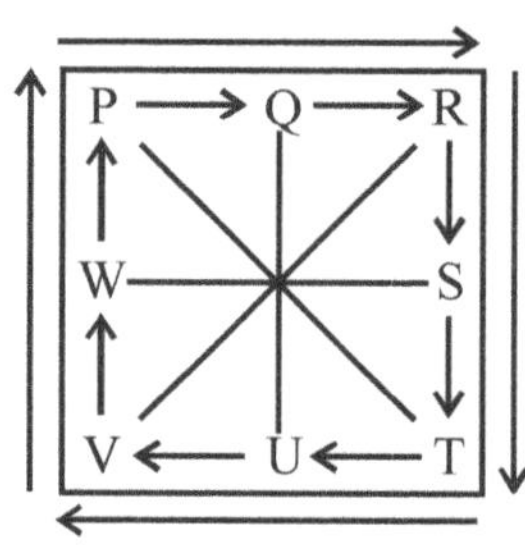

Clockwise Movement

$P \rightarrow Q = \frac{1}{2}$ arm/step

$P \rightarrow R = 1$ arm/step

$P \rightarrow S = 1\frac{1}{2}$ arm/step

$P \rightarrow T = 2$ arm/step

$P \rightarrow S = 2\frac{1}{2}$ arm/step

$P \rightarrow R = 3$ arm/step

$P \rightarrow Q = 3\frac{1}{2}$ arm/step

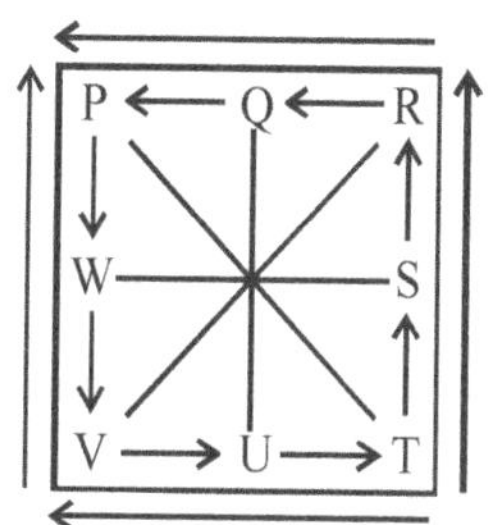

Anti Clockwise Movement

$P \rightarrow W = \frac{1}{2}$ arm/step

$P \rightarrow V = 1$ arm/step

$P \rightarrow U = 1\frac{1}{2}$ arm/step

$P \rightarrow U = 2\frac{1}{2}$ arm/step

$P \rightarrow V = 3$ arm/step

$P \rightarrow W = 3\frac{1}{2}$ arm/step

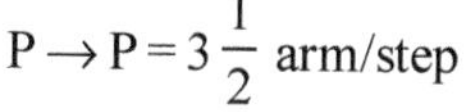

$P \rightarrow P = 3\frac{1}{2}$ arm/step

- **Directional Movement of Elements–**

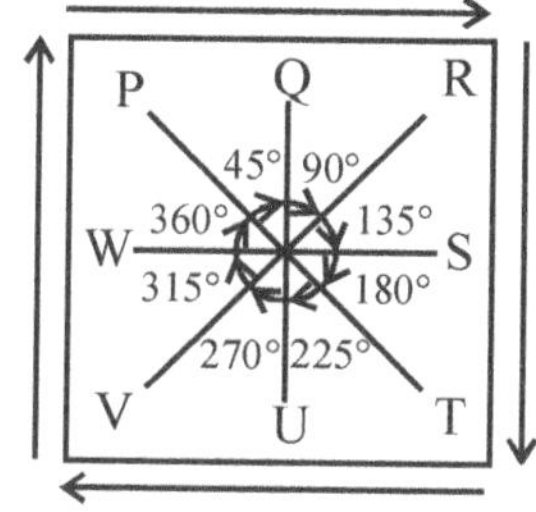

Clockwise Movement

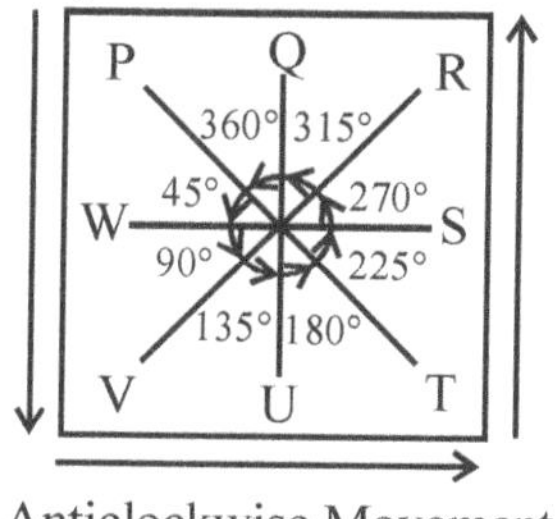

Anticlockwise Movement

TYPES OF SERIES

TYPE-I

A definite relationship between elements in given figures.

EXAMPLE 1.

Study the problem figures marked (A), (B) and (C) carefully and try to establish the relationship between them. From the answer figures marked a, b, c and d, pick out the figure which most appropriately completes the series.

Problem Figures

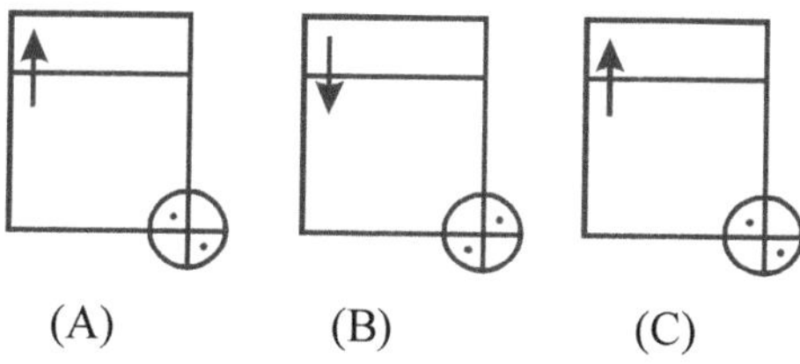

Answer Figures

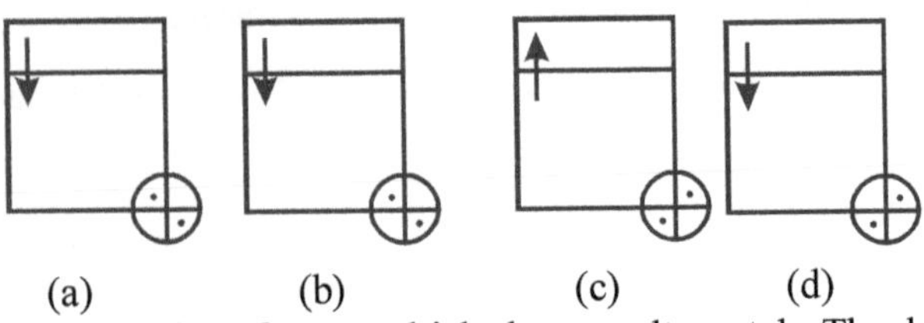

(a) (b) (c) (d)

Sol. The direction of arrow which changes alternately. The dots are also changing alternately. Hence, we are looking for a figure in which the arrow points down and the dots and positioned as in figure (b).

TYPE II. ADDITIONS OF ELEMENTS :

In these type of questions, each figure is obtained by either sustaining the element of preceding figure as it is or adding a part of element or one element or more than one element of the preceding figure in a systematic way.

EXAMPLE 2.

Problem Figures

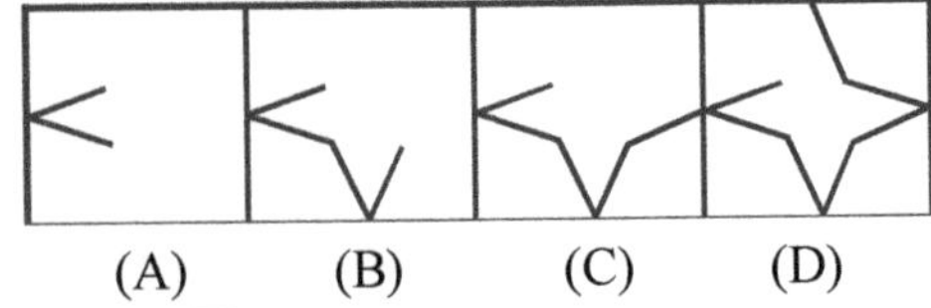

(A) (B) (C) (D)

Answer Figures

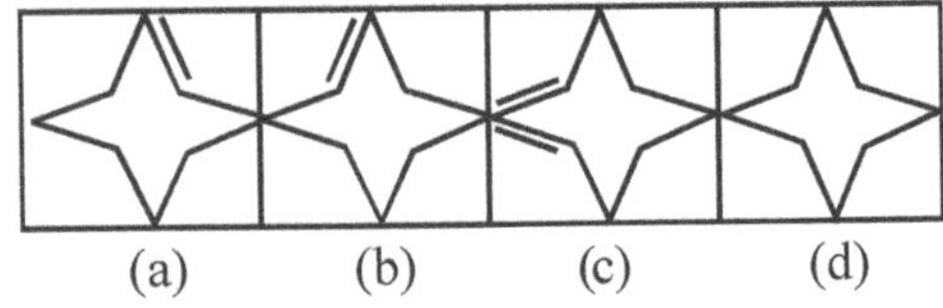

(a) (b) (c) (d)

Sol. Two line segments are added in A to obtain B and one line segment is added in B to obtain C. This process is repeated again to obtain D. Hence, answer figure (d) continues the series.

TYPE III. INCREASING/DECREASING OF ELEMENTS:

In these questions, the items in the diagrams either increase or decrease in number.

EXAMPLE 3.

Problem Figures

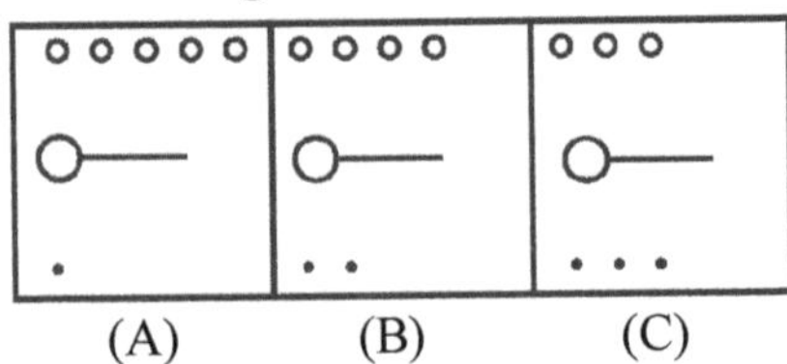

(A) (B) (C)

Answer Figures

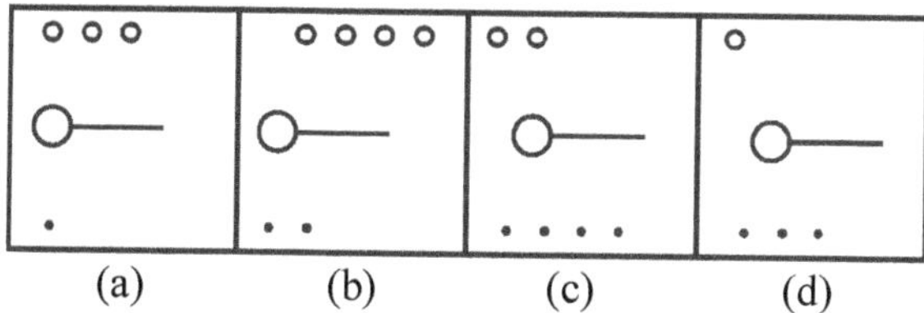

Sol. The small circles are decreasing consecutively and the black dots are increasing. So, figure (c) continues the series.

TYPE IV DELETION OF ELEMENTS :

In these type of questions, each figure is obtained by either sustaining the element of preceding figure as it is or deleting a part of an element or one element or more than one element of the preceding figure in a systematic way.

EXAMPLE 4.

Problem Figures

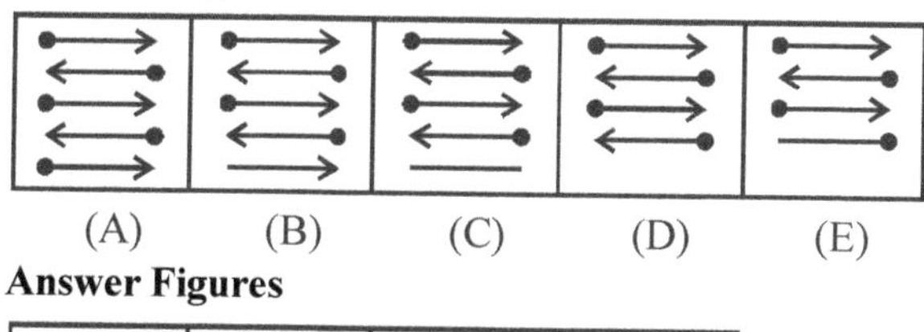

Answer Figures

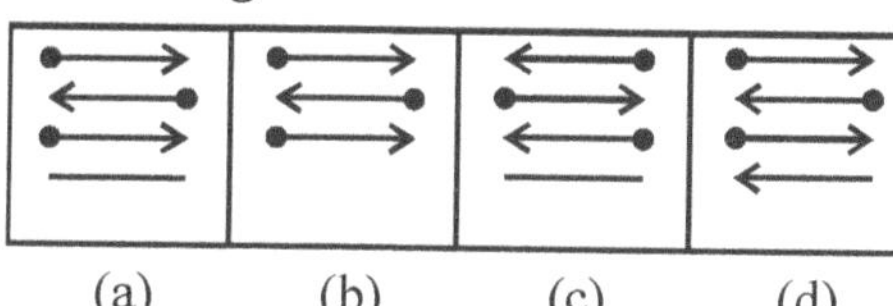

Sol. The qualitative characteristic of various elements in the diagrams change to complete the series. So, figure (a) continues the series.

TYPE V ROTATION TYPE :

The various elements in the diagrams move in a specific manner. They may rotate in clockwise or anti-clockwise direction.

EXAMPLE 5.

Problem Figures

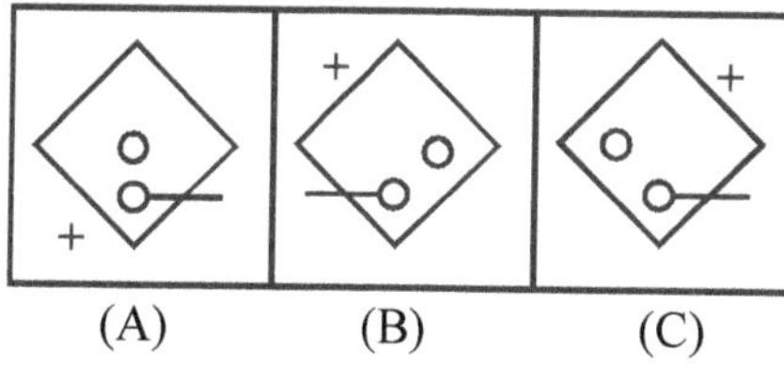

Answer Figures

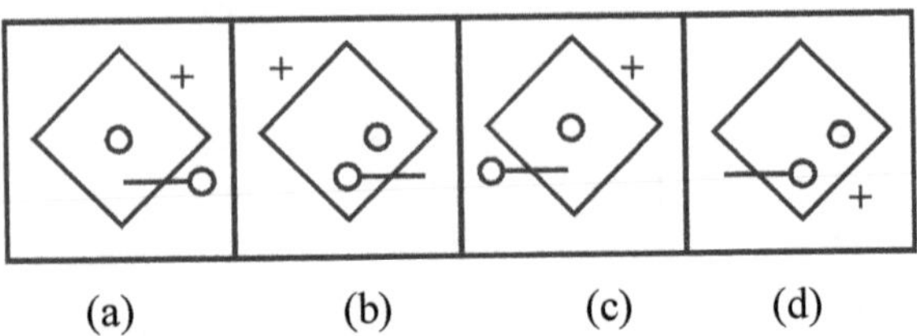

(a) (b) (c) (d)

Sol. The sign of plus is rotating clockwise. The pin changes direction alternately. So, figure (d) coninues the series.

TYPE VI REPLACEMENT OF ELEMENTS :

In these type of questions, each figure is obtained by either sustaining the element of preceding figure as it is or replacing a part of element or one element or more than one element by a new element of the preceding figure in a systematic way.

EXAMPLE 6.

Problem Figures

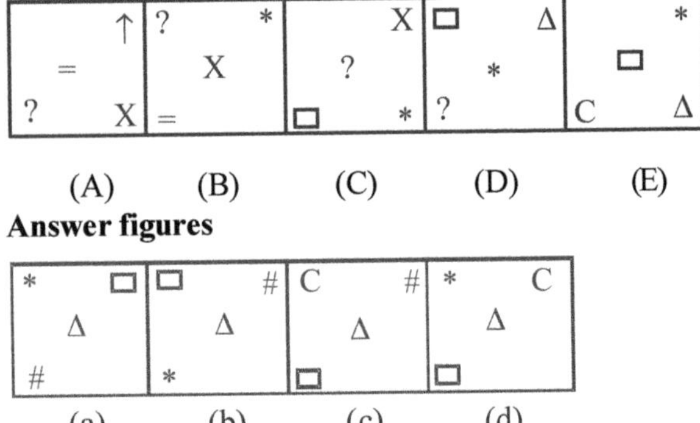

(A) (B) (C) (D) (E)

Answer figures

(a) (b) (c) (d)

Sol. The elements positioned at north-east (NE) corners disappear from the odd-numbered figures. The elements positioned at the south-west (SW) corners disappear from the even-numbered figures. Therefore * should not appear in the answer figure. Hence (a), (b) and (d) cannot be the answers. Also new elements are introduced at the NE corners in even-numbered figures. Therefore, answer figure (c) continues the given series.

PRACTICE EXERCISE

1. Select a figure from amongst the Answer Figures which will continue the same series as established by the five Problem Figures.

Problem Figures:

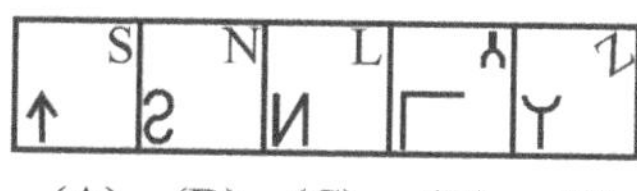

Answer Figures:

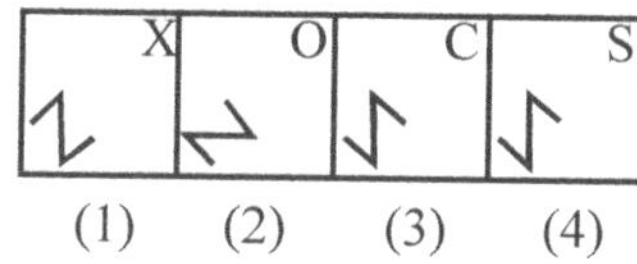

(a) 1 (b) 2
(c) 3 (d) 4

2. Select a figure from amongst the Answer Figures which will continue the same series as established by the five Problem Figures.

Problem Figures:

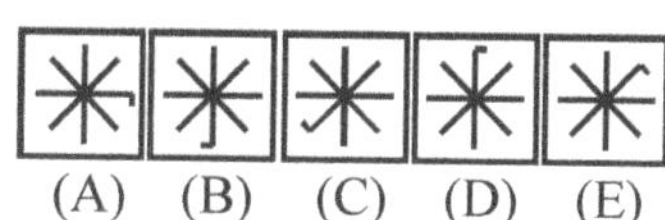

Answer Figures:

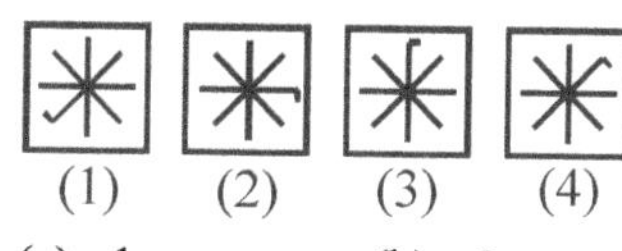

(a) 1 (b) 2
(c) 3 (d) 4

3. Select a figure from amongst the Answer Figures which will continue the same series as established by the five Problem Figures.

Problem Figures:

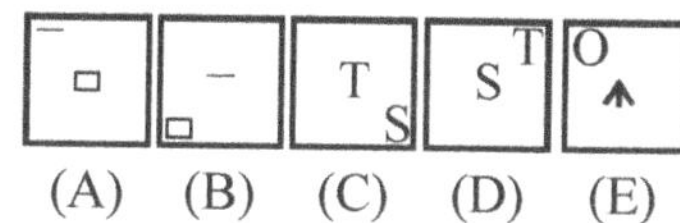

Answer Figures:

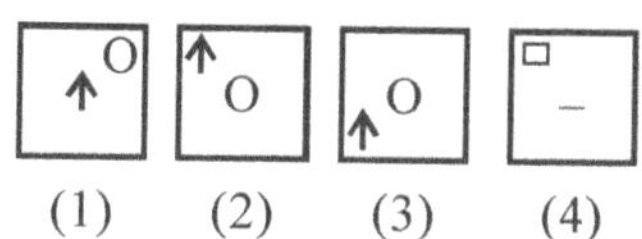

(a) 1 (b) 2
(c) 3 (d) 4

4. Select a figure from amongst the Answer Figures which will continue the same series as established by the five Problem Figures.

Problem Figures:

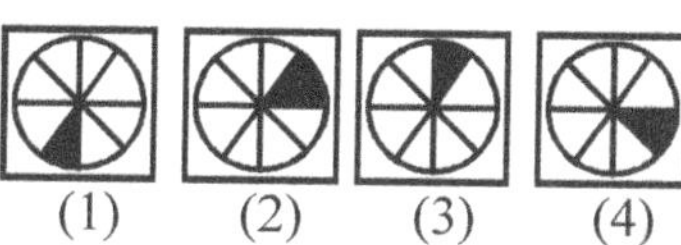

Answer Figures:

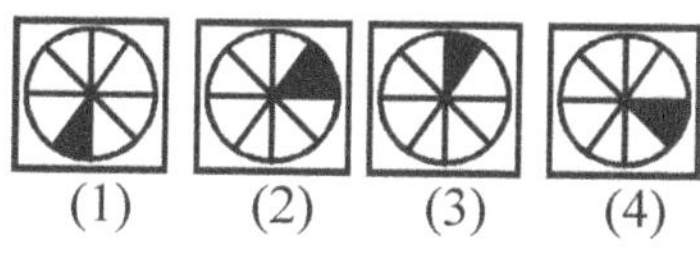

(a) 1 (b) 2
(c) 3 (d) 4

5. Select a figure from amongst the Answer Figures which will continue the same series as established by the five Problem Figures.

Problem Figures:

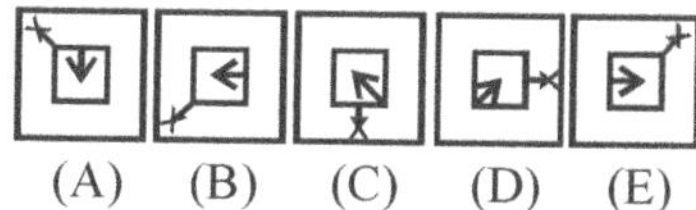

Answer Figures:

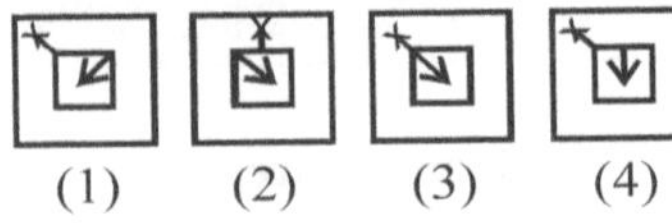

(a) 1 (b) 2
(c) 3 (d) 4

6. Select a figure from amongst the Answer Figures which will continue the same series as established by the five Problem Figures.

Problem Figures:

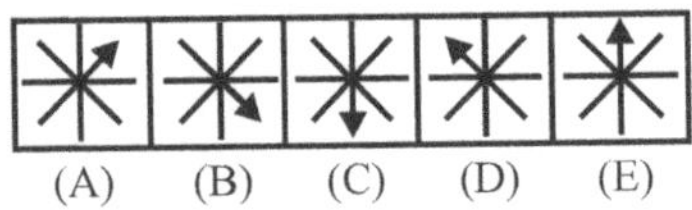

Answer Figures:

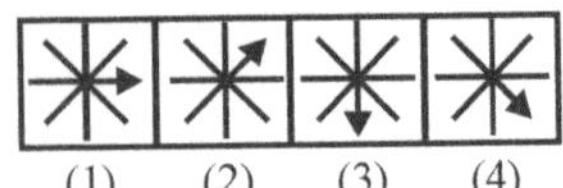

(a) 1 (b) 2
(c) 3 (d) 4

7. Select a figure from amongst the Answer Figures which will continue the same series as established by the five Problem Figures.

Problem Figures:

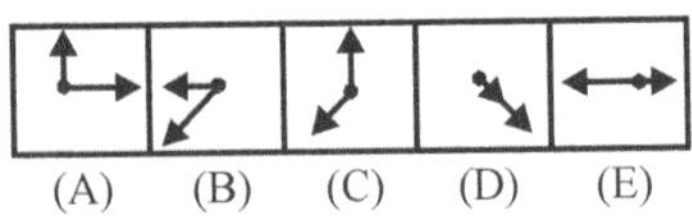

Answer Figures:

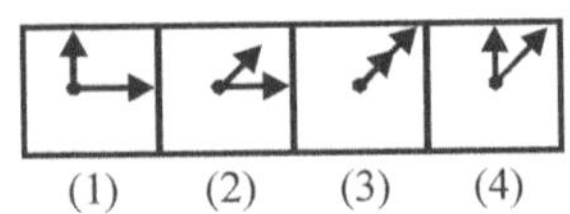

(a) 1 (b) 2
(c) 3 (d) 4

8. Select a figure from amongst the Answer Figures which will continue the same series as established by the five Problem Figures.

Problem Figures:

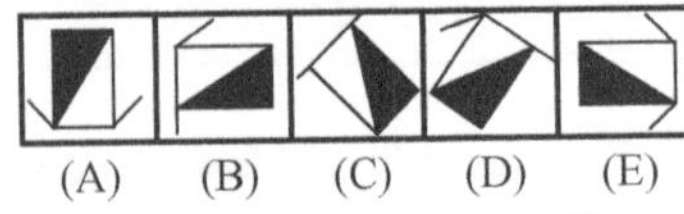

Answer Figures:

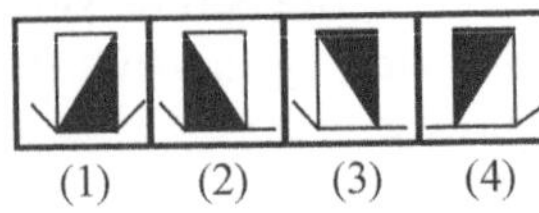

(a) 1 (b) 2
(c) 3 (d) 4

9. Select a figure from amongst the Answer Figures which will continue the same series as established by the five Problem Figures.

Problem Figures:

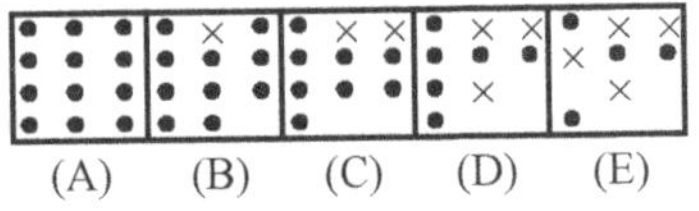

Answer Figures:

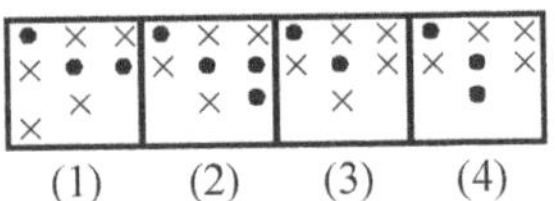

(a) 1 (b) 2
(c) 3 (d) 4

10. Select a figure from amongst the Answer Figures which will continue the same series as established by the five Problem Figures.

Problem Figures:

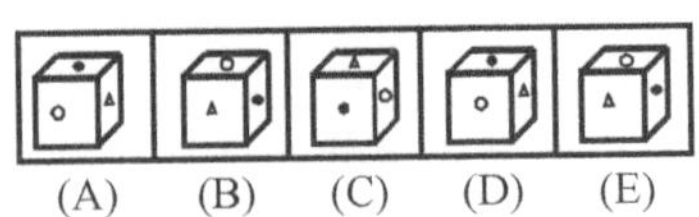

Answer Figures:

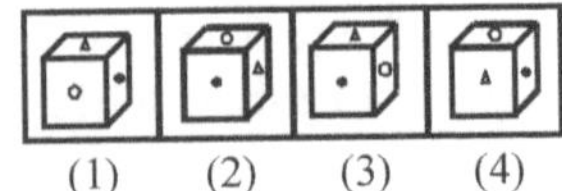

(a) 1 (b) 2
(c) 3 (d) 4

HINTS & SOLUTIONS

1. (c) In each step, element at the upper-right position gets enlarged, inverts vertically and reaches the lower-left corner; the existing element at the lower-left position, is lost and a new small element appears at the upper-right position.

2. (a) 

   The figure rotates sequentially 2, 1, 3, 1, 4… step in a CW (Clock wise) direction.

3. (c) The symbol along with line lie rotate 90° ACW (Anti clock wise) direction in each step, and the symbol interchange position in one step and are replaced by new symbol in the new step.

4. (b) The shading rotates through two and three steps alternatively in CW (clock wise) direction.

5. (d) The cross line mover ACW 90° and 45° alternatively and the pin arrow moves CW 90° and 45° alternatively.

6. (c) The arrow is changing its positions clock wise 90°, 45°, 135°, 45°, ...next should be 180°. So option (c) is correct answer.

7. (d) Small hand is moving anticlock wise 90°, 45°, 90°, 45°,... and Big hand is moving clock wise 135° constantly. So in the next figure, small hand must move 90° anti clockwise, and big hand must move 135°. So option (d) is correct answer.

8. (c) Similar figure reappears in every fourth step and each time a figure reappears, it rotates through 90° ACW.

9. (c) In each step, one dot is lost while another dot is replaced by a cross.

10. (c) All the three symbols in the dice are rotating clockwise. So option (c) is correct answer.

Mirror & Water Images

MIRROR IMAGES

INTRODUCTION

In this category, questions are based on the criteria that a few figures are given and you have to find out which one is the exact image of the given figure in a mirror placed in front of it. This image formation is based on the principle of 'lateral inversion' which implies that size of the image is equal to the size of the object but both sides are interchanged. The left portion of the object is seen on the right side and right portion of the object is seen on the left side. For example, mirror image of ABC = ƆꓭA

> **Note :** There are '11' letters in English Alphabet which have identical mirror images: A, H, I, M, O, T, U, V, W, X, Y.

Characteristics of Reflection by plane mirror

1. Perpendicular distance of object from mirror = Perpendicular distance of image from mirror.
2. The image is laterally inverted.

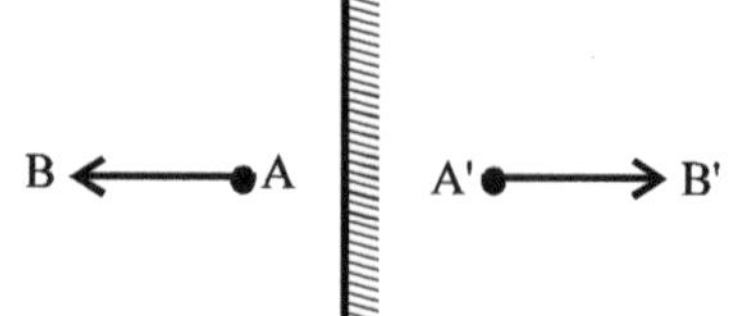

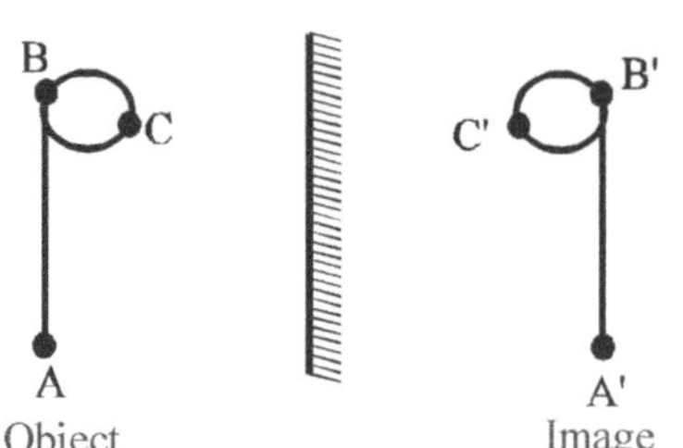

3. The line joining the object point with its image is normal to the reflecting surface.
4. The size of the image is the same as that of the object.

I. Mirror Images of Capital Letters

A	A	N	И
B	ꓭ	O	O
C	Ɔ	P	ꟼ
D	ᗡ	Q	Ϙ
E	Ǝ	R	Я
F	ꟻ	S	Ƨ
G	Ꭾ	T	T
H	H	U	U
I	I	V	V
J	Ⴑ	W	W
K	ꓘ	X	X
L	⅃	Y	Y
M	M	Z	Ƹ

II. Mirror Images of Small Letters

a	ɒ	n	n
b	d	o	o
c	ɔ	p	q
d	b	q	p
e	ɘ	r	ɿ
f	ʇ	s	ƨ
g	ǫ	t	ƚ
h	ʜ	u	u
i	i	v	v
j	ᒑ	w	w
k	ʞ	x	x
l	l	y	ʏ
m	m	z	ᴤ

III. Mirror Images of Numbers

0	0	6	∂
1	I	7	Ꞁ
2	Ƨ	8	8
3	Ɛ	9	ϱ
4	ᔦ	10	01
5	Ƽ		

IV. Mirror Images of Clock:

There are certain questions in which the position of the hour-hand and the minute-hand of a clock as seen in a mirror are given. On the basis of the time indicated by the mirror-image of the clock we have to detect the actual time in the clock. In the solution of such questions we use the fact that if an object A is the mirror-image of another object B then B is the mirror-image of A.

❑ Shortcut Approach

Whenever you have to solve a mirror image question, imagine a mirror placed in front of the object and then try to find its inverted image. The portion of the object that is near the mirror will now be the portion of the image near to the mirror in the inverted form.

EXAMPLE 1.

By looking in a mirror, it appears that it is 6 : 30 in the clock. What is the real time ?

Sol. As,

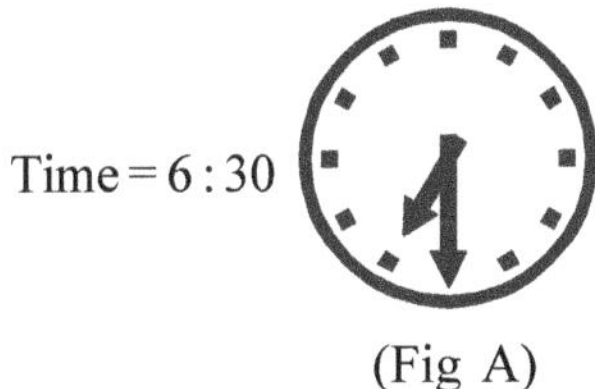

(Fig A)

(Fig B)

Clearly, fig (A) shows the time (6 : 30) in the clock as it appears in a mirror. Then its mirror-image i.e. Fig (B) shows the actual time in the clock i.e. 5 : 30. You can solve it quickly if you remember that the sum of actual time and image time is always 12 hours.

WATER IMAGES

The reflection of an object as seen in water is called its water image. It is the inverted image obtained by turning the object upside down.

Water-images of Capital Letters

Letters	A	B	C	D	E	F	G	H	I	J	K	L	M
Water-image	∀	B	C	D	E	Ŀ	Ꮆ	H	I	ſ	K	Γ	W
Letters	N	O	P	Q	R	S	T	U	V	W	X	Y	Z
Water-image	И	O	b	Ǫ	ʁ	Ƨ	⊥	∩	Λ	M	X	⅄	Z

Water-images of Small Letters

Letters	a	b	c	d	e	f	g	h	i	j	k	l	m
Water-image	ɐ	p	c	q	ә	ƭ	ƃ	ɥ	!	ɾ	ʞ	l	ɯ
Letters	n	o	p	q	r	s	t	u	v	w	x	y	z
Water-image	u	o	b	d	ɹ	ƨ	ʇ	∩	ʌ	ʍ	x	ʎ	z

Water-images of Numbers

Letters	0	1	2	3	4	5	6	7	8	9
Water-image	0	I	Ƨ	3	ᔭ	ƨ	ჲ	˩	8	∂

Note :

1. The letters whose water-images are identical to the letter itself are : C, D, E, H, I, K, O, X
2. Certain words which have water-images identical to the word itself are : KICK, KID, CHIDE, HIKE, CODE, CHICK

❑ *Shortcut Approach*

Whenever we have to analyze the water image of an object, imagine a mirror or a surface that forms an image just under the given object. The portion of the object that is near the water surface will be inverted but will be near the water surface in the image as well.

EXAMPLE 2.

Find the correct option for the water images below:

STORE
/////////////// ← water surface
?

Sol. In case of water image, the water reflection will usually be formed under the object / word.

In this case, the water image of the word will be an outcome of the water images of each of the letters like, the water images of S is Ƨ, T is ⊥, O is O, R is ʁ and E is E. Thus, the water image of the word 'STORE' is 'Ƨ ⊥ O ʁ E.'

STORE
///////////////
Ƨ⊥OʁE

❑ *Shortcut Approach*

(i) While solving a question, try eliminating some options and solving the questions will become easier. To eliminate options, keep in mind the pattern used in the object (given diagram whose image is to be formed) as well as the position of mirror or water such that the portion of the object near to the mirror / water will produce the same portion near the mirror / water in an inverted form.

(ii) Images are images, be it water or mirror, in both the cases an inverted image of the alphabets / numerals / clocks / any other object are formed by inverting the object. Inverting of the object solely depends upon the position of mirror or water surface w.r.t. the object.

PRACTICE EXERCISE

1. If the mirror is placed on the line LM, then which of the answer figures is the right image of the given question figure?

Questions Figure :

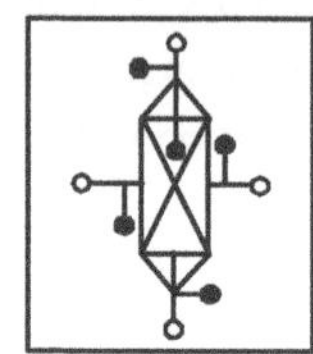

L M

Answer Figures :

(a) 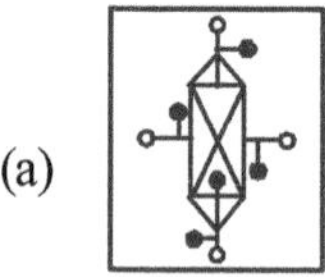 (b) 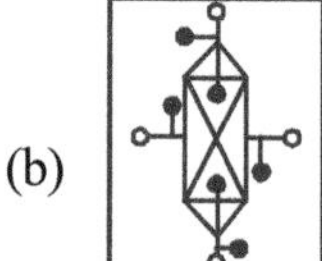

(c) 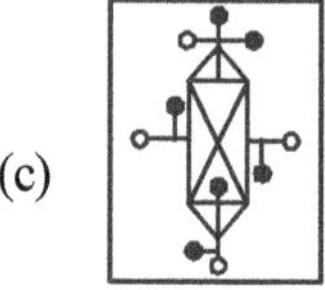 (d) 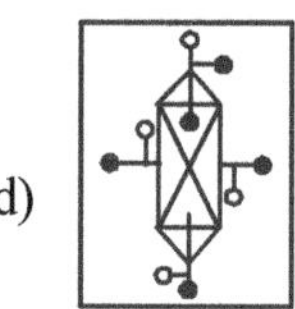

DIRECTIONS (Q. 2) : *If a mirror is placed on the line MN, then which of the answer figures is the correct image of the given question figure ?*

---

2. **Question Figure:**

Answer Figures:

(a) 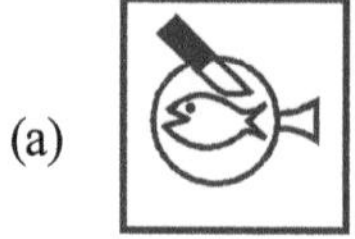 (b) 

(c) 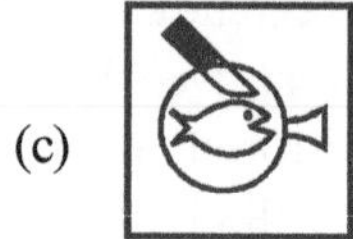 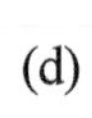 (d) 

DIRECTIONS (Q. 3) : *If a mirror is placed on the line MN, then which of the answer figures is the right image of the given figure ?*

---

3. **Question Figure :**

Answer Figures :

(a)  (b) 

(c) 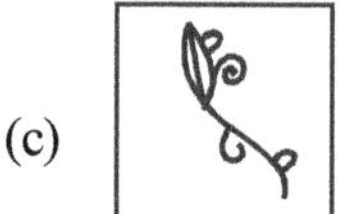 (d) 

4. Select the correct option that will be the mirror reflection of the problem figure.

Question Figure :

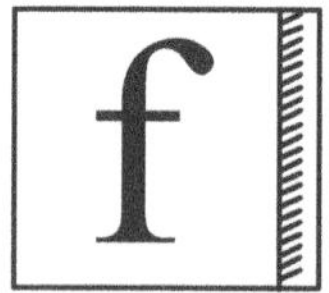

Answer Figures :

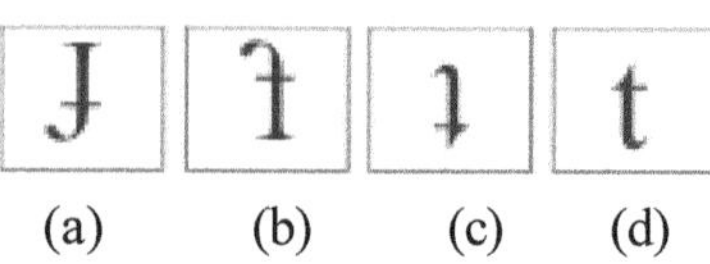

(a) (b) (c) (d)

5. If a mirror is placed on the line AB, then which of the answer figures is the correct image of the given question figure?

Question Figure :

Answer Figures :

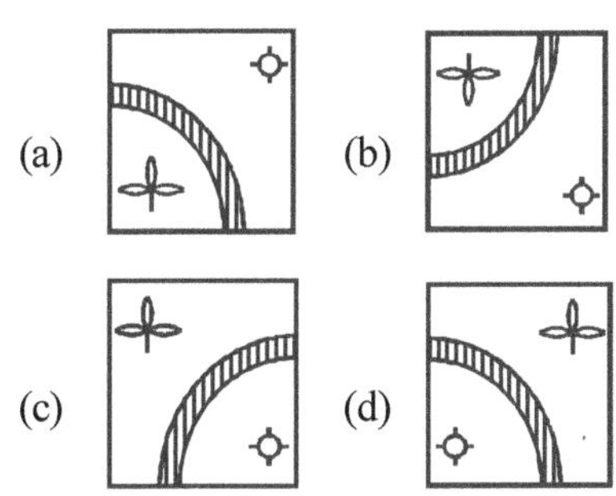

6. Choose the right water-image of the question figure from the given answer figures.

Question Figure :

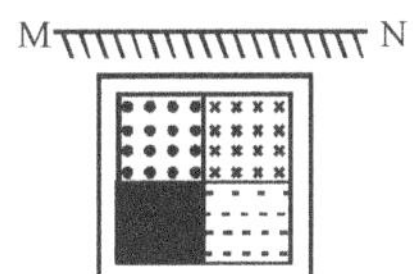

Answer Figure :

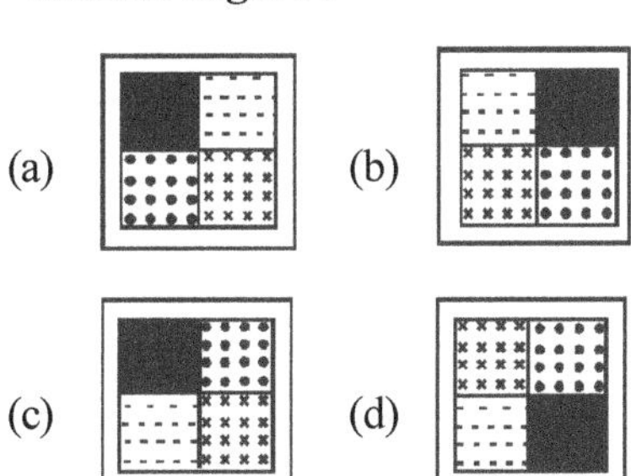

7. From the answer figures, find out the figure which is the exact mirror image of the question figure, when the mirror is placed on the line MN.

Question Figure :

Answer Figures :

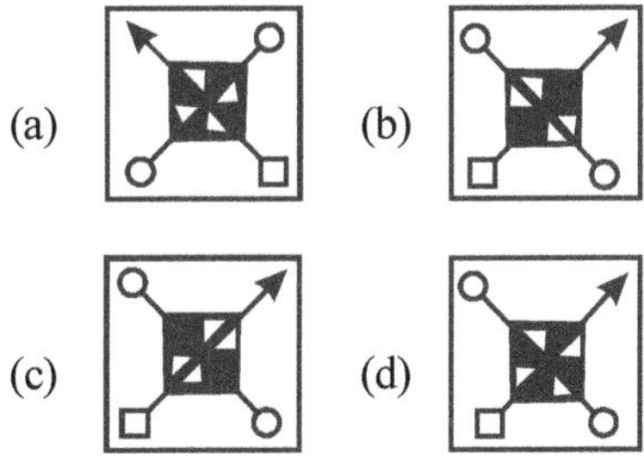

8. If a mirror is placed on the line MN, then which of the answer figures is the right image of the given figure ?

Question figure:

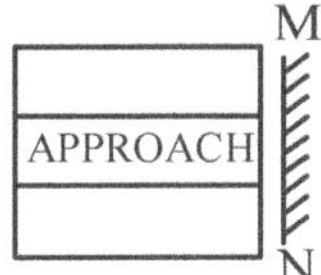

Answer figures:

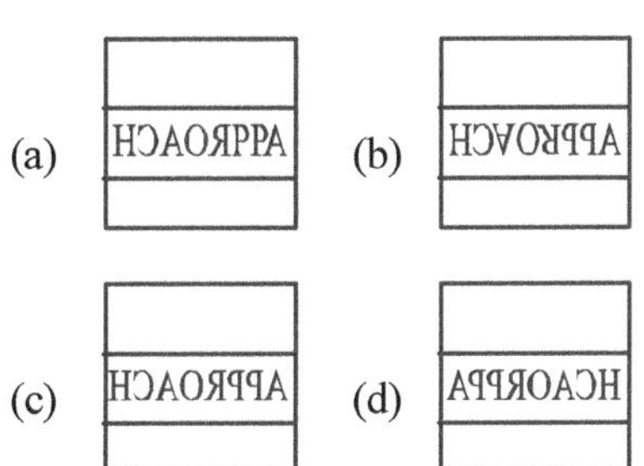

9. Which one of the following is water image of COMMISSION"?

(a) NOISSIMMOƆ

(b) COMMI ƧƧIOИ

(c) CO WWIƧƧIOИ

(d) NOISSIMMOƆ

10. If a mirror is places on the line MN, then which of the answer figures is the right image of the given figure?

Question figure:

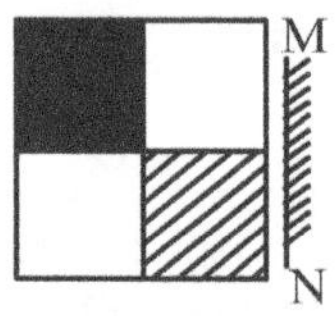

Answer Figures :

(a) 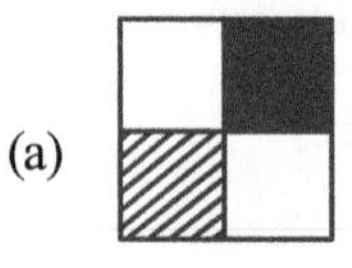

(b) 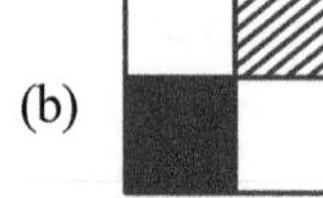

(c) 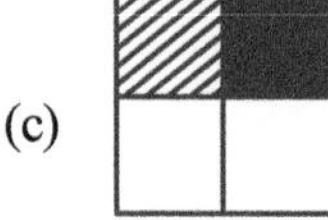

(d) 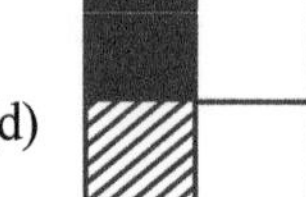

HINTS & SOLUTIONS

1. **(a)** In water image upside becomes downside.

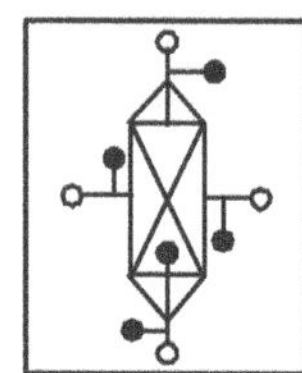

2. **(c)**
3. **(b)**
4. **(b)**
5. **(a)** Option (a) is the correct mirror image of given question figure.

6. **(a)**

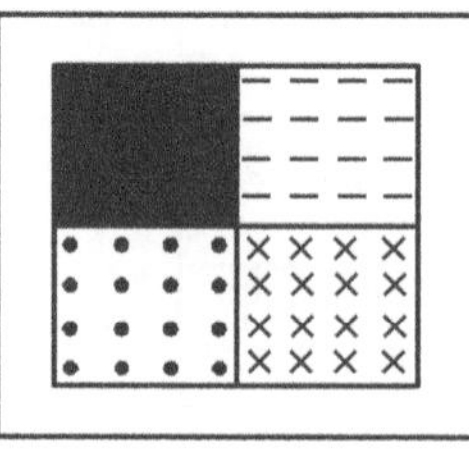

7. **(d)**

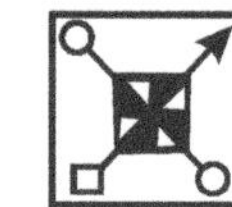

8. **(c)**
9. **(c)** Water image of

10. **(a)**

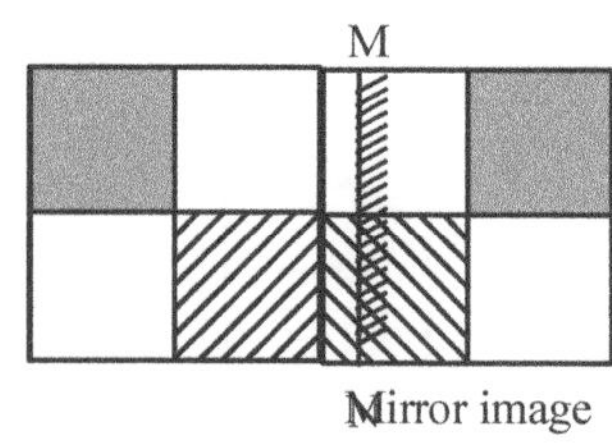

Mirror image

Paper Cutting and Folding

INTRODUCTION

In this section, a sheet of paper is folded in given manner and cuts are made on it. A cut may be of verying designs. We have to analyze how this sheet of paper will look when paper is unfolded.

Note that when a cut is made on folded paper, the designs of the cut will appear on each fold.

EXAMPLE 1.

Directions In the following example, figures A and B show a sequence of folding a square sheet. Figure C shows the manner in which folded paper has been cut. You have to select the appropriate figure from alternatives which would appear when sheet is opened.

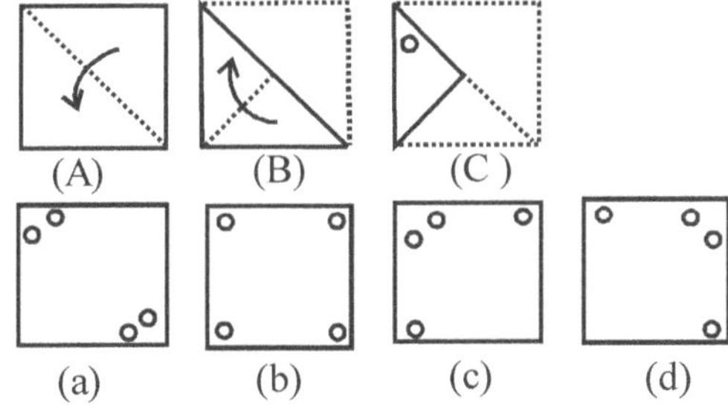

Sol. Step I-When sheet C is unfolded once, it will appear as follows

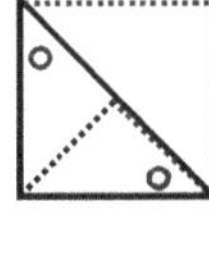

Step II -

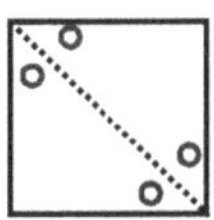

Clearly, the circle will appear in each of the triangular quarters of the paper. So, figure (c) would appear when sheet is opened.

EXAMPLE 2.

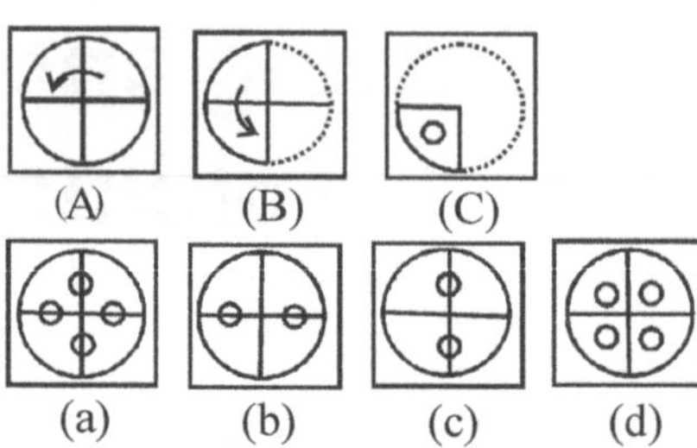

Sol. Here, a circular cut is made on the quarter circle. Hence, this sheet, when completely unfolded, will contain small circle on each quarter and will appear as option (d).

Shortcut Approach

- Consider a mirror placed on the dotted line facing the portion/part which is to be folded and the mirror image thus obtained is superimposed on the design of the other side to get the folded pattern.
- When more than one fold is made before punching then virtually try to unfold each fold one by one and predict the complete unfolded pattern.

PRACTICE EXERCISE

1. A piece of paper is folded and cut as shown below in the question figures. From the given answer figures, indicate how it will appear when opened.

Question figure

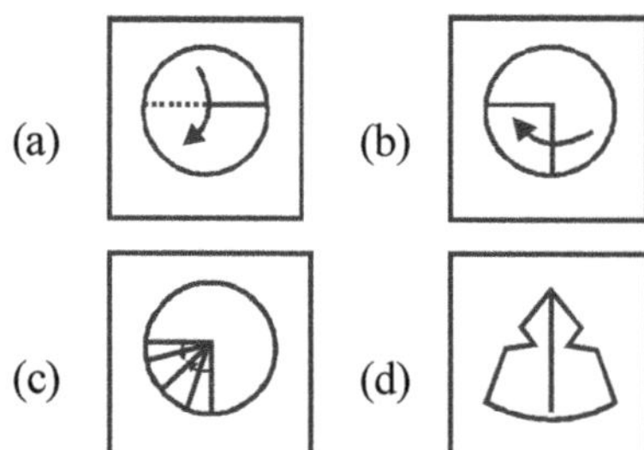

Answer figures

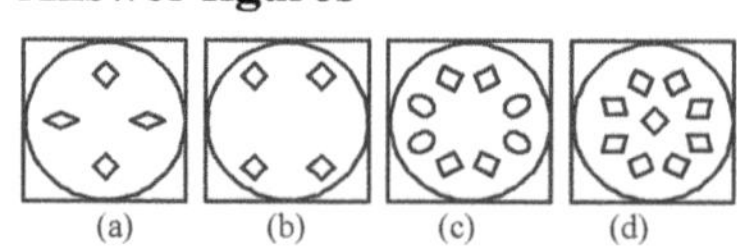

2. A square sheet of paper has been folded and punched as shown in the question figure. You have to figure out from amongst the four answer figures, how it will appear when opened?

Question figure :

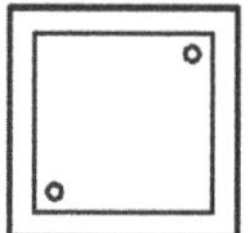

Answer figures :

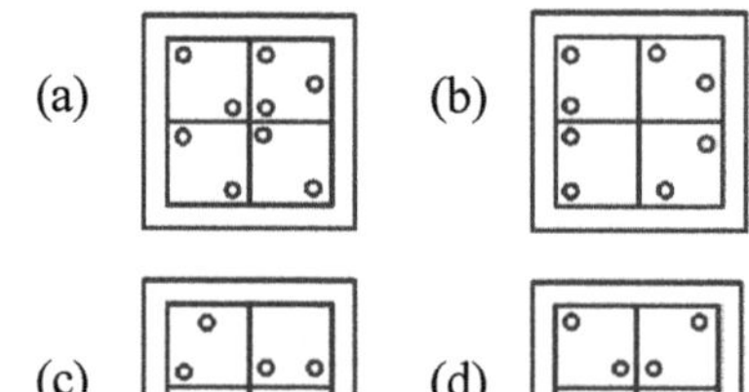

3. A sheet of paper has been folded as shown by the question figures. You have to figure out from amongst the four answer figures how it will appear when opened?

Question figures :

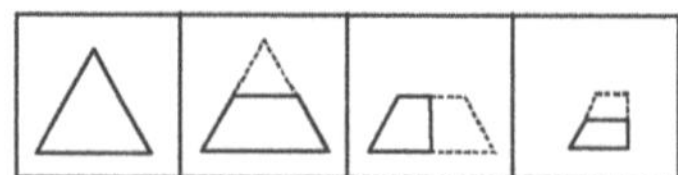

Answer figures :

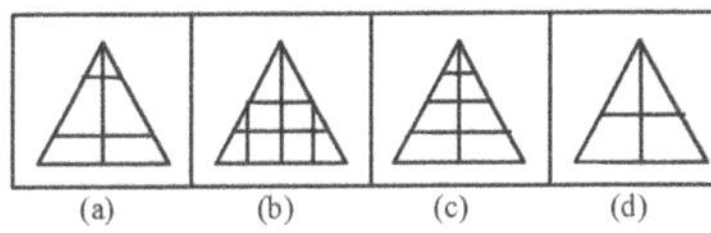

4. A sheet of paper when folded, punched and opened shows the question figure. Choose from the answer figures which punched hole pattern gives this figure.

Question figure (Open pattern) :

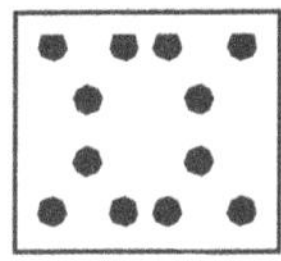

Answer figures (Punched hole patterns) :

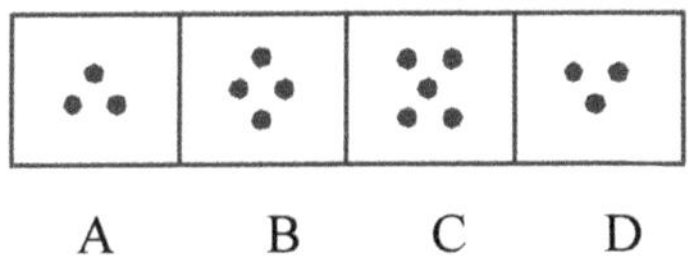

5. A piece of paper is folded and cut as shown below in the question figures. From the given answer figures, indicate how it will appear when opened.

Question Figures :

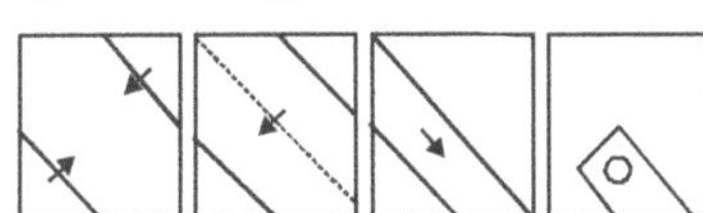

Answer Figures :

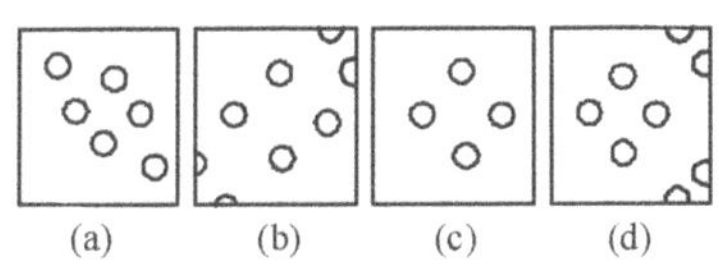

6. A piece of paper is folded and punched as shown below in the question figures. From the given answer figures, indicate how it will appear when opened.

Question Figures :

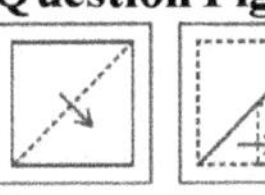
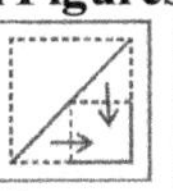
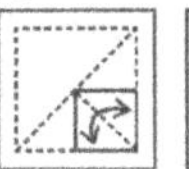
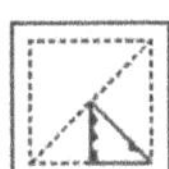

Answer Figures :

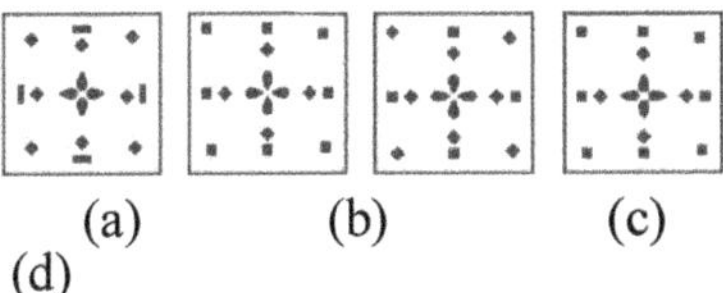

7. A piece of paper is folded and cut as shown below in the question figures. From the given answer figures, indicate how it will appear when opened.

Question figure:

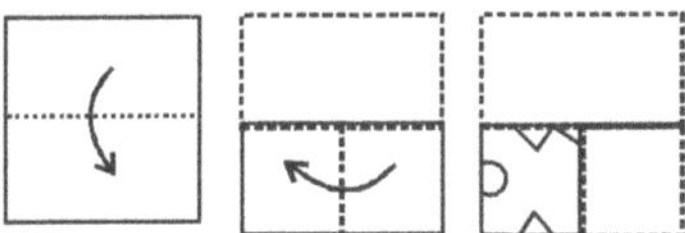

Answer figures:

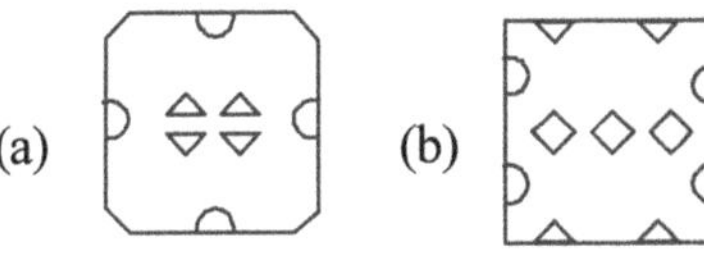

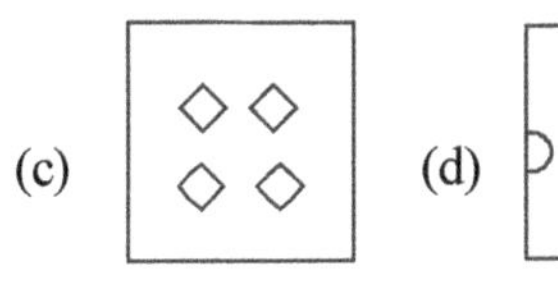

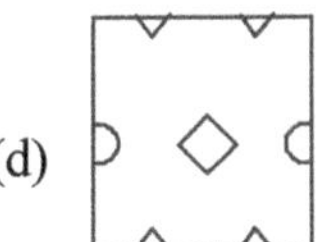

8. A piece of paper is folded and cut as shown below in the question figures. From the given answer figures indicate how it will appear when opened.

Question figure :

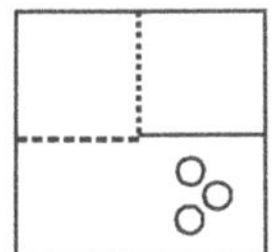

Answer figures :

(a) 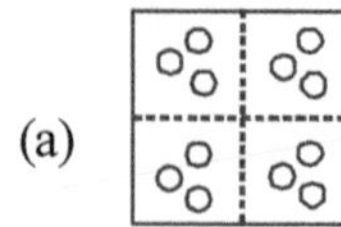 (b)

(c) 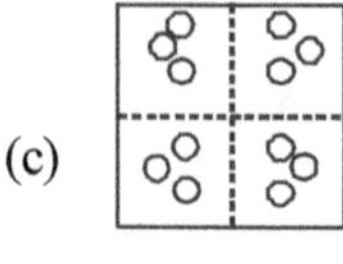 (d)

9. A piece of paper is folded and punched as shown below in the question figures. From the given answer figures, indicate how it will appear when opened?

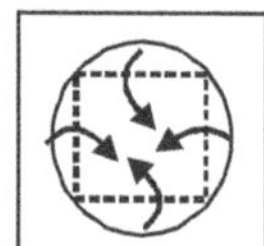 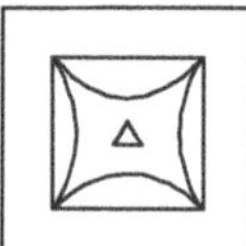

(a)  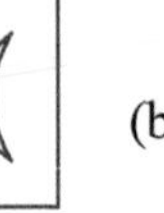 (b) 

(c) 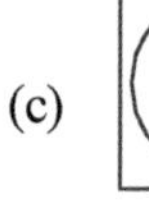 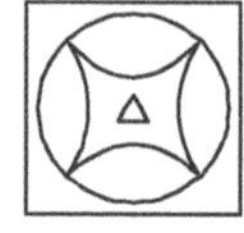 (d) 

10. A piece of paper is folded and punched as shown below in the question figures. From the given answer figures, indicate how it will appear when opened?

(a) 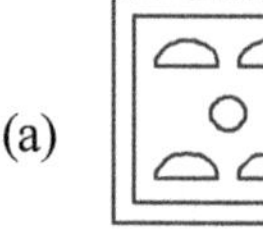 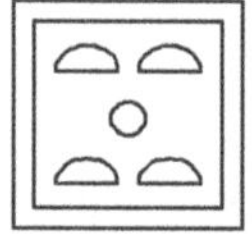 (b) 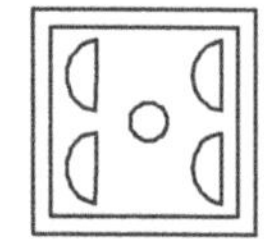

(c)  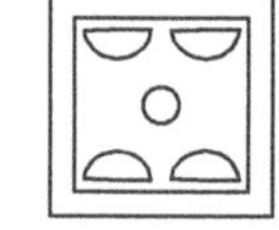 (d)  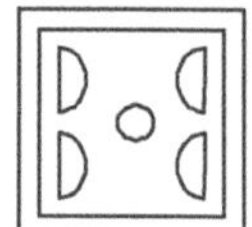

HINTS & SOLUTIONS

1. **(c)** **2.** **(b)** **3.** **(b)** **4.** **(a)** **5.** **(c)**
6. **(c)** **7.** **(b)** **8.** **(c)**

9. **(c)** 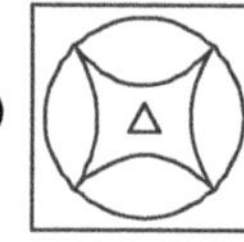

10. **(c)** 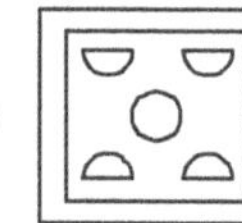

Completion of Figures

INTRODUCTION

In this section, an incomplete figure is given, in which some part is missing. We have to choose the segment, given in choices, that exactly fits into the blank portion of figure so that the main figure is completed.

Note : If you observe carefully, you notice that the missing portion may be the mirror image of any one of the quarters.

EXAMPLE 1.

Select from alternatives the figure (X) that exactly fits in the main figure to complete its original pattern.

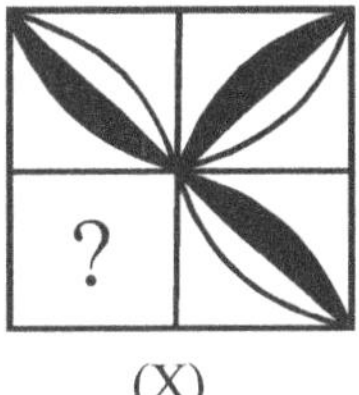

(X)

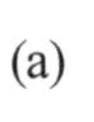    (c)  (d) 

Sol. In this question, half shaded leaf is moved clockwise. So, option (b) is right one.

❑ *Shortcut Approach*

- If answer figures contain similar figure but in rotated forms, then the correct answer figure is that figure which can be substituted at the missing part with least change in orientation.
- The correct option for the missing figure can be given in any rotated from, so student can rotate the figures to check the correctness of option.

PRACTICE EXERCISE

1. Which answer figure completes the form in question figure?

Question Figures :

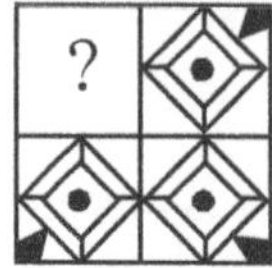

Answer figures :

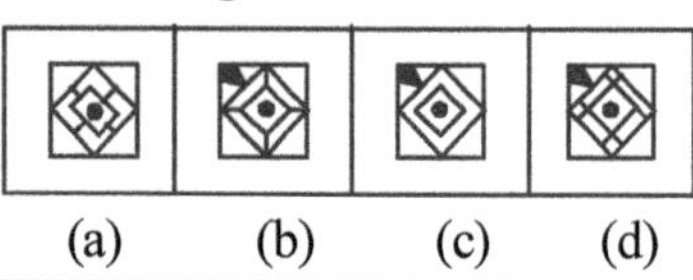

(a) (b) (c) (d)

DIRECTION: *In question no. 2, which answer figure will complete the question figure?*

2. **Question Figure**

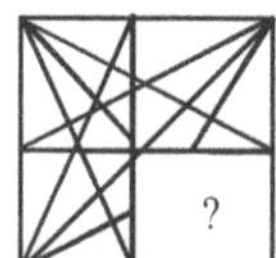

Answer Figures

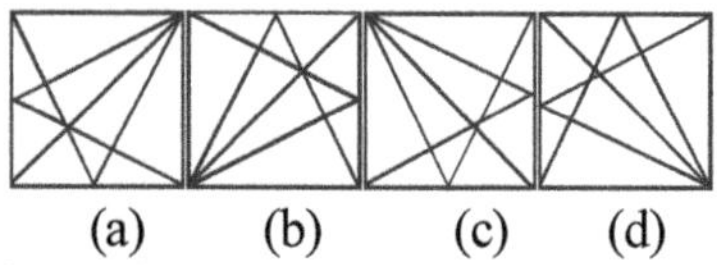

(a) (b) (c) (d)

DIRECTION (Q. 3) : *In the following question which answer figure will complete the question figure?*

3. **Question Figure**

Answer Figure

(a) 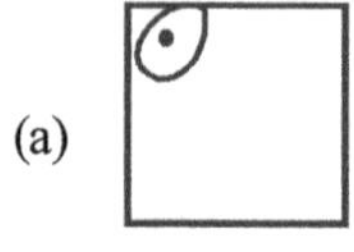 (b) 

(c) (d) 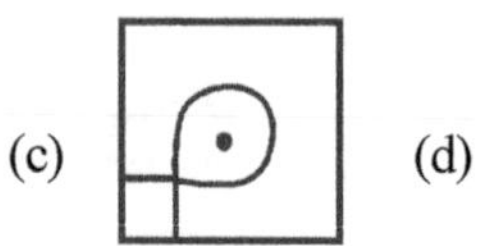

DIRECTION (Q. 4) : *Which answer figure completes the pattern given in the question figure?*

4. **Question Figure :**

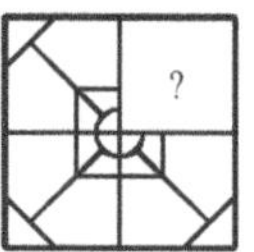

Answer Figures :

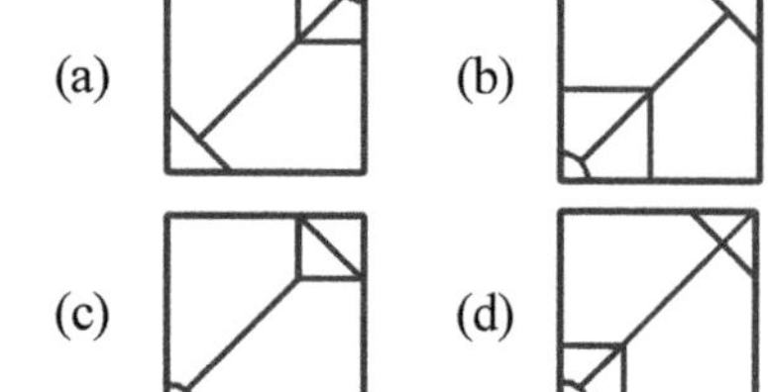

(a) (b) (c) (d)

DIRECTION (Q. 5) : *In each of the following question, which answer figure will complete the question figure?*

5. **Question Figure:**

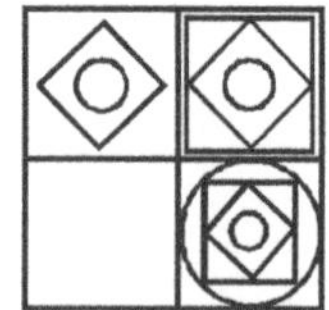

Answer Figures:

(a) 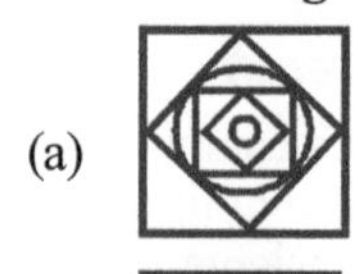  (b) 

 (c)  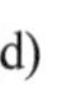 (d) 

DIRECTIONS : *In questions no. 6 and 7, which answer figure will complete the question figure ?*

6. Question Figure :

Answer Figures :

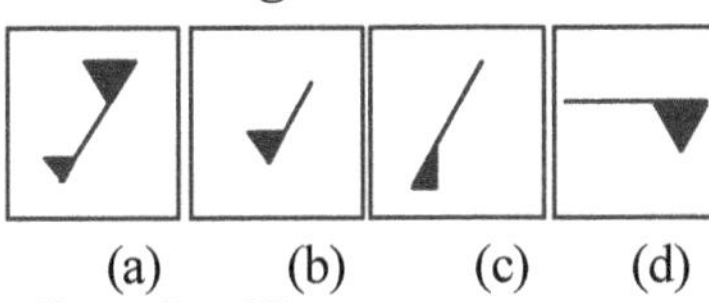

(a) (b) (c) (d)

7. Question Figure :

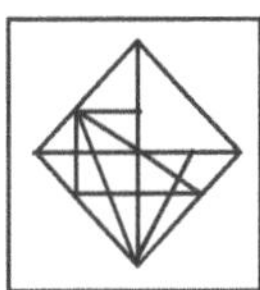

Answer Figures :

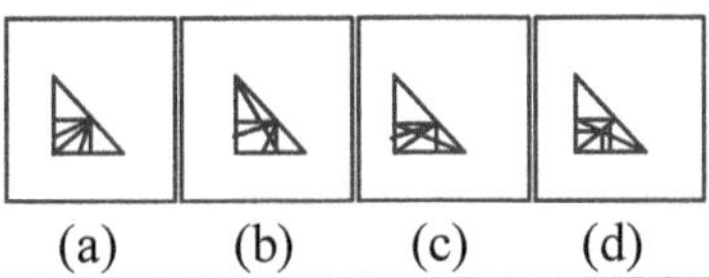

(a) (b) (c) (d)

DIRECTION: *In question no. 8, which answer figure will complete the pattern in the question figure?*

8. Question figure

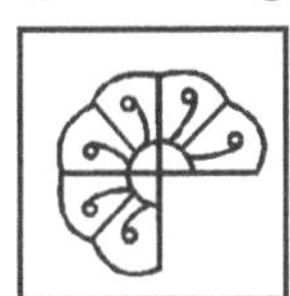

Answer figures

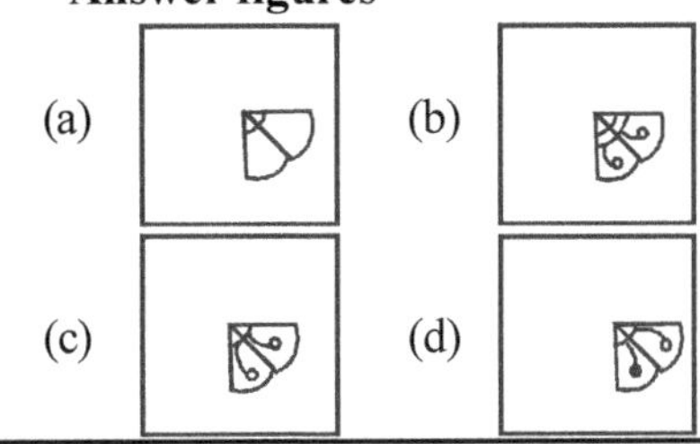

(a) (b) (c) (d)

DIRECTIONS (Qs. 9-10): *In the following Two Questions, which answer figure will complete the pattern in the questiion figure ?*

9. Question Figure

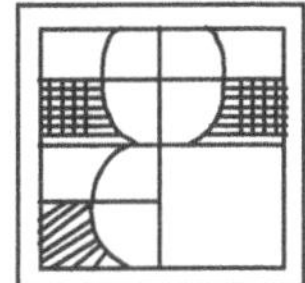

Answer Figures :

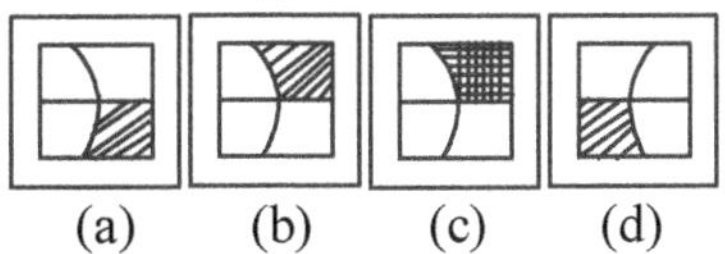

(a) (b) (c) (d)

10. Question Figure

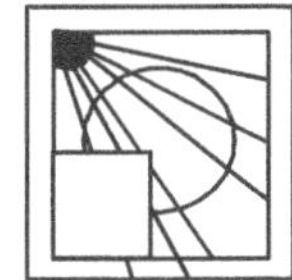

Answer Figures :

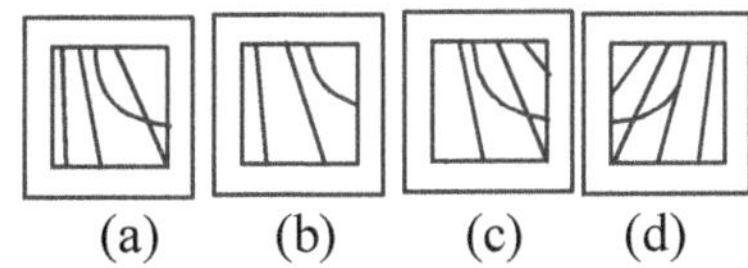

(a) (b) (c) (d)

HINTS & SOLUTIONS

1. **(b)**
2. **(d)** Option (d) will complete the question figure.
3. **(d)**

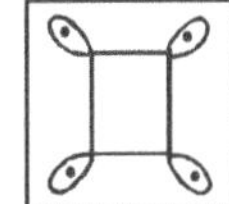

4. **(b)** 5. **(a)**
6. **(b)**

7. **(c)** 8. **(c)** 9. **(a)** 10. **(c)**

Hidden / Embedded Figures

INTRODUCTION

A figure (X) is said to be embedded in a figure Y, if figure Y contains figure (X) as its part. Thus problems on embedded figures contain a figure (X) followed by four complex figures in such a way that fig (X) is embedded in one of these. The figure containing the figure (X) is your answer.

EXAMPLE

Directions : In each of the following examples, fig (X) is embedded in any one of the four alternative figures (a), (b), (c) or (d). Find the alternative which contains fig. (X) as its part.

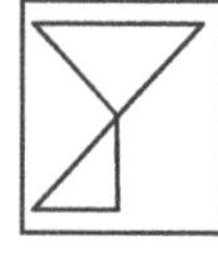

(X)

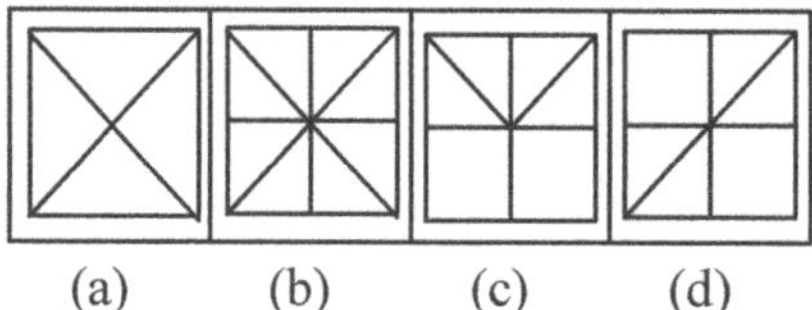

(a) (b) (c) (d)

Sol. Clearly, fig. (X) is embedded fig. (b) as shown below :

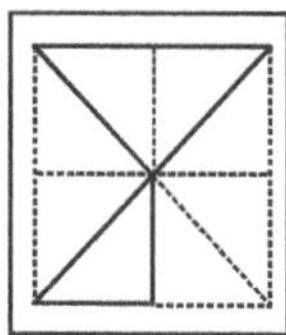

Hence, the answer is (b)

❑ *Shortcut Approach*

- There may be some questions in which the question figure is not directly embedded in any of the answer figure. In these type of questions, change the orientation of question figure to find the correct answer figure.
- In some questions, the question figure embedded in two or more answer figures, then the most appropriate answer is that in which the question figure is embedded with least change in its orientation.

PRACTICE EXERCISE

1. From the given answer figures, select the one in which the question figure is hidden/embedded in the same direction.

Question Figure:

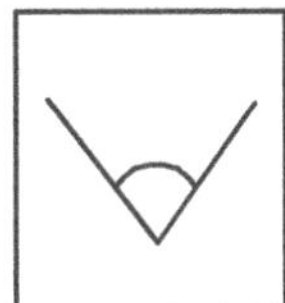

Answer Figures:

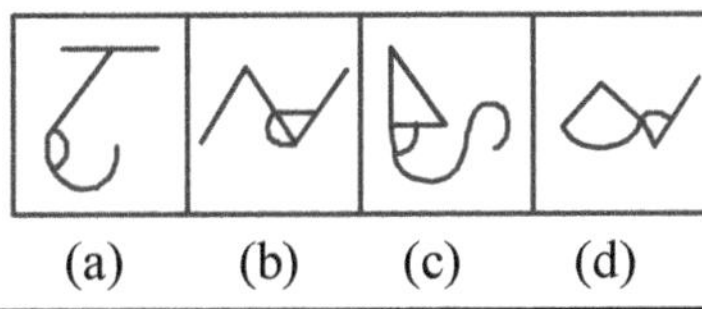

(a) (b) (c) (d)

DIRECTION : *From the given answer figures, select the one in which the question figure is hidden/embedded.*

2. **Question Figure:**

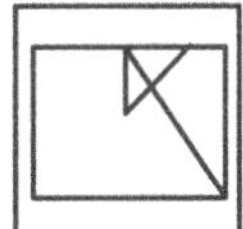

Answer Figures:

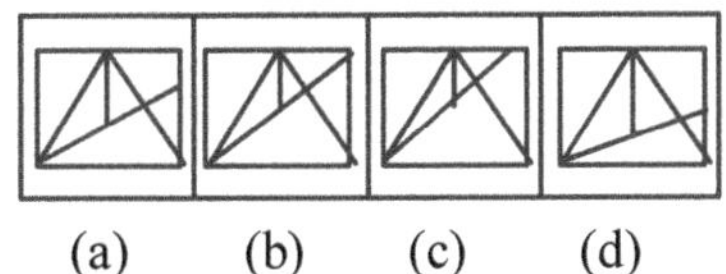

(a) (b) (c) (d)

DIRECTION: *From the given answer figures, select the one in which the question figure is hidden/ embedded.*

3. **Question Figure**

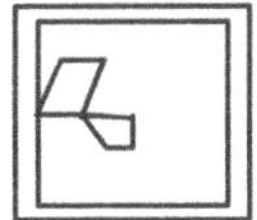

Answer Figures

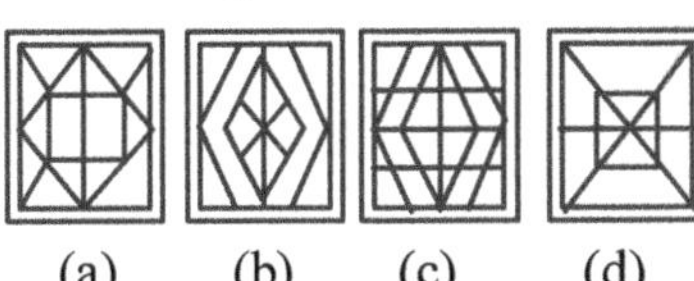

(a) (b) (c) (d)

4. From the given answer figures, select the one in which the question figure is hidden/embedded.

Question Figure :

Answer Figures :

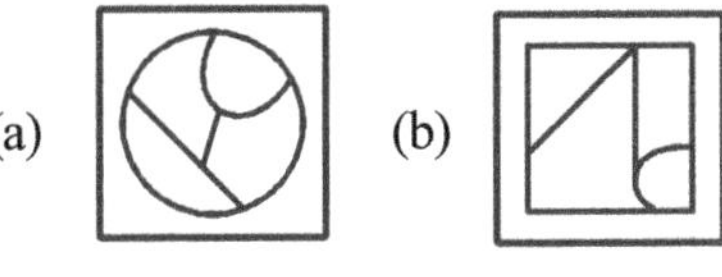

(a) (b)

(c) (d)

5. Select the answer figure in which the question figure is hidden.

Question Figure

Answer Figures

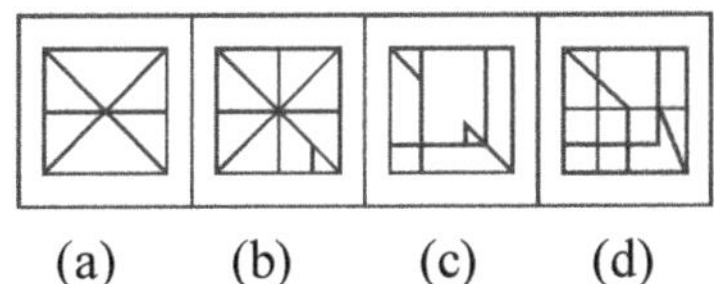

(a) (b) (c) (d)

DIRECTIONS (6-7) : *In each of the following questions, select the answer figure in which the question figure is hidden/embedded.*

(SSC Sub. Ins. 2013)

6. Question Figure:

Answer Figures :

(a) 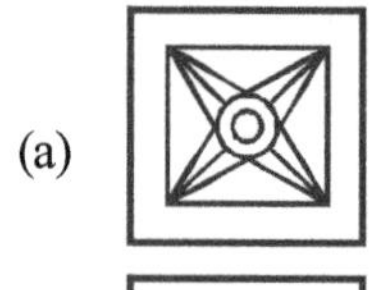 (b) 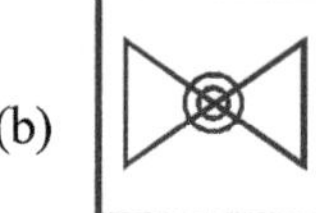

(c) 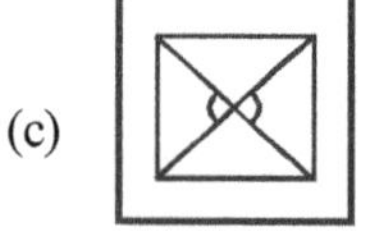 (d) 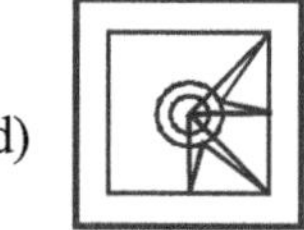

7. Question Figure:

Answer Figures:

(a) 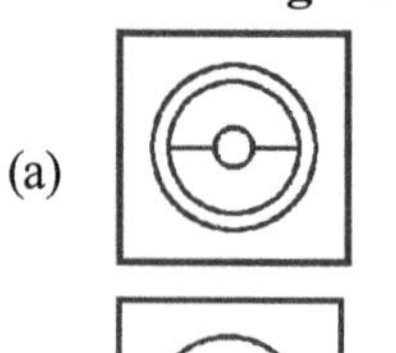 (b) 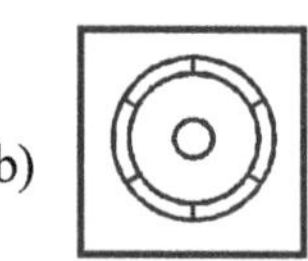

(c) 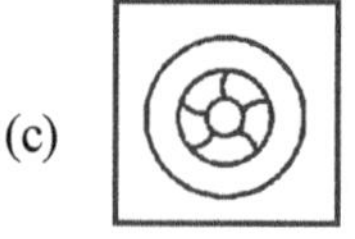 (d) 

8. Which of the answer figures is embedded in the question figure ?

Question Figure :

Answer figures :

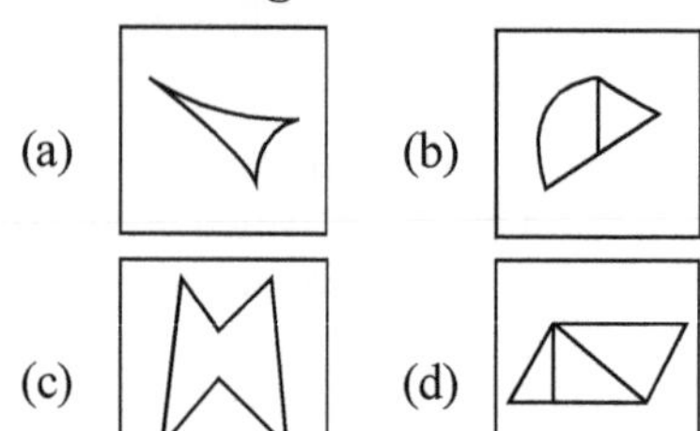

(a) (b) (c) (d)

9. From the given answer figures, select the one in which the question figure is hidden/ embedded.

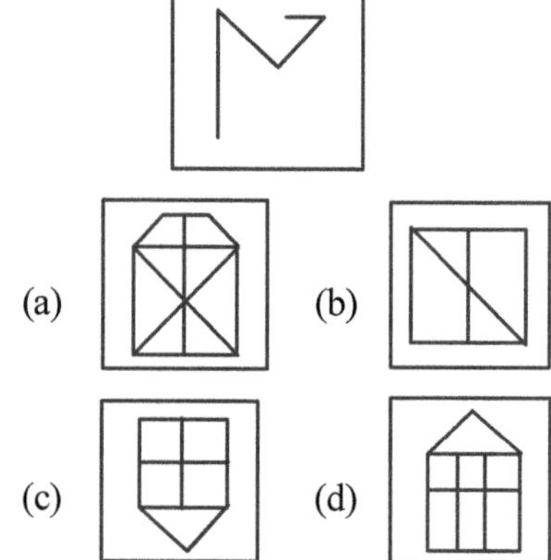

(a) (b) (c) (d)

10. From the given answer figures, select the one in which the question figure is hidden / embedded.

(a) 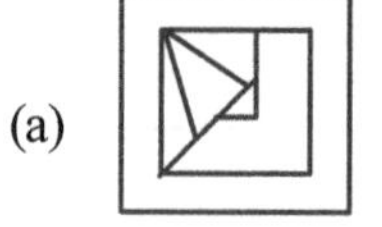 (b) 

(c)  (d) 

HINTS & SOLUTIONS

1. **(d)**

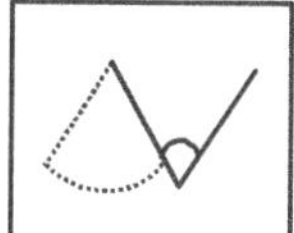

2. **(c)**

3. **(c)**

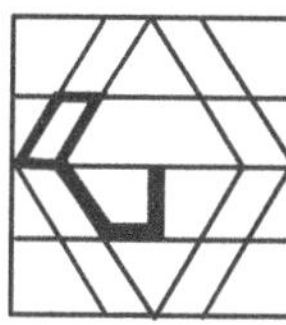

4. **(b)**

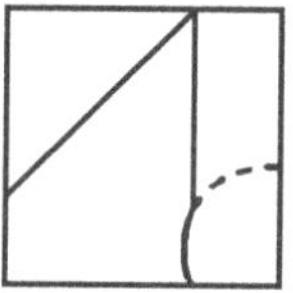

5. **(d)**

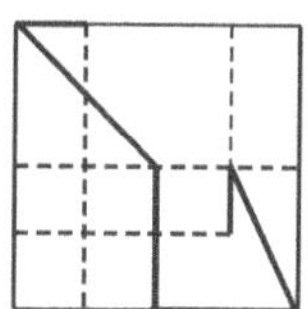

6. **(a)** **7.** **(d)**

8. **(c)**

9. **(a)** The figure  is embedded in 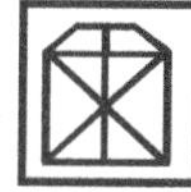

10. **(b)**

Figure Formation and Analysis

INTRODUCTION

In this topic, a question is one of the following types :

I. Formation of triangles/square/ rectangle etc. either by joining of three figures after choosing them from the given five figures or by joining any other pieces after selecting them from given alternatives.

II. Making up a figure from given components.

III. Making up a three dimensional figure by paper folding.

IV. Rearrangement of the parts of given figure.

V. Fragmentation of key figure into simple pieces.

TYPE-I: Formation of triangles/ square/rectangle etc. either by joining of three figures after choosing them from the given five figures or by joining any other pieces after selecting them from given alternatives.

EXAMPLE 1.

A set of five figures (A), (B), (C), (D) and (E) are followed by four combinations as the alternatives. Select the combination of figures which if fitted together, will form a complete triangle.

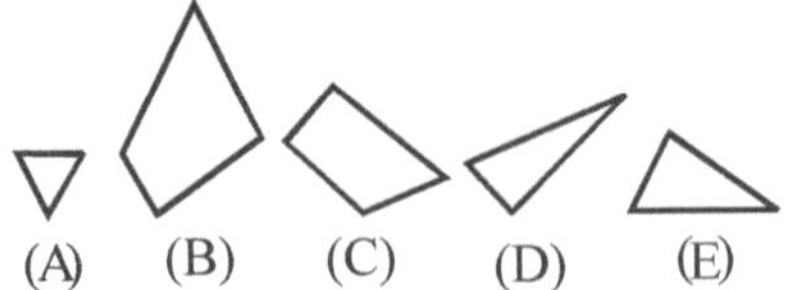

Sol. If figures A, B and E are fitted together, the resultant figure will be a triangle.

TYPE-II: Making up a figure from given components

EXAMPLE 2.

Find out which of the alternatives (a), (b), (c) and (d) can be formed from the pieces given in box 'X'.

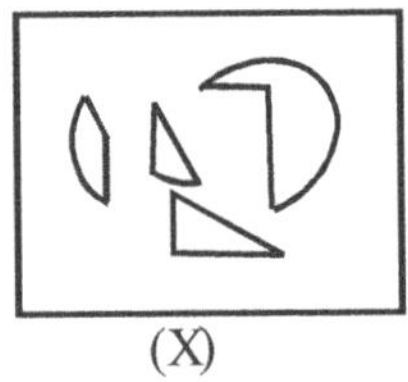
(X)

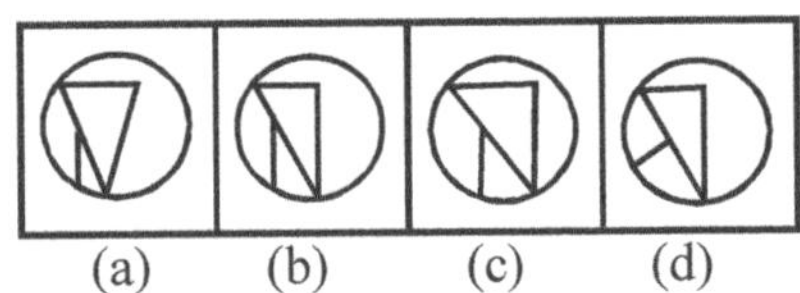

Sol.

Figure (b) can be formed from the pieces the given in box 'X'.

TYPE-III : Making up a three dimensional figure by paper folding. In this type, we have to analyze when a paper folded along the lines, how a three dimensional figure look like. Sometimes, a key figure is given which is made by folding one of the four figures given in alternatives. We have to determine which figure can be used to create the key figure.

EXAMPLE 3.

A figure 'X' is given. You have to choose the correct figure, given in the alternatives, when folded along the lines, will produce the given figure 'X'.

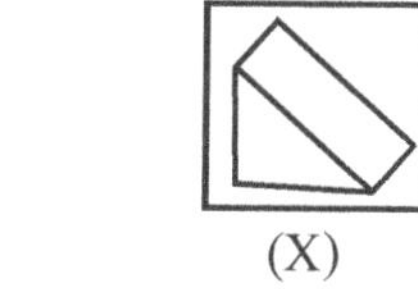
(X)

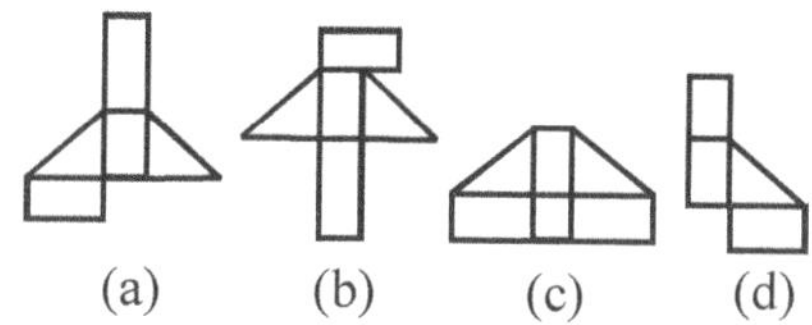
(a) (b) (c) (d)

Sol. Figure (a) will produce the given figure 'X'

TYPE-IV : Rearrangement of the parts of given figure.

In this type of questions, a key figure is given. We have to identify the figure from alternatives that is a rearrangement of parts of key figure.

EXAMPLE 4.

Which figure is the rearrangement of the parts of the given figure.

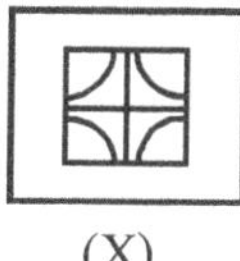
(X)

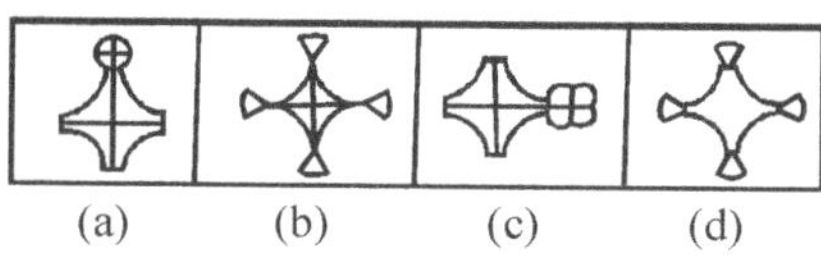
(a) (b) (c) (d)

Sol. Figure (a) is the rearrangement of the parts of the given figure 'X'.

TYPE-V : Fragmentation of key figure into simple pieces.

This type is opposite to **TYPE-II.** In this type, a key figure is given and every alternatives has different pieces. We have to select the set of pieces that can make the given key figure.

EXAMPLE 5.

Find out which of the alternatives will exactly make up the key figure (X)

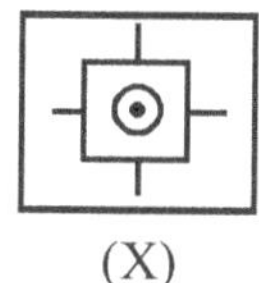
(X)

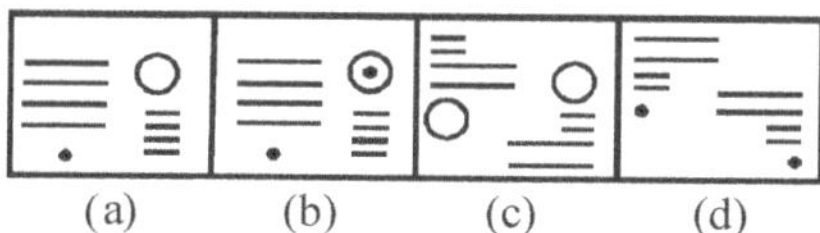
(a) (b) (c) (d)

Sol. Figure (a) will exactly make up the key figure 'X'

Shortcut Approach

- The number of elements given to form a figure must be equal to the elements present in the answer figure. This will help you to easily eliminate some of the option figures.
- The size of pieces of figures in the question figure and the size of pieces used to form a figure may vary but their shapes must have to be similar.

PRACTICE EXERCISE

DIRECTIONS (Qs. 1-4): *Among the four answer figures, which figure can be formed from the cut-pieces given below in the question figure?*

1. **Question Figure:**

Answer Figures:

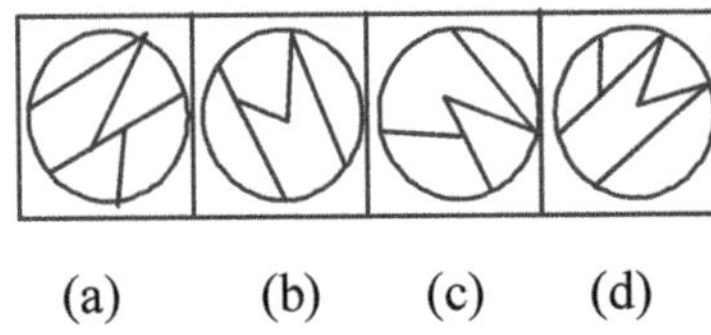

(a) (b) (c) (d)

2. **Questions Figure :**

Answer Figures :

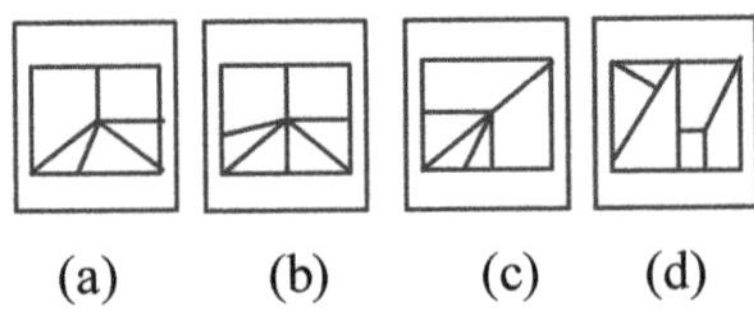

(a) (b) (c) (d)

3. **Question Figure :**

Answer Figures :

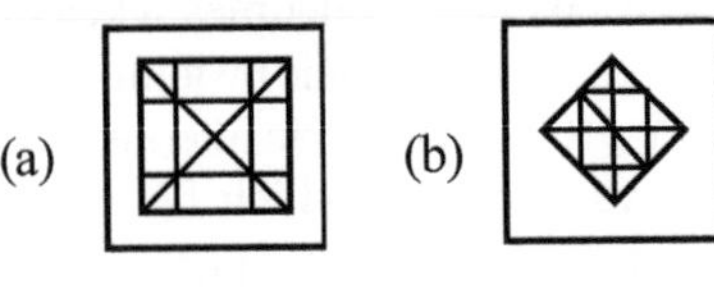

(a) (b)

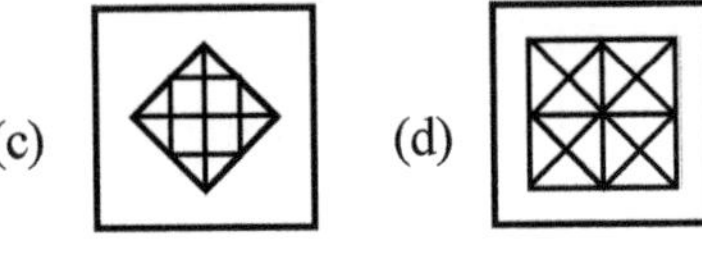

(c) (d)

4. **Question Figure :**

Answer Figures :

(a) (b) (c) (d)

5. Which answer figure includes all the components given in the question figure ?

Question Figure :

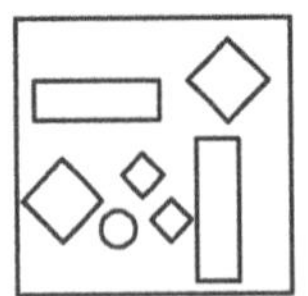

Answer Figures :

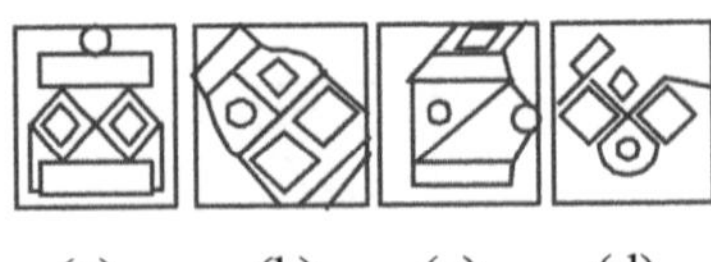

(a) (b) (c) (d)

6. Identify the response figure from which the question figure's pieces have been cut.

Question figure

Answer Figures.

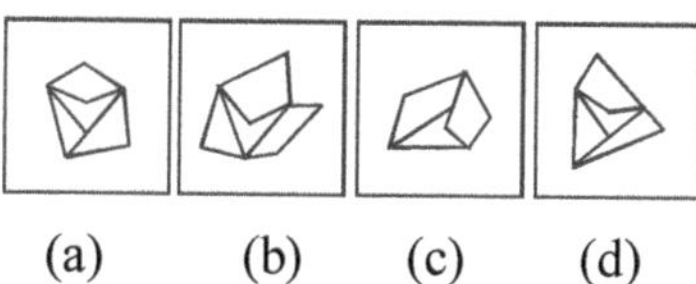

(a) (b) (c) (d)

7. Which of the answer figures include the separate components found in the question figure?

Question figure:

Answer figure:

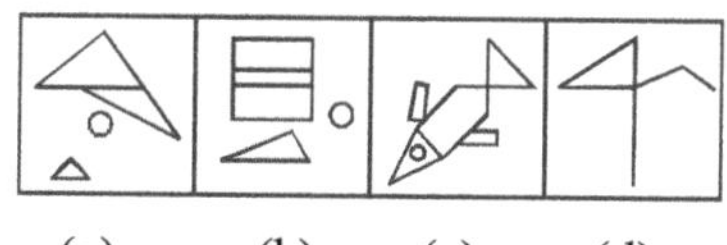

(a) (b) (c) (d)

8. Among the for answer figures, which figure can be formed from the cut - pieces given below in the question figure ?

Question figure :

Answer figures :

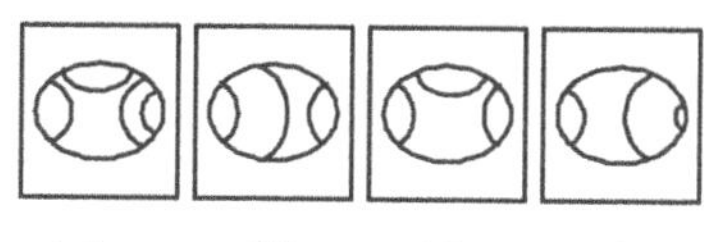

(a) (b) (c) (d)

9. Find out which of the following answer figures will exactly make up the question figure ?

Question Figure :

Answer Figures.

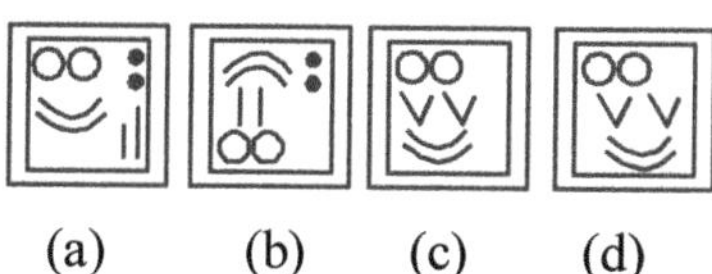

(a) (b) (c) (d)

10. Identify the answer figure from which the pieces given in the question figure have been cut.

Question Figure

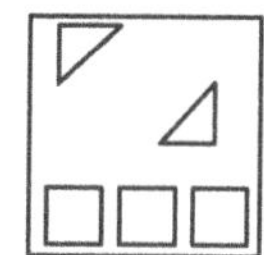

Answer Figure

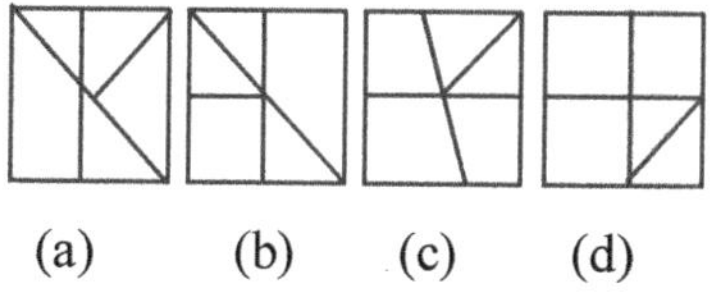

(a) (b) (c) (d)

HINTS & SOLUTIONS

1. (c)

2. (a)

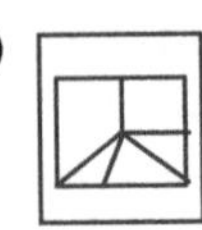

3. (c) 4. (a)

5. (a)

6. (d) All the components of question figure are present in the Answer Figure (d).

7. (c) All the components of Question Figure are present in Answer Figure (c)

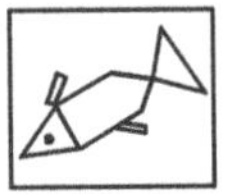

8. (d)

9. (b) All the components of the Question Figure are present in the answer figure (b).

10. (d)

Visual Reasoning

INTRODUCTION

Visual intelligence measures the ability to process visual material and to employ both physical and mental images in thinking. As a result people with a high visualization find it easier to comprehend information and communicate it to others. Your visualization skills determine how well you perceive visual patterns and extract information for further use. Visualization also facilitates the ability to form associations between pieces of information something which helps improve long term memory.

TYPES OF VISUAL REASONING

(A) Odd-Man Out Type
(B) Counting of Figures

(A) Odd-man Out Type

1. ROTATION OF SAME FIGURE

This is the most common type of classification. The similar figures are actually the rotated forms of the same figure in clockwise or anti-clockwise direction. The figure which comes out to be different from other is that figure which cannot be obtained by rotation of either of the other figures,

EXAMPLE 1.

Directions : In the following question, a group of five figures is given. Out of which four figures are similar to each other in a certain way and one is different from other. Find the odd figure out.

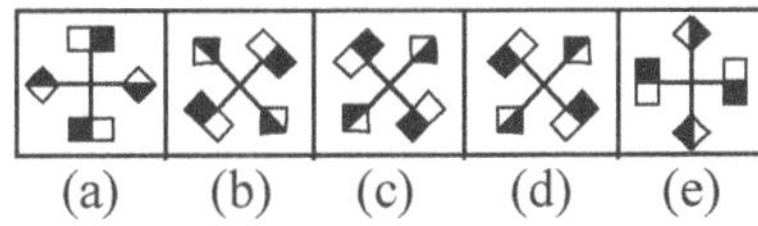

(a) (b) (c) (d) (e)

Sol. After examining the above figure, it is found that except (d) all figures can easily be obtained by clockwise and anti-clockwise movement or each other.

2. NUMBER OF ELEMENTS OR LINES

A group of figure may be classified on the basis of number of elements or the number of lines present in figures. The figures can also be classified on even or odd number of lines or elements present in figures. Classification can also be done on the ratio of number of lines and elements.

EXAMPLE 2

Directions : In the following question, a group of five figures is given. Out of which four figures are similar to each other in a certain way and one is different from other. Find the odd figure out.

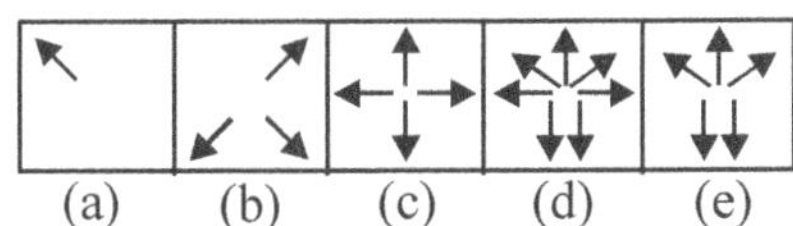

(a) (b) (c) (d) (e)

Sol. All except figure (c) contains odd number of arrows.

3. DIVISION OF FIGURES

This type of classification is done on the equal or inequal division of figures or divisioin of figure in some specified ratio or parts.

EXAMPLE 3.

Directions : In the following question, a group of five figures is given. Out of which four figures are similar to each other in a certain way and one is different from other. Find the odd figure out.

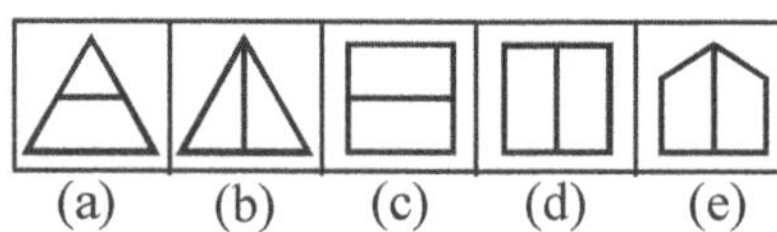

Sol. Except figure (a) all figures are divided into two equal parts.

4. SIMILARITY OF FIGURES

Classification on the basis of similarity of figure is done when orientation, shape, measure of angle or method of presentation of group is same except for the odd figure.

EXAMPLE 4.

Directions : In the following question, a group of five figures is given. Out of which four figures are similar to each other in a certain way and one is different from other. Find the odd figure out.

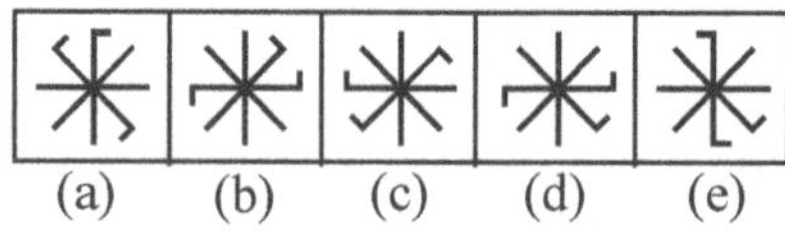

Sol. Let us consider the two adjacent bent lines as a pair. Then, in each figure except (d) there are two straight lines between the bent pair and the remaining bent line when the direction of bent is considered.

5. RELATION BETWEEN ELEMENTS OF FIGURE

In this type of classification, the elements of the figure bears a certain relationship between them in which the odd figure does not posses. This relation can be based on shape of elements presents, inversion of elements etc.

EXAMPLE 5.

Directions : In the following question, a group of five figures is given. Out of which four figures are similar to each other in a certain way and one is different from other. Find the odd figure out.

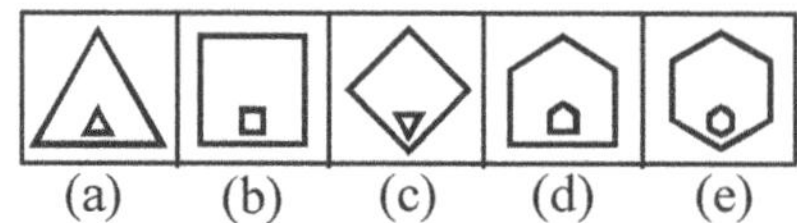

Sol. Except figure (c) in all the figures, both the inside and outside figures are similar but differ in size.

6. INTERIOR-EXTERIOR CONSIDERATION OF ELEMENTS

A figure can be formed from two or more elements, it is likely that some elements may lie in interior of other elements while some may lie in the exterior of the other elements. This consideration can be used for classification of elements from a group.

EXAMPLE 6.

Directions : In the following question, a group of five figures is given. Out of which four figures are similar to each other in a certain way and one is different from other. Find the odd figure out.

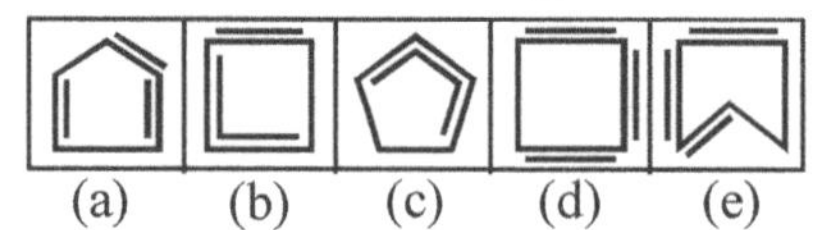

Sol. Only figure (d) does not contain any element present in the interior of the closed figure.

(B) Counting of Figures Type

Type-1: Counting of Straight Lines and Triangles

(a) Straight lines

A. Horizontal line 

B. Vertical line

C. Slant line

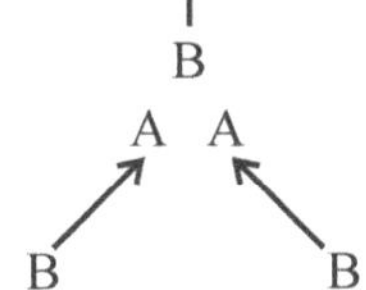

> ❑ ***Shortcut Approach***
>
> - Consider a line (AB) given
>
> 
>
>
> - Then, on counting, it will be counted as one line, i.e., AB and not as a two straight lines AC and CB.

EXAMPLE 1.

How many straight lines are there in the figure ?

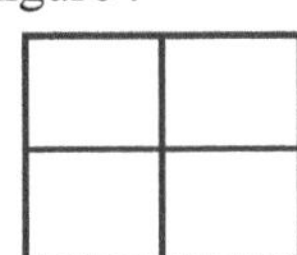

Sol.

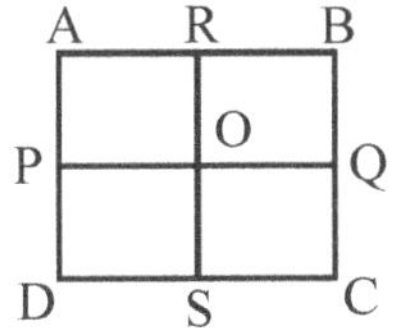

Horizontal lines = AB + PQ + DC = 3
Vertical lines = AD + RS + BC = 3
Slant lines = 0
$\therefore$ Total lines = 3 + 3 + 0 = 6

(b) Triangle –

It is a closed figure bounded by three side.

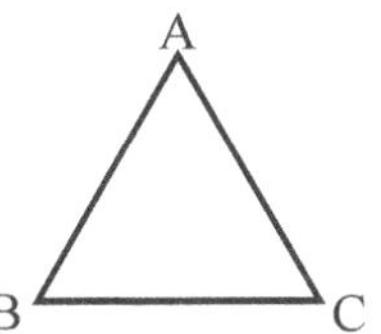

> ❑ ***Shortcut Approach***
>
> - Smallest triangles are counted first.
> - Now, counted those triangles which are formed with the two triangles and further counting goes on in the same way.
> - Largest triangle is counted in the last.

EXAMPLE 2.

How many triangles are there in the figure ?

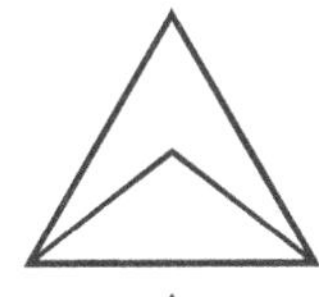

Sol.

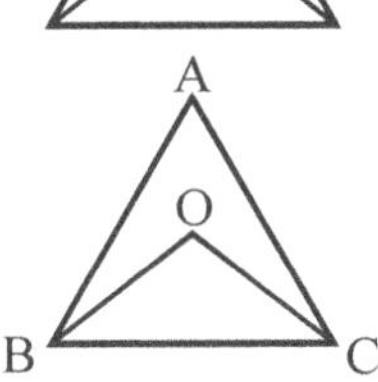

Smallest triangle = BOC = 1
Largest triangle = ABC = 1
$\therefore$ Total triangle = 1 + 1 = 2

Type-2 : Counting of Quadrilaterals and Polygons

(a) Square

It has four equal sides, equal diagonals, and each of the four angles equal to 90°.

❑ Shortcut Approach

- Count smallest squares first.
- Now, count squares which are formed with two squares and further counting goes on in the same way.
- Largest square is counted in the last.

EXAMPLE 3.

How many square are there in the figure ?

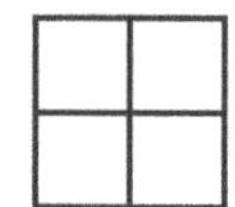

Sol.

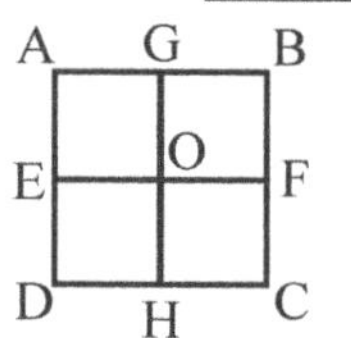

Smallest squares
= AGOE + GBFO + EOHD + OFCH
= 4

Square formed with four squares
= ABCD = 1

∴ Total squares = 4 + 1 = 5

FORMULA FOR COUNTING SQUARES

Let r be the number of rows and c be the number of columns.

Now, total number of squares
$= (r \times c) + \{(r - 1) \times (c - 1) + (r - 2) \times (c - 2) + \ldots\ldots$

The terms are continued upto the term which is equal to zero (0). This method is applicable only to the figure. where each row and column is divided into squares of equal sections.

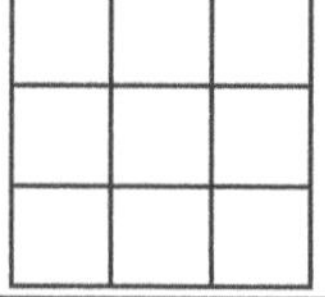

(b) **Rectangle**

It has four sides, and opposite sides are equal. It has equal diagonals and each of the four angles is equal to 90°.

EXAMPLE 4.

How many rectangles are there in the figure?

Sol.

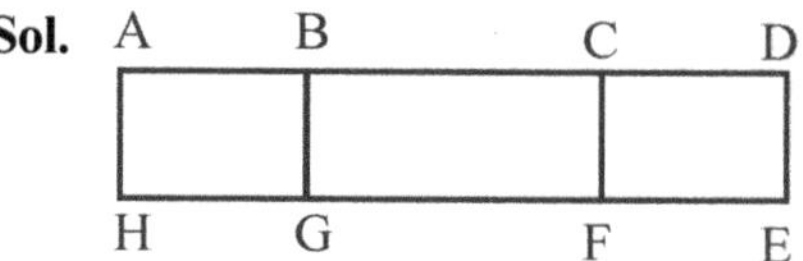

Smallest rectangles = ABGH + BCFG + CDEF = 3

Rectangles formed with two rectangles = ACFH + BDEG = 2

Largest rectangles = ADEH = 1

∴ Total rectangles = 3 + 2 + 1 = 6

FORMULA FOR COUNTING OF RECTANGLES AND PARALLELOGRAMS

Let r be the number of rows and c be the number of columns.Now, total number of rectangles or parallelograms
$= [(r + (r - 1) + (r - 2) + \ldots\ldots + 1] \times [c + (c - 1) + (c - 2) + \ldots\ldots + 1]$

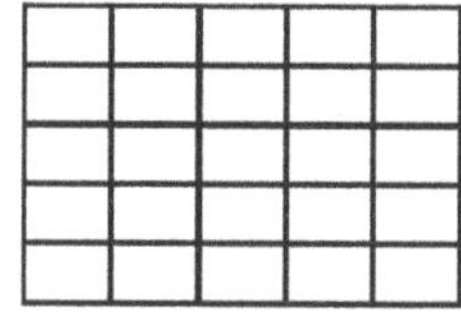

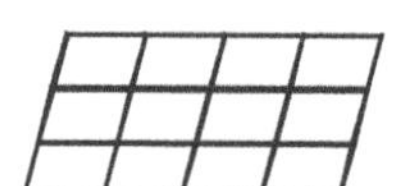

The method is applicable only to the figure, where each row and column is divided into rectangle of equal sections.

Type-3 : Circle

Circle is a closed figure. It has zero sides.

> **Shortcut Approach**
> - Keep writing numbers one by one inside the circles starting from 1 i.e., for 1st circle put 1, for 2nd circle put 2, for 3rd circle put 3 and so on.
> - The number which is put for the last circle is the required number of circles.

EXAMPLE 5.

How many circles are there in the figure ?

Sol. Here, we start counting of circles and mark them, as 1, 2 and so on and finally we end on getting 5 number of circles as shown below:

PRACTICE EXERCISE

1. How many triangles are there in the following figure ?

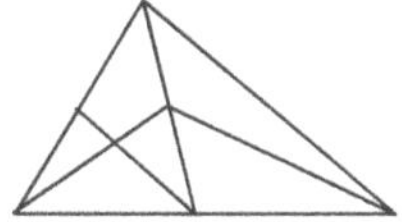

(a) 11 (b) 13
(c) 9 (d) 15

2. How many triangles are there in the following figure ?

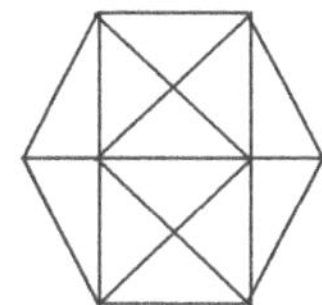

(a) 20 (b) 24
(c) 28 (d) 32

3. How many rectangles are there in the given diagram?

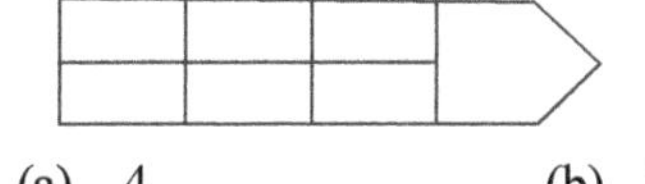

(a) 4 (b) 7
(c) 9 (d) 18

DIRECTION: (Q. 4): *Among the four answer figures, which figure can be formed from the cut-pieces given below in the question figure?*

4. How many cubes are there in the group?

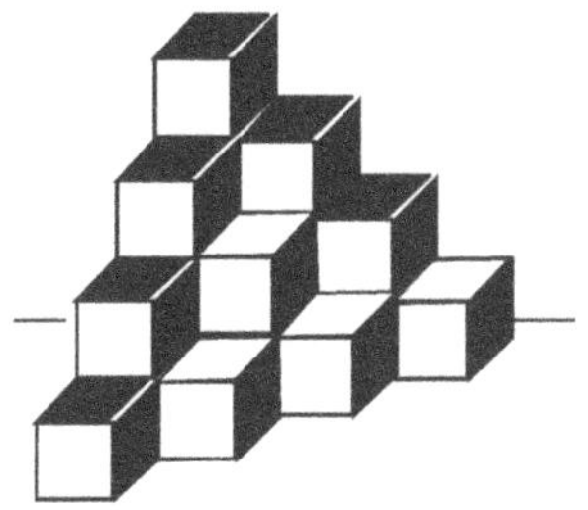

(a) 16 (b) 18
(c) 20 (d) 10

5. How many triangles are there in the given figure ?

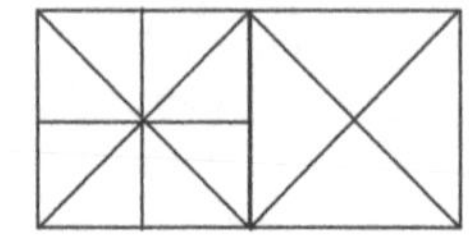

(a) 24 (b) 26
(c) 28 (d) 30

DIRECTIONS (Qs. 6-10): *In each problem, out of the five figures marked (1), (2), (3), (4) and (5), four are similar in a certain manner. However, one figure is not like the other four. Choose the figure which is different from the rest.*

6. Choose the figure which is different from the rest.

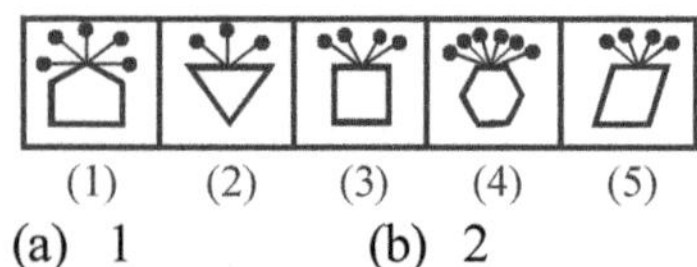

(1) (2) (3) (4) (5)

(a) 1 (b) 2
(c) 3 (d) 4

7. Choose the figure which is different from the rest.

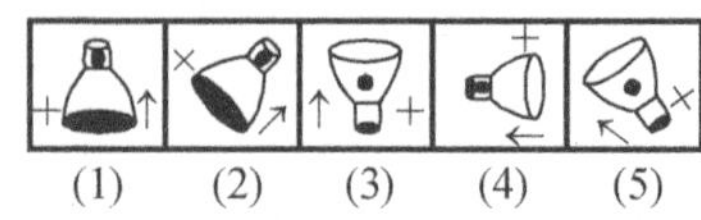

(1) (2) (3) (4) (5)

(a) 1 (b) 2
(c) 3 (d) 4

8. Choose the figure which is different from the rest.

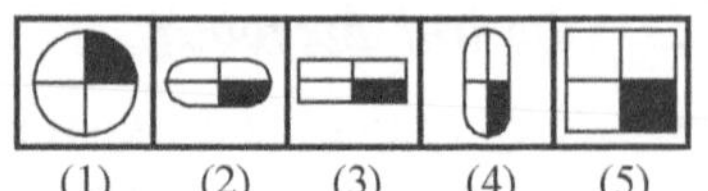

(1) (2) (3) (4) (5)

(a) 1 (b) 2
(c) 3 (d) 4

9. Choose the figure which is different from the rest.

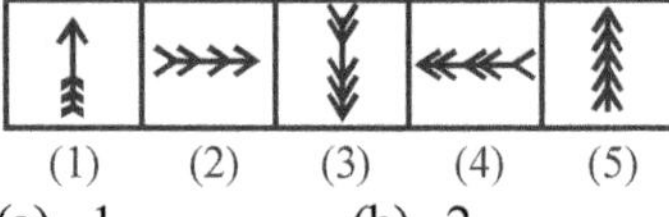

(1) (2) (3) (4) (5)

(a) 1 (b) 2
(c) 3 (d) 4

10. Choose the figure which is different from the rest.

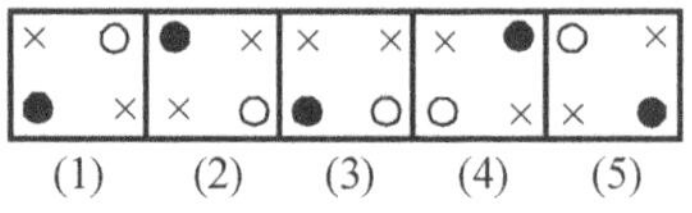

(1) (2) (3) (4) (5)

(a) 1 (b) 2
(c) 3 (d) 4

HINTS & SOLUTIONS

1. **(b)**

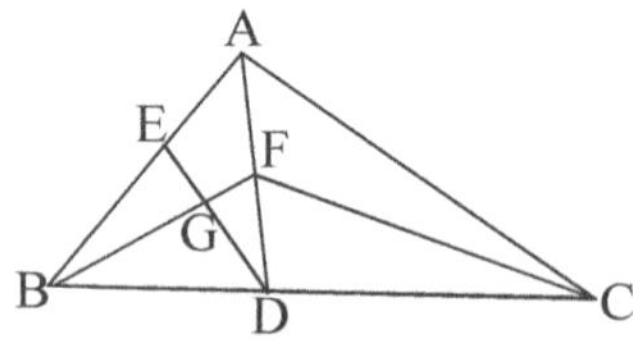

The triangles are :
ΔABC ; ΔABD ; ΔADC ; ΔAFC ; ΔFDC ; ΔAFB ; ΔFDB ; ΔFBC; ΔGBD ; ΔADE ; ΔGBE ; ΔFDG ; ΔDBE ;

2. **(c)** The figure may be labelled as shown.

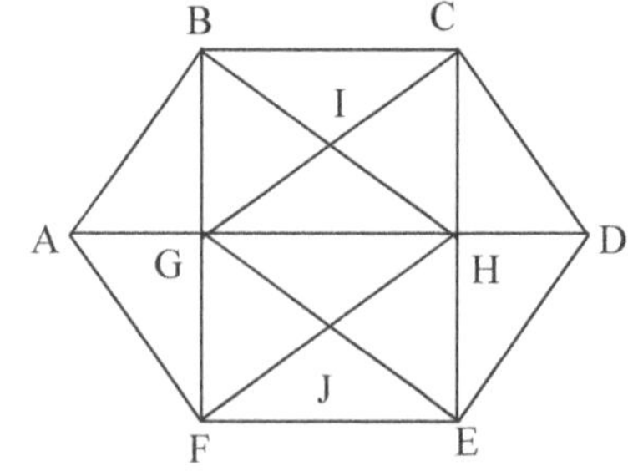

The simplest triangles are ABG, BIG, BIC, CIH, GIH, CDH, HED, GHJ, HJE, FEJ, GFJ and AGF i.e. 12 in number.

The triangles composed of two components each are ABF, CDE, GBC, BCH, GHG, BHG, GHF, GHE, HEF and GEF i.e. 10 in number.

The triangles composed of three components each are ABH, AFH, CDG and GDE i.e. 4 in number.

The triangles composed of four components each are BHF and CGE i.e. 2 in number.

Total number of triangles in the figure = 12 + 10 + 4 + 2 = 28.

Thus, there are 28 triangles.

3. (d)

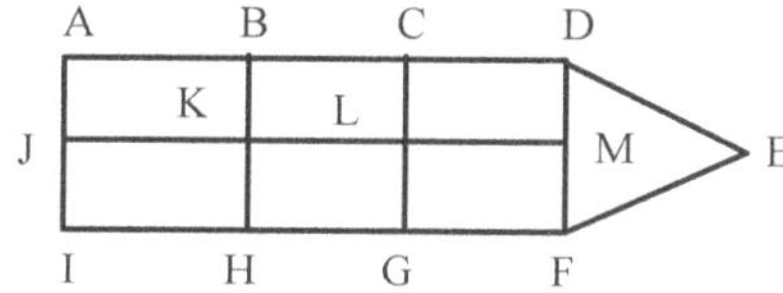

The rectangles are :

ABKJ; JKHI; BCLK;
KLGH; CDML; LMFG;
ACGI; ACLJ; JLGI;
BDFH; BDMK; KMFH;
ADFI; ADMJ; JMFI
ABHI, BCGH and CDFG are squares. We know that every square is a rectanlge. But its reverse is not always true.

Note : *By option only its easy to analyze.*

4. (c) 10 cubes are visible and 10 cubes are hidden. Clearly, there is one column having four cubes.

There are two columns each having three cubes.

There are three columns, each having two cubes.

There are four columns, each having only one cube.

Thus, total number of cubes = 4 + 6 + 6 + 4 = 20 cubes

5. (b)

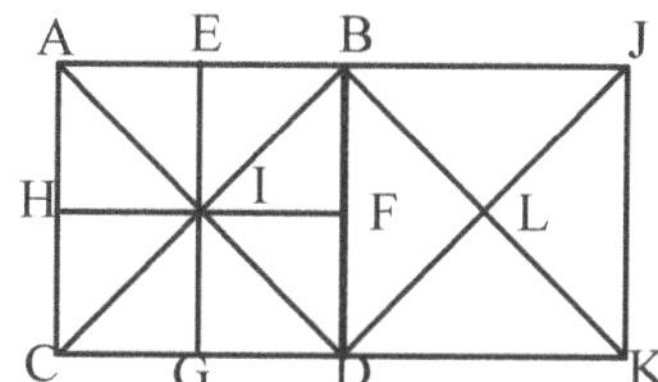

The triangles are :

ΔAIH; ΔAIE; ΔEIB; ΔBFI;
ΔIHC; ΔIGC; ΔIGD; ΔDFI;
ΔIAB; ΔIBD; ΔICD; ΔIAC;
ΔBAC; ΔACD; ΔBDC; ΔBDA;
ΔBLD; ΔLDK; ΔKLJ; ΔJLB;
ΔJBK; ΔBDK; ΔDBJ; ΔDKJ
ΔADJ; ΔCBK.

Thus, there are 26 triangles.

6. (a) The pins, equal in number to the number of sides in the main figure are attached to the midpoint of a side of the main figure in case of figures (2), (3), (4) and (5). In fig. (1), these pins are attached to a vertex of the main figure.

7. (d) In all other figures, the arrow and the V sign lie towards the black end of the main figure.

8. (a) In all other figures, the lower-right quarter portion is shaded.

9. (b) Each one of the figures except fig. (2), consists of five arrowheads.

10. (c) In each one of the figures except fig. (3), the two crosses (x) appear in the diagonally opposite corners.

Chapter 25 Evaluating Inferences

INTRODUCTION

This chapter makes you aware about a special type of question pattern which has become a regular trend of almost all type of competitive examination. An inference is a logical conclusion on evidence. A valid inference is believable and realistic. As per the pattern, a passage is given followed by some inferences (conclusions) and the examinee is asked to decide whether a given inference follows or not in the light of the given passage. Let us see the format below:

What is the Problem Like?

Problem Format/ Sample Problem:-

Directions (Qs 1-5): Below is given a passage followed by several possible inferences which can be drawn from the facts stated in the passage. You have to examine each inference separately in the context of the passage and decide upon its degree of truth or falsity.

Mark answer:

(a) If the inference is definitely true i.e., it properly follows from the statement of facts given.

(b) If the inference is 'probably true' though not definitely true in the light of the facts given.

(c) If the 'data are inadequate' i.e. from the facts given you can not say whether the inference is likely to be true or false.

(d) If the inference is 'probably false' though not definitely false' in the light of the facts given.

(e) If the inference is 'definitely false' i.e., it cannot possibly be drawn from the facts given or it contradicts the given facts.

PASSAGE

In its most ambitions bid ever to house 6 crore slum dwellers and realise the vision of a slum-free India, the government is rolling out a massive plan to build 50 lakh dwelling units in five years across 400 towns and cities. The programme could free up thousands of acres of valuable government land across the country and generate crores worth of business for real estate developers. Proliferation of slums has had an adverse impact on the GDP growth for years. Slum dwellers are characterised by low productivity and susceptibility to poor health conditions. The government believes that better housing facilities will address social issues and also have a multiplier effect and serve as an economic stimulus.

Q 1. Development of land occupied by slums in cities of India will not have any effect on the common public.

Q 2. Majority of the slums in cities and towns in India are on prime private properties.

Q 3. Per capita income of slum dwellers is significantly lower than that of those living in better housing facilities.

Q 4. Cities and towns of developed countries are free from slums.

Q 5. Health and sanitary conditions in slums are far below the acceptable norms of human habitat in Indian cities and towns.

Before solving the sample problem, we must see the pattern of the problem and find out what it puts before you to think.

A minute look will make you clear that here the examiner has graded the choices very closely. He/ she has given two positive choices instead of one.

i. Definitely true
ii. Probably true

Further, he/ she has also given two negative choices instead of one:-

i. Definitely false
ii. Probably false

This pattern requires a deeper thinking as it leaves before you following areas of confusion:-

1. Definitely true or probably true
2. Definitely false or probably false
3. Data inadequate or probably true
4. Data inadequate or probably false

1. Definitely True or Probably True

If the given inferences is a direct consequences of something given in the passage, then it falls under the category of definitely true. But the confusion may arise when the given inference is not directly stated in the passage but it appears 'almost' definitely true to you. Since it is not clearly stated in the passage, you may think that even 'Probably true' could be the answer. To get rid of this confusion, you have to recheck your reasoning. If the given inference has not been mentioned directly in the passage, then you must have assumed something 'extra' to draw this conclusion. Now, ask the following questions from yourself.

(A) Is the extra assumption an universal truth?
(B) Can the extra assumption never be false?

If you find 'yes' for the question (A) and 'no never' for the question (B), then accept it as definitely true, otherwise pick 'Probably true'.

2. Definitely False or Probably False

If the given inference does not follow from the passage, it falls under the category of definitely false. But confusion may arise when the given inference is not given directly in the passage and seems 'almost' definitely false. But as related things are not mentioned clearly in the passage, you think that 'probably false' may be correct. To get rid of this confusion try to recheck your reasoning. If the opposite of the inference has not been mentioned in the passage, then you must assume something extra to reach your conclusion. Just ask the following questions to yourself.

(A) Is this assumption an universal truth?
(B) Can this assumption never be false?

If you find 'yes' for question (A) and 'no, never' for question (B) then select your answer as definitely false, otherwise probably false will be your correct answer.

3. Data Inadequate or Probably True

When an indirect inference is drawn from the passage, this confusion may arise. As the given inference is not explicitly mentioned, you think that data are inadequate because sufficient information has not been given to draw a conclusion. However, the given inference appears to be in sync with the general 'tone' of the passage In such case you may go for 'Probably true'.

To get rid of this conusion, recheck your general mental ability. You can declare the given inference as probably true, if with the help of some extra assumption, the given inference seems likely to be true. Thus, you can some how convince yourself that the inference is likely to be true. On the other hand, you can declare that data are inadequate if no definite conclusion can be drawn from the passage even with the help of some extra assumption.

4. Data Inadequate or Probably False

When the given inference is drawn indirectly from the passage, such confusion may arise. As it is not explicitly said in the passage, you come to the conclusion that data are inadequate because sufficient information has not been provided to draw a definite conclusion. However, the given inference appears to you in contradiction with the general 'tone' of the passage. Therefore, you are tempted to pick up 'probably false' as your answer. To get rid of this confusion recheck your general mental ability. You can declare an inference 'probably false' only if you are able to find out a reasonable assumption, combining which with what is said in the given passage the inference appears likely to be false.

On the other hand, you should pick up the choice 'data are inadequate' only if you can not find any acceptable assumption which, combined with what is said in the passage, may lead to some definite conclusion. In such case, you can not get convinced whether the given inference is likely to be true or false.

Now, lets try to apply the above rules in the passage given above and try to solve the sample problems.

Solution to sample problems:

1. (c) As we have no information about how the freed up land will benefit the common public, hence data inadequate' will be our correct answer choice. The passage do not suggest us any related assumption.
2. (e) The passage says to the contrary getting rid of slums would "Free up ..... valuable government land". The inference does not follow from the passage.
3. (b) The extra assumption that makes this option probably true is : Low productivity is likely to lead to low income. The passage does not directly talk about per capita income.
4. (b) As slums have led to a lower GDP growth in India. The statement is in sync with the 'tone' of the passage. The extra assumption here can be that as develop countries deploy things that improves their GDP. So it can be probably true that all slums vanish.
5. (a) The passage says that the slums dwellers are susceptible "to poor health conditions". This is directly mentioned in the passage.

❑ Shortcut Approach

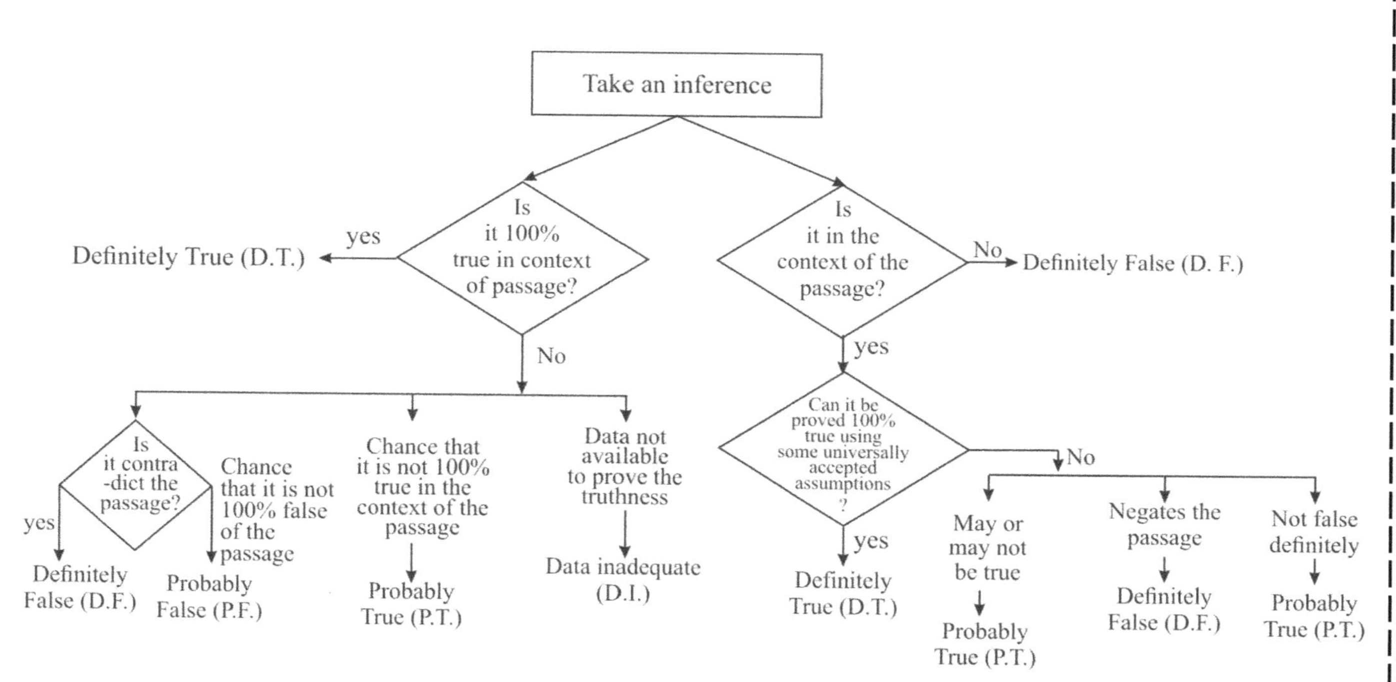

Note: Check the truthness of each inference one by one as above.

PRACTICE EXERCISE

DIRECTIONS (Qs. 1-5) : Below is given a passage followed by several possible inferences which can be drawn from the facts stated in the passage. You have to examine each inference separately in the context of the passage and decide upon its degree of truth or falsity.

Mark answer (1) if the inference is 'definitely true,' i.e. it properly follows from the statement of facts given.

Mark answer (2) if the inference is ' probably true' though not 'definitely true' in the light of the facts given.

Mark answer (3) if the 'data are inadequate, i.e. from the facts given you cannot say whether the inference is likely to be true or false.

Mark answer (4) if the inference is ' probably false' though not 'definitely false' in the light of the facts given.

Mark answer (5) if the inference is 'definitely false, i.e. it cannot possibly be drawn from the facts given or it contradicts the given facts.

The deterioration in the overall asset quality of banks– gross Non–performing Assets (NPAs) are reportedly 27% higher at the end of December 2009 than at the end of December 2008– is not surprising. Any slowdown in growth is bound to trigger a rise in NPAs as more and more companies default on loan repayments. The effect would be pronounced when the slowdown coincides with a severe global recession. But for the restructuring of loans permitted by the Central Bank on fairly generous terms, NPAs would have been still higher. Prudent banks that took care while sanctioning loans and then monitored the post– sanction disbursement diligently should be able to weather the crisis. But it is one thing to have NPAs rise because of a cyclical downturn, it is quite another to have NPAs rise because of policy errors that are entirely within the realm of policy makers. And this is what we need to guard against. Excessiyely low interest rates skew the risk–reward equation by making projects that are actually not viable, appear viable–till interest rates reverse and the same projects cease to be viable! it is now well established that tong periods of unduly low interest rates encourage banks to take more risks. A low interest rate regime driven by an easy money policy rather than macroeconomic fundamentals leads to excessive expansion of credit. It incentivizes banks to take on more risk in search of higher returns and to misprice risk.

1. Higher NPAs indicate shortcomings in disbursement and follow-up of credit given by banks.
2. The Central Bank always allows banks to restructure their loans in the event of rise in NPAs.
3. Lower interest rate cycle projects commercially unviable projects as viable.

4. Low interest rate on credit reduces the capacity to absorb various unaccounted risk factors.
5. Banks' NPAs occur only due to economic factors.

DIRECTIONS (Qs. 6-10) : Below is given a passage followed by several possible interferences which can be drawn from the facts stated in the passage. You have to examine each inference separately in the context of the passage and decide upon its degree of truth or falsity.

Mark answer (a) If the inference is "**definitely true**" i.e. it properly follows from the statement of facts given.

Mark answer (b) If the inference is "**probably true**" though not "**definitely true**" in the light of the facts given.

Mark answer (c) If the **data is inadequate** i.e. from the facts given, you cannot say whether the inference is likely to be true or false.

Mark answer (d) If the inference is "**probably false**" though not "**definitely false**" in the light of the fact given.

Mark answer (e) If the inference is "**definitely false**" i.e., it can not possibly be drawn from the facts given or it contradicts the given facts.

(**Note:** Each of the five questions has only one distinct answer i.e., no two questions can have the same answer. If you get the same answer for more than one question, consider both again and decide which one of the two would more definitely be that answer and in the same way review the others also).

Cardiovascular disease is so prevalent that virtually all businesses are likely to have employees who suffer from, or may develop, this condition. Research shows that between 50-80 percent of all people who suffer a heart attack are able to return to work. However, this may not be possible if they have previously been involved in heavy physical work. In such cases, it may be possible to move the employee to lighter duties, with appropriate retraining where necessary. Similarly, high-pressure, stressful work, even where it does not involve physical activity, should also be avoided. Human Resource managers should be aware of the implications of job roles for employees with a cardiac condition.

6. Employees who suffer from cardiovascular disease are mostly unable to return to work.
7. Employees suffering from Cardio-vascular diseases are unable to handle stressful situations.
8. Employees above the age of 50 are found to suffer from cardiovascular disease.
9. Physical and stressful work definitely leads to a heart attack.
10. Heart disease can affect employees in any type of business.

HINTS & SOLUTIONS

1. (a) From the given data in the passage, it is clear that the Inference is definitely true.
2. (b) The use of term' always' in the inference shows that the Inference is probably true.
3. (a) The inference is definitely true. Consider the following line of the passage:

   "Excessively low interest rates skew the risk reward equation by making projects that are actually not viable, appear viable."
4. (e) The Inference is definitely false. Consider the following line of the passage:

   "It is now well established that long periods of unduly low interest rates encourage banks to take more risks."
5. (a) The Inference is definitely true because rise in NPAs depend upon cyclic factors.
6. (e) It is mentioned in the passage that 50 - 80 per cent of all people who suffer a heart attack are able to return to work. Therefore, the inference is definitely false.
7. (b) It is mentioned in the passage that the persons who have suffered a heart attack should avoid high pressure, stressful work. Therefore, it may be concluded that the inference is probably true.
8. (c) There is no information about this inference.
9. (d) The use of term 'definitely' in the inference makes it doubtful. Therefore, the inference is probable false.
10. (a) Consider the very first line of the passage. It is clear from the first line of the passage that the inference is definitely true.

Statement & Arguments

INTRODUCTION

In this chapter, we are going to study arguments. In fact, this is the study what we call the basics of all logic. Do you know what do we do in logic? In logic, we advocate certain point of view with the help of some evidences and certain assumptions and that is called argumentation. This is a fact that almost all segments of analytical reasoning are someway associated with argumentation and this is the reason why study of argumentation is so important for the examinees preparing for various competitive examinations.

CONCEPT OF ARGUMENT

A sequence of two or more sentences (or statements)/ phrases/clauses that includes a conclusion (or claims), is called an argument. This conclusion of the argument is based on one or more than one statement and these statements may be called premises (propositions). Apart from this, arguments may also have some hidden premises. which may be called assumptions. Let us see the following example:

Example:

Mr. Sharma bought a large quantity of sweets, he must have celebrated some occasion.

Explanation: The foregoing example has two parts:

Part I: "Mr. Sharma bought a large quantity of sweets."

Part II: "He must have celebrated some occasion.

Here, 'Part II' is the conclusion part of the given argument. How has this conclusion (part II) been arrived at? In fact, this conclusion has come out with the help of supporting evidence or premise that is part I of the argument. Did you notice that in this argument part I and part II (Premise and conclusion) are connected by a hidden premise which is not explicitly stated. That hidden premise is "a large quantity of sweets is bought only on occasions" and this premise may be called an assumption. Hence, in reality the given argument has three parts.

Part I: (Premise) Mr. Sharma bought a large quantity of sweets.

Part II: (Assumption or hidden premise) A large quantity of sweets is bought only on occasions.

Part III: (Conclusion) He must have celebrated some occasion.

Point to be noted is that part II is an assumption (a hidden premise) that connects part I (premise) and part III (conclusion) and hence, it is a missing link between part I and part III of the given argument.

No doubt that above mentioned example brings to us the basic characteristics of argumentation but it also leaves some questions before us like:

(i) Is the assumption or hidden premise always present in an argument?

(ii) Is the number of premise only one in an argument?

Our answer for both the questions will be a big 'No'. Why so? Let us see the explanations for both the questions given below:

(i) **Explanation for question:** Just consider an argument given as "Mr. Sharma bought a large quantity of sweets. A large quantity of sweets is bought on occasions only. Hence, he must have celebrated an occasion".

Here, we see that this argument has no assumption (hidden premise) because the premise or supporting evidence (Mr. Sharma bought a large quantity of sweets) and conclusion (Hence, he must have celebrated an occasion) are connected by an explicit statement (A large quantity of sweets is bought on occasions only). Remember, an assumption is a hidden premise. It does mean assumption is a missing link in the chain of logic. Therefore, if an argument is complete in itself and does not have any missing link, then it will not have any assumption. In the given argument, the explicit statement (A large quantity of sweets is bought on occasions only) connects premise or supporting evidence and conclusion to make the argument assumptionless.

(ii) **Explanation for question:** Just consider the argument given as "Vandana is tall. She is slim and has beautiful eyes. She has long hair and charming face as well. So, Vandana is a beautiful girl."

Here,

1st premise: Vandana is tall.

2nd premise: She is slim and has beautiful eyes.

3rd premise: She has long hair and charming face as well.

Conclusion: So, Vandana is a beautiful girl.

This proves that an argument can have more than one premises. Further this explanation is also a reply for question (i) as the given argument has no missing link. This argument is complete in itself and hence, it is free of hidden premise or assumption.

Ways of Argumentation: So far, you must have understood the basic concept of argumentation and come to the conclusion that an argument is usually made to make strong a particular point of view in order to convince someone about something.

(i) **Argument based on Analogy:** Analogy based arguments are often used to make strong a particular point of view. In fact analogy is an inference drawn out of a resemblance between particular things, occasion or events (that are known) to a further (unknown) resemblance. For example, if we find a fat-woman eating very much and meet in another woman who is also fat then, by analogy, we expect that the other fat woman would also be eating very much.

EXAMPLE 1. Sachin scored a century in the 1st test against Australia and so did Dhoni; Sachin scored more than 150 runs in the 2nd test against Australia and so did Dhoni; Sachin has scored a double century in the 3rd test against Australia. So, Dhoni will also hit a double century in this 3rd test match against Australia.

EXAMPLE 2. Australia and England have both lost to India in football and hockey. So, India should defeat both the countries in cricket.

Findings:

In Example 1, Sachin and Dhoni performed very well in the 1st two matches against Australia. In fact, it seems that Dhoni did the same thing what Sachin did in the 1st and 2nd test. As Sachin has played a great inning scoring a double century in the 3rd test match, hence on the basis of similar situation the conclusion has been made that Dhoni will also make a double century.

We also know that performing good or bad is a matter of chance. It is also a matter of chance that two players (Sachin and Dhoni) performed equally good in the last two test matches. Therefore, we cannot say definitely that Dhoni will make a double century because Sachin has done so. In fact, we can say that he may or may not hit a double century. It can also be said that future performances can not be predicted on the basis of past performances. Thus, it is clear that this analogical argument does not seem strong. Similary, in case of example (2) we can say that India may or may not defeat Australia and England in the game of cricket only because India has defeated both the countries in two different games (Football and Hockey). Hence, the argument given in example (2) also seems to be a weak argument.

Final comment: Analogy based arguments are weak arguments.

(ii) **Argument based on cause:** Such arguments relate a cause with a result. Let us see the examples given below:

EXAMPLE 3. India will win the world cup this year because it is the most balanced one day team in the world in present day cricket.

EXAMPLE 4. He came back home late night. He must have gone to watch a movie.

Findings: We see in the foregoing examples that effects have been related with causes. In example (1), the cause (the most balanced one day team) well supports the effect (India will win the world cup) and hence, it is a good argument. But in Example (2) it is argued that since the effect (coming home late night) has taken place, the cause (watching movie) must have occurred. But the point to be noted that effect may occur (he may come home late night) because of the other reason as well. Hence, the argument given in the Example (2) is not a good argument or it may be called a weak argument.

Final Comment: Arguments based on causes may be strong or weak or fallacious.

(iii) **Argument based on example:** Sometimes an argument is given by citing some example/ examples as premise/ premises. Let us see the following examples that will illustrate the concept:

EXAMPLE 5. We should use X brand of cold cream because X brand is used by 'Madhuri Dixit", the famous bollywood actress.

EXAMPLE 6. We must like Roses because Chacha Nehru loved Roses.

Findings: In example (1) we have arrived at the conclusion (we should use X brand of cold cream) by using the premise as example (X brand is used by Madhuri Dixit). In example (2) the conclusion (we must like roses) has come out by using the premise as example (because Chacha Nehru loved it). Here, we can say in case of Example-1 that using certain brand by a particular actress, does not mean that X brand will be liked by all people as likes and dislikes are the personal choices. In example (2), the case is also the same. Everyone cannot like the roses only because Chacha Nehru loved roses.

Final comment: Example based arguments are either weak or fallacious.

Note: In Example-1 and 2, conclusion part is the start of the arguments. Sometimes you can also see that conclusion is given in the middle. It does mean that conclusion part is not always in the last. But it depends on the style of writing of different writers/authors.

(iv) **Argument based on blind advocacy:** Such argument is like a salesman's argument who argues only for the purpose of selling a particular product. He speaks of the advantages and the benefits of his product. Hence, a salesman argument is one where a conclusion comes out because of the positive points and the benefits that it leads to. Such types of arguments are very common in day to day life.

EXAMPLE 7. Exercise is good for health and students need good health to put hard labour in their studies. This is the reason why every educational institution must have a gym.

EXAMPLE 8. There should be a ban on strikes as they disrupt the normal life of the common people.

Findings: In example-1, the conclusion is that every educational institution must have a gym because exercise is good for health and students need good health. No doubt the good health ensures good mind but it is not practically feasible for every educational institution to have a gym. Hence, Example-1 will be a weak argument. In example-2, ban on strikes is being demanded and this demand is reasonable as argument has negative feature of strike. Hence, example-2 is a strong argument.

Final comment: Such arguments can be both weak or strong.

(v) **Argument based on chronology:** Very often we see that a conclusion is drawn only on the basis of chronological order of some events. Let us see the examples given below:

EXAMPLE 9. Computer was invented later than television. Therefore, television has a technology inferior to that of a computer.

EXAMPLE 10. Song 'B' was released two months earlier than song 'C'. So the former could not be the copy of the latter.

Findings: In example-1, it is assumed that a technologically inferior object always comes before the superior objects. This may be true most of the time but this is not true in 100% cases. Hence, the conclusion given in example 1 is questionable making the given argument a weak one. In 2nd case, it is the possibility that song 'C' was recorded earlier although released later than the song 'B'. Hence, in such a situation the possibility of copying can not be denied and this makes argument given in Example-2 a weak argument.

Final comment: This type of arguments are usually weak and unconvincing.

By now, all the standard ways of argumentation have been discussed in detail. We will now take a look at the key words so that you could easily take out the conclusion part from the given argument. The keywords are given below:

So,	**Hence,**
Therefore,	**Consequently**
Thus,	

Apart from above given keywords, the conclusion part can also be identified by the certain phrases given below:

As a result
It can be inferred that
Which means that
Which suggests that
Which proves that
Which shows that
It follows that

If you find one of these keywords/ phrases before any sentence then take that sentence as your conclusion. If the keywords/phrases are absent, then apply your common sense and take out the sentences that can follow one of these keywords/ phrases and that sentence will be your conclusion.

After learning concept of argument we can easily move on to the problems of reasoning which are asked in various exams wherein examinee is required to evaluate the forcefulness of the arguments. On the basis of a statement, arguments are given in the questions and the candidate is required to find out:

(a) **Which argument is strong.**

(b) **Which argument is weak.**

We know that "strong" arguments are those which are both important and directly related to the question. "Weak" arguments are those which are of minor importance and also may not be directly related to the question or may be related to a trivial aspect of the question. To find out if a given argument is strong or not we will move according to the solution steps given below:

Solution steps

Step I: Do the preliminary screening of the given arguments.

Step II: Find out if the given arguments really follow or not.

Step III: Find out if the given arguments are really desirable (in case of positive argument) / harmful (in case of negative arguments)

Step IV: Find out if the statement and argument are properly related.

Now, we will discuss all the steps one by one.

Step I: Preliminary screening of the given arguments

At the very 1st level we test how weak an argument is. If at the very 1st level we find the argument weak, then there is no need to go for further steps. In many cases the weak arguments are very clearly visible and we do not need to think much before arriving at the conclusion that they are weak. Such type of arguments come under the following category:

(i) **Doubtful/Ambiguous arguments:** These arguments do not make it clear that how they are related to a course of action. They also do not give the clear idea about what exactly the author or writer wants to say.

EXAMPLE 11.

Statement: One should enjoy every second of one's life because everyone has to die one day.

Argument: No, because one must think about fulfilling one's ambition in life and should not think about death as one's goal.

Comment: Here, statement and argument are not properly related. Statement suggests to enjoy every second of life. Enjoying life does not mean that one should not follow the path of fulfilling one's ambition. In fact a person can enjoy his/ her life in the course of fulfilling his/her ambition. In fact, we can say without enjoying work of our own choice, we can not fulfill our ambition. Further the given statement does not give any indication that one should see death as one's goal. Hence, in this case statement and argument leave doubtful and confusing impression on our mind making the given argument very weak.

(ii) **Useless/ superfluous arguments:** Such arguments do not do a deep analysis of the given statement. They simply 'glance' at the statement and put them under the category of weak arguments.

EXAMPLE 12.

Statement: Cricket must be banned in India.

Argument: Yes, it has no use.

Comment: Here, the argument does not go deep down into the matter making itself a weak argument.

(iii) **Arguments in the form of question:** Such arguments are very weak in nature as the arguments given in the question form are without any substance and have no technique of argumentation. In fact, in such arguments arguers throw back the question.

EXAMPLE 13.

Statement: Should import be banned in India?

Argument: Yes, why not?

Comment: Here, statement is given in the form of question and arguer throws back the question without giving any convincing statement in the form of argument. Hence, the given argument is very weak.

(iv) **Very simple arguments:** Such arguments are very simple in nature. They are given in small sentences but do not get any support by facts or established notions. Further, such arguments are not ambiguous and they are properly related with the statement but because of their simple nature they come under the category of weak arguments.

EXAMPLE 14.

Statement: Enjoying life should be the principle of our life.

Argument: No this thinking hardly enable us to do anything.

Comment: Here, the given argument is only a simple assertion which contains no substance. Here, it will come under the category of weak arguments.

Step II: Finding out if the given arguments really follow or not.

If the arguments are rejected at the preliminary step then we do not need to test them further. But, if the preliminary step has been cleared, then we move on to step II.

Case I: When the result follows

At the step II, the result will follow in the cases given below:

(i) **Established fact:** An established fact does mean that it must be universally acknowledged/scientifically established. A result will follow a course of action if it is an established fact that this particular result follows this particular course of action.

EXAMPLE 15.

Statement: Should drinking be avoided?

Argument: Yes, it contributes to bad health.

EXAMPLE 16.

Statement: Should Tendulkar be selected in the team even after 10 years from now?

Argument: Yes, Tendulkar is one of the greatest cricketers in the world.

EXAMPLE 17.

Statement: Married people should live separate from their parents.

Argument: Yes, living separate will give married people a greater freedom.

EXAMPLE 18.

Statement: Should smoking be promoted?

Argument: No, smoking is injurious to health.

Comment: In the above examples, all the given arguments are expected to follow as they all are established facts. Therefore, all the arguments presented can be said to pass the test of step II.

NOTE : *Point to be noted that arguments given under Example 1, Example 2, Example 3 & Example 4 have passed the step II only so far but it has not yet been determined whether these arguments are forceful or not (strong or not). They will be called strong only when they will pass step III and step IV.*

(ii) **Prediction on the basis of experience:** Such arguments are very near to established facts type of arguments. But, in reality, they are not established facts as they are not yet so universally acknowledged as to be treated as established fact. In fact, such arguments are given on the basis of experiences. Just see the following example:

EXAMPLE 19.

Statement: Captains should not have given their say in selection of national sports teams.

Argument: Yes, it discourages favouritism towards some particular players.

Comment: The result or consequences given in this example will be a probable result as our experiences suggest this. Hence, this will go for further test.

(iii) **Logically given arguments:** Such arguments are given on the basis of logic. It does mean that the emphasis here is on the logic and not on the established fact or experience. If we see such type of arguments we can easily predict that such cases have occurred in practice. But when we think over such situations with proper logic and reasoning then we arrive at the conclusion that such an argument may be true. Let us see the example given below:

EXAMPLE 20.

Statement: World leaders must try for complete disarmament.

Argument: Yes, complete disarmament will make a war free world.

Comment: The example gives an argument that is logically convincing: The argument is probable as the logic behind it is that if there will be armless world then there will be a war free world. Hence, the argument passes the step II test and will go for further test.

(iv) **Notions of truth:** Such arguments are unquestionable truth because of the simple reason of universal acceptance. It does mean that they are the ideas or thoughts already acknowledged by society. This is the reason why they are very similar to established facts in many ways. The following example illustrates this point:

EXAMPLE 21.

Statement: Should marriages between blood relatives be promoted?

Argument: No, it will promote incest which is a sin.

Comment: No, doubt, the given argument seems strong as it is based on prevailing notion of truth that our society does not allow marriages between blood relatives and consider such marriages as a sin. As, the given argument is likely to be strong it will go for next step test.

Case II (When the result does not follow argument will be rejected).

Following are the cases when results do not follow and arguments are rejected at 2nd level test in step II only.

(i) **Established fact:** If it is an established fact that a particular result will not follow a particular course of action, then the argument will be rejected at step II. Let us see the example given below:

EXAMPLE 22.

Statement: Should smoking be discouraged in the country?

Argument: No, it give relaxation when one gets tired and this way contributes to health.

Comment: It is an established fact that smoking is injurious to health and thus, we can say that this argument is incorrect and weak enough to be rejected at step II.

(ii) **Prediction on the basis of experiences:** If the experiences say that the result will not follow then the given argument will be rejected at the step II. Let us see the example given below:

Statement: Should cricketer A be appointed the next captain of the Indian cricket team?

Argument: Yes, it will end the favouritism in selection of team as cricketer A has made allegations of favouritism against the current captain.

Comment: In this example, the argument suggests that cricketer A should be appointed captain of the Indian cricket team because it will end the favouritism in the team selection. This suggestion has been given on the basis that A has made allegation of favouritism against the current captain. But the experiences say that there have been so many cases when people did the things what they opposed. Hence, saying one thing and doing other is very common. This is the reason why it can not be made sure that

A will not do favouritism in team selection only because he has criticised the current captain for this. It is clear that the given argument is weak enough to be rejected in step II.

> ***Note :*** *This is the exactly opposite to point (ii) in step II (Case I).*

(iii) **Argument with faulty logic:** This is exactly opposite to the point (iii) in step II (case I). Let us see the following example:

Statement: Should the culprits behind the fodder scam in Bihar be punished?

Argument: No, a political vaccum will be created if the culprits get punishment.

Comment: As per the logic, punishing culprits behind the fodder scam in Bihar would please the public and improve the image of the Bihar government. How can it create a political vaccum? This argument has been given with a faulty logic and hence will be rejected in step II only.

(iv) **Argument violating prevailing notions of truth:** Argument that violates unquestionable notions (Ideas that are universally accepted and acknowledged by society) will be rejected in step II. Let us see the example given below:

Statement: Should marriage in blood relations be promoted in India?

Argument: Yes, if the two mature blood relatives are willing to do so, then they can not be prohibited from doing it.

Comment: In our society, it is widely accepted truth (or universally accepted truth) that the marriages between blood relatives are considered to be a sin as it promotes incest. The given argument violates this prevailing notion of truth and is weak enough to be rejected in step II.

(v) **Arguments based on examples/ analogies:** Very often it is seen that an example or a precedent is made the basis of an argument. But point to be noted that analogy or example based arguments come under the category of bad arguments. It must be cleared that just because someone did something in the past, the same can not be said as pursuable. Let us see the example given below:

Statement: Should everyone be optimistic in Life?

Argument: Yes, Indira Gandhi was optimistic and this is the reason why she became the prime minister of India.

Comment: Here, the example of Indira Gandhi is given that makes the argument very weak. Thus, such type of arguments are rejected in step II.

(vi) **Arguments based on individual perceptions (or assumptions):** In some cases it is seen that an assumption or view of the author is the substance of an argument. Such arguments neither have proper logic nor substance of established fact. These arguments are called bad arguments and they can be rejected in step II.

Statement: Should India be declared a Hindu Rashtra?

Argument: No, it will lead to chaos.

Comment: What message author gives through the argument is view of the author. In fact, declaring India a Hindu Rashtra may or may not lead to the result given in the argument. It means that assertion made by argument may or may not follow in actual practice and if the author has a rigid stand on this assertion, it is his/ her individual perception or assumption which makes the argument weak enough to be rejected in step II.

Step III: Given arguments are really desirable/ harmful

In step II, we come to the conclusion that Examples 1-7, have passed the 2nd level test and qualified for the step III (3rd level test). Hence, we will take the examples to be qualified for step III one by one:

EXAMPLE 23. Here, the argument is positive and therefore, we have to check the desirability. As, it is a established fact that drinking contributes to bad health and thus it is desirable to avoid it. It is clear row that Example 1 passed the 3rd level test.

EXAMPLE 24. No doubt that at present Tendulkar is one of the greatest cricketers in the world. He will also remain in the list of great ones in the history of the game of cricket. But it is also a truth that he has spent more than 20 years in this game and is a retired cricketer. This is the reason that after 10 years he will definitely not be in team as his selection is impossible. Hence, despite being an established fact the argument is not desirable and is rejected in step III. (Example 2 is a weak argument)

EXAMPLE 25. Here, it is true that living separately from parents gives married people more freedom but at the same time getting freedom at cost of separation from parents is undesirable. Further, separating from parents does mean avoiding duty of taking care of parents. Hence, argument given in example 3 is not desirable and is weak enough to be rejected in step III.

EXAMPLE 26. As smoking is injurious to health, its promotion is harmful. This reason makes the argument strong enough to pass the step III test.

EXAMPLE 27. It is true that favouritism takes place on the part of captains at times, but that does not mean that they should not be given their say while selecting team. In fact, captains are expected to bring positive and desired result if given their say in team selection. Further, giving their say in team selection makes the captains more responsible for the bad performance of the team and this inspires the captain to draw best out of the players in the team. Hence, the result is not desirable and the given argument proves to be weak enough to be rejected in step III.

EXAMPLE 28. If it is possible to make world free of wars through complete disarmament, it is well and good. But, complete disarmament does not assure that there would be no antisocial elements like murderers, looters, terrorists and the likes. To tackle these kind of anti-social elements, police and different security forces are needed. How do police and other security forces function without arms? No, doubt, it is impossible for such security providing bodies to work without arms. Hence, the argument given in Example 6 is weak and will be rejected in step III.

EXAMPLE 29. Marriages in blood relatives promote incest which is a sin and hence harmful for the established norm of society. On the basis of this logic, argument given in Example 7 is strong enough to pass the 3rd level test step III.

Now, we have,

Examples qualified for step IV test: Example-1, 4 and 7. Rejected examples in step III: Example- 2, 3, 5 and 6.

***Note :** How to decide a positive argument which is really desirable or a negative argument which is really harmful, is only the matter of common sense. Just apply your common sense, think over the argument, try to go by proper logic and general norms of society.*

Step IV: Finding proper relation between statement and argument.

What does proper relation between statement and argument mean? In fact, it does mean that argument must be pinpointed on the main issue involved and it should not focus on any irrelevant, insignificant or minor issues. Now, we move on to step IV or final test. As Example-1, 4 and 7 have qualified for this test, let us check the three examples one by one:

EXAMPLE 30. Drinking and bad health are properly and directly related. Hence, the given argument "Yes, it contributes to bad health" is a strong argument and this is the final conclusion.

EXAMPLE 31. Smoking and bad health (injurious to health) are directly and properly related. Hence, the given argument "No smoking is injurious to health" is a strong argument and this is the final conclusion.

EXAMPLE 32. Marriages in blood relatives and promotion of incest is directly and properly related. Hence, the given argument "No, it will promote incest which is a sin" is a strong argument and this is the final conclusion.

Now, we have come to the end of this chapter. For the understanding of students, below is given a question format for the examination. The question format has been made with the Example 4 given in this chapter.

Question format:

Direction: Each question given below is followed by two arguments numbered I and II. You have to decide which one of the arguments is a 'strong' argument and which is a 'weak' argument.

Give answer (a) If only argument I is strong.

(b) If only argument II is strong.

(c) If either I or II is strong.

(d) If neither I nor II is strong.

(e) If both I and II strong.

Statement: Should smoking be promoted?

Argument: I: No, smoking is injurious to health.

II: Yes, why not?

Solution:

I will follow (the reason already given see Example 4)

II will not follow as it is a question back type of argument and such type of arguments are very weak.

Hence, option (a) is the correct answer.

❑ Shortcut Approach

Step I: Preliminary Screening of argument

Passes / Fails — **Weak Argument**

Step II: The argument follows the statement

Passes / Fails — **Weak Argument**

Step III: The argument is desirable (for positive statements) / harmful (for negative statements)

Passes / Fails — **Weak Argument**

Step IV: The argument is properly related to the statement.

Passes / Fails — **Weak Argument**

Strong Argument

PRACTICE EXERCISE

DIRECTIONS (Qs. 1-5) : In making decisions about important questions, it is desirable to be able to distinguish between 'strong' arguments and 'weak' arguments. 'strong' arguments are those which are both important and directly related to the question. 'Weak' arguments are those which are of minor importance and also may not be directly related to the question or may be related to a trivial aspect of the question.

Each question below is followed by three arguments numbered (A), (B) and (C). You have to decide which of the arguments is a 'strong' argument and which is a 'weak' argument.

1. **Statement :** Should there be a cap on drawing groundwater for irrigation purposes in India ?

   Arguments :

   (A) No, irrigation is of prime importance for food production in India and it is heavily dependent on groundwater in many parts of the country.

   (B) Yes, water tables have gone down to alarmingly low levels in some parts of the country where irrigation is primarily dependent on groundwater, which may lead to serious environmental consequences.

   (C) Yes, India just cannot afford to draw groundwater any further as the international agencies have cautioned India against it.

   (a) Only (A) and (B) are strong
   (b) Only (B) and (C) are strong
   (c) Only (A) and (C) are strong
   (d) All (A), (B) and (C) are strong
   (e) None of these

2. **Statement :** Should there be complete ban on setting up of thermal power plants in India ?

   Arguments :

   (A) Yes, this is the only way to arrest further addition to environmental pollution.

   (B) No, there is a huge shortage of electricity in most parts of the country and hence generation of electricity needs to be augmented.

   (C) No, many developed countries continue to set up thermal power plants in their countries.

   (a) None is strong
   (b) Only (A) is strong
   (c) Only (B) is strong
   (d) Only (C) is strong
   (e) Only either (A) or (B) is strong

3. **Statement:** Should there be a restriction on the construction of high rise buildings in big cities in India.

   Arguments :

   (A) No, big cities in India do not have adequate open land plots to accommodate the growing population.

   (B) Yes, only the builders and developers benefit from the construction of high rise buildings.

   (C) Yes, the Government should first provide adequate infrastructure facilities to existing buildings before allowing the construction of new high rise buildings.

(a) Only (B) is strong
(b) Only (C) is strong
(c) Only (A) and (C) are strong
(d) Only (A) is strong
(e) None of these

4. **Statement :** Should road repair work in big cities be carried out only late at night ?

Arguments :

(A) No, this way the work will never get completed.
(B) No, there will be unnecessary use of electricity.
(C) Yes, the commuters will face lot of problems due to repair work during the day.

(a) None is strong
(b) Only (A) is strong
(c) Only (C) is strong
(d) Only (B) and (C) are strong
(e) Only (A) and (B) are strong

5. **Statement :** Should all the deemed universities be derecognised and attached to any of the central of state universities in India ?

Arguments :

(A) Yes, many of these deemed universities do not conform to the required standards of a full – fledged university and hence the level of education is compromised.
(B) No, these deemed universities have been able to introduce innovative courses suitable to the requirement of various industries as they are free from strict Government controls.
(C) Yes, many such universities are basically money spinning activities and education takes a backseat in these institutions

(a) Only (A) and (B) are strong
(b) Only (B) and (C) are strong
(c) Only (A) and (C) are strong
(d) All (A), (B) and (C) are strong
(e) None of these

DIRECTIONS (Qs. 6-8) : Read the following statements carefully and answer the questions which follow.

6. The ministry of sports has been advised by a committee to take the highest award in the field of sports back from two players who were allegedly-involved in match fixing.

Which of the following statements would **weaken** the argument put forward by the committee to the sports ministry?

(a) A good conduct in the past and a lack of evidence against the players make the case against them very weak.
(b) The ministry of sports has never declined the recommendations made by the committee earlier.
(c) Taking the award back from the players would set a good example to other players for avoiding such actions in the future.
(d) There have been past cases where the award had to be taken back from the players owing to some misconduct later on.
(e) The committee is constituted of some of the most respected from the fields of sports and politics.

7. Many organizations have been resorting to recruitment based upon performance at graduate post-graduate level exams rather than conducting exams for the same purpose.

   Which of the following statements would **strengthen** the argument given in the above statement?

   (a) A recent study shows no link of past performance with the performance in recruitment exams.

   (b) The graduate/post-graduate exams are considered to be severely deficient in training in job related environment

   (c) Organisations which had undertaken recruitment on the basis of graduate / post-graduate exams report a significant drop in the quality of the recruited employees.

   (d) Such policies would add to unemployment amongst students having below average performance in graduation or post-graduation.

   (e) Such policies could save time, money and resources of the organisation which are wasted in the conduct of recruitment examinations.

8. According to a recent government directive, all bank branches in rural areas should be computerized.

   Which of the following statements would **weaken** the government's argument?

   (a) Computerisation of bank branches in urban areas has helped in making their performance more efficient and fast.

   (b) Lack of skilled and qualified manpower has been suitably substituted by computers in banks.

   (c) Non-computerised bank branches in the rural areas have been proved to be as efficient as their computerized counterparts.

   (d) The government has introduced a special test for computer knowledge in all recruitment exams for banks.

   (e) Unemployment in the rural areas could be controlled by training more and more professionals in computers.

DIRECTIONS (Qs. 9-10) : In making decisions about important questions, it is desirable to distinguish between 'strong' argument and 'weak' argument. A 'strong' argument must be both important and directly related to the question. A 'weak argument may not be directly related to the question and may be of minor importance or may be related to the trivial aspect of the question. Each question below is followed by two arguments, numberd I and II. You have to decide which of the arguments is 'strong' and which is 'weak'

Give answer

(a) if only argument I is strong

(b) if only argument II is strong

(c) if either I or II strong

(d) if neither I nor II is strong and

(e) if both I and II are strong.

9. **Statement** Keeping in consideration the longivitity of life in India, should the age limit for retirement in government jobs be increased?

Argument

I. Yes, other countries have decided so long before.

II. Yes, it is the actual demand of lakhs of employees.

10. **Statement** Should the admission to professional courses in India be given only on merit without any concession to any particular group of students?

Argument

I. Yes, this will improve the quality of the professionals as they will be able to complete the courses successfully.

II. No, this will keep large number of socially and economically backward students out of the reach of the professional courses.

HINTS & SOLUTIONS

1. **(a)** Both argument (A) and (B) are strong. Which clearly show the importance of irrigation nad environmental consequences of reducing groundwater level. Argument (c) is not strong.

2. **(c)** Only Argument (B) is strong because thermal power plants in India are one way to increase environmental pollution so cannot be completly banned. Argument (C) is based on example which is a bad argument.

3. **(d)** Argument (A) is strong because due to shortage of space in big cities in India high rise building should be encouraged.

4. **(c)** Only Argument (C) is strong because to avoid the inconvenience of commuters, repair work is advisable in night only.

5. **(c)** Only Argument (A) and (C) are strong because compromise with level of education cannot be done.

6. **(a)** Option (a) would weaken the argument put forward by the committee to the sports ministry.

7. **(e)** Option (e) would strengthen the argument.

8. **(c)** Option (c) would strengthen the argument of government.

9. **(d)** Both the arguments are weak. Other countries have different conditions. And in India population of youth is increasing so, for the benefits of youth age limit for retirement should not be increased in government jobs.

10. **(b)** Our country seaks to support educationally and economically backward classes for their overall growth and development. Therefore, argument I is not strong, in Indian context.

Statement & Assumptions

INTRODUCTION

Assumptions are essential part of analytical reasoning. This is the reason why in various competitive examinations, examinees are asked to identify assumptions. In this chapter, we will see how to identify assumptions. Before we go ahead, we must have a look at a common format of the problem as it will give you a clear idea of the questions to be asked in the examination.

PROBLEM FORMAT (SAMPLE PROBLEM)

Directions: In every question given below a statement (or a passage) is followed by two assumptions number I & II. An assumption is something supposed or taken for granted. You have to consider the statement and the following assumptions and then decide which of the assumptions is implicit in the statement.

Mark answer:

(a) If only assumption I is implicit.
(b) If only assumption II is implicit.
(c) If either assumption I or assumption II is implicit.
(d) If neither of the assumption is implicit
(e) If both the assumptions are implicit.

Statement: "A" television — the largest selling name with the largest range" — an advertisement.

Assumptions:

I. There is a demand for televisions in the market.

II. 'A' television is the only one with wide variations.

The given statement in the problem format is an advertisement. This is the one form of statement. But the statement may be in different forms like it can be in the form of a passage; in the form of a single line; in the form of a notice; in the form of an appeal or in any other different forms.

WHAT DOES AN ASSUMPTION MEAN?

Assumption is the hidden part of an argument. It does mean that an assumption is something which is assumed, supposed and taken for granted. In fact, when a person says something, he does not put everything into words and leaves some part unsaid as why does he ? so?

He does so because he takes this unsaid part for granted. In other words he thinks this unsaid part will be understood without saying and hence there is no need to put this (unsaid part) into words. It does mean this unsaid part is hidden in the given statement and this hidden part is called assumption. Let us understand it in another way. Just remember your childhood days when you used to solve the given arithmetic problem without leaving any single step. But what you do today? Today your approach is totally different. Today you leave easier steps as you assume that the person who see your solution, is very much aware of these elementary operations. Therefore, this is an example of assumption.

To get the concept of assumption more clearly just suppose a thrilling one day international cricket match is going on between India and Australia. The Australian team has scored 300 runs but while chasing the score India has made 280 runs in 48 overs and now, the situation is India has to score 21 runs to win the match in remaining two overs. As Yuvraj Singh is batting, you tell your friend - "No need to worry as Yuvraj is a big hitter. India will definitely win the match". What do you find in this statement. In fact this statement has two parts:-

(i) No need to worry as Yuvraj is a big hitter.

(ii) India will win the match.

Now, this is the time to think over these two parts. How do you relate them? Obviously, by assuming that a big hitter may score 21 runs in the remaining two overs. Therefore, this is another example of assumption. The above statement can be written in three parts as follows:-

(i) No need to worry as Yuvraj is a big hitter.

(ii) A big hitter may score 21 runs in 2 overs (Hidden part/Assumption)

(iii) So, India will win the match.

Let's get more ideas about assumption with some simple examples given below:-

EXAMPLE 1.

Statement: Of all the mobile sets manufactured in India **'M'** brand has the largest sale.

Assumption: The sale of all the mobile sets manufactured in India is known.

Comment: The given assumption is valid. Here the statement makes a claim that of all the mobile sets manufactured in India, **'M'** brand has the largest sale. In fact, without knowing sale figures may be rough data of all mobile brands manufactured in India, no such claim about M brand could be made. Hence, it must have been implicitly assumed in the given statement that sale figure of all brands is known.

EXAMPLE 2.

Statement: Virat is in great form and therefore, India is going to beat New Zealand in upcoming test series.

Assumption:

I. Virat will give a good performance in upcoming series against New Zealand.

II. Virat will score a triple century in the upcoming series against New Zealand.

Comment: Assumption I is valid as the statement says that Virat is in great form and therefore, India is going to beat New Zealand in the upcoming test series. It does mean that it is assumed in the statement that Virat will perform well in the upcoming test series against New Zealand and on the basis of that good performance India will beat New Zealand. But II is invalid because if Virat is in great form, that does not mean he will surely hit a triple century. He may or may not do so. Hence, assumption II is not hidden in the statement.

EXAMPLE 3.

Statement: The next meeting of the governing body of the institute **X** will be held after one year.

Assumption: Institute **X** will remain in function after one year.

Comment: The given assumption is valid as we know that the common practice is to hold meetings of only those bodies that are functional. Hence, it does mean that the announcer must be assuming that the society will remain functional after one year.

EXAMPLE 4.

Statement: The student is too clever to fail in the examination.

Assumption: Very clever students do not fail in the examination.

Comment: This is a valid assumption. As per the given statement the student will not fail (This is an effect) as he / she is very clever (This is a cause). Clearly, it has been assumed in the statement that very clever students do not fail.

HOW DOES A SINGLE WORD OR PHRASE MAKE A DIFFERENCE?

A. Definitive Words Cases:

Just consider the words like 'all', 'only', 'best', 'strongest', 'certainly', 'definitely', etc. These are some words that put a greater degree of emphasis or more weight on the sentence than some others. In fact, these words impart a kind of exclusiveness to the sentence and thereby reduce the scope / range of the sentence. In fact, some kind of certainty is associated with all these words. Let us consider the following examples:

EXAMPLE 5.

Statement: The crisis of onion has worsened and the government should make every effort to boost import of onion.

Assumption:

I. Import is the best solution to avert the onion crisis.

II. Import is a reasonably good solution to the onion crisis.

III. Import is the only solution to overcome the onion crisis.

IV. The onion crisis will definitely be averted by boosting import of onion.

V. The onion crisis will probably be averted by boosting import of onion.

Comment: In the above mentioned example, the assumption II and V are valid. But I, III and IV are not valid. The reason is that there is use of definitive words (best, only and definitely) in case of I, III and IV. The given statement mentions a fact that crisis of onion has worsened and then makes a suggestion that imports of onion should be boosted. In fact the statement assumes that import should help to overcome onion crisis or that import is a good/ reasonably good solution to the onion crisis. But, there is no hint that import is the only solution/ best solution/a definitely effective solution.

Therefore, the example given above illustrates how a definitive word may give a different 'tone' to a sentence.

B. Cases of Conjunctions:

The words like 'because', 'therefore', 'in spite of', 'despite', 'so', 'after', 'even', 'although' 'as', 'as a result of' are some significant conjunctions. When a statement has two clauses and the clauses are connected by a conjunction, then the nature of conjunction helps in detecting the assumption that the author suggests in his statement. Suppose 'x' is one clause of a sentence that mention an event (or fact/suggestion) and 'y' is the another clause of the same sentence which mentions another event (or fact/suggestion), than depending upon the conjunction, we can conclude the following assumption.

(i) x because/ as a result of y ⇒ It is assumed that 'y' leads to x.

EXAMPLE 6.

Statement: You will find improvement in your English after taking classes in institute M.

Valid Assumption: Institute M may help in improving English.

(ii) x therefore/ hence y ⇒ It is assumed that 'x' leads to 'y'.

EXAMPLE 7.

Statement: Sachin Tendulkar has become the 1st man to score 50th test century, therefore all Indians must be feeling very proud on his achievement.

Valid Assumption: An achievement by a fellow countryman makes other citizens proud.

(iii) x even after/ despite/ in spite of y ⇒ It is assumed that usually x does not occurs when y occurs.

EXAMPLE 8.

Statement: There was a theft in the city mall last night inspite of the maximum security arrangement made by the police.

Valid Assumption: Maximum security arrangement is usually sufficient to prevent theft.

(iv) Not 'x' even after/ in spite of/ despite 'y' ⇒ It is assumed that usually x occurs when y does.

EXAMPLE 9.

Statement: There was no outbreak of any epidemic even after the continuous deposition of rain water for six days.

Valid Assumption: Deposition of rain water usually leads to epidemic.

C. Cases of Connotive Phrases:

Sometimes words used by the author are slightly indirect or unconventional. This is the reason you may miss the thing which the author wants to say. Such indirect or unconventional words are called connotative or connotive phrases. For example "It is true that ...." can be put / written as:

(i) It can be claimed with reasonable degree of truth that...

(ii) It would be correct to say that...

(iii) Even the most sceptic of men would agree that....

Similarly, "It is false" is put / written by the author as :

(i) It is baseless to say that ...

(ii) It would be highly misleading to say that....

(iii) Nothing could be farther from truth than...

Note: The role of connotative phrases is very limited in the questions asked because they are given so that they do not escape your eyes whenever one come across them.

Rules Related to Assumptions

(i) Any form of public interest notice/ official notice is assumed to be paid attention to.

(ii) If an appeal is made, it is assumed that the appeal will get response.

(iii) Any form of advertisements are given by assuming that people will respond to such materials.

(iv) If X says something to Y, it means X assumes that B will hear what he (X) says.

Conditions for Invalidity of Assumptions:

(a) Restatement

If the given assumption is a restatement of the given statement, then the given assumption will be invalid. In fact, in such case, same thing is put in different words.

EXAMPLE 10.

Statement: Of all the computer brands, manufactured in India, brand M has the largest sale.

Invalid Assumption: No other brand of computer has as high a sale as brand M.

(b) Long-drawn Conclusion: If an assumption makes too far fetched logic or long drawn conclusion, then it will be considered as invalid assumption.

EXAMPLE 11.

Statement: All teaching should be done in religious spirit as religious instruction leads to a curiosity for knowledge.

Invalid Assumption: Curious persons are good persons.

(c) Observation : It is slightly different from the restatement case. In this case, two of the trio (Subject, verb, predicate) are changed into negative that changes the appearance of the sentence without changing its meaning.

EXAMPLE 12.

Statement: Beauty is lovable.

Invalid Assumptions :

I. Ugliness is not lovable

II. Beauty is not hateable

(d) Conversion : When you study the chapter of syllogism, you see that statements are converted to get immediate inference. In fact, there are three standard cases of conversion:

(i) All M are N, converted into Some N are M.

(ii) Some M are N, converted into Some N are M.

(iii) No M are N, converted into No N are M

Points to be noted that given assumptions will be invalid if they are conversions of the given statements.

❑ Shortcut Approach

Assumption will be implicit if	Assumption will not be implicit if
• it is in context of passge	• not in context of statement or passage
• it is not directly mentioned	• it is directly mentioned in the statement
• it is a mandatory factor condition for the statement to be correct.	• it is not an accepted fact or cannot be truly inferred
	• there is use of definitive words
Note : *The assumption must follow all the above rules for it to be implicit.*	• it is a restatement or a long-drawn conclusion or negative rephrasing or a converted syllogism form.

PRACTICE EXERCISE

DIRECTIONS (Qs. 1-5) : *In each questions bellow is given a statement followed by three assumptions (A), (B) and (C). An assumption is something supposed or taken for granted. You have to consider the statement and the following assumptions and decide which of the assumptions is implicit in the statement.*

1. **Statement :** Police authority cordoned of the entire locality for the entire day and stopped vehicular movement for the visit of a top functionary of the government in view the threat perception and advised all the residents in the area to limit their movement outside their dwellings.

   Which of the following assumption(s) is /are implicit in the above statement ?

   (A) Police personnel may not be able to control the vehicular movement in the locality and may seek help from the armed forces.

   (B) People living in the locality may move out of their houses for the day to avoid inconvenient.

   (C) The Government functionary may request the police authority to lift the ban on movement of residents of the locality outside their dwellings.

   (a) None is implicit

   (b) Only (A) is implicit

   (c) Only (B) is implicit

   (d) Only (C) is implicit

   (e) Only (B) and (C) are implicit

2. **Statement :** The apex body controlling universities in the country has decided to revise the syllabus of all the technical courses to make them focused towards the present needs of the industry thereby making the technical graduates more employable than they are at present.

   Which of the following assumption(s) is /are implicit in the above statement ?

   (A) Technical colleges affiliated to different universities may not welcome the apex body's decision and may continue with the same syllabus as at present.

   (B) The industry may welcome the decision of the apex body and scale up their hiring from these colleges.

   (C) The Government may not allow the apex body to implement its decision in all the colleges as it may lead to chaos.

   (a) None is implicit

   (b) Only (A) is implicit

   (c) Only (B) is implicit

   (d) Only (C) is implicit

   (e) Only (A) and (B) are implicit

3. **Statement :** Government has urged all the citizens to use electronic media for carrying out their daily activities, whenever possible instead of using paper as the manufacture of paper requires the cutting down of a large number of trees causing severe damage to the ecosystem.

Which of the following assumption(s) is /are implicit in the above statement ?

(A) Most people may be capable of using electronic media to carry out various routines.

(B) Most people may have access to electronic media for carrying out their daily routine activities.

(C) People at large may reject the Governments appeal and continue using paper as before.

(a) Only (A) is implicit
(b) Only (B) is implicit
(c) Only (A) and (B) are implicit
(d) Only (C) is implicit
(e) None of these

4. **Statement :** Government has decided to auction construction of highways to private entities in several blocks across the country on build–operate–transfer basis.

Which of the following assumption(s) is /are implicit in the above statement ?

(A) An adequate number of private entities may not respond to the Government's auctions notification.

(B) Many private entities in the country are capable of constructing highways within reasonable time.

(C) The Government's proposal of build–operate–transfer may financially benefit the private entities.

(a) Only (A) and (B) are implicit
(b) Only (B) and (C) are implicit
(c) Only (B) is implicit
(d) Only (A) and (C) are implicit
(e) None of these

5. **Statement :** The airlines have requested all their bona fide passengers to check the status of flight operations before leaving their homes as heavy fog is causing immense problems to normal flight operations.

Which of the following assumption(s) is /are implicit in the above statement ?

(A) The majority of the air passengers may check the flight status before starting their journey to the airport.

(B) The Government may take serious objection to the notice issued by the airline company.

(C) Majority of the passengers may cancel their tickets and postpone their journey till the situation becomes normal.

(a) None is implicit
(b) Only (A) is implicit
(c) Only (B) is implicit
(d) Only (C) is implicit
(e) Only (A) and (C) are implicit

DIRECTIONS (Qs. 6-10): *In each question below is given a statement followed by two assumptions numbered I and II. An assumption is something supposed or taken for granted. You have to consider the statement and the following assumptions and decide which of the assumptions is implicit in the statement.*

Give answer (a) if only Assumption I is implicit.

Give answer (b) if only Assumption II is implicit.

Give answer (c) if either I or II is implicit.

Give answer (d) if neither I nor II is implicit.

Give answer (e) if both I and II are implicit.

6. **Statement** : A nationalised bank issued an advertisement in the national dailies asking the eligible candidates for applying for 100 posts of chartered accountants.
   Assumptions :
   I. The eligible chartered accountants may respond to the advertisement
   II. There may be adequate number of eligible chartered accountants who may want to join a nationalized bank.

7. **Statement** : The municipal authority announced before the onset of monsoon that the roads within the city will be free of potholes during monsoon.
   Assumptions:
   I. The roads were repaired so well that potholes may not reappear.
   II. People may not complain even if the potholes reappear.

8. **Statement :** "Our Europe Holiday Package costs less than some of the holiday Packages within the country" - An advertisement by an Indian travel company.
   Assumptions:
   I. People may prefer to travel to foreign destinations than to the places within the country at comparable cost.
   II. People generally take their travel decisions after getting information from such advertisements.

9. **Statement :** The retail vegetable vendors increased the prices of vegetables by about 20 percent due to non availability of vegetables at lower prices at the wholesale market.
   Assumptions:
   I. The customers may totally stop buying vegetables at higher prices.
   II. The customers may still buy vegetables from the retail vendors.

10. **Statement :** A large number of students and parents stood in the queue to collect forms for admission to various undergraduate courses in the college.
    Assumptons :
    I. The college authority may be able to admit all those who stood in the queue.
    II. The college authority may have adequate number of forms for all those standing in the queue.

HINTS & SOLUTIONS

1. (a) None of the Assumptions (A), (B) and (C) is implicit in the statement. If police authority has cordoned off the entire locality, it implies that police will ably control the vechicular movement in the locality.

   It is assumed that any advice given to the people will be followed.

2. (c) Only Assumption (B) is implicit in the statement.

   The apex body controlling universities has taken the decision assuming that technical colleges will honour it.

3. (c) Only Assumption (A) and (B) are implicit in the statement.. Government urged all the citizens to use electronic media assuming that most people are capable of using electronic media.

4. (c) Only Assumption (B) is implicit in the statement. If the Government has decided to auction construction of highways to private entities, it may be assumed that many private entities in the country are capable of constructing highways within reasonable time.

5. (b) Only Assumption (A) is implicit in the statement. Any appeal/ request is issued assuming that some people will pay heed to it.

6. (e) Both the assumptions are implicit because daily newspapers provide instant reach. Again 100 vacancies of Chartered Accountants were announced assuming sufficient eligible candidates may join the nationalised bank."

7. (a) Only assumption I is implicit because repairing of roads is carried out so efficiently to leave potholes. Assumption II is not implicit because it is people's right to complain against any pothole.

8. (e) Both the assumption are implicit because main consideration for people is cost factor. People would prefer foreign destination at competitive prices. Advertisement provides sufficient information on this.

9. (b) Only assumption II is implicit because customers prefer to buy vegetables from retail vondors as there is a lot of innovation in retail sector.

10. (b) Only assumption II is implicit because college authority cannot admit all those standing in the queue.

Statement & Conclusions

INTRODUCTION

In this type of questions, a statement is given followed by two conclusions. We have to find out which of these conclusions definitely follows from the given statement.

WHAT IS A 'CONCLUSION'?

'Conclusion' means a fact that can be truly inferred from the contents of a given sentence. Conclusion is the art of judging or deciding, based on reasoning.

DIRECTIONS (for Examples 1 to 3) : In each of the following questions, a statement is given followed by two conclusions I and II. Give answer :

(a) if only conclusion I follows;
(b) if only conclusion II follows;
(c) if either I or II follows;
(d) if neither I nor II follows;
(e) if both I and II follows;

EXAMPLE 1.

Statement : The oceans are a store house of practically every mineral including uranium. But like most other minerals, it is found in extremely low concentration – about three gms per 1000 tonnes of water.

Conclusions :

I. The oceans are a cheap source of uranium.

II. The oceans harbour radiation hazards.

Sol. (d) I. Uranium is found in extremely low concentration in oceans. Hence oceans are not a cheap source of uranium. II is out of context of the sentence.

EXAMPLE 2.

Statement : Today, out of the world population of several thousand million, the majority of men have to live under government which refuses them personal liberty and the right to dissent.

Conclusions :

I. People are indifferent to personal liberty and the right to dissent.

II. People desire personal liberty and the right to dissent.

Sol. (b) It is mentioned in the statement that most people are forced to live under governments which refuse them personal liberty and right to dissent. This means that they are not indifferent to these rights but have a desire for them. So, only II follows.

EXAMPLE 3.

Statement : It has been decided by the Government to withdraw 33% of the subsidy on cooking gas from the beginning of next month—a spokesman of the Government.

Conclusions :

I. People no more desire or need such subsidy from government as they can afford increased price of the cooking gas.

II. The price of the cooking gas will increase at least by 33% from the next month.

Sol. (d) I does not follow because a govt's policy is not determined merely by people's needs.

II does not follow. Let the present price be x

∴ Price if subsidy is removed

$= \frac{x}{0.67} = 1.49x$

Hence increase in price will be around 49%

DIRECTIONS (for Examples 4 to 5) : In each of the following questions, a statement is given followed by two conclusions I and II. Give answer :

(a) if only conclusion I follows;
(b) if only conclusion II follows;
(c) if either I or II follows;
(d) if both I and II follow.
(e) if neithter I nor II follows;

EXAMPLE 4.

Statement : Interest rate will be fixed on the basis of our bank's rate prevailing on the date of deposit and refixed every quarter thereafter.

Conclusions:

I. It is left to the depositors to guard their interest.

II. The bank's interest rates are subject to change on a day-to-day basis depending on market position.

Sol. (b) I does not follow because the statement is silent about the depositors. II follows from the phrase "bank's rate prevailing on the date of deposit" which means the rates are subject to day-to-day changes.

EXAMPLE 5.

Statement : The government of country X has recently announced several concessions and offered attractive package tours for foreign visitors.

Conclusions :

I. Now, more number of foreign tourists will visit the country.

II. The government of country X seems to be serious in attracting tourists.

Sol. (e) Clearly, the government has taken the step to attract more tourists. So, both I and II follow.

❑ Shortcut Approach

4 GOLDEN RULES.

1. The conclusion must be in context of the statement. If out of context then it does not follow.

2. The conclusion must support the contents of the statement. If it negates then it does not follow.

3. The conclusion must be truly inferred. If there is some doubt that it may or may not be correct or truly inferred, then it does not follow.

4. The conclusion must not repeat or rephrase the statement. If so, it does not follow.

Now let us apply these rules to the 5 examples solved above.

Ex. 1 I. Rule 2 applies as it negates the statement.

II. Rule 1 applies as it is out of context.

Ex. 2 I. Rule 2 applies as it negates the statement.

II. Fulfils all the conditions in Rule 1-4.

Ex. 3 I. Rule 1, 2 & 4 follow but 3 does not as there can be various reasons to withdraw subsidy.

II. Rule 1, 2 & 4 follow but 3 does not as the price increase is actually 49%

Ex. 4 I. Rule I applies as it is out of context.

II. Follows all the 4 rules perfectly.

Ex. 5 Both I & II follow all the 4 rules and hence follow the statement.

PRACTICE EXERCISE

DIRECTIONS (Qs. 1-10): *In each question below is given a statement followed by two conclusions numbered I and II. You have to assume everything in the statement to be true, then consider the two conclusions together and decide which of them logically follows beyond a reasonable doubt from the information given in the statement.*

Give answer:

(a) If only conclusion I follows
(b) If only conclusion II follows
(c) If either I or II follows
(d) If neither I nor II follows and
(e) If both I and II follow.

1. Statements: Government has spoiled many top ranking financial institutions by appointing bureaucrats as Directors of these institutions.

Conclusions:

I. Government should appoint Directors of the financial institutes taking into consideration the expertise of the person in the area of finance.
II. The Director of the financial institute should have expertise commensurate with the financial work carried out by the institute.

2. Statements: Population increase coupled with depleting resources is going to be the scenario of many developing countries in days to come.

Conclusions:

I. The population of developing countries will not continue to increase in future.
II. It will be very difficult for the governments of developing countries to provide its people decent quality of life.

3. Statements: Prime age school-going children in urban India have now become avid as well as more regular viewers of television, even in households without a TV. As a result there has been an alarming decline in the extent of readership of newspapers.

Conclusions:

I. Method of increasing the readership of newspapers should be devised.
II. A team of experts should be sent to other countries to study the impact of TV. on the readership of newspapers.

4. Statements: In Japan, the incidence of stomach cancer is very high, while that of bowel cancer is very low. But Japanese immigrate to Hawaii, this is reversed - the rate of bowel cancer increases but the rate of stomach cancer is reduced in the next generation. All this is related to nutrition - the diets of Japanese in Hawaii are different than those in Japan.

Conclusions:

I. The same diet as in Hawaii should be propagated in Japan also.
II. Bowel cancer is less severe than stomach cancer

5. Statements: Monitoring has become an integral part in the planning of social development programmes. It is recommended that Management Information System be developed for all programmes. This is likely to give a feedback on the performance of the functionaries and the efficacy with which services are being delivered.

Conclusions:

I. All the social development programmes should be evaluated.

II. There is a need to monitor the performance of workers.

6. **Statements:** In a highly centralised power structure, in which even senior cabinet ministers are prepared to reduce themselves to pathetic countries or yesmen airing views that are primarily intended to anticipate or reflect the Prime Minister's own performances, there can be no place for any consensus that is quite different from real or contrived unanimity of opinion, expressed through a well orchestrated endorsement of the leader's actions.

Conclusions:

I. The Ministers play safe by not giving anti-government views.

II. The Prime Minister does not encourage his colleagues to render their own views.

7. **Statements:** The eligibility for admission to the course is minimum second class Master's degree. However, the candidates who have appeared for the final year examination of Master's degree can also apply.

Conclusions:

I. All candidates who have yet to get their Master's degree will be there in the list of selected candidates.

II. All candidates having obtained second class Master's degree will be there in the list of selected candidates.

8. **Statements:** Applications of applicants who do not fulfill eligibility criteria and/or who do not submit applications before last date will be summarily rejected and will not be called for the written test.

Conclusions:

I. Those who are called for the written test are those who fulfill eligibility criteria and have submitted their applications before last date.

II. Written test will be held only after scrutiny of applications.

9. **Statements:** Although we have rating agencies like Crisil, ICRA, there is demand to have a separate rating agency for IT companies to protect investors.

Conclusions:

I. Assessment of financial worth of IT companies calls for separate set of skills, insight and competencies.

II. Now the investors investing in IT companies will get protection of their investment.

10. **Statements:** Wind is an inexhaustible source of energy and an aero-generator can convert it into electricity. Though not much has been done in this field, the survey shows that there is vast potential for developing wind as alternative source of energy.

Conclusions:

I. Energy by wind is comparatively newly emerging field.

II. The energy crisis can be dealt by exploring more in the field of aero-generation.

HINTS & SOLUTIONS

1. **(e)** According to the statement, Government has spoiled financial institutions by appointing bureaucrats as Directors. This means that only those persons should be appointed as Directors who are experts in finance and are acquainted with the financial work of the institute. So, both I and II follow.
2. **(b)** The fact given in I is quite contrary to the given statement. So, I does not follow. II mentions the direct implications of the state discussed in the statement. Thus, II follows.
3. **(d)** The statement concentrates on the increasing viewership of TV. and does not stress either on increasing the readership of newspapers or making studies regarding the same. So, neither I nor II follows.
4. **(d)** The statement neither propagates the diet of any of the countries nor compares the two types of cancer. So, neither I nor II follows.
5. **(e)** According to the statement, monitoring and evaluation of social development programmes - their function, performance and efficiency - is absolutely essential. So, both I and II follow.
6. **(a)** According to the statement, even senior cabinet ministers are always ready to conform to the Prime Minister's views. So, I follows. However, II contradicts the given statement and so does not follow.
7. **(d)** The statement mentions that the candidates who have obtained second class Master's degree or have appeared for the final year examination of Master's degree, can apply for admission. This implies that both types of candidates may be selected on certain grounds. Thus, some candidates of each type and not all candidates of any one type, may be selected. So, neither I nor II follows.
8. **(e)** The statement clearly mentions that fulfilling the eligibility criteria and submitting the application before the stipulated date are both essential to avoid rejection. So, I follows. Also, since it is given that the candidates whose applications are rejected shall not be called for written test, so II also follows.
9. **(a)** The need for separate rating agency for IT companies clearly indicates that such assessment requires a separate set of skills. So, I follows. However, the statement indicates only the need or demand and neither the future course of action nor its after-effects can be judged. So, II does not follow.
10. **(e)** The phrase 'not much has been done in this field' indicates that wind energy is a comparatively newly emerging field. So, I follows. The expression 'there is vast potential for developing wind as alternative source of energy' proves II to be true.

Courses of Action

INTRODUCTION

In many competitive examinations questions related to courses of action are frequently asked.

The basic reason behind asking such questions is to test your ability to judge a problem correctly in order to determine the root of the given problem and then finding out a proper course of action for that particular problem.

WHAT IS THE FORMAT OF THE PROBLEM?

Directions: In the question given below is given a statement followed by two suggested courses of action number I and II. A course of action is a step or administrative decision to be taken for improvement, follow up, or further action in regard to the problem, policy etc. On the basis of the information given in the statement. Read the situation carefully and then decide which of the given courses of action follow/ follows.

Mark answers:

(a) If only I follows
(b) If only II follows
(c) If either I or II follows
(d) If neither I nor II follows
(e) If both I & II follow.

Statement: The sale of a particular product 'A' has gone down considerably, causing great concern to company 'X'.

Courses of action :

I. Company 'X' should make a proper study of the rival products in the market.

II. The price of product 'A' should be reduced.

NOTE : In the examinations more than two courses of actions may also be given.

TYPES OF PROBLEMS

(1) Problems based on problem and solution relationship.
(2) Problems based on fact & improvement relationship.

1. Problems Based on Problem and Solution Relationship

This is a case when the given statement talks of a problem and the suggested course of action talks of a solution. It is very easy to find out when a suggested course of action is acceptable and when it is not. In fact, the suggested course of action will be acceptable if:

(a) it solves/ reduces or minimises the given problem
(b) it gives a practical and wise solution.

Now, what to do ? Just see the given problem with a serious eye; think over that; apply your day to day experiences; apply your common sense and use your general knowledge to judge whether a suggested course of action solves or reduces or minimises the problem given in the statement. After this step, the next step is checking the practicality. Here, you have to check if the solution suggested by the given course of action is wise enough and applicable in practical way in day to day life.

Infact (a) is the 1st step test and after passing the step I test, the given course of action will have to pass step II (which is (b)). If the given course of action passes both the tests [step I and step II] only then it will be called a correct action.

Step I test

To pass the step I test a suggested course of action must be

(i) based on an established fact or
(ii) based on logical prediction or
(iii) based on experiences
(iv) based on prevailing notions of truth

Let us discuss all the conditions mentioned above:-

(i) Action based on established fact: -

In some of the cases an action taken is an established fact which suggests that the given problem can be reduced or solved by this particular solution. It does mean that the solution suggested by the given course of action is universally acknowledged to the given problem. Let us see the examples given below:

EXAMPLE 1.

Statement: Southern part of India has been coming rapidly into the grip of malaria.

Courses of action:

I. The Southern Indian population must be instructed not to come out of their houses. [wrong action]

II. Anti-mosquito liquids should be sprayed in the southern part of India. [correct action]

EXAMPLE 2.

Statement: A child was caught while stealing money of a respectable person of society.

Courses of action:

I. The child should be sent to child welfare society. (correct action)

II. The child should be put in jail and severly beaten (wrong action)

Comment: In example I, I is rejected as it is an irrelevant action. It does not make it clear how instructing population for not coming out of their houses will solve or reduce the problem of spreading malaria. But II is a proper course of action as it is an established biological fact that malaria can be prevented by using safeguards against mosquitoes. This is the reason that II will go for further test (step II test) proving itself a proper course of action in 1st level test (step I test).

In example 2, II is rejected on the basis that it is totally illogical to beat a child and put into jail as a child is not mature enough to decide what is right and what is wrong. Further, it is an established fact (socially established fact) that child criminals must not be treated as punishable wrong doer but they should be made to mend their ways and on the basis of this I is the correct course of action. Hence, I will qualify for the 2nd round test (Step II test)

(ii) Action based on logical prediction:

In such type of cases, solutions provided for the given problems are neither an established fact nor they can be considered as proper action on the basis of our past experiences. Hence, in such cases examinees are required to apply certain logic and reasoning to find out if the given course of action solves or reduces or minimises the problem. Let us see the example given below:

EXAMPLE 3.

Statement: Jammu & Kashmir is experiencing, again, the rise of terrorism and it is obvious that Pakistan is encouraging it.

Course of action: India must go to the international bodies with all the proof of Pakistani involvement in Jammu & Kashmir and demand that Pakistan must be declared a terrorist nation. [correct action]

Comment : Here, the given course of action is the correct one at step I test. In fact, it is a matter of simple logic of diplomacy that in case of disturbances created by a hostile nation within our country, we put this issue before international bodies so that the hostile nation stands at disadvantage. Thus Ex. 3 will qualify for the next step test (step II or practicality test).

(iii) Action based on experiences: In certain cases, while deciding if a given course of action solves or reduces or minimises the given problem, our experiences work. In fact, in such cases the given problem may be a relatively new one. It will not be totally new but it will not be very old either. This is the reason that the solution can not be said as an established fact. However, based on our past experiences, in the similar kind of situation, we can reach the conclusion that the given problem can be solved/ reduced/ minimised by this particular action. Let us see the example given below:

EXAMPLE 4.

Statement: Several foreign powers having expansionist thinking are threat to India.

Course of action: Efforts should be made that the Indians remain united for any eventuality. [correct action]

Comment: Our past experiences say that we (India) became a sufferer several times because of the foreign powers and at that time we lacked our unity. In another words, India has fallen victim to foreign powers only when our country (India) has not remained united. Hence, on the basis of our past experience, we can conclude that the given course of action solves or reduces the problem making its entry for 2nd level (step II) test.

(iv) Action based on prevailing notions of truth: In such type of cases solutions provided for the given problem is as per the social norms. In other words, the given course of action suggests a solution that is prevailing notion of truth. In fact, they are the ideas that are universally accepted and acknowledged by the society and hence in many ways they are similar to established fact. Let us see the following examples:

EXAMPLE 5.

Statement: Mr Sharma got angry and beat his son mercilesely.

Course of action : Mr.Sharma should be caned publicly [wrong action]

EXAMPLE 6.

Statement : Most of manufacturing companies in India are running in losses.

Course of action: Prospects of privatisation of these companies must be explored. [correct action]

Comment: In example 5, the given solution is against the societal norm as public beating is not considered a good punishment. In other words, it is prevailing notion of truth that public beating is not good. Hence, on the basis of this the given solution is rejected and will not go for 2nd level test (step II test). In example 6, the given course of action suggests privatisation for loss making manufacturing companies and no doubts, it is a prevailing notion of truth that privatisation can reduce or minimise their losses. There is also a chance that privatisation can convert a loss making company into a profitable one. Hence, we conclude the given solution is correct one and will qualify for further test (2nd level test or step II test). Now, we can move on to step II test.

Step II (Test of Practicality)

This is the 2nd part of test. In the 1st part we just found out whether a suggested action really solves/ reduces/ minimises the given problem. But an important part also remains to be checked and that is the test of practicality. Point to be noted that a given course of action may solve/ reduce/ minimise a particular problem but if it is not practically possible, it will be consider useless. This is the reason why this point too, needs sound checking. For this you have to keep the following things in your mind:

A. The problem and solution must be well matched and must be in proportion. In other words, if solutions are too simple for too severe problems, they will be useless. Conversly, we can say that too severe solutions are not good solutions for too simple problems.

B. Even after passing the step I test, the given solution is creating a new problem, then the given solution will not be a good solution and will fail in practicality test.

EXAMPLES FOR (A)

EXAMPLE 7.

Statement : Lack of discipline is a good reason for low productivity in India.

Course of action : Government must take step to make military traing compulsory for all Indian citizens. [wrong action]

EXAMPLE 8.

Statement: As per the report of 'WHO' (World Health Organisation) the life expactancy of an average Indian is continuously declining.

Course of action : A serious effort must be made to prevent children from making noises. [wrong action]

Comment: In Example 7, the given course of action is not a good solution for the given problem. No, doubt that military training wold be a solution for lack of discipline but is it a practical solution? Your answer will be a big 'No' (why?). In reality, at the 1st step test the given course of action may seem true as it solves the given problem but when it comes to the 2nd level test, it becomes clear that it is too severe solution for a relatively small problem. Hence, on this basis the given course of action is rejected finally.

In example 8, the given course of action suggests that problem of declining life expectancy can be solved if children are prevented from making noises. At one stage the given course of action reduces the problem to some extent as it suggests that less noise will increase the chances of low blood pressure and this will result in less deaths. But when we think analytically, we come to the conclusion that the problem is very serious and the given solution is very simple for it. Hence on this basis the given course of action would be declared a wrong one and would be rejected finally.

EXAMPLE FOR (B)

EXAMPLE 9.

Statement: In recent years, people have developed a tendency of tax evasion and this is the reason it has increased at an alarming level.

Course of action : Government must make law to abolish taxes. [wrong action]

Comment: Here, the given problem is about tax evasion. Tax evasion does mean showing less income to pay less tax. Why tax evasion is a problem? Because tax evasion generates black money. The given course of action suggests the abolition of taxes which connot be a good solution as taxes are taken to provide people certain indirect services like the facilities of roads, parks, police etc. Suppose if taxes are not charged, how and where from money will come to provide such indirect services to community. No doubts, the tax abolition will create a new problem. Hence on this basis the given course of action will be rejected finally as it fails the 2nd level test (step II test) of practicality.

Now after understanding what is a practical solution, we can test the courses of action that have passed the step I test and given under examples 1, 2, 3, 4 and 6.

Step II test of Example 1 (Course of action II):

IInd course of action given under example 1 is "Anti mosquito liquids should be sprayed in the southern part of India". In step II, we need to check if it is a practical solution for the given problem. In the past we have also seen that such steps have been taken. Not in the past only even today whenever it seems that mosquito born diseases are imminent, the anti-mosquito liquids are sprayed. Such step is taken only because it is practical. Here, the IInd course of action given under example 1 passes both the test to be finally declared as proper and correct solution.

Step II test of Example 2 [Course of action I]:

Ist course of action given under example 2 is "child should be sent to child welfare society". In step II, we need to check if it is a practical solution. In so many cases we have seen that when a child does a crime like stealing and some other more serious crime, then they are put under such atmosphere that they can understand the seriousness of their crime and try to mend their ways. For such children, child welfare societies and some other such kind of organisations are very helpful. Hence, this course of action passes its final test to be declared a correct course of action.

Step II test of Example 3 :

The course of action given under example 3 is "India must go to the international bodies with all the proof of Pakistani involvement in Jammu & Kashmir and demand that Pakistan must be declared a terrorist nation" and this is a very practical solution. As we have seen in certain circumstances in past that India has put such type of demand from UNO and even from some other nations on individual basis. No doubts, that on such demands India has got support to some extent. Hence it is a very practical solution and this given course of action passes it practicality test to be declared a proper and correct course of action.

Step II test of Example 4 :

The given course of action "efforts should be made that the Indians remain united for any eventualities" is a practical one as we have shown this type of unity in the past. For example, in the freedom struggle we were united. How this unity took place? Only because this was practically possible. Hence, this given course of action, too, passed the practicality test to be declared finally a proper and correct course of action.

Step II test of Example 6:

The given course of action "Prospects of privatisation of these (loss making) companies must be explored is not a correct solution at the end at the 2nd level test (Practicality test) because the course of action and the given statement are not properly linked. The statement does not make it clear that it talks only about public sector manufacturing concerns as even a private sector manufacturing company may be a loss making company. Hence the statement and given course of action creates confusion. Therefore, the given course of action is rejected at 2nd level test.

2. Problem Based on Fact and Improvement Relationship

This is the 2nd type of problem related to course of action. But point to be noted is that this does not require any new skill. The solving method is exactly the same as you have solved the 1st type of problem that is problem solution based. In fact you have to solve this type of problem in two steps:

(i) Find out whether the suggested course of action will help in improvement of the situation.

(ii) Find out whether the two are properly balanced.

In fact problem given under example 7 is such type of problem.

Now we have come to the end of this chapter and this is the time to solve the problem given under 'what is the format of the problem'? Let us solve it:

Statement : The sale of a particular product 'A' has gone down considerably, causing great concern to company 'X'.

Courses of action :

I. Company should make a proper study of rival products in the market.

II. The price of product 'A' should be reduced.

Solution. Option (a) is the correct option as only I follows.

Reason /Explanation: If the sale of 'A' has gone down, then there must be some reasons. The company X must know this reason. As I suggest the similar solution, it follows. But II does not follow. The company should first know if price was a factor behind the drop in sale. Without knowing this, reducing price may turn out to be a wrong and harmful action.

Note : If you see 'an either choice' in the answer options avoid it. It will be a wrong answer. Either choice can be in the form like "Either of I or II (or III or I etc.) follows".

Shortcut Approach

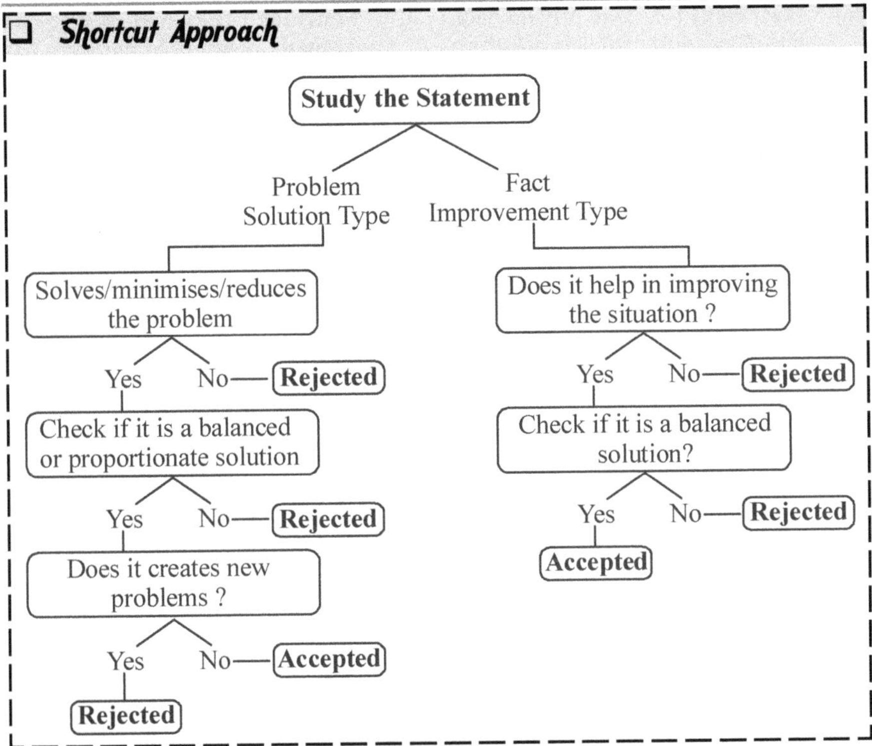

PRACTICE EXERCISE

DIRECTIONS (Qs. 1-5): *In each question below is given a statement followed by three courses of action numbered (A), (B) and (C). A course of action is a step or administrative decision to be taken for improvement, follow-up or further action in regard to the problem, policy, etc. On the basis of the information given in the statement, you have to assume everything in the siatement to be true, then decide which of the suggested courses of action logically follow(s) for pursuing.*

1. **Statement:** A heavy unseasonal downpour during the last two days has paralysed the normal life in the state in which five persons were killed but this has provided a huge relief to the problem of acute water crisis in the state.

Courses of action :

(A) The state government should set up a committee to review the alarming situation.

(B) The state government should immediately remove all the restrictions on use of potable water in all the major cities in the state.

(C) The state government should send relief supplies to all the affected areas in the state.

(a) None
(b) Only (A)
(c) Only (B) and (C)
(d) Only (C)
(e) All (A), (B) and (C)

2. **Statement :** A large private bank has decided to retrench one-third of its employees in view of the huge losses incurred by it during the past three quarters.

Courses of action :

(A) The Government should issue a notification to general public to immediately stop all transactions with the bank.

(B) The Government should direct the bank to refrain from retrenching its employees.

(C) The Government should ask the central bank of the country to initiate an enquiry into the bank's activities and submit its report.

(a) None
(b) Only (A)
(c) Only (B)
(d) Only (C)
(e) Only (A) and (C)

3. **Statement :** Many political activists have decided to stage demonstrations and block traffic movement in the city during peak hours to protest against the steep rise in prices of essential commodities.

Courses of action:

(A) The Government should immediately ban all forms of agitations in the country.

(B) The police authority of the city should deploy additional forces all over the city to help traffic movement in the city.

(C) The state administration should carry out preventive arrests of the known criminals staying in the city.

(a) Only (A)
(b) Only (B)
(c) Only (C)
(d) Only (A) and (B)
(e) None of these

4. **Statement:** The school dropout rate in many districts in the state has increased sharply during the last few years as the parents of these children make them work in the fields owned by others to earn enough for them to get at least one meal a day.

Courses of action :

(A) The Government should put up a mechanism to provide food grains to the poor people in these districts through public distribution system to encourage the parents to send their wards to school.

(B) The Government should close down some of these schools in the district and deploy the teachers of these schools to nearby schools and also ask remaining students to join these schools.

(C) Government should issue arrest warrants for all the parents who force their children to work in fields instead of attending classes.

(a) Only (A)
(b) Only (B)
(c) Only (C)
(d) Only (A) and (B)
(e) None of these

5. **Statement :** One aspirant was killed due to stampede while participating in a recruitment drive of police constables.

Courses of action :

(A) The officials in charge of the recruitment process should immediately be suspended.

(B) A team of officials should be asked to find out the circumstances which led to the death of the aspirant and submit its report within a week.

(C) The Government should ask the home department to stagger the number of aspirants over more number of days to avoid such incidents in future.

(a) Only (A)
(b) Only (B)
(c) Only (C)
(d) Only (B) and (C)
(e) None of these

DIRECTIONS (Qs. 6-10): *In each question below is given a statement followed by two courses of action numbered I and II. A course of action is a step or administrative decision to be taken for improvement, follow-up or further action in regard to the problem, policy, etc. On the basis of the information given in the statement, you have to as some everything in the statement to be true, then decide which of the suggested courses of action logically follow(s) for pursuing.*

Give answer (a) if only course of action I follows.

Give answer (b) if only course of action II follows.

Give answer (c) if either course of action I or II follows.

Give answer (d) if neither course of action I nor II follows.

Give answer (e) if both courses of action I and II follow.

6. **Statement :** Drinking water supply to many parts of town is disrupted due to loss of water because of leakage in pipes supplying water.

Courses of action :

I. The government should order an enquiry into the matter.

II. The civic body should set up a fact-finding team to assess the damage and take effective step.

7. **Statement:** There is an alarming increase in the number of people suffering from malaria in many parts of the city.

Courses of action :

I. The municipal corporation has advised all the government hospitals to store adequate supply of malaria drugs.

II. The municipal corporation has urged people to use mosquito repellants and keep their premises clean.

8. **Statement :** Many people have encroached into the government property and built their houses and business establishments.

Courses of action :

I. The government should take immediate steps to remove all unauthorised constructions on government land.

II. All the encroachers should immediately be put behind bars and also be slapped with a hefty fine.

9. **Statement :** The meteorological department has predicted normal rainfall throughout the country during the current monsoon.

Courses of action :

I. The government should reduce the procurement price of foodgrains for the current year.

II. The government should reduce subsidy on fertilizers for the current year.

10. **Statement :** The number of dropouts in government schools has significantly increased in the urban areas over the past few years.

Courses of action :

I. The government should immediately close down all such schools in the urban areas where the dropout goes beyond 20 per cent.

II. The parents of all the students who dropped out of the government schools in urban areas should be punished.

HINTS & SOLUTIONS

1. **(d)** Immediate course of action to avert the difficult situation is to send relief rupplics in affected areas course of action I is a long term action plan which is time consuming and course of action II is not feasible practically.
2. **(a)** None of course of action is feasible because the government cannot interfere in bank's internal matter but the government can componsate the huge losser incurred by bank.
3. **(b)** The course of action (A) and (C) are not feasible because in a democratic country the government cannot impose ban on these things.
4. **(a)** Course of action (A) is only feasible solution because the government can neither close these schools nor issue arrest warrants for all the parents.
5. **(d)** Clearly course of action (B) and (C) should be followed because terminating official in charge of recruitment procers is not a solution to the problem.
6. **(d)** Both of the course of action are not necessary because ordering an enquiry into the leakage matter would not solve any purpose and secondly no need of setting up fact-finding team when cause of leakage is known to us.
7. **(e)** Both the course of action I and II should be followed because sufficient supply of malaria drugs is necessary to avoid malaria. Secondly use of mosquito repellant and cleanliness are necessary to avoid mosquito breeding.
8. **(a)** Only I course of action is suitable to follow because the government should check all unauthorised construction on government land. II course of action is too harsh to be suitable.
9. **(d)** Both the courses of action are not suitable because when there is no problem, no action is required.
10. **(d)** Both the course of action are not practically possible because government cannot close down all such schools and also parents of such children cannot be punished because there may be genuine reason for dropouts.

Chapter 30

Critical Reasoning

INTRODUCTION

Critical Reasoning (CR) is ability to reason clearly to evaluate and judge arguments. You are using this skill a lot during your everyday life while reading newspapers or watching movies. When you think that the movie is pushing the limit of the Reasonable or the news sounds less reasonable than the movie that was pushing the limit, you are using your Critical Reasoning skills to produce these conclusions. The argument you meet can be anything from a classical argument to an advertisement or a dialog. Critical Reasoning questions will ask you to manipulate the argument to weaken/strengthen it, find the conclusion, assumption, explanation, do an inference or supplement a statement, etc. Whatever it is that you have to do, you will need 2 things to succeed: know the basic structure of arguments and clearly understand the argument.

In general, most of them, arguments consist of evidence, usually 2 pieces, a conclusion - the main point of an argument, and an assumption - the bridge between the evidence and conclusion. The majority of the arguments you encounter on the test will be 3 step arguments:

Evidence 1 + Evidence 2 = Conclusion.

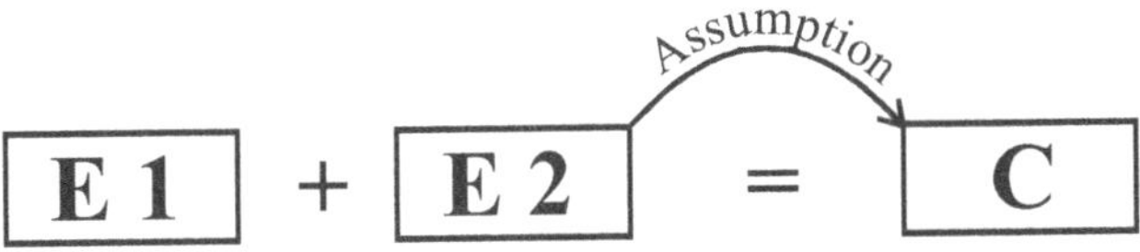

EXAMPLE 1. Last week Mike was detained for shoplifting at a groceries store near his house, but he has been a Christian for 10 years, therefore, the police must have been wrong accusing him in stealing.

> **Note :** There are two pieces of evidence: *'Mike was accused of stealing'* and that *'he is a Christian'*. The conclusion is that **'the police are wrong'**. Therefore, our huge assumption here is that *'a Christian could not have stolen anything.'*

EXAMPLE 2. There are a lot of mosquitoes outside today, please do not turn on the light in the room because a lot of them will fly in.

> **Note :** Here the evidences are *'there are a lot of mosquitoes outside today'* and *'do not turn on the light'*. The conclusion is that '**Many will fly in**' and the assumption is 'mosquitoes will approach the light.'

There is no set scheme for structure in CR, but since the majority of the arguments are only a few sentences long, the conclusion usually comes in the first or the last sentence. However, some of the arguments encountered will not have a conclusion at all or will have just an implied one.

STRATEGY TO CRACK CRITICAL REASONING QUESTIONS

This strategy is not the easiest way to do CR (the easiest would be read-and-answer), but it lets you get the most questions right spending less time per correct answer.

1. Read the questions first; this is needed so that you would know what to look for and what to do: find an assumption, strengthen/weaken, infer something or else; do not worry about the details in the question, read for keywords, such as strengthen, deny, or explain. [Use symbols for convenience, e.g. + for strengthen or – for weaken].
2. Read the passage very attentively because in contrast to Reading Comprehension, there is very little text here and mostly everything is important; try to read only once. Reread if required.

   As you read, look for the problem in the passage (evaluate how convincing it is)
3. Paraphrase (reword) the passage. It is a very important step because when you do a paraphrase, you check whether you understood the passage and at the same time you extract the skeleton of the argument, making it easier to identify the conclusion and the assumption. Very often, the paraphrase of the passage will be pretty close to the conclusion. It is not surprising, since the conclusion is the main point and evidence just supports it.) Your paraphrase should be as close to the text and as simple as possible so that you would understand it easily and at the same time could fully trust it. Do not make it too general nor too detail oriented. When you do a paraphrase, do it in three steps: Evidence1, Evidence2, and Conclusion; put "therefore" word before you start your conclusion, this will help you to set it off.
4. Read the question again (now with more understanding of what is being asked; reading the question 2 times, it will also help you to make sure your answer exactly what is stated and that you understand the question.)
5. Answer before reading the answer choices. There are two reasons for this :
   (i) if you can think of the correct answer or at least the general direction that the answer choice needs to be, you will identify it among the wrong choices much faster, thus spend less time reading the answers, which usually take 30 seconds to cover.
   (ii) Often students are seduced by the author's wording. One reads a few words that were used in the passage and the brain identifies this choice with the passage, thus making it seem more right that it needs to be. The more problems you practice with, the more chance is you will guess the right answer even before reading it.
6. Go through the answers, first time scan them for YOUR answer choice (usually you will guess correctly in 60-70% of cases), if you did not find it, reread them more attentively.
7. Draw a grid to eliminate the wrong answers easier. Use "✓" for a sure answer, "×" for a definitely wrong

answer choice, and "?" for an answer that may be right or questionable. This will help to concentrate only on a few answer choices and will prevent you from reading same answers several times if you get confused or keep having troubles locating the right answer.

TYPES OF CRITICAL REASONING QUESTIONS

Critical reasoning questions will ask you to:

1. Identify the inference / Must be true question
2. Identify the assumption.
3. Strengthen an argument.
4. Weaken an argument.
5. Select the best conclusion/Main Point
6. Identify the paradox
7. Evaluation/ Reasoning
8. Identify a parallel argument/Structure.

1. Identify the Inference / Must be True Question

These type of questions are extremely common. An **Inference** means the same thing as "must be true". **Conclusions** differ from **inferences** in that conclusions are the result of premises and inferences are something that must be true. The following are the typical Inference (Must be true) based Questions:

- If the statements above are true, which of the following must also be true?
- Which of the following is [implied, must be true, implicit, most reasonably drawn] in the passage above?
- Which of the following inferences is best supported by the statement made above?

❑ ***Shortcut Approach***

How to tackle "Identify the inference / Must be true questions":

- Read the stimulus and look for the argument.
- Note that Must Be True questions may not contain an argument. They may just be a series of facts. Nevertheless, try to find the argument.
- Avoid choices which contain absolute statements - never, always, none, only etc. Although these words might appear in some correct choice, you should be very sure about them.
- Some of the options can be eliminated as they go beyond the scope of the passage. Note that an inference can be based on only some of the information provided and not the complete passage.

EXAMPLE 1. Stimulus Argument

Increases in funding for police patrols often lower the rate of crimes of opportunity such as petty theft and vandalism by providing visual deterrence in high-crime neighborhoods. Levels of funding for police patrols in some communities are increased when federal matching grants are made available.

Question : Which of the following can be correctly inferred from the statements above?

Options :

(a) Areas with little vandalism can never benefit from visual deterrence.

(b) Communities that do not increase their police patrols are at higher risk for crimes of opportunity late at night.

(c) Federal matching grants for police patrols lower the rate of crimes of opportunity in some communities.

(d) Only federal matching grants are necessary to reduce crime in most neighborhoods.
(e) None of these

Sol.

(c) is a summary of the information provided; it is the logical end of a chain of reasoning started in the stimulus argument. The sequence of events goes like this :

Increased funding → Increased visual deterrence → Lower crime

The last statement could be mapped as follows:

Federal grants → Increased patrol funds

(c) makes the chain complete by correctly stating that federal grants can lead to lower crime in some communities. Now the logical chain becomes:

Federal grants → Increased funding → Increased visual deterrence → Lower crime

The other answer choices may not be correctly inferred because they go beyond the scope of the argument. They may be objectively, factually correct, or they may be statements that you would tend to agree with. However, you are limited to the argument presented when choosing a correct answer.

2. Identify the Assumption

An assumption is an unstated premise that supports the author's conclusion. It's the connection between the stated premises and the conclusion., which together forms the passage. An assumption is something that the author's conclusion depends upon. Assumption questions are extremely common and have types that look like this:

- Which of the following most accurately states a hidden assumption that the author must make in order to advance the argument above?
- Which of the following is an assumption that, if true, would support the conclusion in the passage above?

❑ **Shortcut Approach**

How to approach "Identify the assumption Questions"

- Look for gaps between the premises and the conclusion. Ask yourself why the conclusion is true. Before you progress to the answer choices, try to get feel of what assumption is necessary to fill that gap between the premises.
- Beware of extreme language in the answer choices of assumption questions. Assumptions usually are not extreme. "Extreme" answer choices usually contain phrases such as always, never, or totally.

EXAMPLE 2. Stimulus Argument

Traditionally, decision making by doctors that is carefully, deductively reasoned has been considered preferable to intuitive decision making. However, a recent study found that senior surgeons used intuition significantly more than did most residents or mid-level doctors. This confirms the alternative view that intuition is actually more effective than careful, methodical reasoning.

Question : The conclusion above is based on which of the following assumptions?

Options :

(a) Senior surgeons are more effective at decision making than are mid-level doctors.
(b) Senior surgeons have the ability to use either intuitive reasoning or

deductive, methodical reasoning in making decisions.

(c) The decisions that are made by mid-level and entry-level doctors can be made as easily by using methodical reasoning as by using intuitive reasoning.

(d) Senior surgeons use intuitive reasoning in making the majority of their decisions.

(e) None of these

Sol.

(a) The correct answer is (a), which provides a missing link in the author's reasoning by making a connection from the evidence: that intuition is used more by senior surgeons than other, less-experienced doctors, and the conclusion: that, therefore, intuition is more effective. None of the other choices helps bridge this gap in the chain of reasoning. Although some of the other statements may be true, they are not responsive to the question. In fact, they mostly focus on irrelevant factors such as appropriateness, ease of application, ability, etc.

3. Strengthen an Argument

Assumptions connect premises to conclusions. An argument is strengthened by strengthening the assumptions. Here are some examples of Strengthen question types :

- The conclusion would be more properly drawn if it were made clear that...
- Which of the following, if true, would most strengthen the conclusion drawn in the passage above?

❑ *Shortcut Approach*

How to approach "Strengthen an argument"

- Once you have identified the argument of the passage, i.e. the evidence(s) + conclusion, try putting in each option with the argument. Check if the assumption(s) you have drawn is (are) strengthened if you accept the content of the option as true.

EXAMPLE 3. Stimulus Argument

Three years after the Bhakra Nangal Dam was built, none of the six fish species native to the area was still reproducing adequately in the river below the dam. Because the dam reduced the average temperature range of the water from approximately 40° to approximately 10°, biologists have hypothesized that sharp increases in water temperature must be involved in signaling the affected species to begin their reproduction activities.

Question :

Which of the following statements, if true, would most strengthen the scientists' hypothesis?

Options :

(a) The native fish species were still able to reproduce in nearby streams where the annual temperature range remains approximately 40°.

(b) Before the dam was built, the river annually overflowed its banks, creating temporary backwaters that were used as breeding areas for the local fish population.

(c) The lowest temperature ever recorded in the river prior to dam construction was 30°; whereas the lowest recorded river temperature after construction was completed has been 40°.

(d) Non-native fish species, introduced after the dam was completed, have begun competing with the native species for food.

(e) None of these

Sol.

(a) most strengthens the conclusion that the scientists reached. It does so a similar population, not subjected to the same change as the population near the dam, did not experience the same type of result. Here the basic assumption about the conclusion that scientists reached is 'because of the reduction of average temperature range of the water, the reproduction of the native fish species has reduced drastically'. Option (a) clearly strengthens the assumption.

4. Weaken an Argument

Assumptions connect premises to conclusions. An argument is weakened by weakening the assumptions. Here are some examples of Weaken question types:

- Which of the following, if true, would weaken the conclusion drawn in the passage above?
- The argument as it is presented in the passage above would be weaken. If which of the following were true?

❑ Shortcut Approach

How to approach "Weaken an argument"

- Once you have identified the argument of the passage, i.e. the evidence(s) + conclusion, try putting in each option with the argument. Check if the assumption(s) you have drawn is (are) weakened if you accept the content of the option as true.

EXAMPLE 4. Stimulus Argument

A drug that is very effective in treating some forms of cancer can, at present, be obtained only from the bark of the Raynhu, a tr ee that is quite rare in the wild. It takes the bark of approximately 5,000 trees to make one pound of the drug. It follows, then, that continued production of the drug must inevitably lead to the raynhu's extinction.

Question :

Which of the following, if true, most seriously weakens the above conclusion?

Options :

(a) The drug made from Raynhu bark is dispensed to doctors from a central authority.

(b) The drug made from the Raynhu bark is expensive to produce.

(c) The Raynhu generally grows in largely inaccessible places.

(d) The Raynhu can be propagated from cuttings and cultivated by farmers.

(e) None of these

Sol.

(d) provides an alternate source of the Raynhu bark. Even though the tree is rare in the wild, the argument is silent on the availability of cultivated trees. The author of the argument must be assuming that there are no Raynhu trees other than those in the wild, in order to make the leap from the stated evidence to the conclusion that the Raynhu is headed for extinction. The option (d) weakens the assupmtion - 'there are limited raynhu trees' - by saying that there are other ways as well for the propogation of Raynhu. The other answer choices all contain information that is irrelevant. Note that the correct choice does not make the conclusion of the argument impossible. In fact, it is possible that there may be domesticated Raynhu trees and the species could still become extinct. Answer choice (d) is correct because it makes the conclusion about extinction less likely to be true.

5. Conclusion / Main Point Question

In Main Point / Conlcusion questions, you have to identify the conclusion of an argument. You are trying to find the author's point and should approach this question in a similar way to the reading comprehension main point questions. They come in several different formats:

- The main point of the passage is that...
- Which of the following statements about... is best supported by the statements above?
- Which of the following best states the author's conclusion in the passage above?
- Which of the following conclusions can be most properly drawn from the data above?

The conclusion of arguments in Main Point questions is usually not directly stated. To find the conclusion, identify the premises and then identify the conclusion drawn from the premises. Main Point questions differ from the other Critical Reasoning questions in that the argument in the stimulus is usually valid. (In most other Critical Reasoning questions the reasoning is flawed.) Conclusion questions require you to choose the answer that is a summary of the argument.

❑ Shortcut Approach

How to approach "Main Point Questions":

- Main Point answers must be within the scope of the passage.
- Your opinions or information outside of the passage are always outside of the scope.
- Some of the options given can be out of the scope of the passage.
- Knock out answers with extreme wording. Main Point answers typically do not use *only, always, never, best* or any strong words that leave little room.

EXAMPLE 5. Stimulus Argument

People should be held accountable for their own behaviour, and if holding people accountable for their own behaviour entails capital punishment, then so be it. However, no person should be held accountable for behaviour over which he or she had no control.

Question : Which of the following is the most logical conclusion of the argument above?

Options :

(a) People should not be held accountable for the behaviour of other people.
(b) People have control over their own behaviour.
(c) People cannot control the behaviour of other people.
(d) People have control over behaviour that is subject to capital punishment.
(e) None of these

Sol.

(b) The correct response is (b). The argument includes the following two premises:

Premise 1: People are accountable for their own behaviour.

Premise 2: People are not accountable for behaviour they cannot control.

Here's the logical conclusion based on these two premises:

Conclusion: People can control their own behaviour.

(a) would require that people never have control over the behaviour of other people. Yet the argument does not provide this premise.
(c) would require that people should not be held accountable for the behaviour of other people. Yet the argument does not provide this premise.
(d) is not inferable.
(e) None of these

6. Identify the Paradox

These questions present you with a paradox, a seeming contradiction or discrepancy in the argument, and ask you to resolve it or explain how that contradiction could exist. In other words, there are two facts that are both true, and yet they appear to be in direct conflict with one another. Here are some examples of the ways in which these questions are worded:

- Which of the following, if true, would help to resolve the apparent paradox presented above?
- Which of the following, if true, contributes most to an explanation of the apparent discrepancy described above?

❑ *Shortcut Approach*

How to approach "Identify the paradox questions"

- Read the argument and find the apparent paradox, discrepancy, or contradiction.
- State the apparent paradox, discrepancy, or contradiction in your own words.
- Use process of elimination. The best answer will explain how both sides of the paradox, discrepancy, or contradiction can be true. Eliminate answers that are out of scope.

EXAMPLE 6. Stimulus Argument

Town Y is populated almost exclusively by retired people and has almost no families with small children. Yet Town Y is home to a thriving business specializing in the rental of furniture for infants and small children.

Question : Which of the following, if true, best reconciles the seeming discrepancy described above?

Options :

(a) The business specializing in the rental of children's furniture buys its furniture from distributors outside of Town Y.

(b) The few children who do reside in Town Y all know each other and often stay over night at each other's houses.

(c) Many residents of Town Y who move frequently prefer to rent their furniture rather than buy it outright.

(d) Many residents of Town Y must provide for the needs of visiting grandchildren several weeks a year.

(e) None of these

Sol.

(d) The correct answer (d), explains why a town of mostly retired residents might need to rent children's furniture. The other answer choices all contain irrelevant information. This further illustrates the fact that, on all question types, if you eliminate the irrelevant choices, the remaining choice will most likely be correct.

7. Evaluation/ Reasoning Based Questions

Reasoning questions ask you to describe how the argument was made, not necessarily what it says. These questions are closely related to assumption, weakening, and strengthening questions. The correct answer identifies a question that must be answered or information that must be gathered to determine how strong the stimulus argument is. The information will be related to an assumption that the author is making. Another type of question that you will encounter asks you to *identify a flaw* in the stimulus argument. The question tells you that there is a problem with the logic of the argument. You just have to choose the answer that describes the flaw. Here are some examples of the ways in which these questions are worded:

- How does the author make his point?
- A major flaw in the argument above is that it...
- A's response has which of the following relationships to B's argument?

Shortcut Approach

How to approach Reasoning Questions

- Read the argument and find the conclusion.
- State the reasoning in your own words.
- Check whether the reasoning given in the various options fall in line with the reasoning described above.

EXAMPLE 7. Stimulus Argument

Some observers have taken the position that the recently elected judge is biased against men in divorce cases that involve child custody. But the statistics reveal that in 40% of such cases, the recently elected judge awards custody to the fathers. Most other judges award custody to fathers in only 20%–30%of their cases. This record demonstrates that the recently elected judge has not discriminated against men in cases of child custody.

Question : The argument above is flawed in that it ignores the possibility that

Options :

(a) A large number of the recently elected judge's cases involve child custody disputes.

(b) The recently elected judge is prejudiced against men in divorce cases that do not involve child custody issues.

(c) The majority of the child custody cases that have reached the recently elected judge's court have been appealed from a lower court.

(d) The evidence shows that men should have won custody in more than 40% of the recently elected judge's cases involving divorcing fathers.

(e) None of these

Sol.

(d) The correct answer (d), points out a flaw in the argument. Specifically, it points out that the author of the argument was comparing the recently elected judge to other judges. The author of the argument made an unwarranted assumption that the recently elected judge did not rule against many men in custody battles where the evidence clearly favored the men. As with strengthening and weakening questions, the correct answer in flaw questions often involves unwarranted assumptions.

EXAMPLE 8. Stimulus Argument

Although dentures produced through a new computer-aided design process will cost more than twice as much as ordinary dentures, they should still be cost effective. Not only will fitting time and X-ray expense be reduced, but the new dentures should fit better, diminishing the need for frequent refitting visits to the dentist's office.

Question : Which of the following must be studied in order to evaluate the argument presented above?

Options :

(a) The amount of time a patient spends in the fitting process versus the amount of money spent on X-rays

(b) The amount by which the cost of producing dentures has declined with the introduction of the new technique for producing them

(c) The degree to which the use of the new dentures is likely to reduce the need for refitting visits when compared to the use of ordinary dentures
(d) The amount by which the new dentures will drop in cost as the production procedures become standardized and applicable on a larger scale
(e) None of these

Sol.

(c) The correct answer (c), highlights an assumption in the stimulus argument. It shows that the author must be assuming that the reduction in refitting with the new dentures compared to ordinary dentures is significant in order to conclude that the difference will help offset an initial outlay that is twice as much. In other words, if you answer the question posed by answer choice (c) with "not much," the argument is weakened. If you answer it with "a tremendous amount," the argument is strengthened. The other answer choices are all irrelevant because no matter what the answers are, there is no impact on the relationship between the evidence presented in the stimulus argument and its conclusion.

8. Identify a Parallel Argument / Structure.

The last type of Critical Reasoning question is the *parallel structure* question. In this type of question, you must choose the answer that has the same structure as the stimulus argument. In other words, you have to find the argument that is analogous to the given argument in that it includes the same relationship between the evidence presented and the conclusion. Here are some examples of the ways in which these questions are worded:

- Which of the following is most like the argument above in its logical structure?
- Which of the following is a parallel argument to the above given argument?

EXAMPLE 9. Stimulus Argument

It is true that it is against international law to provide aid to certain countries that are building nuclear programs. But, if Russian companies do not provide aid, companies in other countries will.

Question : Which of the following is most like the argument above in its logical structure?

Options :

(a) It is true that it is against United States policy to negotiate with kidnappers. But if the United States wants to prevent loss of life, it must negotiate in some cases.
(b) It is true that it is illegal to sell diamonds that originate in certain countries. But there is a long tradition in Russia of stockpiling diamonds.
(c) It is true that it is illegal for an attorney to participate in a transaction in which there is an apparent conflict of interest. But, if the facts are examined carefully, it will clearly be seen that there is no actual conflict of interest in the defendant's case.
(d) It is true that it is against the law to steal cars. But someone else certainly would have stolen that car if the defendant had not done so first.
(e) None of these

Sol.

(d) The correct answer (d), has the same structure as the stimulus argument. If you just replace "aid to developing nuclear powers" with "car theft," and "Russian companies" with the "defendant," it is essentially the same argument. Sometimes the parallel structure is easier to see if you use symbols to represent the terms of the argument: It is true that X is illegal. But, if Y doesn't do it, others will. Here X is stealing cars and Y is the defendant.

Shortcut Approach

How to crack Parallel Argument Question?

- Read the argument and find the conclusion.
- Try to establish a reasoning structure between the premise and the condusion.
- Read out the options and look out for one having the similar reasoning structure.

PRACTICE EXERCISE

DIRECTIONS (Qs. 1-3): *Study the following information carefully and answer the questions given below :*

The centre reportedly wants to continue providing subsidy to consumers for cooking gas and kerosene for five more years. This is not good news from the point of view of reining in the fiscal deficit. Mounting subventions for subsidies means diversion of savings by the government from investment to consumption, raising the cost of capital in the process. The government must cut expenditure on subsidies to create more fiscal space for investments in both physical and social infrastructure. It should outline a plan for comprehensive reform in major subsidies including petroleum, food and fertilizers and set goal posts.

1. Which of the following is a **conclusion** which can be drawn from the facts stated in the above paragraph ?
   (a) Subsidy provided by the government under various heads to the citizen increases the cost of capital
   (b) Government is unable to withdraw subsidies provided to various items.
   (c) Government subsidy on kerosene is purely a political decision.
   (d) Govt. does not have enough resources to continue providing subsidy on petroleum products.
   (e) None of these

2. Which of the following is an inference which can be made from the facts stated in the above paragraph ?
   (a) India's fiscal deficit is negligible in comparison to other emerging economies in the world.
   (b) Subsidy on food and fertilizers are essential for growth of Indian economy.
   (c) Reform in financial sector will weaken India's position in the international arena.
   (d) Gradual withdrawal of subsidy is essential for effectively managing fiscal deficit in India.
   (e) None of these

3. Which of the following is an **assumption** which is implicit in the facts stated in the above paragraph?
   (a) People in India may not be able to pay more for petroleum products.
   (b) Many people in India are rich enough to buy petroleum products at market cost.
   (c) Government may not be able to create more infrastructural facilities if the present level of subsidy continues for a longer time.
   (d) Government of India has sought assistance from

international financial organizations for its infrastructural projects

(e) None of these

DIRECTIONS (Qs. 4-6): *Study the following Information carefully and answer the questions given below:*

Poverty measurement is an unsettled issue, both conceptually and methodologically. Since poverty is a process as well as an outcome; many come out of it while others may be falling into it. The net effect of these two parallel processes is a proportion commonly identified as the 'head count ratio', but these ratios hide the fundamental dynamism that characterises poverty in practice. The most recent poverty reestimates by an expert group has also missed the crucial dynamism. In a study conducted on 13,000 households which represented the entire country in 1993-94 and again on 2004-05, it was found that in the ten-year period 18.2% rural population moved out of poverty whereas another 22.1% fell into it over this period. This net increase of about four percentage points was seen to have a considerable variation across states and regions.

4. Which of the following is a **conclusion** which can be drawn from the facts stated in the above paragraph ?

(a) Accurate estimates of number of people living below poverty line in India is possible to be made.

(b) Many expert groups in India are not interested to measure poverty objectively.

(c) Process of poverty measurement needs to take into account various factors to tackle its dynamic nature.

(d) People living below poverty line remain in that position for a very long time.

(e) None of these

5. Which of the following is an **assumption** which is **implicit** in the facts stated in the above paragraph?

(a) It may not be possible to have an accurate poverty measurement in India.

(b) Level of poverty in India is static over the years.

(c) Researchers avoid making conclusions on poverty measurement data in India.

(d) Government of India has a mechanism to measure level of poverty effectively and accurately.

(e) None of these

6. Which of the following is an **inference** which can be made from the facts stated in the above paragraph ?

(a) Poverty measurement tools in India are outdated.

(b) Increase in number of persons falling into poverty varies considerably across the country over a period of time.

(c) Government of India has stopped measuring poverty related studies.

(d) People living in rural areas are more susceptible to fall into poverty over the time.

(e) None of these

DIRECTIONS (Qs. 7-8): *Read the following information carefully and answer the questions which follow:*

Supermarkets are growing at a fast pace than Kirana Stores. Kirana Stores are such places where customer go to purchase their necessities. In place of five Kirana stores one or two supermarkets are being established. It has been found that customers' requirements are looked after by trained staff. It has been found that food products are low life products which are manufactured from local manufacturers. These products are typically purchased by the customer on the assurance. The markets is appealing to supermarkets and retail outlet owners are setting up their business in other areas where there are less Kirana stores.

7. Which of the following can be a good argument in favour of shopping, from Kirana stores instead of supermarkets?
   (a) People prefer supermarkets because they offer a larger range of products. i.e., products other than FMCG and they can buy everything under one roof.
   (b) People end-up buying other irrelevant things along with those on their shopping lists in Supermarkets and then they have to stand in long queues at the billing counters.
   (c) Most Kirana stores are closed atleast one day in a week whereas supermarkets are open 365 days a year.
   (d) Kirana stores do not accept debit and credit cards.
   (e) Very few Kirana stores sell products at a bargained price.

8. Which of the following can be inferred from the given information? (An inference is something that is not directly stated but can inferred from the given information).
   (a) Most supermarkets and retail outlet owners choose to set up businesses in areas that have very few Kirana stores.
   (b) People tend to trust retail outlets and supermarkets when it comes to buying high value products as opposed to buying them from local shops.
   (c) If there are two or more Kirana stores in a typical residential area the competition among them is very high.
   (d) Kirana stores owners are buying to acquire franchisee of supermarkets as the local shops have lost their charm and business.
   (e) Kirana stores do not sell the products which consumers on their regular shopping lists, so they have to depend on supermarkets.

DIRECTIONS (Qs. 9-10): *Read the following statements carefully and answer the questions given below:*

Mobile technology has played great role in growth and development of society. Earlier cellphone was used as a medium of conversation only. Now mobile phones also support a wide variety of other services, such as, texting, email, internet access etc. The price of mobile phones is also decreasing and people are being encouraged to buy a mobile phone set at a cheaper rate. The mobile technology and smartphones have the capabilities of handling video calls, sharing large files. Mobile technology had made it more efficient to conduct business. Video calls and taking photographs have become possible as mobile phone has in built camera. Therefore, there is no need to carry around a camera everywhere you go,.

9. Which of the following cannot be inferred from the given information? (An inference is something that is not directly stated but can be inferred from the given information)
   (a) One can share photos and videos via mobile phones provided that the other person has a similar device.
   (b) Many features are being added to mobile phones now-a-days
   (c) The other features of mobile phones are used as useful as the built in camera
   (d) Mobile phones can be used for purposes other than making calls
   (e) Technological advances are taking place in fields other than cellphones as well.

10. Which of the following can be concluded from the given information?
   (a) Buying a phone with a camera is more convenient than buying two different devices.
   (b) Mobile phones that are basic last longer than the ones with added features
   (c) Not many people are interested in clicking pictures with mobile phones
   (d) It is possible to share pictures with someone having a similar camera
   (e) No one will buy camera now onwards.

HINTS & SOLUTIONS

1. **(a)** Consider the following line of the passage:
   "Mounting subventions for subsidies means diversion of savings by the government from investment of consumption, raising the coast of Capital in the process".
2. **(d)** Consider the following lines of the passage:
   "The government must cut expenditure on subsidies to create more fiscal space for investments in both physical and social infrastructure".
3. **(c)** The government must reduce expenditure on subsidies so that to create more infrastructural facilities otherwise present level of subsidy cannot continue for a long time.
4. **(c)** Process of poverty measurement needs to take into account various factors to tackle its dynamic nature.
5. **(a)** It may not be possible to have an accurate poverty measurement in India.
6. **(b)** Increase in number of persons falling into poverty varies considerably across the country over a period of time.
7. **(b)** Option (b) strengthens the statement.
8. **(a)** Obviously option (a) can be inferred from the given information.
9. **(e)** From the given information we cannot infer option (e)
10. **(a)** Obviously option (a) is correct.